Joseph Palmer

The Gospel Problems and Their Solution

Being an inquiry into the origin of the four Gospels

Joseph Palmer

The Gospel Problems and Their Solution
Being an inquiry into the origin of the four Gospels

ISBN/EAN: 9783337063801

Printed in Europe, USA, Canada, Australia, Japan

Cover: Foto ©Lupo / pixelio.de

More available books at **www.hansebooks.com**

Joseph Palmer

The Gospel Problems and Their Solution
Being an inquiry into the origin of the four Gospels

ISBN/EAN: 9783337063801

Printed in Europe, USA, Canada, Australia, Japan

Cover: Foto ©Lupo / pixelio.de

More available books at **www.hansebooks.com**

THE GOSPEL PROBLEMS
AND
THEIR SOLUTION

Being an Inquiry into the Origin
of the Four Gospels

BY

JOSEPH PALMER

" I do not call to mind any problem of natural science which has come under my notice, which is more difficult, or more curiously interesting as a mere problem, than that of the origin of the Synoptic Gospels, and that of the historical values of the narratives which they contain. The Christianity of the Churches stands or falls by the results of the purely scientific investigation of these questions.'

—*T. H. Huxley*

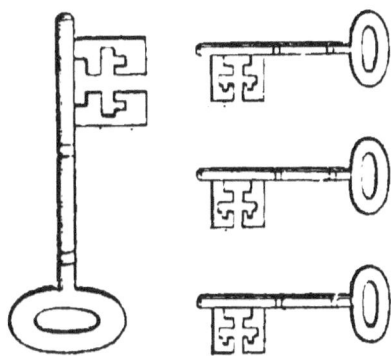

LITERAE SCRIPTAE MANENT

LONDON
H. R. ALLENSON 30 PATERNOSTER ROW
1899

BUTLER & TANNER,
THE SELWOOD PRINTING WORKS,
FROME, AND LONDON.

Preface

I WAS in the first instance led to write on the subject dealt with in this book by a sentence or two in an article by Professor J. T. Marshall in the *Critical Review* for July, 1892. Ever since I was a boy I had had, in common with all who have devoted much attention to the critical study of the Bible, a keen desire to know in what manner the four Gospels had come into existence. I had long felt that all current theories were inadequate; and I had, moreover, a vague impression that at least some portions of the Gospel narratives were written contemporaneously with the events they record. Several years ago this impression was strengthened by a statement which I read somewhere that the art of writing shorthand was practised in the times of the New Testament. But the impression took no definite shape, and I continued to be puzzled by those features of the Gospels which throughout this century have been a leading subject of discussion in the learned world. It was not until I read, soon after its appearance, the article above referred to, that I found the first clue to the solution of the Problems.

The article was a review on a book by Dr. Paul Ewald on *The Chief Problem of the Gospel Question*, in which Professor Marshall, after describing the author's views and arguments, and showing their insufficiency, concludes as follows:—

"Is it not high time that some different method of investigation was attempted? There must be a fault in the method that leads every investigator to a separate goal. We never arrive at certainty. The multitudinous theories all hover between greater or less plausibility. In the pages of the *Expositor*, I have recently advocated the employment of a linguistic method. I must not presume to occupy space here with a repetition of what is accessible to all readers of the *Critical Review*. If substantiated, my theory will, at all events, give us a basis of *facts*. The results thus far arrived at are deeply interesting, as they lead one to believe that a record of most of the events of the Galilean ministry was at one time extant in Aramaic; and that in these portions the Synoptists translated from an Aramaic exemplar. The events of the Judæan ministry, on the other hand, give no evidence of having existed other than in Greek. We wish, however, to proceed with caution, and if we can only lay a substratum of facts which will stand the test of scientific investigation, it will be preferable to the building of a gigantic structure, so attenuated that it only endures till the next investigator assails it.

I had always felt a desire to know in what language Christ was accustomed to speak. But the evidence was conflicting. On the one hand it seemed absolutely certain that He spoke in Aramaic, the language which in Palestine had taken the place of Hebrew. But then again there seemed also to be strong reasons for holding that He spake in Greek. As I read the sentences quoted above the truth flashed into my mind. Our Lord used both languages! According to the people He was addressing, or the subject upon which He was discoursing, He spake—sometimes in Aramaic, sometimes in Greek. And the utterances recorded in Matthew, Mark and Luke were those which He spake in Aramaic, while those recorded in John were those which He spake in Greek. I felt too that the importance of this discovery was inestimable, for, if the fact were so, it was proof absolute and incontrovertible that the reports of Christ's sayings were written at the very time or immediately after they were spoken.

I took the first opportunity to refer to Professor Marshall's articles in the *Expositor*. I was, however, much disappointed to find that the view he maintained was not that which his words in the *Critical Review* seemed, to my mind, naturally to suggest. He held that the first three Gospels were based upon original documents written in Aramaic, while the original manuscripts of the fourth Gospel existed only in Greek ; but he seemed to be of opinion that no portion of either was written until several years after the close of our Lord's life on earth. This obviously was no solution except of a very small part of the difficulties. At the same time the articles struck me as of great value, inasmuch as, making all allowances, they certainly to my mind proved that many of the diversities in parallel passages in the Synoptic Gospels were the result of independent translation of manuscripts which, in the places referred to, were in the originals alike.

During the six years that have elapsed since I first read Professor Marshall's article in the *Critical Review*, I have devoted most of the time I could spare from the duties of a busy life to the study of the subject. I was already fairly well acquainted with the opinions respectively held in the various schools of thought on the different questions that are included in the critical study of the Old and New Testaments. I have since read all the accessible literature that seemed to me able to throw any light on the circumstances surrounding the origin of the four Gospels. Nor was it long before I began to endeavour to make my discovery known. In the years 1893 and 1894 I contributed to the *Baptist* a series of articles on "The Origin of the Four Gospels." The substance of these articles is included in the following pages; it forms, however, but a small portion of the book, and but little of it is repeated in the shape in which it originally appeared.

For a while it was the Chief Problem only for which I was able to find a solution. The explanation of the Synoptic Problem seemed as far off as ever; nevertheless I hoped that, if only the investigation of the subject were followed on the right lines, the solution of this difficulty also would at length be arrived at. In course of time the clue gradually appeared. In the ninth of my articles, written in August, 1893, I ventured to broach the suggestion that it may have been in the reporting in company, by those of the disciples who were accustomed to take notes of the oral narrations of their fellow-disciples, that many of the more perplexing features of co-incidence and variation in the Synoptic Gospels originated. As I continued to unravel the question, I became more and more satisfied that herein lay the solution of the Second Great Problem, till at last all doubt was removed, and I became fully convinced that such was really the case.

There still remained the Chronological Problem, which, I confess, caused me much perplexity. It was quite two years from the time of my first discovery before I found the true explanation of this difficulty. And not even then, nor for some time after, did I notice that many of the transposed sections in Luke are of nearly equal length, making in the nonpareil 32mo edition of the Revised New Testament paragraphs of from 12 to 16 lines each, and so indicating the size of the sheets of papyrus upon which the original notes were written.

Throughout the whole of the time during which I was gradually gaining light on the methods and circumstances in which the Gospels were composed, I never met with anything that tended for one moment to shake my first conclusion as to the date at which the original records were written. Every fresh feature that I noticed in the Gospels themselves, every new book or article that I read, bearing directly or ever so remotely on the subject, added to the certainty of my belief, and increased my wonder that any other opinion could ever have been entertained.

Of the evidential value of the facts herein presented it is needless for me to speak. But I cannot omit to express my profound and reverent admiration of the Providence which has reserved for this critical age the discovery of facts of such supreme importance, and of the Wisdom which has treasured up in the Gospels themselves, even in those very features which were most enigmatical, convincing demonstration of their authenticity, and of the absolute certainty of those great historic events which they record. For it is utterly impossible to imagine that the writers of the Gospel narratives could have perverted, at the very time they were spoken and acted, the words and facts which they daily heard and saw, or have intermixed with them inventions of their own imagination.

I speak in these confident terms because I am well assured

that, whatever may be the fate of this book, the truth for which it contends cannot much longer remain hidden from the world, and that the time is not far distant when the prejudice and superstition that have grown up around the subject of the Gospel histories will have died out, and when it will be universally seen that there was nothing mysterious or unusual in their origin, but that they were honestly composed of reliable materials in a simple and natural manner, like other books of history and biography.

Although I have read much, I have not in the following pages consciously quoted without acknowledgment. I desire to testify to the great assistance I have derived from Mr. S. J. Andrews' *Life of Our Lord upon Earth*, a work that should be in the hands of every student of the subject on which it treats. I have made constant use of Alford's *Greek Testament*, and Smith's *Dictionary of the Bible*, and, to verify my facts, have had frequent recourse to other works too numerous to mention.

In my Scripture quotations I follow usually the Revised Version. The Greek quotations are from Westcott and Hort.

I have to thank Mr. J. G. Griffin, a practised writer for the press, for reading my manuscript and making many suggestions of a literary character, upon most of which I have acted.

August 30, 1898.

Contents

		PAGE
Preface		iii

PART I

THE PROBLEMS AND THE KEYS

Chapter	I.	Introductory	1
,,	II.	The Problems	3
,,	III.	Sources of Information	10
,,	IV.	Current Theories	13
,,	V.	Objections	17
,,	VI.	Froude's Theory	24
,,	VII.	No general belief in Contemporaneous Records	25
,,	VIII.	The Keys	27
,,	IX.	The Genesis of the Gospels	29

PART II

THE MASTER KEY; NAMELY, THAT THE NARRATIVE PARTS OF THE GOSPELS WERE WRITTEN SOON AFTER AND FOR THE MOST PART IMMEDIATELY AFTER THE EVENTS HAPPENED WHICH THEY RELATE; AND THAT THE REPORTS OF CHRIST'S LONGER ADDRESSES WERE TAKEN DOWN AS THEY WERE SPOKEN

Chapter	I.	Ancient Civilization and the Practice of Writing	33
,,	II.	Cause of the Prevailing Misconception	39
,,	III.	Civilization and the Practice of Writing in the Time of Christ	43
,,	IV.	Tautochronistic Reporting	46
,,	V.	Tautochronistic Reports in the Old Testament	50
,,	VI.	The nature of the Gospel narratives	57
,,	VII.	The Birth, Infancy and Early Life of Jesus. The Genealogies	64
,,	VIII.	After the Resurrection	78
,,	IX.	Vividness of Description; Simplicity of Language; Positiveness	82

CONTENTS

		PAGE
Chapter X.	Non-use of Title "Christ" as a Proper Name	84
,, XI.	Accuracy of the reports of our Lord's utterances and of other quotations	90
,, XII.	Editorial notes	96
,, XIII.	The standpoint of the Writers	103
,, XIV.	A distinct allusion to the Reporters	105

PART III

FIRST SPECIAL KEY; NAMELY, THAT OUR LORD WAS ACCUSTOMED TO SPEAK IN BOTH THE LANGUAGES THAT WERE CURRENT IN PALESTINE IN HIS TIME; AND THAT HIS UTTERANCES IN ARAMAIC ARE MOSTLY CONTAINED IN MATTHEW, MARK AND LUKE; WHILE HIS DISCOURSES IN GREEK ARE FOUND ONLY IN JOHN

Chapter I.	Linguistic changes in Palestine before Christ	109
,, II.	The actual position in the time of Christ	116
,, III.	The languages spoken by Christ	121
,, IV.	Respective characteristics of Aramaic and Greek	128
,, V.	Respective use of Aramaic and Greek in the Synoptics and John	131
,, VI.	Summary	139
,, VII.	Outcome of the argument	141

PART IV

THE SECOND SPECIAL KEY; THAT THE RECORDS IN THE SYNOPTIC GOSPELS LARGELY CONSIST OF THE UNITED TESTIMONY OF THE APOSTLES GIVEN AT THE TIME IN COMPANY AND SEVERALLY REPORTED BY THE WRITERS

Chapter I.	Brief statement	145
,, II.	A diary of two days	148

PART V

THE THIRD SPECIAL KEY; THAT THE CHRONOLOGICAL DISORDER IN MATTHEW AND LUKE IS OWING TO THE NOTES USED IN THE COMPILATION OF THOSE GOSPELS HAVING BECOME DISARRANGED; AND IN THE CASE OF LUKE THROUGH THE ORIGINAL WRITER THEREOF BEING BY REASON OF DEATH OR SOME OTHER CAUSE UNABLE TO ASSIST IN THEIR REDACTION

CONTENTS

		PAGE
Chapter I.	The nature of the chronological disorder	161
,, II.	The work of redaction	165
,, III.	Disarrangement of manuscripts	173
,, IV.	The writer of the manuscripts used by Luke	176
,, V.	Luke's difficult task	185

PART VI

THE WRITERS AND REDACTORS

Mary and Joseph	187
The Apostles	189
Matthew	190
Peter and Andrew; James and John	193
Peter	198
Mark	200
James	202
Luke	203
John	205

PART VII

DETAILED APPLICATION OF THE FOREGOING PRINCIPLES TO THE NARRATIVES   209

FOR INDEX TO CHAPTER AND VERSE, SEE PAGES XII TO XVI

CONCLUSION 393

CONTENTS

SUBJECT.	MATTHEW.	MARK.	LUKE.	JOHN.	PAGE.
In the beginning				i. 1-18	210
Luke's Dedication			i. 1-4		211
Matthew's Introduction	i. 1; i. 18a				211
Mark's Introduction		i. 1			211
Birth of John the Baptist; the Genealogies; Birth, Infancy and Childhood of Jesus	i. 2-25 ii. 1-23		i. 5-80; ii. 1-52; iii. 23-38		212
John the Baptist's Ministry and the Baptism of Christ	iii. 1-17	i. 2-11	iii. 1-22	i. 19-36	216
The Temptations	iv. 1-11	i. 12, 13	iv. 1-13		221
John's narrative continued: The first disciples; John, Andrew, Simon, Philip, Nathanael; Marriage at Cana; Removal to and short stay at Capernaum; Passover and first cleansing of the Temple; Observation				i. 37-ii. 25	222
First tautochronistic report					225
Conversation with Nicodemus				iii. 1-21	225
John the Baptist's testimony				iii. 22-36	226
Conversation with Samaritan Woman				iv. 1-38	229
Arrival in Galilee				iv. 39-45	230
Cana: Healing of Nobleman's son at Capernaum				iv. 46-54	232
Jerusalem: Healing of man at pool of Bethesda and discourse to the Jews				v.	233
Observation					235
Return to Galilee and mission there	iv. 12-17	i. 14, 15	iv. 14, 15		236
Calling of four disciples	iv. 18-22	i. 16-20			236
Healing of demoniac at Capernaum		i. 21-28	iv. 31-37		237
Healing of Peter's wife's mother and many others	viii. 14-17	i. 29-39	iv. 38-44		237
First miraculous draught of fishes			v. 1-11		238
Healing of a Leper	viii. 2-4	i. 40-45	v. 12-16		238

CONTENTS

SUBJECT.	MATTHEW.	MARK.	LUKE.	JOHN.	PAGE.
Healing of one sick of the palsy; Calling of Matthew; Feast at his house; Question about fasting	ix. 2-17	ii. 1-22	v. 17-39		238
Disciples pluck corn on Sabbath; Jesus heals man with withered hand; Jesus withdraws to the sea and ascends a mountain, where He spends the night in prayer; In the morning He appoints the twelve apostles, and great multitudes gather round Him	xii. 1-21 iv. 23-v. 1	ii. 23-iii. 19	vi. 1-19		238
The Sermon on the Mount	v. 1-viii. 1		vi. 20-49 xi. 1-13, 33-36 xii. 22-34, 58, xvi. 10-18 [59]		241
Healing of centurion's servant	viii. 5-13		vii. 1-10		245
Nain: Restoring widow's son to life			vii. 11-17		247
Visit of Messengers from John the Baptist and discourse occasioned thereby	xi. 2-30		vii. 18-35 x. 13-15, 21-24		248
Anointing by woman in Pharisee's house			vii. 36-50		252
Healing of man possessed with dumb devil; blasphemy of scribes; discourse	xii. 22-50	iii. 20-35	xi. 14-23, 27-30, 32, 31, 24- viii. 19-21 [26]		253
The disciples exhorted to boldness	x. 24-33		xii. 1-12		261
Parable of the Sower and many other parables	xiii. 1-52		viii. 4-18 xiii. 18-21		261
The hesitating disciples	viii. 18-22		ix. 57-62		266
Crossing the sea and calming the storm	viii. 23-27	iv. 36-41	viii. 22-25		269
Casting out of devils and destruction of swine	viii. 28-ix. 1	v. 1-20	viii. 26-39		271
Raising of daughter of Jairus and healing of woman	ix. 18-26	v. 21-43	viii. 40-56		271
Healing of two blind men and dumb man possessed with devil	ix. 27-34				272

SUBJECT.	MATTHEW.	MARK.	LUKE.	JOHN.	PAGE.
Rejection by men of Nazareth	xiii. 53–58	vi. 1–6a	iv. 16–30		273
Ministry in Galilee and mission of the Twelve	ix. 35–x. 16 x. 34–xi. 1	vi. 6b–13	viii. 1–3; ix. 1–6; xii. 49–53		276
Herod hears of Jesus; Death of John the Baptist; Return of the Twelve	xiv. 1–12	vi. 14–30	ix. 7–10a		277
Crossing Lake Tiberias and feeding the five thousand	xiv. 13–21	vi. 31–44	ix. 10b–17	vi. 1–13	278
Recrossing the lake, walking on the sea, and works at Gennesaret	xiv. 22–36	vi. 45–56		vi. 14–21	286
Discourse in Capernaum				vi. 22–71	280
Observation					287
Enmity of the Jews				vii. 1	
About ablutions	xv. 1–20	vii. 1–23			288
Tour through Northern Galilee and Phœnician border; detour to the East; and return by way of Decapolis and Sea of Galilee	xv. 21–xvi. 12	vii. 24–viii. 21			291
Healing of blind man at Bethsaida		viii. 22–26			291
Attendance at Feast of Tabernacles				vii. 2–52	296
The woman brought before Christ in the Temple				viii. 1–11	296
Discourses and miracles in Jerusalem				viii. 12–x. 21	
Journey through Gaulanitis and Iturea and return viâ Mount Tabor to Capernaum	xvi. 13–xvii. 23	viii. 27–ix. 32	ix. 18–45		296
The Temple tribute	xvii. 24–27				299
Dispute among disciples; discourse	xviii. 1–35	ix. 33–50	ix. 46–50		299
Final departure from Galilee	xix. 1	x. 1a	ix. 51		300
Précis of subsequent proceedings			ix. 52–56		303
Rejection in Samaria; Indignation of James and John; Healing of ten lepers; Mission of the Seventy and their return; Incidents and para- bles delivered during the journey through Perea;			xvii. 11–37 x. 1–12, 16–20, xi. 37–41 [25–37] xii. 13–21, 54–57		304

SUBJECT.	MATTHEW.	MARK.	LUKE.	JOHN.	PAGE.
Incidents and Parables, *continued*—			xiii. 1–17, 22– xiv. 1–35 [33 xv. 1–32 xvi. 1–9, 19–31 xvii. 1–10 xviii. 1–14 x. 38–42		304
Visit to Bethany and commendation of Mary					308
Feast of the Dedication; Discourse to the Jews; They attempt to kill Him; He returns to Perea				x. 22–42	312
In Perea; About divorce; Blessing the children; The rich young man; About riches; Parable of the Householder and Hired Servants	xix. 1–xx. 16	x. 1–31	xviii. 15, 30		317
Raising of Lazarus				xi. 1–44	318
Resolution of the Sanhedrin; Jesus again leaves Judæa and arrives at Ephraim				xi. 45–54	319
Journey from Ephraim to Jericho; Incidents and addresses	xx. 17–34	x. 32–52	xviii. 31–34 xxii. 24–30 xviii. 35–43 xix. 1–27		320
Foreview of the final portions of the Gospels					
Gathering at Jerusalem for the Passover; Arrival of Jesus at Bethany; Supper and anointing; Plotting of Sanhedrin; Treachery of Judas	xxvi. 6–16	xiv. 3–11	xix. 28 xxii. 3–6	xi. 55–57 xii. 1–11	327
Triumphal entry into Jerusalem; Second cleansing of the Temple; Withering of fig-tree; Last ministry in the Temple; Interview with Greeks; Attempt to provoke Jesus; Final departure from Temple	xxi. 1–xxiii. 39	xi. 1–xii. 44	xix. 29–48 xxi. 37, 38 xx. 1–xxi. 4 xi. 42–52 xiii. 34, 35 xi. 53, 54	xii. 12–36a 44–50 36b–43	331

CONTENTS

SUBJECT.	MATTHEW.	MARK.	LUKE.	JOHN.	PAGE.
Discourse to disciples foretelling destruction of Jerusalem and end of the world	xxiv. 1-9 x. 17-23 [46 xxiv. 10-xxv.	xiii. 1-37	xxi. 5-36 xii. 35-48		341
Two days before the Passover; Decided measures of Jewish rulers	xxvi. 1-5	xiv. 1, 2	xxii. 1, 2		343
Wednesday, April 5					343
The Passover Supper					344
Christ's last discourse and His prayer for His disciples	xxvi. 17-29	xiv. 12-25	xxii. 7-23	xiii. 1-35 xiv. 1- xvii. 26	346
Peter's fall foretold	xxvi. 30-35	xiv. 26-31	xxii. 31-38	xiii. 36-38	347
Gethsemane	xxvi. 36-46	xiv. 32-42	xxii. 39-46	xviii. 1, 2	348
The arrest	xxvi. 47-56	xiv. 43-52	xxii. 47-53	xviii. 3-11	349
Before Annas and Caiaphas; Peter's denials	xxvi. 57- xxvii. 1	xiv. 53- xv. 1a	xxii. 54-71	xviii. 12-27 xviii. 28-	350 367
Proceedings before Pilate and Herod; Condemnation, crucifixion, death, and burial of Jesus	xxvii. 2-61	xv. 1b-47	xxiii. 1-56		
The name Golgotha; Calvary	xxvii. 33	xv. 22	xxiii. 33	xix. 42	371
The titles on the cross	xxvii. 37	xv. 26	xxiii. 38	xix. 17	372
Date of the Passover in the year 30				xix. 19	373
The time of the Crucifixion	xxvii. 45, 46	xv. 25, 33, 34	xxiii. 44		376
The Apostles resume writing				xix. 14, 16	380
The Resurrection	xxviii. 1-10	xvi. 1-8	xxiv. 1-12	xx. 1-10	382
From the Resurrection to Pentecost					387
Matthew's narrative of Resurrection and subsequent events	xxviii. 62- xxviii. 20				390
Peter's narrative of Resurrection					390
James's narrative of Resurrection and Ascension					391
John's narrative of Resurrection and subsequent events; Conclusion of John's Gospel		xvi. 1-8	xxiv. 1-53	xx. 1- xxi. 25	392

Part I

THE PROBLEMS AND THE KEYS

Chapter I

INTRODUCTORY

IT may safely be asserted that no question in literature, not even excepting the questions relating to the books of the Old Testament, has given rise to one half the controversy that has gathered round the question of the origin of the four Gospels. During the present century books and magazine articles innumerable have been written on the subject, and still the discussion shows no abatement, nor is there any sign of finality: rather is there a general sense of dissatisfaction with all that has been written and of despair of finding any feasible solution of the problems.

In one respect however the controversy has led to an important result. The early date at which the Gospels were completed is now established beyond all doubt. It is generally admitted by competent persons that Matthew, Mark and Luke were in circulation at the latest before the year 75, and that John was published before the end of the first century. The quotations which are found in extant books of undoubted antiquity prove that the four Gospels in their present shape, and no others, were accepted and recognised as authoritative amongst Christians early in the second century. As they could not have attained that distinction unless they had already been in circulation a considerable number of years it follows that their actual production must have taken place much earlier. Indeed, it is difficult to conceive how they could have found the general acceptance they did unless at the time of their first appearance they were known to have been composed by men who possessed in a high degree the confidence of the Christian Church, and who had had special opportunities of becoming acquainted with the facts narrated. In other words, the very circumstance of the four Gospels being acknowledged as authoritative in the early Church is a strong reason to believe that they were composed either by Apostles or with Apostolic sanction, and could therefore be fully relied on as trustworthy and accurate accounts of the events they relate and the sayings they recite. It is not, in fact, going too far to say that, in the absence of any evidence to the contrary, the strong presumption is that the Gospels were composed by the men whose names they respectively bear. As two of these were of the number of the Twelve and had therefore been in close personal attendance on our Lord during His ministry, and the other two were on terms of friendly intimacy with the Apostles, the historical accuracy of the whole four rests upon a most substantial basis.

But, admitting this, the question as to the manner in which the Evangelists composed the Gospels still remains unanswered. This question resolves itself into two: What were the materials which the Evangelists made use of? and How did those materials themselves originate? These are the questions which have occasioned so much controversy. The extreme difficulty of answering them is due to certain features in the Gospels themselves which must now be described.

Chapter II

THE PROBLEMS

THE most important of the Problems are two in number. The first, which has been styled by Ewald, "The Chief Problem of the Gospel Question," relates to the difficulties observed on comparing, or rather contrasting, the first three Gospels with the fourth. The second, commonly called the "Synoptic Problem," relates to the difficulties presented by a comparison of the first three Gospels amongst themselves.

There is a third problem which really forms part of the Synoptic Problem; but which it will be convenient to deal with separately. It is found in the want of chronological harmony which is manifest in the arrangement of much of the first three Gospels, and may therefore be styled the "Chronological Problem."

The Chief Problem

Every thoughtful reader of the New Testament must observe a marked difference, both in style and substance, between the Gospels of Matthew, Mark and Luke on the one hand, and that of John on the other.

Whilst in Matthew, Mark and Luke a great number of the facts recorded are found to be common either to all or to two of them, most of the facts related in John are found in that Gospel alone. From the beginning of Christ's ministry to the time of His last visit to Jerusalem only three facts narrated in the first three Gospels or either of them are also recorded in the last. The facts referred to are, the feeding of the five thousand, His walking on the sea of Galilee, and the anointing of His feet by Mary at Bethany. This peculiarity is often accounted for by what is called the Supplementary Theory, that is to say that John, writing long after the other Gospels were in circulation, purposely made his narrative of a supplementary character, and recorded as a rule only sayings and doings of Christ which the earlier writers had left untold.

But, not to mention many grave objections which have been raised to the Supplementary Theory, it entirely fails to account for some other striking features of the problem referred to.

The first three Gospels are mainly occupied with our Lord's work in Galilee. If we had no information beyond what they supply, it might have been inferred that He made no visit to Jerusalem except the last, and that the whole duration of His ministry did not exceed some twelve or eighteen months. John, on the other hand, records several visits to Jerusalem during a ministry which must have lasted three or four years, and a large part of his Gospel consists of a narrative of what Jesus said and did in the Holy City on those occasions. And yet the Three give a very full account of what transpired in the Temple during the last visit, whilst the Fourth relates only a single incident that occurred at that time.

What, however, is most perplexing is that the sayings and addresses recorded in the first three Gospels on the one hand, and the fourth Gospel on the other, though presenting so many points of resemblance as to prove them to be accurate reports of the sayings of the same Person, are yet very unlike both in their substance, and in their literary character and composition. The Kingdom of God is the theme of all four Gospels; but whilst the expression 'Kingdom of God' or 'Kingdom of Heaven' is found in the speeches recorded in Matthew thirty-six times, in Mark fourteen times, and in Luke thirty-two times, in John it only occurs twice. In the first three our Lord's sayings refer chiefly to the outward manifestations of the Kingdom, its claims on men's acceptance, the terms of admission to it, its laws, requirements and privileges, and the results of rejecting it. In the fourth the subject is rather the King Himself, His eternal Sonship, His vital union with His people, His purposes concerning them, and His gift to them of the Holy Spirit. Equally marked is the difference in their literary character. In the Three our Lord's teaching consists largely of those homely but wonderful stories which the Evangelists call 'parables.' Matthew and Mark indeed say that He never spoke to the multitude without a parable. In John however the word elsewhere translated 'parable' (παραβολή) never occurs, and, although there is plentiful illustration and much figurative language, not a single parable of the narrative sort, such as are found in the other Gospels, is recorded. Profoundest truth is taught in simple, clear, precise terms.

There is no difficulty in the fact that our Lord should thus have varied the style and substance of His discourse. But it is most remarkable, and has hitherto seemed inexplicable, that the two classes of utterances should have been kept so entirely distinct; the one class being preserved in the first three Gospels alone, and the other exclusively in John. Why is no specimen to be found in the former of discourses like that delivered in the Synagogue of Capernaum after the feeding of the five thousand (John vi)? And why is no parable like that of the Sower, or the Good Samaritan, to be found in John?

These and other difficulties suggested by the facts mentioned in the foregoing remarks constitute "the Chief Problem of the Gospel Question."

The Synoptic Problem

When the Gospel of John is left out of consideration and attention is exclusively directed to Matthew, Mark and Luke, another set of difficulties present themselves.

The first thing we notice is that these three Gospels, as already mentioned, have very much in common. They relate in similar, though rarely in quite identical terms, many of the same facts in our Lord's ministry. For this reason many attempts have been made, from very early times to the present, to construct a harmony by placing the three narratives side by side in parallel columns. Arranged in this way they are said to form a 'Synopsis,' because the three narratives may be looked at together; and as a result the narratives themselves have come to be called the 'Synoptic Gospels.'

An estimate made by Reuss gives the following results: Matthew, Mark and Luke contain respectively 341, 380 and 320 verses relating to the same subjects, and bearing a greater or less resemblance to one another.

Matt. contains 330 verses not found elsewhere.
Mark   „   68   „   „   „   „
Luke   „   541 „   „   „   „
Matt. and Mark contain 170–180 verses not found in Luke.
Matt. and Luke   „   230–244   „   „   „   Mark.
Mark and Luke   „   50   „   „   „   Matt.

Accepting this estimate as nearly enough correct for our purpose, it appears that Luke has far more independent matter than Matthew, whilst Mark has hardly any independent matter at all.

As stated above, the incidents related in two or more of the Gospels are not usually told in precisely similar terms. There is sometimes, moreover, great diversity in details of fact and sometimes there are seeming discrepancies which cannot at first sight be easily reconciled. In no case however is there actual contradiction, and there is no reason to doubt that, were we in possession of all the facts, the harmony in every case would be found to be complete. But the difficulty from a literary point of view consists mainly in this; that with all these diversities there is yet great similarity in the language used by the Synoptic writers when two of them or the whole three relate the same incident. Three examples taken almost at random will suffice to show what we mean.

Take first the accounts of the preaching of John the Baptist (Matt. iii. 1–12; Mark i. 2–8; Luke iii. 2–18.) It will be noted that Mark alone quotes from Malachi, "Behold, I send

my messenger before thy face, who shall prepare thy way"; which words are however found in both Matthew (xi. 10) and Luke (vii. 27) as quoted by our Lord Himself on a subsequent occasion. All three use the word 'wilderness,' but whilst Luke mentions it to describe the place where the word of God came to John, Matthew tells us that that was where he preached, and Mark that it was there that he both baptized and preached. Matthew alone quotes these words of John, "Repent ye; for the Kingdom of Heaven is at hand"; but both Mark and Luke state that he preached "the baptism of repentance for the remission of sins." All three apply to John the prophetic words of Isaiah,
"The voice of one crying in the wilderness,
"Make ye ready the way of the Lord,
" Make his paths straight ";
but Luke continues the quotation,
" Every valley shall be filled,
" And every mountain and hill shall be brought low;
" And the crooked shall become straight,
" And the rough ways smooth;
"And all flesh shall see the salvation of God."
Matthew and Mark alone describe John's clothing and food; whilst Luke gives a much fuller account of the substance of his exhortation than either of the others.

Take next the account of the healing of the withered hand (Matt. xii. 9–13; Mark iii. 1–5; Luke vi. 6–10). Luke is the only one who mentions that it was the man's right hand that was withered. Matthew says, "they asked him, saying, Is it lawful to heal on the sabbath day?"; whereas Mark says, "they watched him whether he would heal him on the sabbath day"; and Luke's words are, "the scribes and Pharisees watched him, whether he would heal on the sabbath." Their motive in doing so is stated in all three; Matthew's and Mark's words being, " that they might accuse him"; and Luke's, "that they might find how to accuse him." The answer of Jesus is thus recorded by Matthew:

"What man shall there be of you, that shall have one sheep, and if this fall into a pit on the sabbath day, will he not lay hold on it, and lift it out? How much then is a man of more value than a sheep? Wherefore it is lawful to do good on the sabbath day." Mark and Luke omit these words and record His answer respectively as follows :—" Is it lawful on the sabbath day to do good, or to do harm? to save life, or to kill?" "Is it lawful on the sabbath to do good, or to do harm? to save a life, or to destroy it?" The account of the actual healing is substantially alike in the three; but Luke first describes Jesus as "looking round about upon them all"; and Mark more fully as "looking round about upon them with anger, being grieved at the hardening of their heart."

Refer lastly to the receiving and blessing of the children (Matt. ix. 13–15; Mark x. 13–16; Luke xviii. 15–17). It will be seen that in the three Gospels the first two verses of the section reporting this incident are nearly, but not exactly, alike. Then follows in Mark and Luke this verse, identical in both, "Verily, I say unto you, Whosoever shall not receive the Kingdom of God as a little child, he shall in no wise enter therein." This ends Luke's account; but Matthew goes on to say, "And he laid his hands on them, and departed thence"; and Mark at greater length, "And he took them in his arms, and blessed them, laying his hands upon them."

Similar peculiarities will be observed all through the Synoptic Gospels, wherever the same fact is recorded by more than one. In a large degree the very same words are used, proving that the narratives are in some way related or governed by some common influence. And yet mingled with these are such distinct diversities, both in fact and phraseology, as to make it certain that the narratives could not have been in any case copied one from another. How is it to be accounted for that these three Gospels are so like and yet so unlike? How is this dependent independence to be explained? This is the Synoptic Problem.

The Chronological Problem

It is only necessary to glance at any one of the numerous Harmonies to be painfully convinced that in at least two of the Gospels very great confusion exists. Not only does the historical order of the first three Gospels disagree; but utterances of Christ are in many instances placed in one Synoptic in a quite different connection from that in which they are found in another. In several cases we are forced to admit, either that in one Gospel portions of a discourse have been violently torn from their context and located elsewhere, or else that in another Gospel utterances spoken on a variety of distinct occasions have been arbitrarily brought together so as to present them as one deliverance. Incidents again, which according to one Gospel occurred on widely different occasions, are grouped together in another. And even where portions of considerable length in the main agree, short sections will be found in one of them most curiously and unaccountably transposed.

Thus the Sermon on the Mount is presented in Matthew as one consecutive discourse; in Luke it is distributed through various parts of the book. And many miracles and parables which appear in Luke before the delivery of the first part of the Sermon are recorded in Matthew several chapters later.

It is this curious want of agreement in the arrangement of the three Synoptic Gospels that constitutes what is here called the Chronological Problem.

Chapter III

SOURCES OF INFORMATION

TO discover how the Gospels originated we are dependent almost entirely upon the internal evidence of the Gospels themselves. Of external evidence it is not too much to say that there is nothing in which we can place implicit confidence. Although it has been inferred from Luke's introduction that there were in his time many writings in circulation besides those contained in the New Testament, none have been preserved, and the more ancient writings following that time which are still in existence, though invaluable as showing that the authenticity and Divine authority of the four Gospels was in an early age recognised in the Church, throw little or no light upon the manner in which they were composed.

Papias' Testimony

The only evidence that seems to deserve serious attention is the testimony of Papias, who lived early in the second century, and in his youth took special pains to learn all that could be known about the Apostles. He wrote a book in five volumes which has long since been lost, but was extant in the time of Eusebius, who flourished in the latter part of the third and the beginning of the fourth century, and who in his *Ecclesiastical History* (Bk. III., c. 39) quotes three extracts. These are as follows :—Extract 1. "But I shall not regret to subjoin to my interpretation also for your benefit, whatsoever I have at any time accurately ascertained and treasured up in my memory, as I have received it from the Elders, and have recorded it in order to give additional confirmation to the truth by my testimony. For I have never like many delighted to hear those that tell many things, but those that teach the truth; neither those that record foreign precepts, but those that are given from the Lord to our faith, and that came from the truth itself. But if I met with anyone who had been a follower of the Elders anywhere, I made it a point to enquire what were the declarations of the Elders; what had been said by Andrew, Peter, or Philip; what by Thomas, James, John, Matthew, or any of the disciples of our Lord; what was said by Aristion and the presbyter John, disciples of the Lord; for I do not think that I derived so much benefit from books as by the living voice of those that were still surviving."

Extract 2. "And John the 'presbyter also said this: Mark being the interpreter of Peter, whatsoever he recorded he wrote with great accuracy, but not however in the order in which it was spoken or done by our Lord, for he neither heard or followed our Lord, but as before said, he was in company with Peter, who gave him such instruction as was necessary, but not to give a history of our Lord's discourses: wherefore Mark has not erred in anything, by writing some things as he has recorded them; for he was carefully attentive to one thing; not to pass by anything that he heard, or to state anything falsely in these accounts."

Extract 3. "Matthew composed the utterances ($τὰ\ λόγια$) in the Hebrew dialect, and every one translated them as he was able."

The last of these extracts gave rise to the belief which was expressed by many subsequent writers that Matthew wrote his Gospel in Hebrew, or rather in Aramaic, for Papias and other ancient writers, in common with the New Testament, applied the term "Hebrew" to the Aramaic language current in Palestine in the time of Christ. The opinion that Matthew's Gospel was written by the Evangelist in Aramaic, and that the Gospel as we have it is a Greek translation made by some unknown person, was pretty generally received until recent times, but is now discarded. It is by no means certain that

Papias himself intended to say this, and there has been much discussion as to what he meant by the term "utterances," or, as some would render it, "oracles."

Papias' statement that Mark acquired from Peter the facts recorded in his Gospel has been generally accepted as correct, there being indications in the Gospel itself which tend to the same conclusion.

Chapter IV

CURRENT THEORIES

IT does not come within the scope of this book to give anything like a full or detailed account of the various theories that have been advanced as to the mode in which the Gospels came into existence. It is necessary however for the information of those who have not studied the subject to glance briefly at the leading opinions current at the present day.

It should at once be said that hardly any one now maintains that any portion of either of the Synoptic Gospels was copied from either of the others. All attempts to show that Matthew and Luke are amplifications of Mark, or that Mark is an abridgement of the other two have been given up as impracticable. The more the three narratives are compared, the more certain does it appear, that in no case did the author of one borrow from either of the others. Some, indeed, like Alford, contend that neither of the three writers could even have seen either of the other histories up to the time at which he composed his own.

The Oral Teaching Theory

A theory that has many advocates, and which a few years ago was more prevalent than it is now, is that the Gospels are composed either directly or indirectly of the oral teaching of the Apostles. It is assumed that after Pentecost the Apostles were largely occupied in narrating the events of our Lord's life and ministry of which they had been the witnesses, and in repeating the teaching they had heard from His lips. Their recitals were repeated by others in the instruction of catechumens, or young people who were being prepared for baptism and admission to the Church. The constant repetition of the same facts, nearly in the same words, would deeply impress them on the minds of both speakers and hearers, and, as people's memories are assumed to have been much more retentive at that time than they are now, the lessons in time acquired a settled stereotype shape. By degrees one and another would commit some of the lessons to writing, and some would even try to connect them into the form of a continuous narrative.

At length a time came when the need was felt of a permanent and authoritative history, and Matthew, Mark and Luke, unknown to one another, in different places, and writing each for a different class of readers, set to work to supply that need. They sought out such written documents as were now in circulation, selected such of them as suited the special purpose each had in view, included some unwritten facts that they had heard or which they remembered themselves, and composed the whole into the works bearing their respective names. In this manner the Synoptic Gospels came into existence.

The Gospel of John according to this theory was composed much later, and consisted more exclusively of the Apostle's own recollections. He too was accustomed to tell the story of the life and ministry of Jesus, dwelling however more upon our Lord's doctrinal discourses than upon the miracles and parables which form so large a portion of the earlier histories. It was not until he was advanced in age that he undertook the task of committing to writing what he had so often repeated with his lips, and produced the Gospel, so precious to believers, known by his name.

This view was strenuously maintained by Alford but of late it has seemingly fallen somewhat out of favour.

The Document Theory

The theory that seems to be most generally favoured now is that the Synoptic Gospels are based partly upon an older Aramaic Gospel and partly upon a number of fragmentary records which are supposed to have been in circulation in the early Church. The older Aramaic Gospel referred to may itself have been composed of fragmentary records, and there may have been besides other narratives of less or greater length also composed of similar original fragments. The fragments are supposed to have been the work of various disciples who either were themselves personally acquainted with the incidents and utterances of our Lord's ministry, or were in a position to learn the particulars from others, and who at an early date committed what was remembered to writing. It is thought that it is to some such document or documents that Papias refers when he speaks of the utterances or oracles in the Hebrew dialect composed by Matthew. As the documents were copied and passed about from hand to hand many slight variations would gradually creep in, until, at length, when Matthew, Mark and Luke prepared their narratives, the changes had become considerable.

The three Evangelists collecting independently and in different places the fragments and older Gospel or Gospels, and copying them into their more complete and ordered works, of course reproduced in the latter the variations in the former. Possibly they themselves added some further alterations in translating separately from Aramaic into Greek, and also as some think in making some slight modifications to suit the needs of the class of readers for whom each respectively wrote. In this way the variations in the parallel portions of the Synoptic Gospels are accounted for.

As to the portions that are not parallel, it is easy to understand that some fragments may have been available for one which were not accessible to another; besides which a selection may have been made by each of those which suited the special design of the Gospel he was writing.

The Document Theory is applied only to the Synoptics. But little favour is shown to the idea that John made use of written records in the composition of his work. The assumption appears to be general that the author of the Fourth Gospel wrote from Divinely assisted memory alone.

Many attempts have been made to work out this theory in detail, with all sorts of curious and unlikely combinations, so as to fit it to the literary features of the books. Some of these remind us of the ingenious attempts of astronomers before Copernicus to harmonise the geocentric theory of the universe with the observed movements of the heavenly bodies. Of all such elaborations it is enough to say that they satisfy no one except their respective authors, and that the Document Theory itself is only accepted provisionally in default of anything better.

Chapter V

OBJECTIONS

IT is not to be wondered at that the theories which we have endeavoured in the last chapter briefly to describe are not accepted with confidence or satisfaction, inasmuch as they are confronted with many insurmountable objections.

One of these is that they utterly fail to account for either of the Problems that require solution. As to the Synoptic Problem, to explain which is the purpose for which they have been specially designed, it should be observed that each Gospel has features peculiar to itself and which plainly belong to the original material of which it was composed, thus proving the independence of the sources.

For instance :

In Matthew there is a tendency to quote spoken words very fully and exactly.

In Mark there are numerous minute details respecting matters of fact.

In Luke there are fewer proper names than in either Matthew or Mark.

Some of the features too of what we have called the Chronological Problem appear to be simply fatal at any rate to the Document Theory.

But there is another and still more serious difficulty. However in some respects the two theories may differ there is one respect in which they, and in fact all current theories, are alike. They are all based upon the assumption that a considerable time elapsed after the termination of our Lord's life on Earth before any written record was made of His doings or sayings. As to the length of the interval opinions vary. Some would grant that certain disciples began very early—perhaps within a year or two—to write their reminiscences. A greater number date the earliest written document from ten to twenty years after the Ascension. But, taking even the earliest date, it is necessary to assume that the writers whoever they were had most wonderful memories. In fact, for the production of the Gospels in any such way as that supposed, a state of society would be requisite which did not exist, and powers of memory for which it is impossible to find a parallel.

Ancient Memories

It is taken for granted by all who endeavour to explain the origin of the Gospels that in our Lord's time and country the practice of writing was almost entirely neglected, and that in consequence men's memories, by constant practice, had acquired a power of accurately retaining facts and sayings of which we in our circumstances can form no conception.

In illustration of this it may suffice to quote from two authors holding quite opposite opinions concerning the Gospel facts and teachings. The first is Plumptre, who in his *Introduction to the New Testament* (p. 149) remarks, "In the East as elsewhere the memory of men is often active and retentive in proportion to the absence of written aid. Men recite long poems or discourses which they have learnt orally, or get into the way of repeating long narratives with comparatively slight variations." The second is Rénan, who asserts that "the strength of man's memory is in inverse proportion to the habit of writing," in proof whereof he cites the opening passage of the Parmenides of Plato as follows: "The Clamozenians had heard tell of one Antiphon, who was connected with a certain Pythadorus, friend of Zeno, who remembered the conversations of Socrates with Zeno and Parmenides, in order to repeat them to Pythadorus. Antiphon knew them by heart, and would repeat them to whomsoever would hear them." (*The Gospels*, Chap. v.)

The assumption, however, that in the time of Christ, or in ancient times generally, men's memories were far more retentive than they are now, or that people who cannot write remember better than those who can, is utterly without foundation. The worthlessness of Rénan's illustration lies on the surface. In the first place, it is quite certain that the habit of writing was anything but uncommon in Athens at the time referred to. Next, there is no reason to suppose that the conversations repeated by Antiphon were anything approaching to exact reports of those which actually took place. Lastly, the quotation plainly implies that Antiphon's strength of memory was regarded at the time as something quite exceptional.

Nor is any analogy afforded by the poems of Homer or the hymns of the Indian Vedas, so often referred to by writers on this subject. Allowing it to be true as alleged that these compositions were not written by their authors, but were transmitted orally from one generation to another: still they would be carefully taught by them by means of frequent repetition to classes of learners, who in their turn would teach them to others, and so on from age to age. But our Lord's sayings were spoken only once; and that publicly in many cases, and as occasion arose. Some of the discourses were of great length, and, dealing with most profound subjects, were above the disciples' power of comprehension. There is not a single instance of His repeating any of His sayings in such a manner as would enable His disciples to learn them by heart. Even the Lord's Prayer does not appear to have been so taught; if it be maintained that it was spoken twice, it must be admitted that the occasions on which it was spoken were distinct. Yet it is assumed that after the lapse, sometimes of years, and always of months, the disciples were able to repeat the utterances of Christ without material alteration.

It seems a pity that those who dwell so much upon the power of human memory in places where writing is not practised do not supply us with some modern illustrations in support of their idea. In Russia, Turkey and most Asiatic countries writing is not in common use except amongst the upper classes. Why are not some examples forthcoming of persons who can listen to lengthy speeches, and, months after, say them off again word for word as first spoken? So far as my enquiries go, there is nothing whatever to justify the assumption that, either in Eastern or Western lands, the memories of the illiterate are in the least degree better than those of the educated.

Ancient Quotations

As it happens, we have a ready means of testing the ability of men in olden times to remember and repeat accurately the words of others. There are a great number of quotations in ancient books: are they as a rule verbally correct? In some cases they are so. Many authors made no scruple in appropriating the composition of others as if it were their own. They as a rule quoted correctly enough for they simply copied out the passages from the manuscripts before them. It is not however to the practice of literary piracy that I am referring, but to acknowledged quotations from recognised authorities introduced to support or illustrate an argument. These were usually made from memory, the inconvenience of copying a passage from the book itself being too great to allow of this being often done. Books were then of course much scarcer than they are now, and to refer to one it might be necessary to travel a greater or less distance to a public library, or to the synagogue if it were a Jewish author desirous of making a scriptural quotation. Even if the author had the book in his possession, it would be a long and tedious process to find a needed passage. Books were formed of strips of parchment or papyrus several feet long with a roller at each end upon which they were wound. The writing — and handwriting is never so clear to the eye as printing—was not commonly punctuated and divided into paragraphs or chapters and verses. To go carefully through such a document and pick out a required sentence would be too arduous a task for an author to undertake every time he wished to quote. Therefore they trusted to memory. Still if men had such wonderful memories as they are assumed to have had in those times their quotations should be fairly accurate. It is notorious however that quotations in ancient books are most inaccurate. It appears from Professor Ryle's work that Philo sinned in this respect to a degree that would be considered intolerable in any modern author.

Even the New Testament writers, though not nearly so inaccurate as Philo—doubtless because they were much more familiar with the Scriptures than he—seldom quote the Old Testament with verbal correctness. Matthew and John rarely give the exact sense either of the Hebrew original or the Greek version. And yet they were accustomed to hear the Scriptures read every Sabbath in the Synagogue, and were doubtless devout students thereof at other times. If then they could not remember well enough to quote correctly the words of the Old Testament books which they had heard many times, is it likely that they would after months and years be able to report correctly the words of Jesus which they had heard but once?

The Promise of the Spirit

There are however a great number of persons who lay much stress upon the supernatural aid which they believe was granted to the Gospel writers. They quote with emphasis the promise of Jesus Christ that the Holy Spirit should bring to the remembrance of the Apostles the words that He had spoken. Is not that sufficient to remove all difficulty suggested by the natural incapacity of their minds to retain and accurately recite His teachings?

In reply to this let me in the first place enquire: What reason is there to regard this text as a promise to the Apostles alone in their official capacity? It forms part of that long address which our Lord delivered at the Last Supper, and which has always been accepted as the priceless heritage of all God's believing children. It is not imagined that His promises to go and prepare a place, to do whatsoever was asked in His name, to send a Comforter, the Spirit of Truth, were meant alone for the little company assembled in the upper room. When we read the words, "Peace I leave with you; My peace I give unto you," we understand them as a legacy for His followers in all ages, as truly as for those who reclined with Him at the table. In speaking of the branches of the True Vine, it is never supposed that He referred merely to the little group, eleven in number, who surrounded Him at the moment; it is doubted by none that He was describing those who, to the end of the world, should be by living faith engrafted to Himself. Why then single out one sentence, and treat it, not like the rest of the discourse, as addressed through the Apostles to the entire Church, but as a promise of special qualification for their own official duty? It is a promise of infinite worth to all believers. Like the kindred sentence, "He shall take of mine and show it unto you," it describes the way in which the Holy Spirit operates. It is by calling to the Christian's remembrance in every time of need the exact teaching of Christ suited for the occasion that the Holy Ghost performs His sanctifying work. Our reading the Bible would be of little practical use to us were it not for this: that in the time of trial, of perplexity or of anguish, words are brought back to our minds by the Great Comforter fitted to strengthen, to guide and to cheer. To limit the promise to a narrower sense than this is to wrench it from the context and to mar the symmetry of the discourse.

There is another grave objection to this view. One of the most striking features of the Bible miracles is their economy. There are no needless marvels, and the fullest use is made of all natural means before the supernatural is brought into play. Our Lord might have provided wine at the Cana wedding by speaking the word and filling empty pitchers. But He chose to have the pitchers filled with water by human hands and simply to gather into the fluid from the atmosphere the elements needful to convert it into wine. When feeding multitudes, He could if He had pleased have created all the food required; but He saw fit rather to multiply the small supply available.

"'Twas springtide when He blessed the bread:
'Twas harvest when He brake."

When the collectors for the Temple tax applied for the half-shekel, He might have produced it then and there, but instead of that He directs Peter to go to the sea and cast a hook and take up a fish, in whose mouth he will find a shekel which doubtless had been accidentally (humanly speaking) dropped into the lake and seized by the fish. It is the same with the Old Testament miracles. Tyndall complains of the enormous expenditure of energy required to cause the sun and moon to stand still at the prayer of Joshua (Josh. x. 12, 13). But by an increase in the refractive power of the atmosphere, and probably in many another way unknown to us, all that the history implies might be effected without any tremendous disturbance of physical forces. It is a general rule all through the Scriptures, that no miracle is related for which some good and sufficient reason is not apparent, or to accomplish any purpose which could be equally well accomplished by natural means. But this certainly could not be said of a miracle such as is necessary to existing theories concerning the origin of the Gospels; namely, that men should remember accurately after the lapse of a long space of time, the substance of numerous addresses spoken on various occasions during a period of three or four years. The miracle would be superfluous for the same result could be attained by the simpler process of suggesting to the minds of the witnesses to make written reports of the sayings at the time they were spoken. Moreover it is a class of miracle of which no other instance is recorded, and the magnitude of which may be measured by the consideration that, just in proportion as mind is superior to matter, so must any miraculous operation on men's mental faculties be more surprising than the like operation on merely material objects.

Chapter VI

FROUDE'S THEORY

BEFORE leaving this part of the subject it may be well to notice a suggestion of Froude with reference to the Synoptic Problem, which, though far from being an adequate solution, has more appearance of probability than other current theories, and is, I think, deserving of more attention than it seems to have been accorded.

His words are as follows :—

"One hypothesis, and so far as we can see one only, would make the mystery intelligible; that immediately on the close of our Lord's life some original sketch of it was drawn up by the congregation, which gradually grew and gathered round it, whatever His mother, His relatives, or His disciples afterwards individually might contribute. This primary history would thus not be the work of any one mind or man; it would be the joint work of the Church, and thus might well be called, 'Memoirs of the Apostles'; and would naturally be quoted without the name of either one of them being specially attached to it. As Christianity spread over the world, and separate Churches were founded by particular Apostles, copies would be multiplied, and copies of those copies; and, unchecked by the presence (before the invention of printing impossible) of any authoritative text, changes would creep in." (*Short Studies on Great Subjects*, Vol. 1, pp. 276, 277.)

Chapter VII

NO GENERAL BELIEF IN CONTEMPORANEOUS RECORDS

IT is surprising that, in the course of the long discussion that has taken place as to the origin of the Gospels, the idea should not have gained currency that they may possibly be based upon written notes or memoranda made at the time of the events which they record, and that the longer speeches which they contain may be verbatim reports taken down at the time of delivery. The idea seems so obvious and natural that it is hardly possible that it should not have often suggested itself to New Testament students. But, be that as it may, such a notion has certainly not been widely entertained, nor has it, so far as I can learn, ever been seriously considered. To Bertholdt, it is true, the honour belongs of having advanced the opinion that the Apostle John took down at the time most of the discourses of Jesus (which he supposed were spoken in Aramaic) and made those notes the foundation of his Gospel. But although this suggestion received the partial approval of Tholuck and some few others, and is even mentioned not unfavourably by Strauss, it was not largely accepted, and Alexander alludes to it almost contemptuously in his article on John's Gospel in Kitto's *Cyclopædia*. With the exception just named, there are but few instances in which such an idea has been even alluded to, and in those it has been summarily dismissed as too improbable to demand serious discussion. Plumptre fairly expresses the general attitude of scholars on this subject. "It is scarcely probable," he says, "though we are not justified in assuming it to be impossible, that any notes of our Lord's discourses or parables or shorter sayings were taken at the time, or that records of His miracles were there and then reduced to writing."

It is the design of this book to demonstrate, by what I do not hesitate to say is overwhelming evidence, that it is a matter of absolute certainty that the records of which the greater part of the Gospels were composed originated exactly in the manner in which Plumptre admits it to be possible, but asserts it to be scarcely probable, that they were written.

Chapter VIII

THE KEYS

TO unlock the problems which have been described in the foregoing pages, four keys are necessary—one master key that applies to all the problems, and a special key for each one separately.

It thus appears that each of the problems is double-locked and to this doubtless must be attributed the difficulty that has hitherto been found in dealing with them.

The Master Key

The Master Key is:—That the narrative parts of the Gospels were written soon after and for the most part immediately after the events happened which they relate; and that the reports of Christ's longer addresses were taken down as they were spoken.

The other keys are all dependent upon this one : if any one of them is true this must be true ; if this fails they all fail.

The First Special Key

The First Special Key; the key by which the Chief Problem must be unlocked, is: That our Lord was accustomed to speak in both the languages which were current in Palestine in His time, that is to say in Aramaic and Greek, and that His addresses in Aramaic are contained in the Synoptic Gospels; whilst His discourses in Greek are found only in John.

The Second Special Key

The Second Special Key ; the key that unlocks the Synoptic Problem, is : That the records in the Synoptic Gospels largely consist of the united testimony of the Apostles, given at the time in company and severally reported by the writers.

The Third Special Key

The Third Special Key; the key that unlocks the Chronological Problem, is : That the notes used by Matthew and Luke in the composition of their Gospels, being written on small slips of paper, became disarranged during the time that elapsed before they were redacted, and that, in the case of Luke, the original writer was unable to assist the redactor in their arrangement.

Chapter IX

THE GENESIS OF THE GOSPELS

IT is desirable, before proceeding further, to describe fully but concisely my theory of the manner in which the Gospel records came into being and finally assumed their present shape.

When the twelve disciples forsook their occupations, their homes, and all that they had, to follow the Lord Jesus, they must in some degree have realized the dignity of Him to Whom they attached themselves, and the importance of the office to which they were called. Inadequate as their notions certainly were, they yet understood that they were chosen to be witnesses of Him of Whom Moses and the prophets wrote, and they felt the need of treasuring up His teachings for the benefit of their fellow-men. Accordingly, before any long time had elapsed, four of their number—there may have been others, but four certainly—who had already acquired the art of using the pen with freedom and celerity, undertook the task of noting down, as opportunity offered, the words which the Great Teacher spoke, and the principal things that He did.

The first to begin making notes was John; but the others soon followed his example. Whether John obtained any help from his colleagues in composing his notes cannot be known; but it is certain that the others did so. From time to time when the disciples were assembled at their leisure, they talked over the events which had more recently happened, while one, two or sometimes three of the number wrote the substance of what was said. The conversation on these occasions was carried on in the Aramaic tongue, and of course the notes then made were written in the same language. John who wrote in Greek may have taken part in these conversations but he did not write at the same time as the others.

The Aramaic and Greek Languages were both in general use in Palestine at that time, Aramaic being almost exclusively used by the rural population, and Greek being the language most frequently spoken in Jerusalem and the larger towns. Our Lord was accustomed to speak, sometimes in one of these languages, sometimes in the other, according to whichever might be best understood by the audience He was addressing, or to which might best suit the subject upon which He was discoursing. The disciples were familiar with both languages; but John was more accustomed to writing in Greek, whilst the others were more accustomed to writing in Aramaic. Hence when our Lord spoke in Greek He was reported by John; when in Aramaic, by one or more of the others. The natural outcome of this was a sort of division of labour, and an understanding, tacit or otherwise, that at times when Greek was spoken, the facts as well as the utterances should be recorded by John, and when Aramaic was spoken they should be recorded by the others.

It is not meant by these remarks that every sentence, or nearly every sentence, of the utterances of Jesus in the Gospels was reported as He spoke. But on many occasions when He spoke at considerable length and circumstances were favourable the disciples reported His addresses on the spot. There would be no obstacle to their doing so. The Twelve and their companions would form a little group near to their Master, and the one or more who were taking notes would be safe from the jostling of the crowd. There would be no disposition to interfere with them. The practice of reporting was such a common one that it would occasion no surprise, and, the scribes or official writers being a numerous and powerful class, their profession, like that of the pressman to-day, was treated with great respect. In the evening those who had thus taken notes would at their leisure fill in details, before they had faded from their memory.

In other cases, when the sayings were of less formal and connected character; when it was deeds rather than words that had to be recorded; no notes would be written until the day's work was done. Then, when the little company were quietly assembled after their evening meal, two or three would take their writing materials, and, with the help of the others, some of whom it may be, had more clearly observed or more accurately remembered the incidents than themselves, write down the chief events of the day. In this way each writer made what was an independent report of the united testimony of the Apostles to the facts; testimony delivered as a rule but a few hours after the facts occurred.

It is probable that copies of some of the sets of notes so made, those of Matthew especially, were written and put into circulation after the day of Pentecost. At first, the majority of the members of the Church being Galileans, Matthew's Aramaic notes would suit them exactly. As to the Greek-speaking Christians, who steadily increased in number from that time forward, it would be necessary for them, as Papias says " each one to translate as he was able."

The original manuscripts however were carefully preserved, until, after a number of years, Matthew, Mark, Luke and John separately undertook the duty of drawing up for the permanent use of the Church a regular history of the Gospel facts. The first to do this was Matthew. He obtained from one of the sons of Joseph, the husband of Mary, manuscripts left by him relating to the genealogy and birth of Jesus, which, together with his own notes, he employed in the composition of the First Gospel. Peter entrusted his notes to his young friend Mark, who under the direction of the former prepared the Gospel bearing his own name. Luke obtained from Mary the mother of our Lord the manuscripts written by her, consisting of an account of the birth and childhood of Jesus and collateral facts, and a copy of her Son's genealogy on her own side.

He also secured the notes of our Lord's ministry made by a disciple whose identity will be considered later on. With these he composed the Third Gospel. Finally, at a much later date, the aged Apostle John set himself to redact the notes which he had himself taken, preserved either on the original papyri, or on parchment copies of early date, and which he had retained with scrupulous care, as a precious treasure in his own keeping.

The Evangelists arranged in order the sets of documents they had thus respectively preserved or acquired, and, translating into Greek those that were written in Aramaic, copied them on to a parchment roll. They prefixed suitable introductions, inserted here and there explanatory notes, and, in some cases, comments pointing out the fulfilment of Old Testament prophecy, and supplied the connecting links necessary to compose of the fragments an orderly narrative. When they had finished their task they handed the book to the publisher to be copied and circulated.

The demonstration of the foregoing statement will appear in the following pages.

As I have not been able to find a word that exactly expresses the idea of a report taken down—not necessarily in shorthand and not always verbatim—but taken down *at the same time* as the delivery of the address reported, I have ventured to coin the word 'tautochronistic' (ταὐτό *the same*, χρόνος *time*), and I propose in the course of the book to use that word when speaking of reports so written.

Part II

THE MASTER KEY; NAMELY THAT THE NARRATIVE PARTS OF THE GOSPELS WERE WRITTEN SOON AFTER AND FOR THE MOST PART IMMEDIATELY AFTER THE EVENTS HAPPENED WHICH THEY RELATE; AND THAT THE REPORTS OF CHRIST'S LONGER ADDRESSES WERE TAKEN DOWN AS THEY WERE SPOKEN.

Chapter I

ANCIENT CIVILIZATION AND THE PRACTICE OF WRITING

BEFORE proceeding with our proofs of the proposition which forms what we have called the Master Key of the problems, it is necessary to say something about the educational and literary conditions of the ancient world. For at the outset we are confronted by a great barrier of prejudice which must be broken through before we can hope to make any headway with our case. That 1900 years ago in Palestine a company of twelve men, several of whom were fishermen, and none of whom appear to have belonged to a high rank of society, should have made a practice of noting down from time to time the events they observed, and sometimes even taken reports of addresses as they were delivered, seems to most people so improbable, not to say absurd, that they will hardly listen to anything that may be said in its support.

34 THE GOSPEL PROBLEMS AND THEIR SOLUTION

At that time, it is said, hardly any one could write, and those who could write, unless writing were their special business, only did so on rare occasions, and to make notes from day to day of passing events would be so alien to people's habits that it cannot for one moment be supposed that it was ever done. As to taking down a discourse while it was being spoken, that would require a knowledge of shorthand, and shorthand is quite a modern invention, and certainly could not have been in use among the Jews in the first century of our era. We may not compare that early period in the history of the human race with this present age of light and civilization, or attribute to the simple state of society which existed then the customs and methods of the nineteenth century. With some such sentences as these is the subject liable to be lightly dismissed, and our first duty therefore is to try to remove the misconception from which they spring.

The archæological discoveries of recent years have thrown a new light on the civilizations of the ancient world. It is no longer permitted to us to think of the great nations of antiquity as of peoples in a state of ignorance and barbarism, among whom the art of writing, if in use at all, was a rare accomplishment and practised only by the learned few. It is now proved beyond all doubt that, ages before the time of Christ, writing was general and formed an essential element in the daily life of oriental communities.

The excavations in Egypt and Western Asia, which have been carried on with so much enthusiasm during this century, have disclosed immense stores of ancient documents, which not only record the history but reflect the manners and customs of nations long since extinct and forgotten.

A large proportion of these documents consist of tablets, originally made of soft clay, and for common use generally of the size and shape of a cake of soap. For writing on them a stylus—that is a pencil made of flint, bone or metal, with a sharp point—was used; the tablets were usually inscribed all over, and sometimes to economise space with letters so minute that it requires a glass to read them. After use they were allowed to dry and harden, and those of importance were usually baked, thus ensuring the permanence of the record.

One of the most valuable deposits of tablets that has as yet been discovered is that which was found in 1885 among the mounds of Tel-el-Amarna in Egypt, and which Professor A. H. Sayce describes thus :—" They consist of clay tablets, inscribed with cuneiform writing of the Babylonian type, and in the Babylonian language. The tablets are copies of letters and dispatches from the Kings and Governors of Babylonia and Assyria, of Syria, Mesopotamia, and Eastern Kappadokia, of Phœnicia and Palestine, and they prove that all over the civilized East, in the Century before the Exodus, active literary intercourse was carried on through the medium of a common literary language, that of Babylonia, and the complicated Babylonian script. It is evident, therefore, that, throughout Western Asia, schools and libraries must have existed, in which clay tablets, inscribed with cuneiform characters, were stored up, and where the language and syllabary of Babylonia were taught and learned. Such a library must have existed in the Canaanitish city of Kirjath-Sepher, or Booktown (Judges i. 11), and, if its site can ever be recovered and excavated, we may expect to find there its collection of books written upon imperishable clay." (*Records of the Past*: New Series: Vol. 2, p. 58.)

Immense stores of tablets have also been found in the sites where, in ancient times, flourished the cities of Babylonia and Assyria. Great libraries have been opened up, filled with such documents, many of which have been brought to the centres of European learning, there to be patiently interpreted by those who have made it the business of their lives to study and decipher the long-forgotten languages and symbols in which they were written. Thus the world is learning anew the history of nations, some of whose very names had been for ages lost to the memory of man.

These documents, however, are not all of a historic or

official character. A large proportion of them, technically known as *demotic*, relate to matters of trade and everyday life, and many of them to most trivial transactions. (I have seen, in the collection of a friend, a tablet, dated 30th of the month Adar in the 34th year of Darius Hystaspes (B.C. 486), which is a memorandum of a payment for drink in two instalments of the value of 2/- and 3/6 respectively). It is impossible therefore to doubt that, long before the time of Christ, writing was in civilized countries practised by all classes of society and applied to the purposes of trade and social life just as it is to-day.

Ancient Papyri

It has been ascertained that the Israelites, during the time they were settled in Palestine, made use principally of papyrus as the material whereon to write. Such manuscripts would long since have perished, and it is to be feared that no great discoveries will ever be made of Israelitish documents written during that period. The unique climate of Egypt however has preserved many ancient papyri, and from some of them an idea may be formed of the extent to which writing was practised, at a date not very distant from the Christian era, among people who were certainly not superior to the Jews in education and culture.

One especially interesting collection is that found at Gurob in the Fayyûm, to the West of the Nile valley, and of which a description is given by Professor Mahaffy in the *New Review* for November 1892. The greater part of the papers are dated from 260 to 223 B.C., but a few are dated as late as 186 B.C. Among them are not only fragments of literary works and official letters and records, but the correspondence, the business contracts, and the family papers of all sorts and conditions of men. They include, Professor Mahaffy informs us, letters from sons to fathers, letters from stewards giving accounts of their farms to their masters, wills, contracts, accounts —some those of tax-gatherers giving the sums paid to them, some those of contractors for the supply of fodder to horses, food for drivers, and medicaments for curing hurts or lameness —many more are mere private accounts, generally scrawled on the back of some other document.

What gives this find especial interest for us is the class of people to whom the papers originally belonged. The Fayyûm though situated in Egypt was occupied by a colony of Greek mercenary soldiers who "were a population mixed in a most extraordinary way, being in fact the descendants either in blood or in habit of the soldiers of Alexander, who gathered under his standard all the enterprising spirits of his wide domains. Thus there lived side by side in the Fayyûm, speaking good Greek, and using Greek customs, not only Macedonians, the most privileged of all, but Thessalians, Thracians, Arcadians, Illyrians, Carians, Persians, Lycians, Campanians, Artolians, all remembering and specifying their original homes, which they had permanently abandoned." Professor Mahaffy goes on to remark, "We may say without ear of exaggeration that no settlement of soldiers in the present day would produce anything like so civilized a society —I mean of course of mercenary or professional soldiers, not of those citizen armies where soldiering is but a transitory phase in each man's life. But these veterans were soldiers and nothing else, and yet they show, when surprised in their everyday life, and their ordinary conversation, how widely diffused a thing Hellenistic culture was, and what an engine for civilizing the world."

The foregoing refers to only a small proportion of the vast mass of evidence—evidence which is being added to year by year with the progress of Oriental exploration—that the knowledge and civilization of the ancient world had attained a much higher level than, a few years ago, was deemed possible, and that, as regards the practice of writing, the lands of the East, prior to the time of Christ, were far in advance of European countries in the middle ages or of Oriental countries at the present day.

Discoveries such as these have been a severe blow to the

destructive criticism in which modern scholars have so much delighted. It is not merely that many historical facts which have thus been brought to light are found to harmonise with and confirm statements of Scripture which the critics have impugned. The discoveries prove that the critics themselves have had no sympathetic insight into the spirit of the times which formed the subject of their study. How utterly out of touch with the educational condition of the Jews in the time of Josiah must they be, for instance, who can suppose it possible that the priests of that epoch should have forged the Sermons attributed to Moses in the book of Deuteronomy, and have been able to convince both King and people that they were the original work of their ancient lawgiver, accidentally found by them in clearing away the rubbish in the Lord's house.

I cannot for one moment doubt that the book of Daniel, notwithstanding the difficulty which even Professor Sayce and Major Conder find in reconciling some of its statements with the Babylonian records, will, with fuller information, be found to be authentic. The seeming discrepancies are insignificant, compared with the immense weight of evidence for the authenticity of the book, presented by Pusey in his Lectures on Daniel, evidence which cannot be refuted, which indeed no one has ever attempted to refute. But over and above the evidence, it is simply incredible that a historical romance written in the second century B.C. should within 200 years have come to be generally regarded as the genuine production of a great official who served at the court of Babylon in the sixth century B.C. The idea in fact refutes itself. An age that is capable of producing a work of wondrous brilliancy, like Daniel, is not an age when a spurious writing will readily be accepted as genuine.

Chapter II

CAUSE OF THE PREVAILING MIS-CONCEPTION

ALTHOUGH it is only within quite recent years that such an immense flood of light has been thrown upon the civilizations of antiquity, there was not at any time sufficient justification for the low views which prevailed, and for that matter even still very largely prevail, on that subject. It should always have been obvious that the great empires could never have established and maintained their power, or reached the high level of material grandeur which they were known to have attained, if writing had not been in extensive use among the people. It may be well therefore to pause and enquire how it is that, even among men of learning, men who had made the literature of ancient times the study of their lives, so inadequate an estimate could have been formed concerning the educational conditions of the times referred to.

The Intervening Gloom

A chief cause of these mistaken notions is the difficulty of piercing through the gloom of intervening ages so as to see clearly the state of the world as it was in those distant times.

It sometimes falls to the lot of miners, following a formation in the earth's crust, to find that formation, hitherto regular and well defined, together with the strata in which it is embedded, suddenly and completely cut off and brought to a termination by some geological disturbance or intrusion of foreign material. With almost equal suddenness and completeness three great historical disturbances cut off and ended the civilizations of the ancient world.

The first of these was the desolation of Judea, begun by the invasion under Vespasian and Titus, and completed seventy years after with the final destruction of Jerusalem in the time of Hadrian. The glory which had shone forth rom Zion over the heathenism and corruption of surrounding peoples came to a termination with the burning of the Temple. The old Jewish polity which had survived the fierce cruelty of Antiochus and the crafty tyranny of Herod was totally destroyed; the children of Israel were scattered among the nations; and the land of their fathers became the possession of strangers.

The next great disturbance was the overthrow of the Roman Empire in the 5th century, which brought to a close the brilliant day of Latin civilization, to be followed by a long night of ignorance, superstition and social debasement. During that time reading and writing might almost have been reckoned amongst the lost arts. As Voltaire remarks, "Nothing more clearly proves the low state of brutal ignorance to which the peoples of Europe had sunk, than the famous 'benefit of clergy' by which a criminal condemned to death obtained his pardon if he was able to read."

Lastly the rise and spread of the Mohammedan power overwhelmed and extinguished the culture and learning of the nations of the East. The effects of this catastrophe were more widespread and prolonged than even those that followed the breaking up of the Roman Empire. It is true that for a time embers of the old Oriental civilization struggled here and there to keep alight, and it has even been sometimes supposed that the world is indebted to Mohammedanism for the labours of men who rose above its withering influence to work in the cause of science and literature. But the fact cannot be gainsaid that, for several hundred years past, nothing whatever of value has been added by the people of any Mohammedan country to the knowledge or advancement of the world.

CAUSE OF THE PREVAILING MISCONCEPTION 41

Dense ignorance, stubborn prejudice, and gross superstition are the characteristics of the great mass of the people wherever the False Prophet holds his sway.

The dark ages in Europe lasted for more than half a millennium. The first grey streaks of dawn appeared about the tenth or eleventh century; but it was not until after the invention of printing in the fifteenth century that light began to be generally diffused. Even then the spread of daylight was slow, and it is only within the memory of the present generation that education in the Western countries of Europe has become universal. Therefore, although in our land every child is now taught to read and write, and knowledge of every kind is accessible to the poorest person, it is not forgotten that this state of things is new, and confined to a section of the race. It is patent to every one, and ever present in their thought, when they look back upon the past, that even a century ago the number who could read and write was but a small minority. And when they turn to Eastern lands they think of vast populations even now sunk in still denser ignorance. With these impressions vaguely hovering in the mind, it is difficult to realize how high a level as regards culture and education was occupied by the great civilizations prior to the historical events referred to.

Just as viewing from an eminence a distant tract of country the features of the foreground are present to the eye, and blend with outlines many miles away, so the mind, in throwing itself back to those remote times, insensibly gathers up and carries with it, from the long intervening period, ideas and impressions which mingle with its perception of the epoch on which it directs its gaze.

One illustration of this may suffice. In the middle ages many fraudulent documents were produced of no literary merit, but which, owing to the then prevailing ignorance, were successfully imposed upon the public credulity. Of these, one of the most notable instances is the forged Decretals of Isidore, published in the ninth century. Now because such deceptions were possible in those times, it is often imagined that similar deceptions could be perpetrated in the earlier centuries of the Christian era, whereas the period before the Fall of Rome bore no resemblance to the dark ages which followed that event.

That the earliest Christian believers were not liable to be easily imposed on in literary matters is proved by the discrimination they displayed in their treatment of the writings which claimed apostolic or inspired authority. Many such writings were rejected as spurious or excluded from the Canon as the work of good but uninspired men. Of the books which the New Testament includes the greater number were from the first recognised as genuine and inspired; but a few were always regarded as of doubtful authorship, though generally accepted as possessing divine authority. And now, after a century of unsparing and often hostile criticism, the results which have been arrived at are precisely the same as those that were reached in the second, third and fourth centuries. The books that were then acknowledged to be the genuine works of the men under whose name they stand in our New Testament are by common consent admitted to be so. The books whose authorship was then thought doubtful are similarly regarded still, though now as then they are generally accepted as canonical. Nor has it been discovered that any books were improperly omitted from the Canon. It is no slight testimony to the acumen and learning of those times that the ancient Church did not include within the covers of the New Testament a single book which her successors have seen reason to eliminate; or reject any which it has since been thought proper to include. It proves that immediately after the time of Christ, and therefore in the time of Christ itself, there was no lack of intelligence, and gives us reason to conclude that men in the circumstances of the Apostles would not neglect taking such means to record the acts and sayings of their Master as we should expect from men in similar circumstances now.

Chapter III

CIVILIZATION AND THE PRACTICE OF WRITING IN THE TIME OF CHRIST

THE epoch in which our Lord came into the world was that which is distinguished in history as the Augustan era. It is described by Lightfoot as the "moment when the world had reached its highest point of civilization and culture, when political and legislative ability were achieving their most signal triumphs; an age of remarkable progress and enlightenment which was unequalled in ancient, and has only been equalled quite recently in modern times."

Excepting a few minor wars in some of the outlying provinces, the Roman Empire had enjoyed at the beginning of Christ's Ministry half a century of peace. The world had not known a similar experience since the age of Solomon, and has hardly enjoyed the like since, even in the nineteenth century. As a consequence riches had accumulated, and numbers of men possessed wealth and leisure to devote themselves to the cultivation of literature, science and the arts. Intellectual activity was stimulated, I doubt not, in no small degree by the presence of Jews in every city of the Roman Empire. The security afforded by the domination of Rome, together with the wide-spread use of the Greek language, encouraged commerce and facilitated travel in the pursuit of pleasure and knowledge. Hence there was a free interchange of ideas and information amongst the nations of the earth. Schools abounded for the education of the young. Even slaves were often taught to read and write in order to qualify them for the duties required of them by their masters. Publishers employed large numbers of slaves to multiply copies of the works of the poets, philosophers, historians and other authors who adorned the period; hence books were cheap and read by citizens in all ranks of society. It goes without saying that at such a period there was of necessity a large written correspondence. Printing not having been invented it is possible even that among some classes writing was more often practised then than now. Many a man would write a letter where now he would simply send a newspaper.

Writing in Palestine

It is quite certain that the Jews were not behind other nations in education and culture. It was not by chance that the children of Israel were brought successively into such close relations, at the period of their highest splendour, with all the great contemporary civilizations. Called out, and kept separate from the rest of humanity, to fulfil their mission of blessing to the nations, there was a tendency on the part of the chosen people to become insular and narrow-minded, a tendency however which was counteracted by their enforced contact with the culture of Egypt, of Assyria, of Babylonia, of Greece, and of Rome. In the centuries immediately preceding Christ, millions of the race were scattered throughout the civilized world, and kept up constant communication with their brethren in the Holy Land. There is abundant evidence in both the New Testament and Josephus that a large written correspondence was at that time continually going on between Palestine and other countries.

The Holy Land itself was not, as many seem to imagine, an obscure and isolated country. To quote the words of the Apostle Paul, the great events recorded in the Gospels were "not done in a corner." Palestine held the most central position in the map of the ancient world. It was the great highway between the three continents. From the time of Jacob and long before, merchants had passed through its borders on their journey from Asia to Egypt. Travellers rom Europe to Asia and Africa also passed through or near to the land of Israel. The merchant princes of Phœnicia in the North were the great connecting link of commerce between the countries of the Mediterranean seaboard and Central Asia; whilst the port of Joppa, from its nearness to Jerusalem, brought the capital city itself into easy communication with the Western World.

Galilee, the native province of nearly all the Apostles, was a great highway of trade, along which travellers of all nationalities were daily passing to and fro. Coming in frequent contact with these, and with foreigners residing at Tiberias and other Greek cities in Galilee itself, the dwellers about the Sea of Galilee would gain large and varied experience of worldly affairs.

There is abundant evidence that the education of the young was not neglected. The synagogues, with which the smallest towns were provided, and where the ordinances of religion were observed on the Sabbath, appear to have been used as schools during the week. It is probable that the whole population of Palestine could read, and that all but the lowest had been taught to write.

The Apostles

The Apostles themselves were men of superior intelligence. Their wits had been sharpened in the struggle for life. They had left their ordinary pursuits and given up their worldly prospects, social connections and the comforts of home to ollow Him whom they believed to be the long-looked-for Messiah, the Saviour of the world, and to devote themselves to the mission of proclaiming the glad tidings to their fellowmen. Let us try, by the "scientific use of the imagination" to throw ourselves into their times and circumstances, and then ask ourselves the question : Is it credible that, during the three or four years of their attendance on the Great Master, and for long after, it never occurred to one of them to make written notes of the wonderfuul words and facts they were privileged to hear and see?

Chapter IV

TAUTOCHRONISTIC REPORTING

IT has been implied in a previous chapter, that the practice of reporting speakers at the time of utterance was not uncommon in the time of Christ. It would be strange indeed if in so brilliant an age so obvious and necessary a practice were neglected. That anyone should suppose that it was neglected can only be accounted for by that prevailing misconception to which we have adverted, and to a vague idea which has sprung out of the Evolution hypothesis, that men 2000 years ago were less intelligent than they are now. But there is no room for doubt. There is abundant proof, not only that it was customary to take down written reports of speeches as they were delivered, but that systems of shorthand were elaborated for the purpose.

Reporting amongst the Romans

Seneca, quoted by Macaulay in his Essay on Lord Bacon, affecting to complain of the utilitarian spirit of the age, speaks of shorthand having been brought to such perfection, that a writer could keep pace with the most rapid speaker. Shorthand, however, was practised in Rome long before the time of Seneca, who lived when the New Testament was being written. Ennius the poet (239-169 B.C.), among other literary accomplishments, amused himself with an elementary system of shorthand. (*Latin Literature*, J. W. MacKail, p. 7.)

Many of the recorded speeches of the ancient orators must have been reported by means of shorthand. Some of Cicero's orations, for instance, were delivered in circumstances that made previous preparation or subsequent record of them, either by speaker or hearers, impossible. Thus his first oration against Lucius Catiline was provoked, on the spur of the moment, by the unexpected appearance of his enemy in the meeting of the senate. Its character proves that it was unprepared, and adapted at the time to Catiline's behaviour at the meeting. Nor could it have been committed to writing afterwards from memory. The city was in a state bordering on anarchy; Cicero himself was in hourly danger of assassination, and as Consul had to exercise the utmost diligence to thwart the designs of the conspirators. It is known that he had in his service a freedman named Tiro, who wrote shorthand and invented certain signs for the purpose which were named after him, *notæ Tironianæ*, and there is no reason to doubt the correctness of Plutarch's assertion (Life of Cato, c. 23) that the speech was reported by shorthand writers, several of whom had been dispersed about the senate-house by Cicero.

Reporting amongst the Greeks

Amongst the Greeks, shorthand writing was of very early date. A recent writer states that "a fragment of an inscription found recently in the Acropolis at Athens has been shown by Gompers to be a portion of an explanation of a kind of shorthand, composed of arbitrary signs, as old as the fourth century B.C." According to the same authority, "the first undoubted mention of a Greek shorthand writer, occurs in a passage in Galen, wherein he refers to a copy, made by one who could write swiftly in signs." By A.D. 100, a perfected system of shorthand was in use as is proved by "the occurrence in papyri of certain symbols as marks of contraction, or to represent entire words, and particularly the large number of them found in the papyrus of Aristotle's work on the constitution of Athens." (*Handbook of Greek and Latin Palæography* by E. M. Thompson, D.C.L., etc., pages 82, 83.)

48 THE GOSPEL PROBLEMS AND THEIR SOLUTION

Reporting amongst the Jews

It having been shown that tautochronistic reporting was in general use amongst the Greeks and Romans it becomes very unlikely that it was not also practised by the Jews. The influence in Palestine of Greek and Roman culture was at that time immense. As will be shown at greater length hereafter there had been for several centuries a Hellenistic party, constantly growing in strength, which endeavoured to introduce Greek customs and culture. Though stoutly opposed by the conservative and more religious portion of the people, its influence steadily increased, until, in the time of Christ, there were Hellenistic Synagogues in Jerusalem, and the office of High Priest, and the controlling power of the Temple, had fallen into its hands. Indeed by that time, not only had the Greek language supplanted Aramaic in Jerusalem and the larger towns, but Greek customs had become firmly settled in the life of the people. It appears, for instance, from the New Testament that the practice of reclining at meals had then become general. As there is no hint in the Old Testament of any such habit (certainly not in Ezek. xxiii. 41, where the verb used is *yashabh*, to sit) it may safely be said that it was not an ancient national custom. Doubtless the Greeks learned the habit from the Persians, and the Hebrews like the Romans learned it from the Greeks.

On top of this Greek influence came the Roman domination which had now lasted well nigh a century. Roman officials and Roman soldiers were permanent residents in the country. The methodical business-like ways of that nation, so celebrated for administrative ability, could not fail to impress the subject people and provoke imitation.

It is then not open to us to imagine that the Jews neglected a practice so useful and so necessary to a civilized community as tautochronistic reporting. And, if direct proof be required, we have it in the maxim of the Rabbinical schools, "commit nothing to writing." Men are not forbidden to do things which no one thinks of doing. Such an injunction proves that it was the custom in that age and country, as it has been in every other age and country, for disciples to make written notes of their masters' teachings.

Nor does the case end here : there is abundant circumstantial evidence that reporting at the moment of utterance was in use among the Israelites, long before the date at which the earliest trace of it appears among the civilized nations of Europe. This evidence we shall now proceed to consider.

Chapter V

TAUTOCHRONISTIC REPORTS IN THE OLD TESTAMENT

IT is a favourite and oft-repeated assertion of the Higher Criticism, that the speeches recorded in the Old Testament, and attributed to various historical personages, are not to be taken as the actual deliverance of those personages, but must be understood to be the composition of the historians, who, to embellish their narratives, fabricated such addresses and discourses as seemed to them to suit the occasions, and put them into the mouths of their heroes. This is a view, however, that will not bear serious and honest examination. The subject cannot here be discussed at length: nevertheless my argument will be incomplete without some reference to it, and, as the Sermons attributed to Moses in Deuteronomy have been made a special object of attack, I crave for them a few moments of attention.

Deuteronomy

With regard to the Sermons recorded in Deuteronomy, it is singular how completely the critics ignore the fact that these are not presented as the written compositions of Moses, but as his spoken addresses. Dr. Driver for example (*International Commentary*, Deuteronomy, p. xxxv.), while admitting that the representations in Numbers xiii. 1-3 and Deut. i. 22, 23 are capable in the abstract of being harmonized, goes on to say, "It remains remarkable, if the two accounts were written by one and the same person, that they should be so worded as to suggest to the reader *two different ideas of what had taken place;* and (especially) that Moses, while mentioning (Deut. i. 23) that the proposal had his own approval, should not mention that it had Jehovah's also." Nor is this the only instance in which his objections to the Mosaic authorship of the Sermons are based upon the assumption that they claim to be the written composition of the law-giver.

As a matter of fact they make no such claim. What they do claim is that they are reports of Moses' oral addresses, which is quite a different thing, It is expressly asserted that they were *spoken* by him publicly to "all Israel," that is, the assembled representatives of the nation : it is not said that they were *read* from a document which he had written, as would have been said had such been the case. The implication is that the Sermons were reported verbatim by a shorthand writer as they were orally delivered by the speaker.

That Moses had the Book of the Law before him and sometimes referred to it in the course of his Sermons is likely enough, and seems to be implied (xxix. 21, 27, 29, xxx. 10). It is also said that Moses "wrote this law" (xxxi. 9, 24), by which is meant probably the book referred to. But although it is further stated that he wrote the Song recorded Chapter xxxii., and afterwards taught it to the people, it is nowhere hinted that he wrote the Sermons.

Considering Moses' age and office it is probable that even those parts which Moses is said to have written were not actually written with his hand, but by a scribe at his dictation.

The recognition of this, that the Sermons in Deuteronomy are not the written composition of Moses but the reports of his spoken utterances, cuts the ground from under most of the objections that are brought against their authenticity. So much more latitude is always allowable to a speaker than to a writer. Take for instance the reference to the exclusion of Moses from Canaan referred to i. 37, and the appointment of Joshua as his substitute to lead the people thither, i. 38, parenthetically mentioned in connection with events that happened thirty-seven years previously. Granted that Dr. Driver and other critics may be right in thinking it improbable that dates would thus be confused in a *written* statement; in an *oral* statement this is precisely what ought to be expected.

History of Reporting among the Hebrews

If the speeches in the Old Testament are not the genuine utterances of the persons to whom they are ascribed, why is it that no long address of any kind is recorded of earlier date than the discourse delivered by Jacob on his death-bed? When speeches were being fabricated it would have been easy to have invented one for Adam, Enoch or Noah. At any rate it is inexplicable that the claims of Abraham in this respect should have been ignored. He held the very highest place in the estimation of the Israelites. The story of his life is unusually long, occupying the greater part of thirteen chapters. Yet, though many of his sayings are recorded, they are all comparatively short, and such as could easily be retained for a time in the memory. Similar remarks apply also to the life of Isaac and the earlier part of the life of Jacob. How is it that the first lengthy utterance recorded in Scripture was spoken soon after the chosen people had made their home in Egypt? This is a question that cannot be answered on any theory that denies the truth of the histories or the genuineness of the speeches, and should go a long way to prove that all such theories are false. But from the believing standpoint the explanation is easy.

It appears from the discoveries at Tel-el-Amarna that, prior to the time of Jacob's migration to Egypt, paper was not in common use in Palestine; but that clay tablets were generally employed as the material whereon to write. But it would be impossible to write rapidly with a stylus on clay and therefore tautochronistic reporting could not at that time be practised. Dialogues and short poetical sayings could be and sometimes were remembered for a while and afterwards committed to writing. Thus the conversations between the

Almighty and Abraham, recorded Genesis xvii. and xviii., were kept in the mind of the Patriarch until he had an opportunity to inscribe them on a tablet. These are the longest records of the kind which have come down to us from that time. Lengthy discourses such as are recorded at later dates could not be retained in the memory, and, as there was then no method available for writing down the words as they were spoken, all such discourses were lost.

In Egypt, however, the case was different. The thick fleshy stalks of the *Cyperus Papyrus*, which grew so abundantly, and still grows, in the marshes of the Nile Delta, split into sheets and properly prepared, formed a material upon which, with a reed, or quill, one might write as readily as we now write on ordinary paper, with a steel pen. The syllabic characters in use amongst the ancient Egyptians were peculiarly adapted for fast writing, being themselves equivalent to a system of shorthand. The alphabet was not at that time invented and a single sign was used to express a syllable that would require two or three alphabetic letters to spell it. Numerous specimens have been brought to light of cursive syllabic writing on papyrus. That sort of writing is known as hieratic and has been described by a modern author, as the shorthand of hieroglyphics. The ready writers of Egypt probably formed a numerous class, whose services would be required even in connection with the inscriptions which abound on the ancient monuments. The historical record or pious declaration which it was desired to perpetuate would in the first instance be dictated either by the sovereign or eminent personage himself, or by some official at his command, to a writer who would note the words down as spoken, in hieratic or cursive syllabic letters. Afterwards he would make a fair copy in hieroglyphic characters and the copy so made would be the exemplar handed to the engraver to inscribe on the tomb or temple.

It is then not unreasonable to suppose that Joseph, when he learned that his dying father was about to make an inspired

54 THE GOSPEL PROBLEMS AND THEIR SOLUTION

deliverance concerning the future of his descendants, sent for a fast writer acquainted with Hebrew, who wrote down by the bedside of the Patriarch a verbatim report of his last utterances as recorded in Genesis xlviii. and xlix.

When, some centuries later, the Israelites went out of Egypt, there were many among them who had acquired a knowledge of the various arts in use in that highly cultured land. Moses, who was himself "instructed in all the wisdom of the Egyptians," and was moreover an able administrator, turned the talents of his people to account, and doubtless employed some who were fast writers in reporting the addresses preserved in Deuteronomy.

After a time, when the Israelites had been long settled in Canaan, they borrowed from their neighbours, the Phœnicians, the alphabetic mode of writing, and then some new system of shorthand must have come into use. Of this no specimens have been discovered for the reason already mentioned that most papyri of that ancient date, outside the land of Egypt, have perished. But there is a clear reference to shorthand in Psalm xlv., "My tongue is the pen of a ready writer." The word *mahir* translated "ready" means properly quick or rapid. It is derived from a verb *mahar* which means to hasten or to be quick. The verb is found in this sense in numerous places, as, for instance Gen. xix. 22, "Haste thee, escape thither"; Josh. iv. 10, "The people hasted and passed over; 1 Sam. xvii. 48, "David hasted and ran towards the army to meet the Philistine"; Malachi iii. 5, "I will be a swift witness" (literally, "I will be swift to witness"). It does not appear that the Psalmist means to compare his fluency of speech to the speed of a writer's pen, nor is it easy to see any point in such a comparison. It seems rather that he meant to imply that he used the services of a rapid writer to record his utterances. As though he should say, "When I discourse on so noble a theme as the glory of the King it is not enough to speak orally to the few hundreds who may be gathered in the great congregation. The tongue that I use for this purpose is not 'this poor, lisping, stammering tongue,' that will soon ' lie silent in the grave,' but the pen of the rapid writer, by whose aid my song of praise shall be heard by all nations and be remembered to all generations."

By the aid of such writers David's dying charge to Solomon, Solomon's prayer at the dedication of the Temple, and the prayer of the Levites at the Feast of Tabernacles after the Return, were reported. Jeremiah employed such a writer, a man named Baruch, to record his prophecies. When asked, "Tell us now, how didst thou write all these words at his mouth?" Baruch answered, "He pronounced all these words unto me with his mouth, and I wrote them with ink in the book." (Jer. xxxvi. 18.)

Daniel's interpretation of Nebuchadnezzar's dream; Nebuchadnezzar's narrative in Daniel; Daniel's address to Belshazzar; and Daniel's report of his own dream in chapter vii.; were reported by some of the shorthand writers in constant attendance at the Court of Babylon.

Be it understood that the object of the argument in this chapter is not to prove that the disciples had learnt a systematic form of shorthand, but to show that the practice of tautochronistic reporting was not unusual, and therefore not unlikely to have been adopted in the case of our Lord's utterances. If it should be thought improbable that men in their circumstances should have learned shorthand, I reply that it is not essential to our purpose to assume that they had done so. I have known competent reporters for the daily press who never learned Pitman's or any other recognised system : by long practice in the use of abbreviations and signs of their own invention, they had acquired the art of writing fast enough to report even rapid speakers. Later on I shall show that the occupations of the few men, to whom, as I believe, we are chiefly indebted for the Gospel narratives, were such as would necessitate, and educate them in, the art of rapid writing.

It is not at all likely that our Lord was as a rule a rapid

speaker. His longer addresses have the appearance of having been spoken deliberately and slowly : we might almost imagine, as we read the Sermon on the Mount, or the Address at the Last Supper, that He paused after each sentence, thus allowing His reporters time to take down His words.

Chapter VI

THE NATURE OF THE GOSPEL NARRATIVES

HAVING cleared the way by showing that there was nothing in the circumstances of the time to render it improbable that the Apostles would record the events of our Lord's ministry at the time they happened, or even that they should make tautochronistic reports of His utterances, we have now to prove from the internal evidence of the Gospels themselves that they actually did so.

It is remarkable that not one of the Gospels attempts to give anything like a biography of our Lord Jesus Christ. Two of them, Mark and John, are perfectly silent as to the first thirty years of His life. Except with regard to His birth and infancy Matthew is equally silent. Luke in this respect differs from Matthew only in that he relates in addition a single incident that happened when Jesus was twelve years old, and informs us that He went down with His parents to Nazareth, and · was subject unto them, and that He advanced in wisdom and stature and in favour with God and men. It may be inferred from a single quoted sentence in Matthew and Mark that Jesus worked at His reputed father's trade. But even on that point as well as about His education and the events of His early manhood there is not one direct statement.

No attempt is made to tell even the story of His ministry in systematic form or consecutive order. It is not even stated how long the ministry lasted; it is only by careful study and comparison that any idea on that point can be gained, and then there remains some uncertainty and room for difference of opinion. The narratives are fragmentary, consisting for the most part of incidents and sayings, each complete in itself, and sometimes minutely reported, but having little or no connection with that which precedes or follows. Of the 1,100 or 1,200 days, usually supposed to be comprised in our Lord's ministry, the number about which we are told anything whatever is less than 100; except that in two or three instances it is said that, during a period which is not defined, He went about in all Galilee, or all the cities and the villages, preaching the Gospel of the Kingdom and healing all manner of diseases. And of many of the days that are mentioned we get but a glimpse, a snapshot as it were of a single incident which occupied but a few minutes in the enacting. Other days it is true appear crowded with events; parable after parable or miracle after miracle pass before us in succession; but even of such days the number is very few of which there is anything like a consecutive account. The few days preceding the Crucifixion are the only portion of our Lord's life which is narrated with any approach to historical form.

On any of the current theories as to the origin of the Gospels these features are incomprehensible. Whether the Synoptic Gospels are based on the reminiscences of some of the disciples, on the oral teaching of the Apostles, or merely on tradition or legend; whether they were composed twenty years or fifty years after the Crucifixion; whether the fourth Gospel was written by John the Apostle, or by some one else long after his death; there is no denying one thing, namely, that the Gospels are four distinct works, composed by four separate individuals. This would be no less true even if it could be shown that Matthew and Luke were but amplifications of Mark, or that Mark was an abridgment of Matthew and Luke. Four Christian believers set themselves independently to prepare a narrative of the facts upon which their religion is based; and of the manner in which its Founder established it. Yet they give nothing at all resembling a history of the Founder's life; but only (with the exceptions mentioned above) a number of detached recitals of various things He said and did during His last three or four years, and a very full account of His death and resurrection.

It would have been surprising enough if this description had applied to only one or two of the narratives. But that it should apply to the whole four; that all the Synoptics should be alike in this respect, and that John, though differing so much from the Synoptics in other ways, should also in this respect resemble them; this is a problem which, though it has not been so much discussed, is if possible more perplexing than all the others.

There can be no question about the desire of believers to learn all that could be told concerning the life of Christ. People always wish to know every detail of the history of any person in whom they feel a surpassing interest. It was to satisfy this craving in the early Church that spurious works like the Gospel of the Infancy were produced. The desire for a connected history is exemplified by one of the oldest Christian books extant—the Diatessaron of Tatian—which is simply an attempt to form a consecutive narrative out of the four Gospels.

The ignoring of these considerations by the Evangelists is an enigma without parallel in literature, and for which, except on one hypothesis, there is absolutely no solution. And it cannot be too strongly insisted on, that the enigma grows in difficulty in proportion to the lateness of the date assigned to the composition of the Gospels, and to the doubts entertained as to their literal accuracy. For traditions grow fuller with the lapse of time; and, just in proportion to a historian's indifference to the strict claims of truth, will he yield to the popular demand for, and his own inclination to supply, a complete and consecutive story.

Now what is the true solution of this very singular and interesting problem? It is that Mathew, Mark, Luke and John were so profoundly impressed with the solemn responsibility of their task, that they carefully avoided inserting anything in their narratives for which they had not undoubted authority. No tradition, however well supported; no recollection, not even their own, might find a place there. Nothing but reports in black and white, written by trustworthy persons at the very time the events happened, were worthy of insertion in their books. So far from their narratives being composed of reminiscences and oral tradition, reminiscences and oral tradition were the very things they were specially careful to exclude.

Still, why this Incompleteness?

But it may be said, "This is no real solution of the difficulty; it only throws it back to an earlier date. Granted that it relieves the redactors of the Gospels of responsibility for the features described, it only casts it instead on the original reporters. If the Apostles saw it to be their duty to make written records of the facts of the Lord's ministry, how is it that they did the work so imperfectly? If, as this theory assumes, they were conscious even in a limited degree of the greatness and majesty of Him Whom they followed; if they realized however dimly that the duty rested upon them to hand down to the ages a record of the sayings and doings of the Word made Flesh; why did they not carefully follow His footsteps day by day and make full and systematic reports of His proceedings? It is said, "if all the things which Jesus did should be written every one, even the world itself would hardly contain the books that should be written!" With such an abundance of material why was so little preserved? Why are we left in absolute darkness as to Christ's actions on eleven out of every twelve days of those in which He manifested Himself to men as the Saviour of the world?

This is a fair question and demands a reply.

Lost Manuscripts?

There is one possible explanation, which, however, I should be very reluctant to admit. It is that a great number of the original manuscripts were lost, and that only the few that escaped that fate were used in the composition of the Gospels.

THE NATURE OF THE GOSPEL NARRATIVES 61

There can be little doubt that some ancient manuscripts relating to Christ's ministry were lost. It is remarkable that the only saying of Jesus directly quoted by the Apostle Paul is from a manuscript not included in the Gospels (Acts xx. 35). Nevertheless it is not likely that any of the reports written by the disciples whose manuscripts form the substance of the four Gospels were allowed to perish. The early Church would value such documents too highly not to take of them most scrupulous care. Besides, the characteristics of the Gospels are not such as to suggest this explanation. If the original reports had been continuous and connected it is probable that the surviving portions would present a consecutive narrative for a given considerable space of time; whilst for another considerable space of time there would be absolute silence. Instead of this the narratives supply a succession of disconnected facts sprinkled as it were all through the course of the ministry.

The Mission of the Apostles

There is another and far more feasible answer to this question. It should not be forgotten that the twelve disciples were sent by our Lord on a mission which would greatly interfere with their task of reporting His doings, and sayings. They were called to be "Apostles" (ἀπόστολοι). They were "sent forth" to preach the Gospel; to announce that the Kingdom of Heaven was at hand. In their narratives they carefully keep themselves and their doings as much as possible out of sight, so we are afforded very little information as to the experiences which befell them, and none at all as to the time they occupied in carrying out their instructions. It may be that this mission kept them so much employed that they were far less constantly in the company of Jesus than is commonly supposed, and, as they took no hearsay notes, their narratives are for that reason more meagre than they might otherwise have been.

Circumstances sometimes Unfavourable for Reporting

Another reason, still more potent than the last, for the disconnected and fragmentary nature of the Gospel narratives, is to be found in the fact that circumstances were often unfavourable for making written reports. This applies especially to our Lord's own sayings. It is a significant fact that the Gospels do not contain a single address of even moderate length that was spoken in circumstances adverse to the taking of a report on the spot. Many journeys to and fro in Galilee, and between Galilee and Judea, did Christ and the Apostles make in company. Many trips on the blue waters of Gennesaret did they take in the craft of the fishermen. Was our Lord silent on those occasions? Is it not as certain as anything can be, of which no definite assertion is made, that He often availed Himself of such opportunities to instruct His followers? Do not their relations as Master ($\Delta\iota\delta\acute{a}\sigma\kappa a\lambda o\varsigma$) and disciples ($\mu a\theta\eta\tau a\acute{\iota}$) imply that He did so? Yet all that Christ is reported to have said when travelling either by land or water is comprised in about a dozen solitary sentences. Sitting on a mountain or in a boat moored near the shore; standing in the Temple or a synagogue; reclining in a friend's house or in an upper room with His disciples—it was in such postures as these that His recorded lengthy speeches were delivered.

An Illustration

As illustrating this general law, compare two parallel cases. One is related only by Luke (v. 1–3), and the other by both Matthew (xiii. 1–52) and Mark (iv. 1–32). In both instances our Lord addressed, from a boat floating on the lake, great multitudes of people standing on the shore. They were two distinct incidents; for the preaching was followed, in the one case, by the miraculous draught of fishes, and the disciples leaving all and following Him; in the other, by their taking Him with them "even as He was in the boat" (Mark iv. 36). But in the case mentioned by Luke not a word of His teaching is preserved; whereas in that related by Matthew and Mark we find the parable of the Sower, of the Tares, of the Mustard Seed, of the Leaven, of the Hidden Treasure, of the Pearl, of the Drag-net, of the Lamp, and of the Seed growing in Secret. Why are the two cases so differently treated? Read back and you will see. In the former instance the disciples were unprepared for writing. When Jesus entered Simon's boat and asked him to put out a little from the land, he and the other fishermen were standing in the water washing their nets after toiling all night at their occupation. In the other case there is nothing to show that the disciples were not, as usually, in attendance on their Lord, and ready to take notes of His discourses.

Chapter VII

THE BIRTH, INFANCY AND EARLY LIFE OF JESUS. THE GENEALOGIES

NOTHING could more fully demonstrate how extremely scrupulous the Evangelists were to use only authentic written materials in the composition of their works than the manner in which they severally deal with the birth, infancy and childhood of our Lord. No fact is more essential to the claims and to the doctrines of Christianity than the supernatural birth of its Founder. Without that the cardinal truths of the New Testament fail, and the Christian scheme of salvation falls to the ground. Other essential facts are recorded in detail by all the Evangelists; while the primary fact, the exceptional manner of the Christ's coming into the world, the miraculous method of His incarnation, is not even mentioned by Mark and John. Yet none had a higher conception than John of the transcendent dignity of his Lord. The strong antagonism that Naturalists have at all times shown towards the fourth Gospel has ever gathered round its teaching concerning the exalted nature and attributes of the Word that was made flesh and dwelt amongst men. If there is any element of truth in the old tradition that Mark's Gospel contains the substance of Peter's preaching, the omission from this Gospel of any mention of the birth of Christ is hardly less remarkable than the silence of John. For Peter's views of the divine majesty of Jesus were quite as pronounced as John's, as a perusal of his two Epistles will prove. Nor can it be questioned that, at the time when Mark's, much more John's, narrative is supposed to have been written or redacted, very clear and decided views prevailed amongst believers on this subject. There is but one way of explaining this omission. It is that Mark and John had no written material to make use of and each declined to include in his book anything built on a less substantial basis.

This leads to the enquiry, Whence and how did Matthew and Luke obtain their accounts of our Lord's birth and infancy? These accounts when compared are found to be most remarkable and interesting. They dovetail into one another almost as if they had originally formed a single consecutive story. They are easily pieced together thus :

LUKE I.

5 There was in the days of Herod, King of Judæa, a certain priest named Zacharias, of the course of Abijah: and he had a wife of the
6 daughters of Aaron, and her name was Elisabeth. And they were both righteous before God, walking in all the commandments and ordinances
7 of the Lord blameless. And they had no child, because that Elisabeth was barren, and they both were *now* well stricken in years.
8 Now it came to pass, while he executed the priest's office before God
9 in the order of his course, according to the custom of the priest's office, his lot was to enter into the temple of the Lord and burn incense.
10 And the whole multitude of the people were praying without at the
11 hour of incense. And there appeared unto him an angel of the Lord
12 standing on the right side of the altar of incense. And Zacharias was
13 troubled when he saw *him*, and fear fell upon him. But the angel said unto him, Fear not, Zacharias : because thy supplication is heard, and thy wife Elisabeth shall bear thee a son, and thou shalt call his name
14 John. And thou shalt have joy and gladness ; and many shall rejoice
15 at his birth. For he shall be great in the sight of the Lord, and he shall drink no wine nor strong drink ; and he shall be filled with the
16 Holy Ghost, even from his mother's womb. And many of the children
17 of Israel shall he turn unto the Lord their God. And he shall go before his face in the spirit and power of Elijah, to turn the hearts of the fathers to the children, and the disobedient *to walk* in the wisdom of the just ; to make ready for the Lord a people prepared *for him*.
18 And Zacharias said unto the angel, Whereby shall I know this ? for I
19 am an old man, and my wife well stricken in years. And the angel answering said unto him, I am Gabriel, that stand in the presence of God ; and I was sent to speak unto thee, and to bring thee these good
20 tidings. And behold, thou shalt be silent and not able to speak, until

the day that these things shall come to pass, because thou believedst
21 not my words, which shall be fulfilled in their season. And the people were waiting for Zacharias, and they marvelled while he tarried in the
22 temple. And when he came out, he could not speak unto them: and they perceived that he had seen a vision in the temple: and he con-
23 tinued making signs unto them, and remained dumb. And it came to pass, when the days of his ministration were fulfilled, he departed unto his house.

24 And after these days Elisabeth his wife conceived; and she hid her-
25 self five months, saying, Thus hath the Lord done unto me in the days wherein he looked upon *me*, to take away my reproach among men.

26 Now in the sixth month the angel Gabriel was sent from God unto
27 a city of Galilee, named Nazareth, to a virgin betrothed to a man whose name was Joseph, of the house of David; and the virgin's name was
28 Mary. And he came in unto her, and said, Hail, thou that art highly
29 favoured, the Lord *is* with thee. But she was greatly troubled at the saying, and cast in her mind what manner of salutation this might be.
30 And the angel said unto her, Fear not, Mary: for thou hast found
31 favour with God. And behold, thou shalt conceive in thy womb, and
32 bring forth a son, and shalt call his name JESUS. He shall be great, and shall be called the Son of the Most High: and the Lord God shall
33 give unto him the throne of his father David: and he shall reign over the house of Jacob for ever; and of his kingdom there shall be no end.
34 And Mary said unto the angel, How shall this be, seeing I know not
35 a man? And the angel answered and said unto her, The Holy Ghost shall come upon thee, and the power of the Most High shall overshadow thee: wherefore also that which is to be born shall be called holy, the
36 Son of God. And behold, Elisabeth thy kinswoman, she also hath conceived a son in her old age: and this is the sixth month with her
37 that was called barren. For no word from God shall be void of power.
38 And Mary said, Behold, the handmaid of the Lord; be it unto me according to thy word. And the angel departed from her.

39 And Mary arose in these days and went into the hill country with
40 haste, into a city of Judah; and entered into the house of Zacharias and
41 saluted Elisabeth. And it came to pass, when Elisabeth heard the salutation of Mary, the babe leaped in her womb; and Elisabeth was
42 filled with the Holy Ghost; and she lifted up her voice with a loud cry, and said, Blessed *art* thou among women, and blessed *is* the fruit
43 of thy womb. And whence is this to me, that the mother of my
44 Lord should come unto me? For behold, when the voice of thy salutation came into mine ears, the babe leaped in my womb for joy.
45 And blessed *is* she that believed; for there shall be a fulfilment of the things which have been spoken to her from the Lord.

THE BIRTH AND EARLY LIFE OF JESUS

46 And Mary said,
   My soul doth magnify the Lord,
47 And my spirit hath rejoiced in God my Saviour.
48 For he hath looked upon the low estate of his handmaiden:
   For behold, from henceforth all generations shall call me blessed.
49 For he that is mighty hath done to me great things;
   And holy is his name.
50 And his mercy is unto generations and generations
   On them that fear him.
51 He hath shewed strength with his arm;
   He hath scattered the proud in the imagination of their heart.
52 He hath put down princes from *their* thrones,
   And hath exalted them of low degree.
53 The hungry he hath filled with good things;
   And the rich he hath sent empty away.
54 He hath holpen Israel his servant,
   That he might remember mercy
55 (As he spake unto our fathers)
   Toward Abraham and his seed for ever.
56 And Mary abode with her about three months, and returned unto her house.

MATTHEW I.

18 Now the birth of Jesus Christ was on this wise: When his mother Mary had been betrothed to Joseph, before they came together she was
19 found with child of the Holy Ghost. And Joseph her husband, being a righteous man, and not willing to make her a public example, was
20 minded to put her away privily. But when he thought on these things, behold, an angel of the Lord appeared unto him in a dream, saying, Joseph, thou son of David, fear not to take unto thee Mary thy wife:
21 for that which is conceived in her is of the Holy Ghost. And she shall bring forth a son; and thou shalt call his name JESUS; for it is he that
22 shall save his people from their sins. Now all this is come to pass, that it might be fulfilled which was spoken by the Lord through the prophet, saying,
23 Behold, the virgin shall be with child, and shall bring forth a son,
   And they shall call his name Immanuel;
24 which is, being interpreted, God with us. And Joseph arose from his sleep, and did as the angel of the Lord commanded him, and took unto him his wife.

LUKE I.

57 Now Elisabeth's time was fulfilled that she should be delivered; and
58 she brought forth a son. And her neighbours and her kinsfolk heard

that the Lord had magnified his mercy towards her; and they rejoiced
59 with her. And it came to pass on the eighth day, that they came to
circumcise the child; and they would have called him Zacharias, after
60 the name of his father. And his mother answered and said, Not so;
61 but he shall be called John. And they said unto her, There is none of
62 thy kindred that is called by this name. And they made signs to his
63 father, what he would have him called. And he asked for a writing
tablet, and wrote, saying, His name is John. And they marvelled all.
64 And his mouth was opened immediately, and his tongue *loosed*, and he
65 spake, blessing God. And fear came on all that dwelt around about
them: and all these sayings were noised abroad throughout all the hill
66 country of Judæa. And all that heard them laid them up in their
heart, saying, What then shall this child be? For the hand of the Lord
was with him.
67 And his father Zacharias was filled with the Holy Ghost, and prophesied, saying,
68 Blessed *be* the Lord, the God of Israel;
For he hath visited and wrought redemption for his people,
69 And hath raised up a horn of salvation for us
In the house of his servant David.
70 (As he spake by the mouth of his holy prophets which have been since the world began),
71 Salvation from our enemies, and from the hand of all that hate us;
72 To shew mercy towards our fathers,
And to remember his holy covenant;
73 The oath which he sware unto Abraham our father,
74 To grant unto us that we being delivered out of the hand of our enemies
Should serve him without fear,
75 In holiness and righteousness before him all our days.
76 Yea and thou, child, shalt be called the prophet of the Most High:
For thou shalt go before the face of the Lord to make ready his ways;
77 To give knowledge of salvation unto his people
In the remission of their sins,
78 Because of the tender mercy of our God,
Whereby the dayspring from on high shall visit us,
79 To shine upon them that sit in darkness and the shadow of death;
To guide our feet into the way of peace.
80 And the child grew, and waxed strong in spirit, and was in the deserts till the day of his shewing unto Israel.
II. Now it came to pass in those days, there went out a decree from
2 Cæsar Augustus, that all the world should be enrolled. This was
3 the first enrolment made when Quirinius was governor of Syria. And

4 all went to enrol themselves, every one to his own city. And Joseph also went up from Galilee, out of the city of Nazareth, unto Judæa, to the city of David, which is called Bethlehem, because he was of the
5 house and family of David; to enrol himself with Mary, who was betrothed to him, being great with child.

MATTHEW I.	LUKE II.
	6 And it came to pass, while they were there, the days were fulfilled that she should be delivered.
25 And knew her not till she had brought forth a son: and he called his name JESUS.	7 And she brought forth her firstborn son; and she wrapped him in swaddling clothes, and laid him in a manger, because there was no room for them in the inn.

LUKE II.

8 And there were shepherds in the same country abiding in the field,
9 and keeping watch by night over their flock. And an angel of the Lord stood by them, and the glory of the Lord shone round about
10 them: and they were sore afraid. And the angel said unto them, Be not afraid; for behold, I bring you good tidings of great joy which shall
11 be to all people: for there is born to you this day in the city of David
12 a Saviour, which is Christ the Lord. And this *is* the sign unto you; Ye shall find a babe wrapped in swaddling clothes, and lying in a
13 manger. And suddenly there was with the angel a multitude of the heavenly host praising God, and saying,
14 Glory to God in the highest,
And on earth peace among men in whom he is well pleased.
15 And it came to pass, when the angels went away from them into heaven, the shepherds said one to another, Let us now go even unto Bethlehem, and see this thing that has come to pass, which the Lord
16 hath made known unto us. And they came with haste, and found both
17 Mary and Joseph, and the babe lying in the manger. And when they saw it, they made known concerning the saying which was spoken to
18 them about this child. And all that heard it wondered at the things
19 which were spoken unto them by the shepherds. But Mary kept all
20 these sayings, pondering them in her heart. And the shepherds returned, glorifying and praising God for all the things that they had heard and seen, even as it was spoken unto them.
21 And when eight days were fulfilled for circumcising him, his name was called JESUS, which was so called by the angel before he was conceived in the womb.

22 And when the days of their purification according to the law of
Moses were fulfilled, they brought him up to Jerusalem to present
23 him to the Lord (as it is written in the law of the Lord, Every male
that openeth the womb shall be called holy to the Lord), and to offer
24 a sacrifice according to that which is said in the law of the Lord,
25 A pair of turtledoves or two young pigeons. And behold, there was
a man in Jerusalem, whose name was Simeon; and this man was
righteous and devout, looking for the consolation of Israel : and the
26 Holy Spirit was upon him. And it had been revealed unto him by
the Holy Spirit, that he should not see death, before he had seen the
27 Lord's Christ. And he came in the Spirit into the temple : and when
the parents brought in the child Jesus, that they might do concerning
28 him after the custom of the law, then he received him into his arms,
and blessed God, and said,
29   Now lettest thou thy servant depart, O Lord,
    According to thy word, in peace ;
30   For mine eyes have seen thy salvation,
31   Which thou hast prepared before the face of all people :
32   A light for revelation to the Gentiles,
    And the glory of thy people Israel.
33 And his father and his mother were marvelling at the things which
were spoken concerning him ; and Simeon blessed them, and said unto
Mary his mother, Behold, this *child* is set for the falling and rising up
35 of many in Israel ; and for a sign which is spoken against : yea and a
sword shall pierce through thine own soul ; that thoughts out of many
36 hearts may be revealed. And there was one Anna, a prophetess, the
daughter of Phanuel, of the tribe of Asher (she was of a great age,
37 having lived with a husband seven years from her virginity, and she
had been a widow even for fourscore and four years), which departed
not from the temple, worshipping with fastings and supplications night
38 and day. And coming up at that very hour she gave thanks unto God,
and spake of him to all them that were looking for the redemption of
39 Jerusalem. And when they had accomplished all things that were
according to the law of the Lord,

MATTHEW II.

1 Now when Jesus was born in Bethlehem of Judæa in the days of
2 Herod the king, behold wise men from the east came to Jerusalem,
saying, Where is he that is born King of the Jews? for we saw his
3 star in the east, and are come to worship him. And when Herod the
4 king heard it, he was troubled, and all Jerusalem with him. And
gathering together all the chief priests and scribes of the people, he
5 inquired of them where the Christ should be born. And they said

THE BIRTH AND EARLY LIFE OF JESUS 71

unto him, In Bethlehem of Judaea : for thus it is written by the prophet,

6 And thou Bethlehem, land of Judah,
Art in no wise least among the princes of Judah :
For out of thee shall come forth a governor,
Which shall be shepherd of my people Israel.

7 Then Herod privily called the wise men, and learned of them carefully
8 what time the star appeared. And he sent them to Bethlehem, and said, Go and search out carefully concerning the young child ; and when ye have found *him*, bring me word, that I also may come and
9 worship him. And they, having heard the king, went their way ; and lo, the star, which they saw in the east, went before them, till it came
10 and stood over where the young child was. And when they saw the
11 star, they rejoiced with exceeding great joy. And they came into the house and saw the young child with Mary his mother ; and they fell down and worshipped him ; and opening their treasures they offered
12 unto him gifts, gold and frankincense and myrrh. And being warned *of God* in a dream that they should not return to Herod, they departed into their own country another way.
13 Now when they were departed, behold, an angel of the Lord appeareth to Joseph in a dream, saying, Arise and take the young child and his mother, and flee into Egypt, and be thou there until I tell
14 thee : for Herod will seek the young child to destroy him. And he arose and took the young child and his mother by night, and departed
15 into Egypt ; and was there until the death of Herod : that it might be fulfilled which was spoken by the Lord through the prophet, saying,
16 Out of Egypt did I call my son. Then Herod, when he saw that he was mocked of the wise men, was exceeding wroth, and sent forth, and slew all the male children that were in Bethlehem, and in all the borders thereof, from two years old and under, according to the time
17 which he had carefully learned of the wise men. Then was fulfilled that which was spoken by Jeremiah the prophet, saying,
18 A voice was heard in Ramah,
Weeping and great mourning,
Rachel weeping for her children ;
And she would not be comforted, because they are not.
19 But when Herod was dead, behold, an angel of the Lord appeareth
20 in a dream to Joseph in Egypt, saying, Arise and take the young child and his mother, and go into the land of Israel : for they are dead that
21 sought the young child's life. And he arose and took the young child and his mother, and came into the land of Israel.

72 THE GOSPEL PROBLEMS AND THEIR SOLUTION

MATTHEW II.	LUKE II
22 But when he heard that Archelaus was reigning over Judæa in the room of his father Herod, he was afraid to go thither; and being warned *of God* in a dream, he withdrew 23 into the parts of Galilee, and came and dwelt in a city called Nazareth: that it might be fulfilled which was spoken by the prophets, that he should be called a Nazarene.	they returned into Galilee, to their own city Nazareth. 40 And the child grew, and waxed strong, filled with wisdom: and the grace of God was upon him.

LUKE II

41 And his parents went every year to Jerusalem at the feast of the
42 passover. And when he was twelve years old, they went up after the
43 custom of the feast; and when they had fulfilled the days, as they were
44 returning, the boy Jesus tarried behind in Jerusalem; and his parents knew it not; but supposing him to be in the company, they went a day's journey; and they sought for him among their kinsfolk and
45 acquaintance: and when they found him not, they returned to Jeru-
46 salem, seeking for him. And it came to pass, after three days they found him in the temple, sitting in the midst of the doctors, both hear-
47 ing them, and asking them questions: and all that heard him were
48 amazed at his understanding and his answers. And when they saw him, they were astonished: and his mother said unto him, Son, why hast thou thus dealt with us? behold, thy father and I sought thee
49 sorrowing. And he said unto them, How is it that ye sought me?
50 wist ye not that I must be in my Father's house? And they under-
51 stood not the saying which he spake unto them. And he went down with them, and came to Nazareth; and he was subject unto them: and his mother kept all *these* sayings in her heart.
52 And Jesus advanced in wisdom and stature, and in favour with God and men.

If the story be read in the order in which it is presented above it will be seen that, while, on the one hand, there is not one word of contradiction between the two narratives, on the other, not one event is related by both except the fact of the miraculous birth itself, that it occurred at Bethlehem, that the Child was named Jesus, and the final return to Nazareth.

THE BIRTH AND EARLY LIFE OF JESUS 73

Nearly all the facts related by one are completely ignored by the other; and yet the two accounts are in no respect inconsistent. In Luke's narrative no mention whatever is made of the flight into Egypt; it seems to be implied that the holy family went back to Nazareth immediately after the presentation in the Temple. There is not even any hint that they returned from Jerusalem to their temporary dwelling at Bethlehem before starting on their journey to Galilee, though it is obviously probable that they would do so. Nevertheless, without violence to the text, the return to Bethlehem may be allowed for, and the flight into Egypt and the journey back to Palestine may be inserted, between the first and second members of verse 39, chapter ii. In Matthew, again, no mention is made of the incidents told in detail in Luke. And yet a knowledge of some of the earlier incidents is necessary to make Matthew's story intelligible. We might have been sure too that the requirements of the Law were duly observed; and, as, in the nature of things, some weeks must have elapsed between the birth of Christ and the flight into Egypt, there is plenty of room between i. 25 and ii. 1 for the insertion of Luke ii. 8-39.

Features like these are quite incompatible with the theory that the narratives were based upon the current apostolic teaching of the time when Luke and Matthew wrote; still more so that they are composed of tradition, legend or myth. In any such case the two stories would certainly have touched one another either in the way of agreement or contradiction, at other points besides those two at which they do exactly coincide.

There is but one feasible explanation of their origin. It is that the story in Luke is a translation of a written statement made by Mary herself soon after the events, and that the story in Matthew embodies a supplementary statement written by her husband.

Luke's narrative, so far as it relates Mary's personal experiences and that of her cousin Elisabeth, could have been supplied only by Mary. I cannot however believe with Farrar that Luke received the story from Mary's own lips. Its character is such that she could hardly have told it otherwise than in writing to any man except her husband. It was doubtless written either by Mary herself, or, which comes to the same thing, by Joseph at her dictation. The rest of Luke's narrative might also very suitably have been written by Mary. The facts naturally made a deeper impression on the mind of the Virgin Mother than on that of Joseph. The story told by the shepherds was no exception to this, and it is specially mentioned that "Mary kept all these sayings pondering them in her heart." A similar remark is made following the account of the Temple incident when Jesus was twelve years old, clearly implying that it was Mary who supplied the particulars recorded there.

It should be added that, if the Song of Mary, the Prophecy of Zacharias, and the Prayer of Simeon are to be regarded as the authentic compositions of the persons named, they must have been written at the time. On any theory whatever, it would be too absurd to suppose them to have been correctly remembered for more than half a century before they were first committed to paper. It may be said with reference to these compositions that, looking at them from a strictly literary point of view, the presumption is that they are authentic. Not only are they declared in the narrative to have been spoken by Mary, Zacharias and Simeon respectively, but they profess to be the expression of their thoughts. The burden of disproving their authenticity rests with those who deny it, or at least it is incumbent upon such to make some alternative proposition. They were written by some one; if not by those to whom they are attributed by whom were they written? It will hardly be suggested that they were composed by Luke, seeing that they bear no resemblance to his style, he being perhaps the least poetical of all the New Testament writers. That there were poets in the early Church is likely enough; but, if the hymns of praise in the first two chapters of Luke were composed by one or more of them, it is strange that no other specimen of their work should have been preserved either in Luke or either of the other Gospels. Moreover there is a certain contrast between the two longer of these compositions. With the exception of the latter clause of verse 48, the first clause of verse 49, and two or three short phrases, the Magnificat consists entirely of quotations from the Song of Hannah, the Psalms, and other parts of the Old Testament. The Prophecy of Zacharias on the other hand is for the most part original. The style of the Nunc Dimittis again is unlike either of the other pieces. Thus it appears that in these two chapters there are three poetical compositions, all so dissimilar as to lead to the conclusion that no two of them are the work of the same author, whilst in the remainder of the Gospel there is no poetical composition at all, except such as are acknowledged quotations from the Old Testament. In view of all these circumstances it is hard to see how any one coming to the consideration of the subject without prejudice can fail to form the opinion that each of the pieces had its origin in the manner stated in the text.

The story in Matthew relates facts of which Joseph would be more directly cognisant than Mary. First comes his own dream before the birth of Jesus. Then, following the birth, which is barely mentioned, comes the arrival of the wise men at Jerusalem and the proceedings of Herod occasioned thereby, matters of a public nature that would reach the ears of Joseph before those of the Virgin Mother. The visit of the magi to the Bethlehem birth-place would be to Joseph a matter of special interest, inasmuch as their gifts furnished the means wherewith to pay the expenses of the journey to Egypt, the sojourn there, and the return to Palestine—incidents which this narrative also relates. Equally fitting is it that Joseph rather than Mary should tell the shocking story of the murder of the innocents, and the political circumstances which, together with the warning dream, caused him to take his wife and the young child to reside in Galilee.

In exact harmony with this is the general belief of those who hold to the historical truth of the Gospels that the genealogy in Luke is that of Joseph as the son-in-law of Mary's father, and therefore that of Mary herself; and that the genealogy in Matthew is that of Joseph by his own father. There is no need here to discuss the question of the genealogies, a careful study of which by any one having a sympathetic acquaintance with Jewish ideas and customs will remove most of the difficulties which at first seem so perplexing, and show that the two pedigrees were essential; that of Mary to prove that her Son was really descended from David through His Mother; and that of Joseph to prove His title, as David's legal successor through His putative, and by Jewish law legitimate, father, to the theocratic throne. Whether the originals of the two lists were, as supposed by many, preserved in the public archives, does not concern us. The documents from which the lists in Luke and Matthew were copied were those belonging to the family, whether received by transmission through the family itself or copied from official records.

It should seem then that the first two chapters of Matthew, including the genealogy and the events which happened about the time of our Lord's birth, embody the substance of documents originally in the possession of and partly drawn up by Joseph; and that the first two chapters and the latter part of the third chapter of Luke, which also include a genealogy and relate events beginning some time previous to our Lord's birth, and ending with His twelfth or thirteenth year, is a translation of manuscripts belonging to and partly written by or at the dictation of Mary.

Now the question is, How came the two sets of manuscripts to be separated and to fall into the hands of two different Evangelists? Probably it happened in this way: It is generally supposed that Joseph's decease had occurred previously to the time of our Lord's ministry. If so, his personal effects, including all manuscripts belonging to him, would, in accordance with the Jewish law, have fallen into the hands of his eldest son. Mary however would naturally retain her own genealogical record, and would be sure to keep manuscripts that she had herself written, such as those concerning the miraculous birth, the infancy and the childhood of her Divine Son. Matthew, who would be on intimate terms with Joseph's children, would have no difficulty in obtaining the documents or a copy of the documents in the possession of one of them; but for some unknown reason he had not an opportunity to obtain Mary's papers also. But when Luke came to Jerusalem in the year 58, and undertook the task of writing a Gospel, he naturally tried to get all the documents he could bearing on the subject, and was entrusted by Mary who, if still alive, was residing with John at Jerusalem, or, if she were dead, by John, in whose care she had left them, with the precious manuscripts referred to. We shall have more to say on this point later on.

It is now easy to understand why neither Mark nor John gives any account of the birth or early life of Christ. Mark was merely the editor of Peter's notes which related only facts that he himself observed. The same is true of John's notes which he edited himself, perhaps in a distant land, and after those who could have supplied him with information had passed away. And although John must have heard from Mary, during the time she resided in his home, many details of the early life of her Son, he would not insert in his narrative anything for which he had not documentary authority.

If the force of the foregoing argument be admitted the special point to be noted is this, that the fact that original manuscripts were used in the composition of the first portion of two of the Gospels, and that the other two Gospels are totally silent on a most important subject concerning which no original manuscripts were for them available, makes it at least not unlikely that original manuscripts were the materials of which the four Gospels were composed throughout.

Chapter VIII

AFTER THE RESURRECTION

IF it were possible for any feature of the Gospels to be more perplexing, on the current theories as to their origin, than the manner in which they begin, it would be the abrupt, and, from a literary point of view, unsatisfactory way in which they terminate.

Neither Matthew nor John mentions the Ascension of our Lord. They relate the facts connected with His Resurrection, and describe some of the instances in which He manifested Himself to His disciples. Then they come to a sudden close.

The authentic Gospel of Mark, which ends chapter xvi. 8, terminates even more abruptly than Matthew and John. The last twelve verses of Mark in our New Testament are well understood to be a subsequent addition made in early times, not part of the work as originally published. In the Revised Version this portion is divided from the authentic Gospel by a space, and in the margin is found the following note: "The two oldest Greek manuscripts, and some other authorities, omit from verse 9 to the end. Some other authorities have a different ending to the Gospel." But it is the internal evidence that is decisive. Even the English reader feels that he is in a different atmosphere here than in the rest of the Gospel. As to the original Greek it is enough to quote the words of Alford: "Internal evidence is, I think, very weighty against Mark's being the author. No less than twenty-one words and expressions occur in it (and some of them several times) which are never elsewhere used by Mark, whose adherence to his own peculiar phrases is remarkable." The truth is that, in the second, third or fourth century, some well-intentioned publisher, thinking some further statement needful, concocted this addendum from the other Gospels, and affixed it to the copies of Mark which he put into circulation, whence it found its way into the few surviving manuscripts which contain it. Rejecting then these last twelve verses, Mark has less to say about the Resurrection and the events that followed than any other Gospel. It does not mention any one of the appearances of Jesus and indeed does not directly assert the fact of the Resurrection at all; although it is manifest that the writer believed it, and was just on the point of describing some of the appearances of Jesus when he brought his story to an end. And it may be added that Peter, as if to prevent any erroneous inference being drawn from the silence of the Gospel of which he was the real author, asserts the fact of the Resurrection in his first Epistle.

It thus appears that Luke is the only Gospel that mentions the Ascension. And the account in Luke, for so wonderful and important an event, is singularly brief and inadequate.

Admitting however that Luke does bring the history to a suitable conclusion, can anything be more surprising than the sudden and unfinished ending of the other three? That one should merely state in an oblique and inferential way that Christ was risen from the dead; that another should relate the fact in detail and add only a short account of an appointed interview with the Eleven in Galilee; and that a third should narrate at length the intercourse which, on several occasions after His resurrection, He had with the disciples in Galilee; and that the three should then come to a full stop, without a single word to intimate what afterwards became of Him, is marvellous in the extreme.

We, who have been familiar with the Gospels from infancy, and in reading them have our minds charged with all the facts of the story, including the details of the Ascension as narrated in the Acts, may never have been struck with this peculiarity. But let us try to imagine the case of a person who, having no prior knowledge of the facts, sees and reads either Matthew, Mark or John for the first time in mature age. For it must be remembered that, in the early years of Christianity, it was precisely into the hands of such persons that a single Gospel would frequently fall. How amazed and perplexed such a reader would be! Especially if, as would sometimes happen, he had no opportunity of learning by inquiry what had finally become of Him who formed the subject of the narrative. How he would wonder, and form in his mind such questions as these: Did Jesus die again, or is He still alive; and, if alive, where is He now and what is He doing? Moreover, Matthew, Mark and John must have foreseen this; they knew that the very name of Jesus was as yet unknown to the great majority of men, and that such questionings must certainly arise when their books were put into circulation. How is it that they failed to supply so essential a piece of information as the fact of Christ's Ascension to the skies?

If it had been one Gospel only that was left in this incomplete state, it might have been suspected that the final page of the manuscript had been accidentally lost. But, it being the case with three Gospels, no such explanation is possible. On any theory whatever (except one) the fact is absolutely unaccountable. As to the unbelieving theories, such as those of Strauss, Baur and Rénan, respecting the origin of the Gospels, they are simply shut out of court by this one peculiarity.

Unbelieving critics have never been tired of calling attention to the weakness of the testimony to the fact of our Lord's Ascension; and it must be admitted that this event is not supported by so strong a chain of evidence as some of the other facts connected with our Lord's life on earth. But it should be noted that, just in proportion as the evidence for the Ascension is weak, so the evidence for the fact of the Resurrection becomes increasingly strong. For the meagreness of the information that is afforded in the Gospels as to the termination of our Lord's earthly career is proof positive that the original narrators, of whose stories the Gospels are composed, finished their work before that career had in fact terminated, and therefore that they wrote their accounts of the Resurrection directly after it happened.

After the Ascension, the Apostles had no time to spare for writing. For the first few days they were fully occupied with meetings and prayer and the election of Matthias to the vacant Apostleship. Then came the day of Pentecost, with the outpouring of the Spirit, and a large ingathering of converts to the Church, causing them an immense amount of work. Hence the Gospel narratives, with the exception of the third, were never completed, and even the few sentences which form the conclusion to the third appear to have been hastily added. When, after the lapse of a number of years, the narratives were finally redacted, the redactors conscientiously declined to add any new statement to the original records.

Chapter IX

VIVIDNESS OF DESCRIPTION; SIMPLICITY OF LANGUAGE; POSITIVENESS

THE whole style and character of the narratives are in harmony with the idea that they were written at the time the events occurred. They have the freshness of a diary; the life and movement of an instantaneous photograph. They abound in minute details, just such as would strike an observer at the time; but which no memory could long retain or imagination invent. Facts are related with the utmost simplicity. The personality of the writer never appears. There is no sign of passion; no expression of admiration for the Master, or resentment towards His opponents; of delight when He confounds His enemies, or of sympathy with Him when the object of their insult. There is no striving after effect; no attempt at embellishment. Adjectives are rare; adverbs and adverbial phrases are almost absent. There is nought but a bare statement of facts, plain and unvarnished like the evidence of an honest witness in a court of justice. And yet the stories are not cold, stiff or formal. Their very simplicity adds to their warmth and vigour, and secures the sympathies of the reader.

Note also the positive manner in which facts are asserted. There is never the least doubt or hesitation in any statement. Not once do we find the expression λέγεται (*on dit*; it is said), so common with the Greek historians. There are no references to authorities, as in some of the historical books of the Old Testament. There is not the slightest hint that the

VIVIDNESS OF DESCRIPTION

narratives are derived from hearsay or secondary evidence. They are to all appearance the testimony of witnesses speaking from their own knowledge, and they bear on every sentence the impress of truth, as even unbelievers have hardly ventured to deny.

In short they have all the characteristics of reports written by eye-witnesses directly after the events happened; and none of the characteristics of traditions or recollections written after a long lapse of time.

Chapter X

NON-USE OF TITLE "CHRIST" AS A PROPER NAME

A VERY strong proof of the early origin of the substance of the Gospels is found in the non-use, by the writers of the title "Christ" as a proper name. This fact, together with the usage of the New Testament generally respecting the names by which our Lord is designated, is very significant and demands careful consideration.

It is hardly necessary to remind the reader that the word "Christ (Χριστός) is the verbal adjective of the Greek word χρίω to anoint and means "the Anointed One." It is the exact equivalent of the Hebrew word Messiah from the verb *mashach* to anoint. In Old Testament times it was customary, when any one was set aside by divine command to hold one of the great offices of the old dispensation, to pour olive oil, sometimes mingled with spices, on the head. Thus Aaron, David and Elisha, the three men who in a special sense were types of Christ in their respective offices of priest, king, and prophet, were each anointed. This anointing was typical of the bestowment of the Holy Spirit. Our Lord's anointing took place at His baptism, when the Holy Ghost was seen by John to descend in bodily form as a dove and rest upon Him.

The word *Messiah* is used in the Old Testament to denote the promised Deliverer of Israel and of the world. We first find it so used in Psalm ii. 2 :—

"The kings of the earth set themselves,
And the rulers take counsel together,
Against the Lord and against His Anointed."
It is found again in Daniel ix. 25 and 26, where the exact time is foretold at which the Messiah was to appear. Consequently the Jews were accustomed to speak of the "Hope of Israel," whose coming they looked forward to with such passionate desire, as "the Anointed One," "the Messiah," "the Christ." Owing to the maturity of the period mentioned in the prediction in Daniel, and to other signs of the times, there was, at the time when our Lord actually came, a general belief that the fulfilment of the prophecies was at hand, and that the Messiah, the Christ, was about to appear. So, when John the Baptist made his appearance, "all men reasoned in their hearts concerning John whether haply he were the Christ" (Luke iii. 15), and the Jews sent unto him from Jerusalem priests and Levites to ask him, "Who art thou?" to whom he replied, "I am not the Christ" (John i. 19, 20).

Our Lord's ministry had scarcely begun when it was perceived by some that He was indeed the Christ. Andrew had no sooner had his attention directed by John the Baptist to the Lamb of God, than he found his brother Simon and told him the good news, "We have found the Messiah" (John i. 41). The first recorded assertion by our Lord that He was the Christ was made in His conversation with the woman of Samaria. But His claim to the title must already have come to be understood by His disciples and the people generally; for, not long after, the followers of John the Baptist, reporting His works to their master in prison, spoke of Him as "the Christ." There could be no mistaking the meaning of the answer which Jesus gave to the messengers whom John sent to Him in consequence. Simon Peter was the first among the disciples boldly to declare his belief that Jesus was the Messiah. Later on, when asked by the Jewish authorities to say plainly whether He were the Christ or not, our Lord answered that He had already told them, but yet they had not believed, and then proceeded to declare Himself in such distinct terms, that the Jews took up stones again to stone Him. It is manifest from the honours paid to Him at His entry into Jerusalem on His last visit to that city, from the action of the rulers, and from other indications (see for instance John xii. 34) that before His death everyone well knew that He claimed to be the Christ. In fact, it was because of His assertion of that claim that the Jewish Elders determined that He must die.

Bearing these facts in mind let us now look at the manner in which the word "Christ" is used. And first it is necessary to mark the distinction between its use as a title and its use as a name. When used as a title it is preceded by the definite article: "the Christ" (ὁ Χριστός). When used as a name the article is absent and it stands alone or joined with the name "Jesus."

Now the striking fact is this, that the word is never used as a proper name, that is without the article, by the writers of the narrative parts of the Gospels. In these He is usually spoken of by the name of "Jesus." It would seem that during His life upon earth the sublime import of the name Jesus as applied to Him was not recognised. It could not then have been generally known even by His disciples that the name had been given Him by the direct command of God to Mary and Joseph. It was a name that was in common use among the Jews. We read in the Acts of one "Simon Bar-Jesus," and in Colossians of "Jesus which is called Justus." Josephus mentions at least twelve men bearing the name. It was applied to our Lord, therefore, during His earthly life as a matter of course just as other men were spoken of by the names they bore.

By the time the Epistles were written it was well-known by believers that the name "Jesus" had been given to Him by God, as suitably describing the purpose for which He came into the world, and it was recognised as the Name that is above every name, the Name at which every knee should bow.

Moreover, Christ's abasement was Christ's glory, and the name by which He was known as He walked among men was the more honourable by its very homeliness. Hence the name "Jesus" came to be regarded with peculiar reverence, and was seldom used except in conjunction with that other name which denoted the dignity of His office. In the Epistles and Revelation the name "Jesus" alone occurs but seldom; but "Jesus Christ," "Christ Jesus" and "the Lord Jesus Christ" occur frequently. The word "Christ" alone and without the article occurs oftener still, showing that the use of this appellation as a proper name was now a settled thing in the Church.

Although during our Lord's ministry the disciples did not thus use the word "Christ" as a proper name, He Himself so used it twice (Mark ix. 41; John xvii. 3). And the people seem also to have begun in this way to make use of it. For He was in mockery addressed by that name in the house of Caiaphas (Matt. xxvi. 68), and Pilate twice spoke of Him to the multitude as "Jesus, which is called Christ" (Matt. xxvii 17, 22).

After the Ascension this use of the word soon became general, although the use singly of the name "Jesus" continued also for a time to be not infrequent. On the Day of Pentecost, Peter declared to the multitude the Messiahship of Jesus; "Let all the house of Israel therefore know assuredly that God hath made Him both Lord and Christ, this Jesus whom ye crucified" (Acts ii. 36). The same day, when the people asked what they should do, Peter replied, "Repent ye, and be baptised every one of you in the name of Jesus Christ." From this time forward, Peter continued so to use the word. Speaking to the lame man at the Temple gate, he said, "In the name of Jesus Christ of Nazareth, walk" (iii. 7). Addressing the rulers, elders and scribes, the next day, he used the same designation (iv. 10). Speaking to Æneas, he said, "Jesus Christ healeth thee" (ix. 34), and in the house of Cornelius he spoke of the "good tidings of peace by Jesus

Christ," and commanded the converts "to be baptised in the name of Jesus Christ" (x. 36, 48). In his answer to the Apostles and brethren explaining his visit to Cornelius he spoke of the gift of the Holy Ghost to those who "believed on the Lord Jesus Christ" (xi. 17). Although in the earlier chapters of the Acts there is no instance of the name being thus employed by anyone except Peter, there can be no doubt that it was constantly in the mouth of the early believers, for, within fifteen years of the Ascension, they came to be themselves named after it (Acts xi. 26).

Now, as the title "Christ" is in no single instance used as a proper name by the writer of the narrative parts of either of the Gospels, it seems certain that these must have been written before it had become customary thus to employ it. But we have seen that this was done by the world even in the latter part of our Lord's ministry, and that the disciples began to adopt the practice immediately after the Ascension. We are therefore forced to the conclusion that the parts referred to were written before that event. This applies to every one of the Gospels, to John as well as to the Synoptics. The fact is the more striking, because the word is used as a name by three of the Evangelists in parts which were added by them when redacting the books for publication. The name Jesus Christ is found in the first verse, and perhaps in the first member of the eighteenth verse, of the first chapter of Matthew, passages which are plainly editorial additions to the original text. It is found also in the first verse of the first chapter of Mark, which is a heading also prefixed by the redactor. And it is found in the Prologue to John, which, as everyone admits, is quite distinct from the rest of the book. That John was accustomed to use the word as a name is proved by its occurrence six times in the first Epistle of John. It is found also in the second Epistle and the Apocalypse. In short, if there were no other evidence than that educed in this chapter—the usage of the New Testament as to our Lord's names—it should be considered sufficient to prove that the Gospels of Matthew, Mark, Luke and John are all and each of them composed of contemporary records, and that we have in them reports, made at the time, of what our Lord said, and narratives, written on the spot by eye-witnesses, of what He did.

Chapter XI

ACCURACY OF THE REPORTS OF OUR LORD'S UTTERANCES AND OF OTHER QUOTATIONS

THE great practical gain accruing from proof of the fact that our Lord's sayings were written down as He uttered them is of course the assurance it gives us of the accuracy of the reports so made. Conversely, if the accuracy of the reports can be established, that will go a long way to prove that they were written at the time the sayings were spoken.

That the Gospels do in the main correctly report the sayings of our Lord is seriously denied by no one. It is felt by all that it would be a far greater marvel for such a collection of sayings to have been the production of several men than of only one man. Such an idea is like the theory, which at one time was not without advocates, that Shakespeare's Plays were the joint work of a society consisting of several individuals. It was obvious that if that were so, instead of the latter half of the sixteenth century producing one man of extraordinary genius it produced several; and that of these extraordinary men all with but one exception succeeded in effacing themselves and their very name from the knowledge and memory of men. The improbability of this was so extreme that the theory quickly died a natural death. It is just as incredible that in the first century a number of men lived each of whom was capable of uttering some of the sublime truths attributed to Christ in the Gospels. Hence the most pronounced unbelievers admit that Jesus lived and that He spake the substance of all that is attributed to Him in the Synoptics, and at least a nucleus of the discourses in John.

Even Rénan admits as much as that: "One remarkable fact which proves that the so-called synoptical Gospels really contain an echo of the words of Jesus, results from the comparison of the Gospel of Luke with the Acts of the Apostles. On both sides the author is the same. Yet when we compare the discourses of Jesus in the Gospels with the discourses of the Apostles in the Acts, the difference is absolute; here the charm of the most utter simplicity, there (I should say in the discourses of the Acts, especially towards the last chapters) a certain rhetoric, at times cold enough. Whence can the difference arise? Evidently, in the second case, because Luke makes the discourses himself, while in the first he follows a tradition. The words of Jesus were written before Luke; those of the Apostles were not." (*The Gospels*, chap. xiii.) · The fact of course is that both the discourses in the Gospels and those in the Acts are genuine; but the former were the utterances of the Master; the latter, of His disciples.

A careful examination, however, will show that these reports contain many indications, not merely of general accuracy, but of scrupulous exactness. There is a large field here for students to explore; I will mention only a few examples.

Expressions found in Quotations not used by the Evangelists themselves

Whenever certain expressions are found with more or less frequency in the quotations of others, which however are never used by the writers of the Gospels themselves in the narrative portions of the Gospels, it is reasonable to conclude that such expressions were actually used by the speakers quoted, and therefore that the entire quotations are accurate reports. There are several striking examples of this.

Name " Christ "

It has been already shown that the title 'Christ' is never used by either Matthew, Mark, Luke or John as a proper name in the narrative parts of their respective Gospels. But in quoting the words of others, Matthew repeats the title in this sense three times (xxvi. 68; xxvii. 17; xxvii. 22); Mark once (ix. 41); and John once (xvii. 3).

"*Amen*"—*Verily*

The Hebrew word "Amen" is never used, as our Lord used it, in the sense of "verily," by any other speaker, or by any writer in either the Old or the New Testament. But the formula, "Verily (Amen) I say unto you" is a frequent expression of Christ's according to all the Gospels; with however this remarkable distinction, that in the Synoptics it is always single, "Verily, I say unto you," whereas in John it is always repeated, "Verily, verily, I say unto you."

"*Son of Man*"

The title "Son of Man" is the name by which our Lord was wont to designate Himself. It is found in all the Gospels: in Matthew thirty-two times; in Mark fifteen times; in Luke twenty-six times; and in John ten times. It is never so used in the Gospels except by our Lord Himself, and it occurs in that sense only thrice elsewhere in the New Testament. The use of this term by Him is most appropriate, and yet it is one that would never have suggested itself to His disciples. They were duly impressed with a sense of His deity, and spoke of Him without hesitation as the "Son of God"; but it could not have seemed to them to add to His dignity to call Him, what any other person might be called, "Son of Man." But on His part the use of that name was an emphatic assertion that He was something more than man; it declared His heavenly origin.

To make this clear let us take an illustration from recent history. In the year 1863 the Imperial Government of China, finding itself unable to repress the great Tai-Ping rebellion, which was desolating the land and threatened the destruction of the Government itself, secured the services of an Englishman, Charles George Gordon, to organise and command their army. Gordon's name was already famous as a bold and skilful soldier who had fought in the Crimea and elsewhere. On accepting the commission of the Chinese Emperor, Gordon went to that country; became a Chinese military officer; wore the Chinese uniform; and generally identified himself with the interests of the Chinese people. The result was that he acquired in England the name of "Chinese Gordon." It was a strange and unusual thing for a cultured English gentleman; one who had moved in high circles of society, and had distinguished himself by deeds of valour in the service of his country, to throw in his lot with a race so unlike his own in every respect—in appearance, in dress, in religion, in language, in manner and custom—as the Chinese. Hence it was that the adjective "Chinese" was prefixed in common parlance to his name. Even in China he would be spoken of by Europeans as "Chinese Gordon." But he would certainly never be thus designated by the Chinese themselves. What would be strange to them would be, not his Chinese dress, or any of those respects in which he conformed to Chinese ways; but his Aryan features, his European methods, and whatever else betokened his English origin. They would speak of him as "the Englishman," or as their "English general." To the Chinaman the thing that was striking was that their commander, the saviour of their country, was by race, birth and education, English. But to the Englishman the thing that was striking was that Gordon, a fellow-Englishman, had become as it were Chinese. Hence the name of Chinese Gordon was given him and by that name he was known until his last fatal expedition to Khartoum.

When our Lord was upon earth, the marvel from the earthly and human standpoint was, that One should be seen in the midst of men, who was in all respects a man like His brethren, yet whose holiness of character, superhuman power, and effulgence of glory, revealed His divine origin. Those who perceived this expressed their sense of wonder in calling Him the, "Son of God." But from the heavenly and divine standpoint the marvellous thing about the appearance of our

Lord on earth was that He, who was from all eternity in the bosom of the Father, should have humbled Himself to become fashioned as a man. And our Lord, conscious of His deity, expressed that sense of wonder, when He called Himself the "Son of Man."

Applying our illustration: From the Chinese standpoint Gordon was "English Gordon"; from the English standpoint he was "Chinese Gordon." So, from the human standpoint Jesus was the "Son of God"; but from the divine standpoint He was the "Son of Man."

In strict harmony with this conception are those three instances in which our Lord is called by this title by others than Himself. The martyr Stephen, permitted in his last moments to see into the glory of the upper sanctuary, beheld the "Son of Man" standing at the right hand of God (Acts vii. 56). So also the Apostle John speaks of Him, whom in the Apocalyptic vision he twice saw amid the glorious surroundings of the spiritual world (Rev. i. 13; xiv. 14). The contrast of a human figure in the midst of a scene all angelic so impressed the beholders, that the name by which they had so often heard Him designate Himself at once recurred to their memories.

But when Jesus walked amongst men as a man there could be nothing to suggest such a title to others and it was therefore never applied to Him except by Himself, and its use in His quoted utterances only is a sign of the accuracy with which those utterances are recorded.

Old Testament Quotations

It is said by Alford (*Greek Testament*; vol. i. Proleg. pp. 28, 29), that "whereas the Evangelists themselves, in citing the Old Testament, usually quote from the Hebrew text, our Lord in His discourses almost uniformly quotes the Septuagint, even where it differs from the Hebrew." This statement, so far as it is borne out by fact, confirms the literal accuracy of the reports of Christ's utterances.

"Arise, let us go hence"

Sometimes the reporters seem to have done their work almost mechanically. An instance of this is found in the sentence at the end of John xiv. 31, which reads as if it were part of the discourse Christ was delivering to His disciples, there being nothing else to show that our Lord and His disciples rose at that moment from their reclining posture at the table.

Chapter XII

EDITORIAL NOTES

THE mistaken ideas which have hitherto prevailed as to the origin of the Gospels have been partly occasioned by erroneous impressions produced by a number of passages and phrases, found here and there in the course of the narratives, and which manifestly could not have been written until a considerable time after the termination of our Lord's life on earth.

The following list may not be complete, but it contains most of the passages referred to :—

MATTHEW

i.	1.	"The book of the generation of Jesus Christ, the son of David, the son of Abraham."
	16.	"The husband of Mary, of whom was born Jesus, who is called Christ."
	17.	"So all the generations from Abraham unto David are fourteen generations; and from David unto the carrying away to Babylon fourteen generations; and from the carrying away to Babylon unto the Christ fourteen generations."
	18.	"Now the birth of Jesus Christ was on this wise : "
ii.	15.	Old Testament quotation.
	17, 18.	Old Testament quotation.
	23.	Old Testament reference.
iv.	14–16.	Old Testament quotation.
viii.	17.	Old Testament quotation.
x.	4.	"Who also betrayed him."
xii.	17-21.	Old Testament quotation.
xiii.	35.	Old Testament quotation.
xxi.	4, 5.	Old Testament quotation.

xxviii. 15*b*. "and this saying was spread abroad among the Jews and continueth until this day."

MARK

i. 1. "The beginning of the gospel of Jesus Christ, the Son of God."
iii. 19. "Which also betrayed him."
vii. 3, 4. "For the Pharisees, and all the Jews, except they wash their hands diligently, eat not, holding the tradition of the elders : and when they come from the market-place, except they wash themselves, they eat not : and many other things there be, which they have received to hold, washings of cups, and pots, and brasen vessels."
11. "That is to say, Given to God."
19. "This he said, making all meats clean."
ix. 10. "And they kept the saying, questioning among themselves what the rising again from the dead should mean."
xv. 21. "The father of Alexander and Rufus."

LUKE

i. 1–4. Introduction.
iii. 23. "And Jesus himself, when he began to teach, was about thirty years of age, being the son (as was supposed) of Joseph."
vi. 16. "Which was the traitor."
ix. 51. "And it came to pass, when the days were well-nigh come that he should be received up, he stedfastly set his face to go to Jerusalem."

JOHN

i. 1–18. Prologue.
ii. 6. "After the Jews' manner of purifying."
21, 22. "But he spake of the temple of his body. When therefore he was raised from the dead, his disciples remembered that he spake this ; and they believed the scripture, and the word which Jesus had said."
24, 25. "But Jesus did not trust himself unto them, for that he knew all men, and because he needed not that any one should bear witness concerning man ; for he himself knew what was in man."
iv. 9. "(For Jews have no dealings with Samaritans.)"
vi. 71. "Now he spake of Judas the son of Simon Iscariot : for he it was that should betray him, being one of the twelve."

98 THE GOSPEL PROBLEMS AND THEIR SOLUTION

vii. 30.   "Because his hour was not yet come."
    39.   "But this spake he of the Spirit, which they that believed on him were to receive : for the Spirit was not yet given ; because Jesus was not yet glorified."
viii. 20.   "Because his hour was not yet come."
xi. 18.   "Now Bethany was nigh unto Jerusalem, about fifteen furlongs off."
    51, 52.   "Now this he said not of himself : but being high priest that year, he prophesied that Jesus should die for the nation ; and not for the nation only, but that he might also gather together into one the children of God that are scattered abroad."
xii. 33.   "But this he said, signifying by what manner of death he should die."
    37–41.   Old Testament quotations.
xix. 40.   "As the custom of the Jews is to bury."
xx. 30, 31.   "Many other signs therefore did Jesus in the presence of the disciples, which are not written in this book : but these are written, that ye may believe that Jesus is the Christ, the Son of God ; and that believing ye may have life in his name."
xxi. 19.   "Now this he spake, signifying by what manner of death he should glorify God."
    23–25.   "This saying therefore went forth among the brethren, that that disciple should not die : yet Jesus said not unto him, that he should not die ; but, If I will that he tarry till I come, what is that to thee?
"This is the disciple which beareth witness of these things, and wrote these things : and we know that his witness is true.
"And there are also many other things which Jesus did, the which if they should be written every one, I suppose that even the world itself would not contain the books that should be written."

Now it cannot be denied that, if all the above passages formed part of the original material of which the Gospels were composed, that material could not have been written until long after the time at which the events therein recorded happened.

But they did not form part of the original material. They are editorial notes, added by the redactors at the time when they were engaged arranging the records into the form of books for publication. In Part V., dealing with the Third Special Key, the manner in which the Gospels were composed will be treated of more fully; here it will be sufficient to furnish the proof of our assertion that the passages cited were not first written at the same time as the great body of the books.

Dissimilarity of Editorial Notes in the Synoptics

In describing what is called the Synoptic Problem it has been pointed out that the first three Gospels are in many parts so much alike that the first impression produced on reading them is that they are copies one of another. Many passages are almost word for word the same, and in others the resemblance between parallel passages in two or three Gospels is most remarkable. Nor do these similar portions form only a small proportion of the whole. It has been shown that more than half of Luke, over two-thirds of Matthew, and about nine-tenths of Mark consists of matter more or less similar to what is found in one or both of the others. Now, if the passages which are admittedly of late date formed part of the original material, it is obvious that they also would sometimes bear some resemblance in the several Gospels. This however, with one exception, is not the case; but they are altogether as unlike one another as it is possible for them to be.

Before we go further let us dispose of the exception. I refer to the designation of Judas as the traitor in the enumeration of the apostles. The words are as follows :—

Matthew x. 4. " Who also betrayed Him " (ὁ καὶ παραδοὺς αὐτόν).
Mark iii. 19. " Which also betrayed Him," (ὃς καὶ παρέδωκεν αὐτόν)
Luke vi. 16. " Which was the traitor " (ὃς ἐγένετο προδότης).

The three designations are not exactly alike, but the resemblance is close enough. The question is, could such words have been independently inserted by three separate editors? I think it will be seen, not only that in the circumstances such an addition could, but that it almost certainly would, have been made.

Be it remembered that there was another Judas among the Apostles. In Matthew and Mark he is called Thaddæus, but in Luke he is called Judas, the son (or perhaps brother) of James. That he commonly bore the name Judas is proved by its use [John xiv. 22 : "Judas (not Iscariot)"] in the report of our Lord's last discourse delivered some two years after the Apostles were chosen. He was probably living when the Gospels were redacted, and it would be necessary to distinguish the traitor from him.

Doubtless in the early Church, while Judas the son of James was living, the other Judas would never be mentioned without some such expression as "the traitor," being affixed to his name; this designation would thus acquire in time the character almost of a surname.

What then could be more natural than that any and every man engaged in the duty of translating and arranging the original records should add such words to the name of one who, then as now, was never spoken of without a sense of horror.

But in all other instances the passages which show signs of a date subsequent to the time of our Lord's life on earth have no resemblance to one another in the respective Gospels. With the exception mentioned, there is not in any one of the Gospels a single sentence or word having its duplicate or parallel in one of the others, that may not have been written before our Lord's Ascension, or that even suggests the idea that it was written later. Too much stress cannot be laid upon this. It should be sufficient to convince any unbiassed person that at any rate those portions of the Gospels which relate in similar terms the same facts or utterances were all written during the period to which I have assigned them.

Not only is there no verbal similarity in the passages of late insertion; in their general character they are as unlike one another as can be. In Matthew they are nearly all Old Testament quotations. In Mark they are usually short notes explanatory of Jewish customs for the enlightenment of Gentile readers. Luke's notes are chronological or historical. John's are mostly didactic or explanatory: the Old Testament is sometimes appealed to, but in a manner different from Matthew's.

Editorial Notes in John

Of course the foregoing argument applies only to the Synoptics : it affords no proof that passages in John which are manifestly of late date were also inserted some time after the bulk of the narrative was written. There is however at least one instance that makes it seem probable that such was the case.

The passage referred to is verse 2 of chap. xi., forming part of the commencement of the story of the raising of Lazarus. Verses 1-3 are here quoted :—

"Now a certain man was sick, Lazarus of Bethany, of the village of Mary and her sister Martha. And it was that Mary which anointed the Lord with ointment, and wiped his feet with her hair, whose brother Lazarus was sick. The sisters therefore sent unto him, saying, Lord, behold, he whom thou lovest is sick."

It is evident that the anointing here referred to is either that previous anointing, performed by an unknown woman, and which is recorded only in Luke (vii. 36-50), or else the subsequent anointing by Mary at Bethany, related by John himself (xii. 1-8), as well as by Matthew and Mark. The former view accords with an ancient tradition approved by Pope Gregory the Great and is followed by most Roman Catholic commentators. Nearly all other expositors however hold the latter opinion.

Now if the former view be correct, it is manifest that verse 2, and therefore the entire chapter of which it forms part, must have been written before the occurrence of the anointing at Bethany recorded John xii. 1-8. It is impossible that John, writing after the latter event could, in terms of xi. 2, have referred to a previous anointing not mentioned by him at all. It must then be confessed that those who hold the traditional view are unwittingly, but not the less certainly, committed to the principle we maintain as to the contemporaneous character of the Gospel records.

If, however, the more probable view be accepted, that the anointing referred to is that by Mary at Bethany, recorded by John himself (xii. 1-8), then it follows that verse 2 of chap. xi. was not written at the same time as the rest of that chapter, but was inserted afterwards. For I suppose no one, whatever opinion he may hold as to the origin of the fourth Gospel, will dispute that chap. xi. 1-44, as a whole, was written before chap. xii. 1-8. But xi. 2 obviously alludes to xii. 3 as a writing already in existence, therefore xi. 2 must have been written after xii. 3 and *à fortiori* after the main portion of xi. 1-44, in which it is consequently a later insertion.

We are therefore shut up to one of two alternatives. Either xi. 1-44, including verse 2, was written before the anointing took place described in xii. 1-8; or else xi. 2 is an explanatory statement of later date than the main portion of the narrative, and therefore a proof that John, either when revising his manuscripts, or redacting them for publication, sometimes inserted explanatory remarks, which remarks must not be taken as an indication of the time when the manuscripts were originally written.

A glance at the three verses quoted above will show that the mention of the sisters in verse 3 follows verse 1 more naturally without the break caused by the introduction of verse 2 than with it; thus confirming the opinion that verse 2 is a parenthetical addition of later date. This appears to have been the opinion of both the translators of the Authorised Version and the Revisers, for the former enclose the verse in marks of parenthesis, and the latter render the Greek δέ by the conjunction "and" at the beginning of the verse.

Chapter XIII

THE STANDPOINT OF THE WRITERS

THE argument in the foregoing chapter is mainly of a negative character. It proves that all passages of a late date in the Synoptic Gospels certainly, and in John probably, formed no part of the original woof of the narratives, and therefore furnish no clue as to the date when they were first written.

What is most remarkable is that the number of these additions is so small. If they had been far more numerous they would not furnish a solid argument against the contemporaneousness of the records. As it is they serve to throw into greater relief the entire absence in the original manuscripts of any allusion to events that happened after the Ascension, or to the conditions existing in the Church at any of the dates assigned by current theories for their composition.

It shows how averse the redactors were from making any alteration that, for instance, when mentioning the names of persons, they so seldom hint at any subsequent event, even for the purpose of identification.

In every Gospel the standpoint of the writer is always that of the time of the event which he is relating.

From this cause there is in several places a certain obscurity which contrasts with the extreme lucidity which is usually such a striking feature. Some of these will be noticed as we deal with the narratives in detail. One instance here may suffice. In Matthew xvii. 24 a certain tax is mentioned, described as the 'half-shekel' or 'didrachma.' This is understood to have been the annual poll-tax for the Temple, and the force of our

Lord's reply depends on that interpretation. But no information as to the tax referred to is afforded in the text; simply because, writing at the time he did, and in the midst of people who knew all about it, it never occurred to the writer that some explanation was needed. This proves, not only that the passage was written at a time when the tax was in force, and therefore before the destruction of the Temple; but also that it was written before the Gospel had spread abroad into lands where Jewish customs were unknown.

In two places at least the reader is made to feel distinctly this early standpoint of the narrator. The one is Luke iii. 20, where the fact is stated that Herod had shut up John in prison; but no mention is made of his beheading John. The other is John xix. 26, 27, where the touching incident is recorded of our Saviour's committal of His mother to the care of the disciple whom He loved. "And from that hour," we are told, "the disciple took her unto his own home." Is it conceivable that no more than this would have been said if the account had been written years after? Should we not have been afforded some slight glimpse of Mary's subsequent life? Surely some such words as these would have followed: "Where she abideth until this day"; or, "And there she abode until her death."

This early standpoint of the writers cannot be explained away in the easy manner in which the standpoint of the Sermons in Deuteronomy is accounted for. In the case of the latter, the critics argue that, as the author puts them in the mouth of Moses, he was of course careful to avoid allusions that would betray their later origin. But the authors of the Gospels make no claim or assertion as to the date of their work, and that they had no idea of trying to produce an impression that it was of earlier date than was really the case, is proved by the fact that they have completely failed to do so.

Chapter XIV

A DISTINCT ALLUSION TO THE REPORTERS

THERE is one expression in the discourse of Jesus to His disciples delivered on the Mount of Olives (Matt. xxiv. 3–xxv. 46; Mark xiii. 3–37; Luke xxi. 7–36) which of itself makes it certain that He was being reported as He spake. "Let him that readeth understand." That this is really part of our Lord's own utterance, as indeed it professes to be, is proved by its existence in both Matthew (xxiv. 15) and Mark (xiii. 14); for, as already shown, later additions and editorial notes are never found in duplicate. It is besides exceedingly unlikely that the redactors or composers of the Gospels should insert such an addition as this. For they composed the Gospels either before the Siege of Jerusalem or after it. If before, they would not themselves know what was meant by "the abomination of desolation standing where it ought not," and would therefore be extremely unlikely thus to call attention to it. If after, the expression, which could only be useful as a warning, would be meaningless, and quite out of keeping with the entire absence, which we find all through the reports of this discourse, of attempts to read into the prophecy any of the events which were its manifest fulfilment.

Alford saw how utterly irreconcilable this expression was with his theory as to the origin of the Gospels. His comment is as follows:—

"'Ὁ ἀναγινώσκων νοείτω. This I believe to have been an ecclesiastical note, which, like the doxology in ch. vi. 13, has found its way into the the text. If the two first Gospels were published before the destruction of Jerusalem, such an admonition would be very intelligible. The words *may* be part of the Lord's discourse directing attention to the prophecy of Daniel; but this is not likely, especially as the reference to Daniel does not occur in Mark, where these words are also found. They cannot well be the words of the Evangelist, inserted to bespeak attention, as this in the first three Gospels is wholly without example." Alford's belief that the words are an interpolation will not, however, bear a moment's thought. There is no text in the New Testament better attested than this. There is not the least analogy between this and the doxology added to the Lord's Prayer which he cites. It is upon documentary evidence alone that the latter text is rejected as spurious. Alford himself says in his note thereon: "The doxology must on every ground of sound criticism be omitted. Had it formed part of the original text, it is absolutely inconceivable that all the ancient authorities should with one consent have omitted it. They could have had no reason for doing so; whereas the habit of terminating liturgical prayers with ascriptions of praise would naturally suggest some such ending, and make its insertion almost certain in course of time." He goes on to say that, "Stier eloquently defends its insertion, but solely on subjective grounds"; and adds, "in dealing with the sacred text we must not allow any *à priori* consideration, of which we are such poor judges, to outweigh the almost unanimous testimony of antiquity." But the testimony of antiquity to the genuineness of the words, "Let him that readeth understand," is not almost but quite unanimous. They are not wanting in a single manuscript. They exist in two Gospels, whereas the doxology was inserted in Matthew only. It is, as Alford observes, easy to understand the pious but mistaken motive which led to the insertion of the doxology; but there is no conceivable reason for the insertion of the words before us. There is in fact no alternative imaginable but that the words were spoken by our Lord Himself, and that their reference was to the written report that was at that moment being made of His discourse by three of His disciples. So understood, the expression is clear enough.

Our Lord in this discourse foretold two signs by which Christians were to know that they must at once escape from Judea. Each of the Gospels reports one only of the signs. Luke gives the first: "When ye see Jerusalem compassed with armies, then know that her desolation is at hand" (xxi. 20). Matthew and Mark give the second: "When therefore ye see the abomination of desolation, which was spoken of by Daniel the prophet, standing in the holy place (let him that readeth understand)" (Matt. xxiv. 15); "When ye see the abomination of desolation standing where he ought not (let him that readeth understand)" (Mark xiii. 14). When these two signs appeared, then without the loss of a moment's time they were to flee to the mountains.

The fulfilment of the prediction as to the first sign is well-known. At the end of the year 66, Cestius Gallus, the Governor of Syria, marched to Jerusalem to suppress the revolt caused by the misgovernment and cruelty of Gessius Florus. He besieged the city, but, when its inhabitants were at the very point of opening the gates to him, he suddenly and without apparent cause withdrew his army. By him Jerusalem had been "compassed with armies," and his retirement now allowed the Christians the opportunity of acting on the warning their Lord had given.

In what way the other sign was manifested is not exactly known : probably it was by the first of those gross desecrations of the Temple, of which there were soon after so many examples. But the signs were recognised, and, according to Eusebius, the Christians hastened from Judea, finding refuge at Pella in Perea. They had read the merciful warning of their Lord, as reported by His disciples at the time ; they saw the abomination of desolation set up in the holy place, they understood the sign, and fled. "Before John of Giscala had shut the gates of Jerusalem, and Simon of Gerasa had begun to murder the fugitives, so that 'he who escaped the tyrant within the wall was destroyed by the other that lay before the gates'—before the Roman Eagle flapped her wing over the doomed city, or the infamies of lust and murder had driven every worshipper in horror from the Temple Courts—the Christians had taken timely warning, and in the little Perean town of Pella, were beyond the reach of all the robbery, and murder, and famine, and cannibalism and extermination, which made the siege of Jerusalem a scene of greater tribulation than any that has been since the beginning of the world." (Farrar.)

Part III

FIRST SPECIAL KEY; NAMELY, THAT OUR LORD WAS ACCUSTOMED TO SPEAK IN BOTH THE LANGUAGES THAT WERE CURRENT IN PALESTINE IN HIS TIME; AND THAT HIS UTTERANCES IN ARAMAIC ARE MOSTLY CONTAINED IN MATTHEW, MARK AND LUKE; WHILE HIS DISCOURSES IN GREEK ARE FOUND ONLY IN JOHN.

Chapter I

LINGUISTIC CHANGES IN PALESTINE BEFORE CHRIST

IT is beyond dispute that, in the time of Christ, a large part of the population of Palestine was bi-lingual. The language most in use was Aramaic. In the New Testament, Josephus and other writings of the period this is called Hebrew, but though similar to, it was really a different language from, the Hebrew of the Old Testament. It was a form of Aramaic that had its own distinctive peculiarities, having undergone in Palestine a development of several centuries, and received during that time the addition of many Hebrew words and some Hebrew inflexions. The other language in use was Greek; not, however, Greek in its pure Attic or classical form, but enriched by the admixture of Hebrew and Aramaic words and idioms. In modern times the Greek spoken by the Jews has been called "Hellenistic."

Aramaic

In the later Old Testament times Aramaic was the international and diplomatic language of Western Asia. Accordingly the officers of Hezekiah requested Rabshakeh to address them in Aramaic when he stood before the walls of Jerusalem demanding the surrender of the city to his master, the Assyrian King, "for," they said, "we understand it," and they did not wish the townsmen sitting on the wall to comprehend his threatening words.

The policy of the great monarchs of those times, which was to transfer the inhabitants of conquered countries from their own lands to other parts of the empire, tended to squeeze out local dialects and promote uniformity of speech. Aramaic accordingly, which, like French, was easy to learn, flexible and graceful, gained, under the Assyrian and Babylonian ascendancy, general acceptance amongst the peoples that fell beneath the yoke of the conqueror.

In the time of Hezekiah, Aramaic was already superseding Hebrew in Samaria, many of the inhabitants of which had been deported and replaced by men from other conquered provinces. This occurred about 721 B.C. Forty-five years later the national existence of the ten tribes was finally destroyed by the invasion of Ephraim under Esarhaddon, and the carrying into captivity of another detachment of Israelites.

In the year 605 the seventy years' captivity of Judah began. It is impossible to say to what extent the ancient language of the nation survived during that long term of banishment; but that it gradually ceased to be generally spoken may be inferred from Nehemiah viii. 8, where we are told that, after the Return, the Levites, reading the law to the assembled multitude, "gave the sense, so that they understood the meaning." Hebrew, however, was by no means extinct when that occurred. It was at any rate still cultivated by the priestly and prophetic orders, and, with the exception of parts of Ezra, the later books of the Old Testament were written in that tongue. But after the close of the Canon, say about 400 B.C., no book so far as is known was written in Hebrew, which from that time may be regarded as a dead language. At any rate, by the time of the Maccabees, Aramaic, mixed with many Hebrew words and modes of expression, had become the prevailing language of the Jews and neighbouring nations.

Greek

But before the time of the Maccabees a new influence had appeared. Formerly the waves of conquest that overwhelmed Asia had flowed from East to West. Except by means of Phœnician commerce, there had been little communication with Europe; the languages of Asia therefore appear to have remained free from the influence of those of Greece and other Western countries. Greece and Italy had themselves learned much from Asia; but the gain had been on their side alone. When, however, Alexander crossed the Hellespont (B.C. 334), and extended his dominion over the greater part of Western Asia, the Greek language, literature and civilization obtained a permanent and thenceforth a growing footing in the Eastern Continent.

It was the dream of Alexander to Hellenise the world, and his successors, less able than himself, tried without ruth or scruple to carry out his policy. They were aided in their attempt to do this in Palestine by a section of the Jews, who, partly from inclination and partly to curry favour with their rulers, did all they could to promote Greek customs and the Greek language. The accession of Antiochus Epiphanes to the throne of the Syrian empire (175 B.C.) greatly strengthened the party, and, encouraged by them, he and his successors made strenuous efforts to stamp out the Jewish religion and institutions. Cruel persecutions were suffered by those of the Jews who remained faithful to the God of their fathers, until at length, under the Maccabees, they succeeded after many years of conflict in gaining a measure of repose. The nation had by this time become divided broadly into two great parties ; a Hellenising party, who read the Greek literature and affected Greek ways of living; and a Hebraising party, who opposed all innovations and did their utmost to conserve the Mosaic laws and institutions. It was from these two parties respectively that the sects of the Sadducees and Pharisees eventually sprang.

Growth of Greek Culture

After a while the remembrance of the wrongs endured under their Greek oppressors died out, and the aversion even of Hebraists to everything Greek became less pronounced. Under the Roman domination, and especially under the rule of Herod the Great, Greek culture made rapid progress. Herod was as cruel and unscrupulous as Antiochus, but far more politic, and, all his sympathies being in the direction of Greek civilization, the leading Jews soon found it expedient, in the competition for power and place, to modify somewhat their national prejudices. Hence, notwithstanding all his crimes and cruelties, the Pharisees did not display so much hostility to Herod as might have been expected, and did not refuse altogether to conform to his views. No less a person than Gamaliel made a study of Greek literature, and his immense influence must have done much to overcome the repugnance of his countrymen.

The Dispersion

There was another circumstance which helped to strengthen the influence of the Greek civilization. Alexander the Great and Ptolemy Soter had forcibly conveyed a great number of Jews to Egypt, where they continued in a state of slavery until, in the former part of the third century B.C., they were set free by Ptolemy Philadelphus. According to Josephus the number released from servitude was 120,000, to which must be added the number of those who had settled there of their own free will. Thereafter these were steadily augmented, both by the natural increase and by a stream of immigration from Palestine. Greek influence was paramount in Egypt, and the Jewish colony spoke the Greek language and became acquainted with Greek literature. It was for their use that the Old Testament writings were first translated into Greek.

Nor was it only in Egypt that Jews were to be found. In the century before Christ great multitudes scattered themselves through every part of the Roman Empire. In the towns where they settled, not in Europe alone, but also in Asia, Greek had become the prevailing language. It is said by Rawlinson, "Strolling companies of Greek players were at this time frequent in the East, where they were sure of patronage in the many Greek cities, and might sometimes find an appreciative audience among the natives." (*Parthia*, p. 176). Except in the rural districts, Greek was in fact spoken everywhere, and the Jews, whose principal occupation was trade, made it the language of their everyday life.

But the Jews of the Dispersion, though they spoke in a heathen tongue, did not forget the land, still less the religion, of their fathers. They were faithful to the law of Moses, and those who were able made frequent visits to Jerusalem to attend the great feasts. Hence it would often happen that the people gathered in Jerusalem from foreign lands would outnumber the native population, and the latter would be forced to adopt the language, and conform to the ways of those upon whose money they would be largely dependent for their livelihood.

Hellenist Residents

It should also be remarked that many Jews who had been born and educated abroad had taken their permanent residence in Judea. Although but little is said about these in the Gospels, they occupy a conspicuous place in the Acts of the Apostles. These were the "Hellenists," or, as they are called in the English version, "Grecians." This term must be carefully distinguished from the word "Greeks," which always means persons of Gentile birth, for even proselytes—foreigners who had embraced the Jewish religion and conformed to the Jewish law and ritual—are never called "Grecians." The number and influence of the Hellenists or Grecians appear to have been great. Many of them were converted, and the Christian Church had not long been founded ere dissension and jealousy arose between them and the Hebraists. The Hellenists thought that their widows were not fairly treated in the distribution that was made daily to supply the wants of the poorer members. To allay this dissatisfaction seven men were chosen to attend to the business, and it is remarkable that they all bore Greek names. The duty of serving tables was not so onerous but that one of the Seven found time to engage in preaching, and it was amongst Jews who had come from other lands to reside at Jerusalem that his work chiefly lay.

In this connection we learn that there were in the Holy City a number of Synagogues used by Jews ot foreign nationalities. The influence of those attending them was sufficiently powerful to cause the arrest of Stephen, his trial before the Sanhedrin, and his violent death. Some time later a young Jew from Cilicia who had voted for Stephen's condemnation was himself converted, and in course of time might have been seen daily in Jerusalem disputing with the Grecian Jews.

That Greek was the language usually spoken by Hellenists, whether natives of Judea or immigrants from abroad, can hardly be doubted, and seeing that they formed such a large element in the population of Jerusalem, it follows that Greek must have been in frequent use amongst the citizens generally. It may therefore be safely assumed that in Jerusalem, to quote the words of Dr. Angus, "Greek was the language of books of business, and of common life."

Greek Cities

The same was more or less true of the larger towns throughout Palestine. In Judea especially would this be the case; the influence of the capital being naturally greater there than in the other provinces. But in Samaria and Galilee there were also powerful centres of Greek influence. Herod the Great had built several cities; erected in them temples to pagan deities; and planted in them a Gentile population. Amongst them Tiberias by the Sea of Galilee claims notice on account of its nearness to the scene of so large a portion of our Lord's ministry. Samaria should also be mentioned as the capital city of the province so named. Herod had rebuilt Samaria with great magnificence and re-named it Sebaste. The Gentile and heathen character of the cities with which Herod had thus desecrated the land which God had given to His chosen people were the deep aversion of the Jews, who would not needlessly enter them. Still they were there; they drew their food supplies from the country; and Jewish traders could not afford to be ignorant of their language.

Roman Officials

Lastly, let it be remembered that Greek was the language of the Roman centurions and officials stationed in every important centre of the land. By the common soldiers Latin was doubtless more often spoken, and for this reason Pilate wrote the superscription on the cross in that language as well as in Hebrew and Greek. But it is pretty certain that the disciples were not proficient in Latin, and this may well explain why no mention is made of any conversation between our Lord and any common soldier. Otherwise it would be difficult to understand why He, who seemed by preference to work amongst the lower ranks of men, should, in His dealings with the representatives of the Imperial power, have neglected apparently all but the select few who held positions of command.

Chapter II

THE ACTUAL POSITION IN THE TIME OF CHRIST

Greek

IT is often said, on the authority of the Talmud, that the Jews were forbidden to read Greek, and that a curse was pronounced upon any father who should allow his son to learn the language. But that refers to a later period. In the time of Trajan (A.D. 117) there was an outbreak of the Jews against the Greeks of Egypt, Cyrene and Cyprus, which was mercilessly repressed and followed by most terrible reprisals. These resulted in a feeling of bitter animosity against everything Greek. Thenceforth, "whilst Christianity became more and more Greek and Latin, and its writers conformed to a good Hellenistic style, the Jew interdicted the study of Greek, and shut himself up obstinately in his unintelligible Syro-Hebraic dialect. The root of all good intellectual culture is cut off for him for a thousand years. It is especially in this period that the decisions were given which present Greek as an impurity, or at best as a frivolity." (Rénan, *The Gospels and the Second Christian Generation*, chap. xxix.)

Literature

But in our Lord's time there was no severe interdict against Greek. Its widespread use is confirmed by the literature of the period. There is no surviving Aramaic literature of that age. The apocryphal books have come down to us in Greek only; and it is probable that most if not all of them were first written in that tongue. All the books of the New Testament

THE ACTUAL POSITION IN THE TIME OF CHRIST 117

were composed in Greek. Even if it were admitted that the Gospel of Matthew was first written in Aramaic it would not affect the argument, seeing that the Aramaic original so soon perished, and that the Greek replica existed at so early an age. It has never been doubted that the works of the other companions of Christ, those of John, Peter, James and Jude, were written in Greek. It is nothing to the point to question the authenticity of the writings attributed to these Apostles, in view of the fact that they were recognised as theirs at a very early age, when, whatever other mistakes there might be, none could exist as to the language or languages spoken in Palestine in their day. It is inconceivable that people living early in the second century would have accepted as genuine books ostensibly written in the first century, but in a language not then in common use by the class of men to which the assumed authors belonged.

The style moreover of these compositions shows that the writers had considerable acquaintance with the language and were practised in its use. Döllinger, referring to the Epistle of James, says, "The readiness and easy flow of the original Greek style proves (unless St. James like St. Peter availed himself of the services of a Hellenistic Jew) how widely spread was the power of writing Greek among the Jews of Palestine." (*First Age of Christianity*, p. 176.)

Aramaic

But, although Greek had supplanted the Semitic tongue in many of the larger centres of population, Aramaic still flourished in villages and rural districts. In this respect Aramaic resembled all national languages, which, like national customs and national superstitions, die hard among those classes who, from the nature of their pursuits, mix but little with their fellow-men. The fact is so well known, and the evidence is so abundant, that Aramaic was the language generally spoken by the rural population, "the common people," of Palestine, that nothing is needed here but a few words to make the matter clear to general readers.

The statement of Papias as to the language in which Matthew wrote the *Logia*, generally accepted as it was in the second and third centuries, is as strong evidence of the prevalence of Aramaic, as the fact that the Gospels and Epistles were written in Greek is of the prevalence of that language also.

Josephus, who held a command in Galilee for several years during the troublous times preceding the siege of Jerusalem, states that after he was taken prisoner, and during the siege, he was the only man in the Roman camp who was able to understand the deserters from the city. (*C. Apion*, I. 9.) Elsewhere he confesses that he had so long accustomed himself to speak the tongue of his own people, that he was unable to pronounce Greek with accuracy or elegance (*Ant.* xx. 11. 2). In the preface to his History of the Jewish War he explains that the work is a Greek translation of a book which he had originally written in the language of his country, and which had had an extensive circulation. All which goes to show that, largely as Greek had come into use amongst the urban and official classes, Aramaic still held its place as the vernacular.

Even to those Jews who did not usually speak Aramaic it was not an unknown tongue. They regarded it with affection as the language proper to their country for many generations, and as a close connection of the language spoken by Moses, David and Isaiah. Its alphabet was the same, it was written in the same characters, and its grammatical inflexions were similar to Hebrew. They tried even to cheat themselves into the belief that it was Hebrew, and called it by that name, although it was certainly different. Even Jews in foreign lands were taught it, just as most Jews in the present day earn Hebrew.

The attitude of Greek-speaking Jews in this respect may be judged by the conduct of the crowd whom Paul addressed from the stairs of the Tower of Antonia (Acts xxii. 2). They expected him to speak to them in Greek, and were agreeably surprised to hear him in their beloved mother tongue. But it was perhaps not for that reason alone that "they were the more quiet," but because, being less familiar with it, they needed to follow him with closer attention to catch his meaning. That the multitude on that occasion were Greek-speaking is evident from what is told us in the previous chapter (xxi. 31-36). Tidings having reached the chief captain of the Roman cohort that all Jerusalem was in an uproar, he took soldiers and centurions and ran down into the city. Having rescued Paul from the mob and ordered his officers to bind him with two chains, on the suspicion that he was a desperate Egyptian outlaw, he inquired of the crowd who he was and what he had done. In reply "some shouted one thing, some another, among the crowd." Both question and answers were spoken in Greek; for it was not because he did not understand the language in which they spoke; but, as we are expressly informed, because of the noise and confusion, that he could not obtain any definite idea on the subject about which he inquired. If the crowd in their excitement had tried to explain matters to the Roman commander in Aramaic there would have been no need for the explanation, "he could not know the certainty for the uproar": his ignorance of their language would have been sufficient reason. That he did not understand Aramaic is evident (xxii. 21-24), for after Paul had spoken to the people in that language he was unable to guess the reason why they so shouted against him, though he would have known well enough if he had understood the last sentence of Paul's address. However he understood on the following day what was said in the Council (xxiii. 28, 29), showing that the language used on such occasions was Greek.

A Bi-Lingual Population

The conclusion then to which we are led is that both Greek and Aramaic flourished side by side in Palestine in the time of Christ. Amongst the rulers, the priests and the educated and trading classes, in Jerusalem and the larger towns, Greek was generally spoken. Amongst the rural population and in the villages and smaller towns, Aramaic was the tongue in ordinary use. The various religious orders would of course in this respect conform to the customs of those amongst whom they lived and performed their duties. The priests and scribes who officiated at synagogues in towns and villages where Aramaic was the prevailing tongue would at home speak Aramaic like the rest of the people; but when they visited Jerusalem they would be well able to converse with their brethren there in Greek.

In fact a large proportion of the population were able to speak in both languages, in which respect they did not differ greatly from the inhabitants of many modern Oriental towns. I have been told by a missionary to the Punjaub that at Peshawur four languages are in common use and children in the streets may be heard speaking them all. Miss Bellamy, a missionary who has worked for 21 years in Syria, tells me that in that country—in addition to the vernacular Arabic—Turkish, French, Greek, English and German are also in use, and that the children will often speak two, three or four of them. Similar information with reference to the Bulgarians has been furnished me by a literary friend who lived for a time in Turkey. It should not be forgotten that there was a period even in England when two languages were in general use. Professor Maitland points out that, for several centuries after the Norman Conquest, French was the language of law, and tells us that in the thirteenth century, "Some power of speaking a decent French seems to have been common among all classes of men, save the very poorest; men spoke it who had few, if any, drops of foreign blood in their veins." (*Social England*, vol. i., p. 279.)

Chapter III

THE LANGUAGES SPOKEN BY CHRIST

IT being established that two languages were in general use in Palestine in our Lord's time, it follows almost as a matter of course that He spake in both. He came to present His claims as Messiah to the chief men of the nation, to demand from the husbandmen in His Father's name the fruits of the vineyard; to them He must speak in Greek. He also came to preach glad tidings to the poor, to reveal to the common people the things of the Kingdom of God; to them He must speak in Aramaic.

His Use of Aramaic in Galilee

That our Lord sometimes spoke in Aramaic is indicated by the retention in two instances of the original words in that language. "Talitha cumi" (Mark v. 41) is one example. The cry of agony on the cross is the other (Matt. xxvii. 46; Mark xv. 34). It was doubtless also in Aramaic that the ascended Jesus of Nazareth called to Saul of Tarsus while proceeding on his journey to Damascus (Acts xxvi. 14).

The reception which He gained when preaching in Galilee is another proof that He spoke in the language of the people. It is very improbable that such vast crowds would have left their homes and their work and followed Him for miles to the mountains, to the sea-side and to desert places if He had spoken in Greek on those occasions. Those who have read of the powerful influence produced by great Welsh preachers —Christmas Evans for instance—two or three generations

ago, when the ancient British tongue was more universally spoken in the Principality than now, may be better able perhaps than others to see the force of this. Like all primitive languages Aramaic was most effective in impressing the minds of great masses of men. Accordingly, when used by our Lord the results that followed His teaching were very great. For it must not be supposed that the impression He made was a transient one. Of the thousands who thronged into the Church after Pentecost it cannot be doubted that a large proportion were those who had listened to the teaching of Christ in Galilee.

His Use of Greek in Jerusalem

But when Jesus visited the Temple at Jerusalem (except on the last occasion) He spoke in Hellenistic Greek: Because it was the language in daily use by the elders and rulers to whom He designed to declare His mission: Because it was the language most prevalent among the citizens generally: And because it was the language usually spoken and best understood by the great number of Jews from foreign countries, who were always present at the great Temple Feasts.

Aramaic Dialects

There is another reason why He would use Greek in Jerusalem in preference to Aramaic. There was considerable difference between the Judean and the Galilean pronunciation of the latter tongue. In the Holy Land, small as was its area, there were at least three dialects of Aramaic—the Judean, the Samaritan, and the Galilean—differing so much from one another as to make communication by its means between persons of different provinces both difficult and unpleasant. The Judean adhered most nearly to the ancient Semitic type with its deep gutturals, so unlike the musical accent of Greece and Italy. The dialect of Galilee on the other hand had been softened by the influence of Western intercourse, a result of its closer proximity to the maritime ports of Phœnicia.

Hence a man's Aramaic speech at once betrayed to what province he belonged (Matt. xxvi. 73).

"The dialect of Jerusalem and Judea," says Rohr, "was most correct; but that which prevailed in Samaria, and particularly that of Galilee, was much more rude than the former, full of contradictions and mutilations; letters were omitted in it, and one guttural exchanged for another; so that for example, according to the careless and irregular pronunciation of the Galilean dialect, the same word might denote an ass, wine, wool, and a lamb to be sacrificed. A Galilean was therefore easily recognised by his pronunciation (Matt. xxvi. 73)." Professor Marshall quotes from the Babylonian Talmud a story of a Galilean who was lowering a table by a rope into the street from an upper floor. "He fastened the rope so that the feet of the table were a short distance from the ground, and, while he was coming down stairs, a man outside cut the rope and ran off with the table. The Galilean sent his wife to report the theft, and the man to whom she reported it understood her to call him a silly man whom a heretic stole and carried off, with his feet scarcely touching the ground." (*Expositor*, 1891, vol. iv., p. 209).

Now it was in this Galilean dialect of Aramaic, that Christ and His disciples were accustomed to speak that language. But it is manifest that if He had used the Galilean dialect in Judea He would have been liable to have been often misunderstood, and it is therefore unlikely that He did so. On the other hand, it is just as unlikely that He used the more correct pronunciation of Judea, for this reason, if for no other, that His own disciples would have found it difficult to understand Him if He had done so. It seems certain, therefore, that He did not use Aramaic at all when addressing people of Judea, and if so He must have spoken in Greek.

No Reported Evangelisation in Country Parts of Judea

Herein doubtless lies the reason why there is no record in either the Synoptics or John of any evangelistic work in the rural districts of Judea. Our Lord never appears to have made long missionary tours through the towns and villages of that province, as He did in Galilee. The nearest approach is found John iii. 22, where it is said that He tarried with His disciples in the land of Judea and baptized. It may also perhaps be implied by the remark in John vii. 1, that there were other occasions on which His journeyings in Judea were not confined to the road from the Jordan, or the Samaritan boundary, to the Holy City. But if He preached to the multitudes at such times, no record is preserved of what He said. The cause of this in all probability is that the rural population, the " common people " of Judea, like that of Galilee, spoke in Aramaic, but in a dialect so different, as to make communication difficult between the respective inhabitants of those two provinces; wherefore, either He did not make a practice of preaching in the country parts of Judea; or else, if He did so, His disciples were unable to report His utterances.

"Will He Teach the Greeks?"

An undeniable proof that our Lord usually spoke Greek when addressing the Jewish rulers in the Temple is found in the remarkable question recorded John vii. 35 :—

"The Jews,'therefore, said among themselves, Whither will this man go that we shall not find him? Will he go unto the Dispersion among the Greeks, and teach the Greeks?"

Such an idea as this could not have entered the minds of the Jews, unless they were accustomed to hear Him speak in Greek. Let it be noted, their question was not " Will He teach the Jews, dispersed among the Greeks ? " but " Will He teach the Greeks?" that is to say the Gentiles—people who were mostly ignorant of Aramaic, and who, in the aggregate, could be approached by means of the Greek language only. It may be quite true, as Alford says, that they did not believe the hypothesis, and only suggested it to convey contempt and mockery. Nevertheless, there would have been no sense in such a remark, even in irony; if they did not know Him to be a fluent speaker in Greek. Most probably it was His thorough command and ready use of that language that gave rise to the thought.

Our Lord and His Disciples

In conversation with His disciples there can be no doubt that the language usually employed was Aramaic. Brought up in small towns of Galilee and belonging to the humbler ranks of life, it was the tongue with which they were by far the most familiar. Their knowledge of Greek had been acquired and was availed of only when required for purposes of business, and perhaps also for the reading of the Scriptures, and when attending the services of the Synagogue. In their family and social intercourse they would speak in the common language of their country.

But there are indications that, during the progress of Christ's ministry, as the disciples went with Him from place to place, on several occasions accompanying Him to Jerusalem, they gradually improved their knowledge of Greek, until they became as familiar with it as they had been with their native dialect. And so, while there are no signs whatever that in the earlier period of the ministry Jesus ever spoke to His disciples alone except in Aramaic, it can hardly be questioned that it was in Greek that He, subsequently to His Resurrection, addressed Peter immediately after the great draught of fishes (John xxi. 15-18).

Although it may be slightly in advance of the point we have reached in our argument, it may here be observed that no discourse of Jesus to His disciples is contained in the earlier part of John's Gospel. There is the discourse to Nicodemus and there are a number of public addresses. But the longest utterance to His own immediate followers is that contained in the five verses, iv. 34-38, the substance of which might easily be retained for a day or two in a hearer's memory, and be recorded in a different language from that in which it was spoken. That our Lord frequently spoke at length to the disciples privately cannot be doubted, and several such addresses are reported in the Synoptics. (See Matt. xiii. 11-23, 36-52, xviii. 1-35, and parallels). But these were spoken in Aramaic; it was not until on the eve of His crucifixion that He delivered a long discourse to His disciples in Greek—the discourse reported John xiv.-xvi. By that time they had acquired a much greater familiarity with the Hellenistic tongue. They had listened repeatedly to our Lord's conversations and discussions with the Greek-speaking men of Jerusalem. They had journeyed with Him through Samaria and into the parts of Tyre and Sidon. And the frequent use, both in listening and in communicating with others, which they had thus been led to make of Greek, had resulted in their becoming so much at home with it, that our Lord could use that language in His intercourse with them alone.

So perfect had their knowledge of Greek by that time become that they were prepared after the Ascension to adopt it almost to the entire discontinuance of Aramaic. Rénan indeed supposes that the Apostles made in this respect a sudden and complete change: " The primitive nucleus of the Church had been exclusively composed of Hebrews; and the Aramaic dialect, which was the language of Jesus, had been the only one in use. But during the second or third year after the death of Jesus, Greek was introduced into the little community, and soon became the dominant tongue. . . . It was evident that the dialect of Palestine must be abandoned by those who dreamed of a wide-spread propaganda. A provincial patois which was scarcely ever written, and only in use in Syria, was palpably insufficient for such an undertaking. Greek, on the contrary, was almost a necessity to Christianity. It was the universal language of the age, at least around the basin of the Mediterranean; and it was especially the language of the Jews dispersed throughout the Roman Empire." (*Apostles*, chap. vi.)

It is however improbable on the face of it that the Apostles passed from one language to the other in the manner and short space of time stated by Rénan; we may rest assured that they knew Greek from the first, and that they never forgot Aramaic; and that the transition from the dominant use of the one to the dominant use of the other was gradual.

Chapter IV

RESPECTIVE CHARACTERISTICS OF ARAMAIC AND GREEK

THE truth is that each of the languages used by our Lord was admirably suited to the office it was called upon to fill.

Aramaic

In spite of the contemptuous terms in which Rénan speaks of it, Aramaic was a noble language, calculated by its simplicity and strength to strike men's imaginations and reach their hearts. In its essential qualities it did not differ from the language in which the literature of the Old Testament was composed—a literature which, viewed from a purely secular standpoint, is equalled in the New Testament alone. Concerning that language a scholarly writer (William Carpenter) has said: "The Hebrew language is allowed to possess great simplicity and effectiveness. Of all known languages it is the best adapted to indicate the nature and qualities of objects." For the purpose of relating parables, or of announcing moral precepts, for warning men of their sins, calling them to repentance, and exhorting them to righteousness, a more fitting tongue than Aramaic could not have been chosen.

But for the purpose of conveying instruction in the profounder doctrines of Christianity, Aramaic was not so suitable. It was wanting in precision and liable to some ambiguity—matters of but little importance in historic or figurative narration, but of the utmost consequence in the direct statement of theologic truth.

Greek

For the purpose of precise dogmatic teaching no language ever existed so suitable as the later Greek, developed as it was to a high degree of excellence by the influence of philosophic thought, and, in its Hellenistic form, enriched by contact with the East and the addition of Hebrew ideas and modes of expression.

Of this language Döllinger speaks as follows: " Everything had conspired to make the Greek language, that masterpiece of human speech—and at its highest point of development, as the creation of a literature unrivalled for richness in mental power in the ancient world—to make that queen of languages the first instrument for receiving Christian ideas, and giving them form and colour. The idiom the Apostles wrote in was not, indeed, the language of Plato and Xenophon, with its Attic grace and refinement; it was the so-called 'common speech,' which arose after Alexander out of the dissolution and fusion of the old dialects, and in its Hellenistic form, that is, as the Jews then scattered over the heathen world had learnt it from the mouth of the people, and adopted it for oral use, with a mixture of old Hebraisms and new Aramaic forms. It was therefore more like a provincial dialect than the language of books. But the widely spread Alexandrian version of the Old Testament, with its strongly marked Hebraist character, had made this dialect into a vehicle for literature. Its vocabulary supplied the foundation for the language of the Apostles and early Christian writers." (*First Age of Christianity and the Church.*)

The language thus described, so capable of expressing the most delicate shades of meaning, and thus conveying to a nicety whatever the teacher on any subject might wish his hearers or readers to understand, seems to have been specially prepared by Providence to enable our Lord to reveal in their fulness the deep things of God.

Assuming the facts to be as here stated, a careful study of our Lord's sayings will reveal a beautiful harmony and consistency. When talking to the people He used the people's tongue, and spoke about things, and in a way, that the people might understand. When conversing with the cultured men who sat in Moses' seat, He used the language of the learned, and discoursed upon subjects and in a manner adapted to their supposed intelligence. A like distinction will be seen in His intercourse with His disciples; as He talked with them by the way, and in His daily counsel and instruction; when foretelling the judgments that should overtake the nation, and the coming of the Son of man in His glory—in fact, whenever it was possible to do so, He spake in the language of their childhood and their homes. But when He proceeded to reveal the mystery of the three Persons of the Godhead, and to discourse on such doctrines as election, sanctification, and final perseverance, as recorded in the fourteenth and three following chapters of John's Gospel, He used the one language above all others capable of setting forth in clear, distinct terms, the truths He intended to teach.

Chapter V

RESPECTIVE USE OF ARAMAIC AND GREEK IN THE SYNOPTICS AND JOHN

NOW, as has been already remarked, our Lord's addresses to the "common people" in Galilee form a large portion of the Synoptic narratives; whilst His discourses to the Jewish rulers in the Temple occupy a large part of the Gospel of John. There are it is true instances in which at first sight the reverse of this appears to be the case. But it is not so in reality. When we come to consider the narratives in detail we shall find that the discourse reported in John vi., though delivered in Galilee, was not addressed chiefly to the common people of Galilee. And it will even be more evident that the addresses delivered in the Temple on His last visit were not addressed to the audience that on former occasions surrounded Him in the sacred precincts, but to the crowds who had come from the Northern province to the Feast.

We are accordingly drawing near to the conclusion that the utterances of our Lord recorded in the Synoptic Gospels are those which He spake in Aramaic; and the discourses in John are those which He spake in Greek. That such was really the case will appear from other considerations, to which attention must now be called.

Marks of Translation in the Synoptics

The Gospels of Matthew, Mark and Luke abound with Aramaic idioms, and have every appearance of having been translated from that language. Of all the New Testament writers, Luke is considered to have had the greatest command of classical Greek, and some of his passages are admired for the elegance of their composition. The introduction to his Gospel is an instance, concerning which Alford says, "The peculiar style of this preface, which is purer Greek than the contents of the Gospel, and more laboured and formal, may be accounted for, partly because it is the composition of the Evangelist himself, and not translated from Hebrew sources like the rest." Thomson, in Smith's *Dictionary of the Bible*, observes that the style of the Gospel is less pure than the latter part of the Acts of the Apostles, where Luke describes entirely in his own words scenes of which he was himself an eye-witness. In the former there are Hebrew idioms which in the latter disappear. That Luke's Gospel does not exhibit that pure and correct diction which is characteristic of his own proper style is due to its being composed of a translation made by him of documents in another language. He was more careful to reproduce faithfully the meaning of the original than to preserve his own reputation as a classical writer; hence he allowed the Semitic features in the documents before him to reappear when rendered in Hellenistic Greek.

The signs of translation from Aramaic documents are at least as strong in Matthew and Mark as they are in Luke. According to Michaelis, "The Gospels of Matthew and Mark exhibit strong vestiges of the Hebraic style; the former presents harsher Hebraisms than the latter; and the Gospel of Mark abounds with still more striking Hebraisms."

Many of the variations in parallel passages are manifestly the result of independent translations from similar, though not identical originals. The synonyms used by the three Evangelists are altogether inconsistent with the idea that the Synoptic Gospels are composed of materials in the language in which they are themselves written. A single illustration will suffice. Luke alone of all the Evangelists sometimes uses the word 'Epistates' ('Ἐπιστάτης) to express the term by which the disciples were accustomed to address their Lord and Master. The word is found in Luke viii. 24, whilst in the parallel passage, Matthew viii. 25, we find 'Kurios' (Κύριος), and in Mark iv. 38 'Didaskalos' (Διδάσκαλος). Ἐπιστάτης appears again in Luke ix. 33, the parallel in Matthew xvii. 4 being again Κύριος, whereas in Mark ix. 5 the original Aramaic 'Ραββί is retained. In the parallel passage to Luke ix. 49, Mark again uses Διδάσκαλος (ix. 38).

No Marks of Translation in John

In John, on the other hand, there are no indications of translation from another language. The Hebrew nationality of the writer and the Principal Speaker, whose words are recorded, are evident enough; but the diction is pure Hellenistic Greek. In proof of this, I cannot do better than quote from Godet's work on this Gospel: " On the one hand, Rénan tells us, 'The style contains nothing that is Hebraic, Jewish or Talmudic.' And he is right, if by style we simply understand the wholly external forms of the language. There is not to be found in the fourth Gospel, as in certain parts of Luke . . . Hebraisms, properly so called, imported just as they are into the Greek text. . . . . On the other hand, a scholar who has not less profoundly studied the spirit of the Semitic language, Ewald, thus expresses himself: 'No language can be, in respect of the spirit and breath which animate it, more purely Hebraic than that of our author.' And he is equally right, if we consider the internal qualities of the style. . .
In John's language, the clothing alone is Greek, the body is Hebrew; or, as Luthardt says, there is a Hebrew soul in the Greek language of the Evangelist. Keim has devoted to the style of the fourth Gospel, a beautiful page ; he sees in it 'the ease and flexibility of the purest Hellenism adapted to the Hebrew mode of expression, with all its candour, simplicity, profusion of imagery, and sometimes also its awkwardness.'"

Anyone reading in the original Greek, and with the help of a good commentary, the discourses of Christ recorded in John, cannot fail to be struck by the effective use which is made of the wealth of expression for which that language is distinguished.

It is scarcely possible that the fine distinctions in the choice of words, the grammar and the construction which even the English language is sometimes inadequate fully to convey, existed in the first place in a tongue so wanting in precision as Aramaic. And, even if they existed, it is hardly credible that delicate shades of meaning, which it has taken centuries of English learning to reproduce with the accuracy to which our Revised Version has been brought, should have been imported so exactly by John into a translation. Modern writers attempt to account for this, and also for the difference in style between the sayings in John and those in the Synoptics, by supposing that the former are in a greater or less degree coloured by the mind of the Apostle. But the marvellous character of these compositions forbids that supposition. Doctrine so profound expressed in words so simple; such conscious majesty joined with such tender sympathy;—as we reverently read, we seem, like those who saw the Word become flesh dwelling among men, to behold His glory, glory as of the only begotten of the Father, full of grace and truth. Religious sentiment and reason alike shrink from the idea that the teaching of the Master, as recorded in John, bears any impress of the mind even of the Disciple who reclined in the bosom of Jesus.

As illustrating the precision with which our Lord's thoughts are expressed, notice the fine distinction between the word twice rendered in the Revised Version 'go away,' and the word rendered 'go' in John xvi. 7 :—

"Nevertheless, I tell you the truth, it is expedient for you that I go away : for if I go not away, the Comforter will not come unto you ; but if I go, I will send Him unto you."

Note also the three pairs of parallel expressions in John xxi. 15-17 :—

"So when they had broken their fast, Jesus saith to Simon Peter, Simon, son of John, lovest thou me more than these ? He saith unto him, Yea Lord ; thou knowest that I love thee. He saith unto him, Feed my lambs. He saith to him again a second time, Simon, son of John, lovest thou me? He saith unto him, Yea, Lord; thou knowest that I love thee. He saith unto him, Tend my sheep. He saith unto him the third time, Simon, son of John, lovest thou me? Peter was grieved, because he said unto him the third time, Lovest thou me? And he said unto him, Lord, thou knowest all things; thou knowest that I love thee. Jesus saith unto him, Feed my sheep.

Here we have the "lambs" and the "sheep"; the "feeding" and the "tending"; the "loving" ($ἀγαπᾷς$) and the "loving" ($φιλεῖς$); for which last synonyms no two English equivalents exist. Surely in such places we have in our Greek Testament, not a translation merely, but the identical words Jesus spoke.

Without discussing the question, Godet takes for granted the common opinion that our Lord delivered in Aramaic the discourses contained in John. Accordingly while contending for their essential accuracy he admits that "it is certain from the very nature of things that the style peculiar to the translator has coloured that of the Preacher while reproducing His discourses" (*John*, vol. i., p. 160). Nevertheless Godet's chapter on the Characteristics of the Fourth Gospel is a convincing argument that John's report of Christ's sayings is not coloured, not even a translation, but an exact transcript of the very words used. The chapter referred to should be read by those who wish to form a right conclusion on the subject.

As showing the faithfulness of the reports, Godet dwells on the fact, often noticed by other writers, that John never makes Jesus describe Himself by the term Logos or Word, the name which John himself applies to Christ in the prologue of the Gospel. Let me add to this that the word $ῥῆμα$ is used by Jesus and others in this Gospel eleven times in the ordinary sense of $λόγος$, whereas John, where not quoting others, uses it in the Gospel only once, never in his Epistles, and once only in Revelation. It is to be hoped that those who on similar ground contend so strenuously for the composite character of the books of the Old Testament will allow due weight to such evidence as this, that the author of the Gospel, Epistles, and Revelation of John, was not in any sense the author, or even the translator of the speeches attributed to Christ in the Gospel.

Verbal Indications

On comparing the Synoptics with John many verbal indications will be found that the former are composed from Aramaic originals while the latter is not.

For instance, the name Alphæus in the Synoptics is the same as Clopas in John, Alphæus being the Greek rendering of the written Aramaic name (חלפי) while Clopas expresses better the sound as pronounced in the hearing of the writer.

Döllinger observes with reference to our Lord's words to Peter, quoted Matt. xvi. 18:—

"And I also say unto thee, that thou art Peter, and upon this rock I will build my church; and the gates of Hades shall not prevail against it,"

that "the Greek translator of the Aramaic text was obliged to use πέτρος and πέτρα: in the original, Cephas stood in each place without change of gender. 'Thou art stone, and on this stone, etc.'; Cephas being both name and title." (*First Age of Christianity*, p. 47, note.) No similar example exists in John.

Again the Synoptics when they mention the Sea of Galilee always call it by that name, or by its other Hebrew name, Gennesaret. John alone speaks of it by its Greek name, Tiberias.

In three instances where John mentions a place by its Aramaic name he explains that it is the Hebrew name, and in two of those places he gives the Greek equivalent first:

v. 2. Now there is in Jerusalem, by the sheep gate a pool, which is called in Hebrew Bethesda, having five porches.

xix. 13. When Pilate therefore heard these words, he brought Jesus out, and sat down on the judgment-seat at a place called The Pavement, but in Hebrew Gabbatha.

xix. 17. They took Jesus, therefore: and he went out, bearing the cross for himself, unto the place called The place of a skull, which is called in Hebrew Golgotha :

There is no similar example in the Synoptics.

However, in quoting the words of Mary Magdalene to Jesus on the Resurrection morning, John recites the Hebrew word used by her first and gives its Greek interpretation after.

xx. 16. Jesus saith unto her, Mary. She turneth herself, and saith unto him in Hebrew, Rabboni ; which is to say, Master.

Similar instances are found :

i. 41. He findeth first his own brother Simon, and saith unto him, We have found the Messiah (which is, being interpreted, Christ).

And i. 42. He brought him unto Jesus. Jesus looked upon him, and said, Thou art Simon the son of John : thou shalt be called Cephas (which is by interpretation, Peter).

Quoting the words of the Samaritan woman he records exactly what she said, " I know that Messiah cometh (which is called Christ.)" Conversing in Greek with a stranger, she naturally translated into Greek for His benefit (as she thought) the Hebrew name she employed.

The weights and measures mentioned by John are always Greek, whereas the Synoptics use Hebrew, Aramaic, Greek and Latin words denoting weights or dimensions.

Exceptions

The statement that the Aramaic sayings of Jesus are found in the Synoptic Gospels and His Greek sayings in John, must not be understood to apply without exception to every recorded sentence spoken by Him. The Gospels consist of an account, partly of what Christ said, and partly of what He did. But in the narrative of His actions the words that He spake while doing them are usually recorded. Such utterances hold, if we may so say, a subordinate place; they are recorded as an element in the narrative, rather than as forming part of the doctrinal truth that He taught. Although even in such cases the general principle seems to hold good, there are many exceptions. This is specially the case with regard to those facts which are essential to the scheme of Christianity, and which all the Evangelists, so far as they were able, made a point of narrating. The testimony of John the Baptist for instance was much too important to be omitted by any of the four; and, above all, the facts relating to the Saviour's death and resurrection could not be left out. They all recognised that it was in order to die that Jesus came into the world, and each one accordingly gives a fuller account of the incidents which led up to and were connected with His crucifixion than of anything else in His career. And they all realised the importance of the Resurrection as the seal of God the Father's acceptance of His Son's Atoning Sacrifice, and as the convincing testimony to men of the truth of the Gospel. Therefore each Evangelist closes his narrative with a statement of facts which testify to the historical truth of that event.

Chapter VI

SUMMARY

THE evidence that most of the sayings of Christ recorded in Matthew, Mark and Luke were spoken in Aramaic may be summarised thus :—

1. They are mostly addressed to popular audiences of unlearned people whose vernacular was almost certainly Aramaic.

2. They consist largely of parables or stories, for which Aramaic is a very suitable language.

3. They abound with Hebraistic or Aramaic idioms.

4. The diversities found in the reports in two or three Gospels of the same sayings can often be explained on the supposition that they are translations made by different persons of the same Aramaic original.

5. The preservation in one instance of the original Aramaic words, and our ascended Lord's use of that tongue in His call to Saul of Tarsus, prove that he sometimes spoke in Aramaic.

6. The ancient tradition that Matthew originally wrote his Gospel in Aramaic can be best accounted for by supposing that although he actually wrote it in Greek, in doing so he made use of notes which he had previously written in Aramaic.

The following is a summary of the arguments that our Lord's discourses in John were generally spoken in Greek:

1. They all appear to have been spoken either to educated men who must have understood Greek, or to His own disciples, some of whom certainly, and all of whom probably, also understood Greek.

2. A large proportion of them were spoken in the Temple to the Jewish authorities, whose ordinary language was Greek.

3. The difference between the Judean and Galilean dialects of Aramaic makes it likely that our Lord, who spoke Aramaic in the latter dialect, conversed in that language with the men of Jerusalem, who, when they used it at all, spoke in the former dialect.

4. The difference in their style from that of the sayings in the Synoptic Gospels, is best explained by the supposition that they were written in a different language.

5. Their clear logical character, and the absence of parables such as are found in the other Gospels is appropriate to the genius of the Greek language.

6. The purity of their diction and the absence of all traces of translation accords with this view.

7. The manifest accuracy of the reports forbids the supposition that they have been modified even by a translator's hand.

8. The question quoted John vii. 35: "Will He go unto the Dispersion among the Greeks and teach the Greeks?' implies the use by our Lord of the Greek language among those by whom the question was asked.

Chapter VII

OUTCOME OF THE ARGUMENT

IF the truth of that for which we have been contending be admitted, namely, that the sayings of our Lord reported in Matthew, Mark and Luke were as a rule spoken in Aramaic, whereas the discourses reported in John were spoken in Greek, it will no longer be possible to deny that the reports were written at the time the sayings and discourses were spoken, and that each of the Gospels consists mainly of notes taken at the time or immediately after the events happened. If this be not the case the problem is more puzzling than ever. No matter in what language the original reporters of Christ's sayings wrote, if they did not relate the facts until years or even months after they happened, there is no reason why they should have confined their narration mainly to events in which only one language was used. Persons who are in the habit of reading in more than one language will often remember what they have read and yet be unable to recollect in what language they read it. It is ideas that fix themselves in the memory; the words in which the ideas are conveyed soon fade away and are forgotten. The substance of Christ's sayings, whether spoken in Greek or Aramaic, would accordingly be stamped with equal clearness upon the disciples' minds, and when they repeated them orally, or committed them to writing, they would not discriminate between the languages in which they were spoken. If, however, the disciples were accustomed to report the sayings of Jesus as He spoke, or at the first leisure moment thereafter, when the very words He used were fresh in their memory, all becomes plain.

It seems absolutely certain that all the disciples were able to speak and understand both Greek and Aramaic, and it is probable that several were able also to write in both languages. It is true that Dr. T. K. Abbott, in his work "On the Original Texts of the Old and New Testaments" maintains that "the Apostles were able to speak Greek fluently and to write it, and that it is not likely that they had equal command over any other language." But a high authority, Professor Marcus Dods, while admitting the correctness of this view so far as it affirms a general knowledge of Greek, considers that Dr. Abbott "underrates the likelihood of men in the circumstances of the Apostles being bi-lingual," and adds, "Had he been writing in Scotland instead of in Ireland, he would probably have come to a different conclusion and allowed them a knowledge of Aramaic as well." But whilst the evidence is strong that Professor Dods' opinion is the correct one, it is very unlikely that any one of the disciples could write so swiftly in both Aramaic and Greek as to be able to report at the moment the utterances of a speaker in either language indifferently.

For the two languages are as unlike to one another as possible. Aramaic abounds in aspirates and gutturals, whereas in Greek there are no gutturals, only the two breathings used in modern European speech. The pronunciation of the two was therefore entirely different. But to a reporter the pronunciation would be the least part of the difficulty. In Aramaic there are twenty-two letters, none of which are vowels. In Greek there are twenty-four letters, including five vowels. The shapes of the letters are different. And to complete the contrast, the writing runs in contrary ways across the page. Aramaic is written from right to left like the verses of Lars Porsena's prophets:

> "'Traced from the right on linen white,
> By mighty seers of yore."

Greek, of course, is written from left to right.

A man might be well able to write in both these languages; but to write so rapidly as to be able to report in both would be quite another matter, and it should need no argument to convince any one that the Apostles, whose accomplishment of fast writing had been previously applied to business purposes only, could not do so. Hence a division of labour became necessary, and either tacitly or by agreement it came to be understood that those who wrote readily in Aramaic should report the Lord's utterances in the one tongue, and that the one who was at home in Greek should report His discourses in the other.

It appears then that to unlock the Chief Problem of the Gospel Question both the Master Key and this First Special Key are needed. The two propositions stand or fall together. If it be true that our Lord used two languages, and that Matthew, Mark and Luke contain almost exclusively His Aramaic, and John His Greek utterances, there is no escaping the conclusion that the Gospels are based upon contemporary and verbatim reports of what our Lord did and taught. On the other hand, sufficient has been said to prove that, if the records are not vague reminiscences, modified by the mental bias and standpoint of the writers, but faithful and accurate reports of what He really said and did, the addresses in the Synoptics and the discourses in John were respectively spoken in different languages, one of which must have been Aramaic and the other Greek.

All the attempts hitherto made to account for the contrast in form and substance between Matthew, Mark and Luke on the one hand, and John on the other, have been failures. The most usual explanation has been that each evangelist had a special and distinct design in the Gospel which he wrote, or that he intended it for a certain class of readers, and selected his materials accordingly. But this, even if it were so, would go but a short way towards solving the problem. There is nothing, however, to warrant the supposition that the writers of the Gospels had any other design than to give as faithful an account as they were able of the facts of our Lord's life. They write with the simplicity of men whose desire is to let their story speak for itself, and who never dream of twisting it to suit their own views. Their own opinions never appear except it may be in occasional comments which are kept carefully apart from the narrative itself. The theory of design or of doctrinal bias is but a sort of forlorn hope to cope with a question that seemed to defy criticism.

The true solution is a very simple and prosaic one, namely, that it passed the skill of the disciples to write quickly in two totally dissimilar languages, expressed in different characters, running in reverse directions.

Part IV

THE SECOND SPECIAL KEY THAT THE RECORDS IN THE SYNOPTIC GOSPELS LARGELY CONSIST OF THE UNITED TESTIMONY OF THE APOSTLES GIVEN AT THE TIME IN COMPANY AND SEVERALLY REPORTED BY THE WRITERS

Chapter I

BRIEF STATEMENT

IF it is probable that some of the Apostles made a practice of recording the sayings and doings of Christ, it is also probable that those who did so obtained the help of their colleagues in that undertaking. For they were certainly inexperienced in work of that character; and, although for reporting a speech verbatim their inexperience might be a matter of little moment (provided they could write fast enough), for relating facts, and for reporting sayings which they did not take down at the moment of utterance, they would find their want of practice a serious inconvenience. It is highly probable that some who were expert in writing did not possess in so large a degree as some of the others either the faculty for observing and remembering facts, or the command of language necessary for describing them. Those therefore who undertook the task of writing from time to time a narrative of our Lord's sayings and doings needed all the assistance their fellow-Apostles could afford.

The Twelve on our theory did precisely what under the circumstances it was most likely and most natural that they would do. One of the first things that occurred to them, after being called and set apart to their distinguished office, was the necessity of making a record of the acts and utterances of Christ their Master. They began by enquiring who among them were most ready with the pen, and fixed their attention on four who, by reason of their former occupations or otherwise, were known to be expert writers. These however had each a keen sense of his insufficiency for the task. True, they could in their business jot down quickly notes of their dealings; but work of the description now called for they had never done. They were not literary men, and what was now required was literary work. But the others encouraged them to try. " In reporting the Master's addresses you will have but to write just what He says; and for the rest we will all help you as best we can." So it was arranged that, whenever convenient, tautochronistic reports of our Lord's addresses should be made by one or more of the four; and that on suitable occasions the Apostles should unitedly review the events that had recently occurred, and that reports of those events, based upon the conversations which took place on those occasions, should then be written.

The four who thus undertook to write what may be called the Apostolic journals or chronicles were Matthew, John, Peter, and, I think, James the son of Zebedee. Matthew and John speak for themselves, and Peter is named by ancient tradition and general consent as the original author of the records of Mark. My reasons for assuming that James was the writer of the notes which form the substance of the greater part of the third Gospel will be stated in our next Part, when considering the Third Special Key—the Key which unlocks the Chronological Problem.

At present it is impossible to say for certain to what extent John availed himself of the help of his brethren when he wrote the notes of which his Gospel is composed. In some places there are indications that he knew what the others were writing; but in others there are strong indications that he did not. The probability is that he was generally present at the conferences when Matthew, Peter and James wrote, but that, as the conversation at such times was in Aramaic and he wrote in Greek, he himself as a rule wrote by himself alone.

The principal portions of the first three Gospels consist then in part of separate tautochronistic reports of our Lord's utterances, and in part of reports, also tautochronistic and severally made, of the testimony of the Apostles given in conference. When writing the latter the writers also revised and finished off —perhaps re-wrote—the former, and arranged the manuscripts in order.

The proof that the Synoptic narratives were for the most part written in the way described will be found to be convincing by those who will take the trouble, patiently and without bias, to compare, section by section and word by word, the parallel portions of Matthew, Mark and Luke. An attempt is made in the final Part of this book to assist the reader in this undertaking. Meanwhile, in the hope of bringing home to his mind the manner in which, as I believe, the original authors of the Synoptic narratives did their work, I will try to describe their proceedings during a given period. In this attempt I scrupulously follow the letter of the Gospel stories, and my inferences are always those which are, in my opinion, naturally suggested by the text.

The following are the portions chosen:—Matthew xx. 17–34; Mark x. 32–52; Luke xviii. 31–34, xxii. 24–30, xviii. 35–43, xix. 1–27. They relate the doings of two days of the time occupied in the last journey of Christ to Jerusalem. (The reason for the displacement of parts of Luke's narrative will be given in Part V.)

Thanks to the learning and research that have been devoted to the subject by commentators, we are able to fix, almost to a certainty, the dates upon which the events here recorded took place. My reasons for believing that the "City called Ephraim" (John xi. 54) was situated near the east bank of the Jordan, and was the starting point of this journey, will be found in Part VII.

Chapter II

A DIARY OF TWO DAYS

IT is the morning of Wednesday, the 29th March, A.D. 30, when Jesus with the twelve Apostles set out from the "city called Ephraim" in Peræa, on their journey to Jerusalem With them are a number of other disciples, some of them women, who have followed Him from Galilee, and joined the party here. As they proceed on their way they find themselves in the company of other travellers, who like themselves are going to the Temple to observe the Passover. Many of these are also from Galilee where they have often listened to the preaching of Jesus and seen His works; they are therefore friendly disposed towards Him and some are believers on Him.

As the Apostles mingle with these fellow pilgrims, exchanging greetings, and asking and answering questions about mutual acquaintance, the Master walks on in advance. Presently they observe something unusual in His manner. He is hurrying on fast; He appears abstracted, and as it were set upon some fixed purpose; and His bearing is such as to cause a vague feeling of surprise and painful apprehension in their hearts. After a while He stops and waits until they come up with Him; then, calling the Twelve apart from the other travellers, he discloses to them in plainer terms than He has done hitherto, the events that lie before Him during the next few days. He says :—

"Behold, we go up to Jerusalem, and all the things that are written by the prophets shall be accomplished unto the Son of man. For he shall be delivered up to the chief priests and the scribes; and they shall condemn him to death, and shall deliver him unto the Gentiles; and he shall be mocked, and shamefully entreated, and spit upon ; and they shall scourge and crucify and kill him ; and the third day he shall rise again."

Shortly after, as they proceed on their way, Salome, the mother of Zebedee's children, with her two sons, approaching Jesus, asks Him to promise that they may sit, the one on His right hand and the other on His left, in His Kingdon. To this request Jesus replies, "Ye know not what ye ask. Are ye able to drink the cup that I drink ? or to be baptized with the baptism that I am baptized with ?" They answer, "We are able." Jesus then says unto them : "The cup that I drink ye shall drink ; and with the baptism that I am baptized withal shall ye be baptized : but to sit on my right hand and on my left hand is not mine to give, but it is for them for whom it hath been prepared of my Father."

This request of James and John causes much indignation amongst the other ten disciples, who at the moment can see in it only a selfish desire for pre-eminence. But Jesus calls them all together, and speaks to them as follows :—

"Ye know that they which are accounted to rule over the Gentiles lord it over them ; and their great ones exercise authority over them. But it is not so among you : but whosoever would become great among you, shall be your minister : and whosoever would be first among you, shall be servant of all. For verily the Son of man came not to be ministered unto, but to minister, and to give his life a ransom for many. For whether is greater, he that sitteth at meat, or he that serveth ? is not he that sitteth at meat ? but I am in the midst of you as he that serveth. But ye are they which have continued with me in my temptations ; and I appoint unto you a kingdom, even as my Father appointed unto me, that ye may eat and drink at my table in my kingdom : and ye shall sit on thrones judging the twelve tribes of Israel."

Nothing further of unusual importance occurs on this day's journey. As evening approaches, after a walk of twenty or twenty-five miles, they arrive at Bethany "beyond Jordan." Here they have many friends ; for near to this place John the Baptist, three or four years ago, preached and baptized. So there is no lack of hospitality, and the party stay here for the night.

After rest and supper, the Apostles assemble in the principal room of the house where they are guests. Mats or thin cushions are laid upon the floor, and upon these they leisurely recline. The Lord is not in their midst : He probably has withdrawn, as is His wont, to meet with His Father in prayer. Three of the party, Matthew, Peter and James, have pen, ink and paper before them, and near them is a brightly burning lamp. And now they begin to talk over the leading events of the day.

The first subject of conversation is the strange intimation that their Master has given them of the things that are shortly to happen to Him. They recall the feeling of amazement and fear with which they observed His demeanour as He walked in advance in the morning. Of these experiences Peter alone makes a note :—

"And they were in the way going up to Jerusalem ; and Jesus was going before them : and they were amazed, and they that followed were afraid." (Mark x. 32.)

They then speak of the intimation itself, and one and another repeat, as nearly as they can remember, the words that Jesus spoke. Following their recital, the three record His words respectively as shown in parallel columns on page 151.

When these portions have been written, the question is asked by one, "What did the Lord mean by this ?" The question is repeated by others, but no answer is forthcoming, and they all express their inability to understand His allusions. On several former occasions they have taken the Master's figurative language literally ; now that He has spoken literally they cannot realise that such is the case, but think He had some allegorical lesson to convey. James alone mentions their perplexity in the following terms :—

"And they understood none of these things ; and this saying was hid rom them and they perceived not the things that were said." (Luke xviii. 34.)

And now they go on to recall the request which was made to Jesus, only some three or four hours ago, that He would grant to two of their number a place of special favour in His Kingdom. All feeling of anger has passed away; perhaps they see that they too harshly judged the motive of James and John; they try now to remember and repeat the words which Jesus spake to them and to all. As they do so the three continue to write, Matthew and Peter following closely the recital of those whose excellent memories enable them to repeat almost with verbal accuracy what Jesus said. James, however, depends more on his own recollection. He does not mention the application made by John and himself; in general terms he alludes to the occasion which called forth our Lord's admonition, and records some sentences thereof that appear to have escaped the notice of the rest. The three reports are presented on pages 152, 153.

Bethany, where they are passing the night, is a town on the left bank of the Jordan, and close to the fords of that river. On the opposite side, some six or seven miles distant, is the important town of Jericho.

The Jordan, at least on the lower part, as it widens out on its course towards the Dead Sea,

152 THE GOSPEL PROBLEMS AND THEIR SOLUTION

(Matt. xx. 20-28).

Then came to him the mother of the sons of Zebedee with her sons, worshipping *him*, and asking a certain thing of him. And he said unto her, What wouldest thou? She saith unto him, Command that these my two sons may sit, one on thy right hand, and one on thy left hand, in thy kingdom. But Jesus answered and said, Ye know not what ye ask. Are ye able to drink the cup that I am about to drink? They say unto him, We are able. He saith unto them, My cup indeed ye shall drink: but to sit on my right hand, and on *my* left hand, is not mine to give, but *it is for them* for whom it hath been prepared of my Father. And when the ten heard it, they were moved with indignation concerning the two brethren. But Jesus called them unto him, and said, Ye know that the rulers of the Gentiles lord it over them, and their great ones exercise authority over them. Not so shall it be among you: but whosoever would

(Mark x. 35-45).

And there come near unto him James and John, the sons of Zebedee, saying unto him, Master, we would that thou shouldest do for us whatsoever we shall ask of thee. And he said unto them, What would ye that I should do for you? And they said unto him, Grant unto us that we may sit, one on thy right hand, and one on *thy* left hand, in thy glory. But Jesus said unto them, Ye know not what ye ask. Are ye able to drink the cup that I drink? or to be baptized with the baptism that I am baptized with? And they said unto him, We are able. And Jesus said unto them, The cup that I drink ye shall drink; and with the baptism that I am baptized withal shall ye be baptized: but to sit on my right hand or on *my* left hand is not mine to give: but *it is for them* for whom it hath been prepared. And when the ten heard it, they began to be moved with indignation concerning James and John. And Jesus called them

(Luke xxii. 24-30).

And there arose also a contention among them, which of them is accounted to be greatest. And he said unto them, The kings of the Gentiles have lordship over them; and they that have authority over them are called Benefactors. But ye *shall* not *be* so: but he that is the greater among you, let him become as the younger; and he that is chief, as he that doth serve. For whether is greater, he that sitteth at meat, or he that serveth? is not he that sitteth at meat? but I am in the midst of you as he that serveth. But ye are they which have continued with me in my temptations; and I appoint unto you a kingdom, even as my Father appointed unto me, that ye may eat and drink at my table in my kingdom; and ye shall sit on thrones judging the twelve tribes of Israel.

is, at the time of our narrative, and hitherto always has been, entirely without bridges. This is not owing to any lack of engineering skill, as is proved by the architectural works of the country. It is probably owing to a cause similar to that which, in the nineteenth century, will prevent the construction of a tunnel beneath the English Channel. It has been felt in all ages that the river is to Western Palestine a great protection against invasion. A defending army may always advantageously dispute the onward march of an enemy when he attempts the passage of the Jordan. Rather than annul that safeguard the inhabitants have preferred to submit to the inconvenience of having themselves to cross in the most primitive fashion.

The river being at this point shallow and easily crossed, a large part of the traffic between Judea and the outside world converges to it. Another reason for this is that the range of mountains to the west of and running parallel with the Jordan, and which obstructs the entrance to that

---

become great among you shall be your minister; and whosoever would be first among you shall be your servant: even as the Son of man came not to be ministered unto, but to minister, and to give his life a ransom for many.

to him, and saith unto them, Ye know that they which are accounted to rule over the Gentiles lord it over them; and their great ones exercise authority over them. But it is not so among you: but whosoever would become great among you, shall be your minister: and whosoever would be first among you, shall be servant of all. For verily the Son of man came not to be ministered unto, but to minister, and to give his life a ransom for many.

part of Judea, is here broken by a pass along which a road runs from Jericho to Jerusalem.

To return to our story : Jesus and the disciples having passed the night at Bethany, and partaken of breakfast in the morning, resume their journey. But first they must cross the river. Here a large crowd is collected, some of whom wade through the waters, while others wait their turn to be ferried over by the many boats now gathered at the spot. The women of our Lord's party doubtless cross in boats, and perhaps the men also. This takes time, and the morning is somewhat advanced when the company are all collected and continue their journey. Some two or three hours' walking brings them to Jericho, a large and flourishing town, surrounded by a wall, and situated near to the entrance of the pass aforesaid. Here some interesting incidents happen.

It is not strange that two blind men should sit begging, one at the entrance and another at the exit of an important town like Jericho, especially at Passover time, when a large stream of pilgrims are passing through on their way to the Temple. The multitude who are now travelling thither have gathered closely around Jesus, and when they force their way through the narrow gate of the city, and proceed along its equally narrow street, the crowd becomes densely packed. The Apostles thus become separated and will see at different points diverse phases of the miracle about to be performed. As Jesus enters the town, the first blind man, having learned who it is that is passing, cries out, " Jesus, thou son of David, have mercy on me." As appears by Luke's narrative, he follows Jesus crying out, while they that go before rebuke him, and tell him to hold his peace. Being blind, he is unable to push through the crowd, so as to overtake Jesus and attract His attention, until the further gate of the town has been reached. Just outside this gate the other blind man is sitting. He does not at first rise and follow Jesus ; but, retaining his seat, cries out in similar terms, " Jesus, thou son of David, have mercy on me." The Lord hears the appeal, and, standing still, says, "Call ye him "; whereupon the man casts away his garments, springs up and comes to Jesus. The halt gives time for the first blind man to come up, assisted now doubtless by the people, and Jesus heals them both.

While Jesus has been passing through Jericho, the chief publican, Zacchæus, has tried to come near Him, desiring from mere curiosity to see Him, who He is. But, owing to the smallness of his stature and the density of the crowd, he has failed to gratify his wish; so he has run on before and just outside the city, where, having climbed a convenient sycamore tree growing by the roadside, he awaits the coming of Christ, who, as he knows, must pass that way. There he sees Jesus heal the two blind men, and is deeply impressed by the miracle, and convinced that the Rabbi is no ordinary man. Great then is his surprise and joy when the Lord calls him by name and announces His intention to stay the rest of the day at his house.

The house of Zacchæus is situated, not in Jericho itself, but a short distance off on the western side. The nature of his occupation makes this necessary. His business is to collect the duties on merchandise conveyed along the road to and from Judea. This traffic has all to pass through the defile in the mountains to which we have already referred, and to which the entrance is just outside the town. To intercept this it would be of no use for Zacchæus and his staff to reside in the city. Jericho is in a plain, and could by a slight detour be easily avoided by carriers, and thus the payment of an obnoxious tax would be evaded. It is necessary therefore to live at the foot of the mountain, and at the very entrance to the pass, so as to supervise all persons entering or emerging from it.

The manifestation of condescension and mercy which Jesus has made to Zacchæus has produced a complete change in his character. It is a case of instantaneous conversion. As the Lord enters his house, Zacchæus says: " Behold, Lord, the half of my goods I give to the poor; and if I have wrongfully exacted aught of any man, I restore fourfold"; to which words our Lord answers, "To-day is salvation come to this house, forasmuch as he also is a son of Abraham. For the Son of man came to seek and save that which was lost."

However the mark of favour which Jesus is showing to this tax-collector causes much dissatisfaction in the crowd. It is not confined to Pharisees and other hostile persons. They *all* murmur, saying, "He is gone in to lodge with a man that is a sinner." Most of the pilgrims who are following Jesus are well disposed towards Him. True, they do not clearly understand the spiritual nature of His mission, and many of them do not in the higher sense of the word believe on Him; still they are His friends. They well know His way of associating with the poor, the afflicted and the sinful. But this publican is not poor or afflicted, and his sinfulness is of an exceptional and very flagrant character. He has grown rich by acting as the hireling of their Roman oppressors. And he has, as his own confession implies, been guilty of those crimes for which the tax-collectors are notorious. By false representation he has extorted payments in excess even of the imposts to which he is legally entitled. All this the travellers learn from the people of Jericho, many of whom come with them out of the city, and they cannot understand the action of Christ in becoming the guest of such a man as he.

But now, although it is not late, the pilgrims must finish their journey for the day. For there is here a convenient camping place—a verdant fruitful plain with plenty of water—whilst, beyond, the road runs for many miles through rugged mountain passes. So those who have tents pitch them, and others choose suitable places where, when night falls, they may sleep, rolled in their sheepskin rugs. Then they eat their afternoon meal, which needs little preparation, for they have bought food in the town as they came through. When they have finished their dinner they assemble in groups and chat; and now the conversation which passed between Jesus and Zacchæus at the door of the latter's house, and which was heard only by a few bystanders, is told by one to another. Thus the pilgrims learn that Zacchæus is truly penitent, and has promised to make amends, and more than ample compensation to those whom he has wronged, and they begin to see that they were mistaken in their hasty judgment, and that, as always, the Master "hath done all things well."

While this report is circulating ("as they heard these things"; ἀκουόντων δὲ αὐτῶν ταῦτα), Jesus and His disciples, having finished their meal, come out into the verandah of the house; and, observing Him, the people gather round to hear what He has to say. No doubt He has often addressed the multitudes about Him on the way hither, but the Apostles have had no opportunity to report His sayings. Now, however, one of them (James, as I believe) reclines in the verandah with his writing materials before him, and records Christ's every word; and the parable of the Nobleman who went into a far country and returned, is for ever preserved.

To-day is the 30th of March; the sun sets at six o'clock, and at the foot of this range of hills it then becomes almost instantly dark. So the disciples retire into the house; the Master goes apart, while Zacchæus with his other guests assemble in the drawing-room. This gives the Apostles another opportunity to write their reports. Once more we see them in reclining posture, and hear them rehearsing the events of the day, while Matthew, Peter and James are busily engaged with pen, ink and paper.

The subject of their talk is the miracle that has been wrought that day.

"It was just before we reached Jericho," says one, "that I first noticed the blind man. He was sitting by the wayside begging, and hearing a multitude go by he inquired what this meant. And they told him that Jesus of Nazareth passed by, upon which he cried out, 'Jesus, thou son of David, have mercy on me.' And he tried to run after Jesus, but those before told him to hold his peace. But he cried out the more a great deal, 'Thou son of David, have mercy on me.'"

"That was not the man I saw," says another. "I was walking close to the Master and, in the bustle of the crowd, heard no one calling. But as we came out of the city I saw a blind man sitting by the road side and he cried out, 'Jesus, thou son of David, have mercy on me.'"

Now Zacchæus speaks: "That was Bartimæus; I know him well. He has begged for many a year."

Then others in turn go on to tell how the crowd tried to silence Bartimæus; how he, like the first blind man, only cried out the more; how Jesus stood still and commanded to call him; how those, who before had rebuked Bartimæus, now encouraged him; how he cast away his garments, sprang up and came to Jesus; how the first blind man now came up and joined his fellow; how Jesus asked them what they wished Him to do for them; how they answered, "Lord, that our eyes may be opened"; and how Jesus, moved with compassion, touched their eyes so that their sight was restored, and they followed Him.

And as all this is recited the three penmen, who have themselves each seen but a part of the incident, write down what they hear, and produce three accounts, partly in the same words, and identical in their essential facts, yet each possessing some details wanting in the others, and bearing notably this peculiarity, that James mentions only the man who sat at the Eastern gate, Peter only the man who sat at the Western gate, while Matthew—always a good listener—mentions them both. The three accounts appear on page 159.

Matthew and Peter have now finished their work for the day. Not so James. It is his desire to write an account of the conversion of Zacchæus. The gentle delicacy which usually characterises the Galilean followers of Christ has precluded their discussing this subject in the presence of their host. But James now enters into quiet conversation with him; gains from him such information as he needs; and with his help writes the story.

Finally, James writes the short passage explaining the

MATTHEW'S REPORT.
Matthew xx. 29-34.

And as they went out from Jericho, a great multitude followed him. And behold, two blind men sitting by the way side, when they heard that Jesus was passing by, cried out, saying, Lord, have mercy on us, thou son of David. And the multitude rebuked them, that they should hold their peace: but they cried out the more, saying, Lord, have mercy on us, thou son of David. And Jesus stood still, and called them, and said, What will ye that I should do unto you? They say unto him, Lord, that our eyes may be opened. And Jesus, being moved with compassion, touched their eyes: and straightway they received their sight, and followed him.

PETER'S REPORT.
Mark x. 46-52.

And they come to Jericho: and as he went out from Jericho, with his disciples and a great multitude, the son of Timæus, Bartimæus, a blind beggar, was sitting by the way side. And when he heard that it was Jesus of Nazareth, he began to cry out, and say, Jesus, thou son of David, have mercy on me. And many rebuked him, that he should hold his peace: but he cried out the more a great deal, Thou son of David, have mercy on me. And Jesus stood still, and said, Call ye him. And they call the blind man, saying unto him, Be of good cheer: rise, he calleth thee. And he, casting away his garment, sprang up, and came to Jesus. And Jesus answered him, and said, What wilt thou that I should do unto thee? And the blind man said unto him, Rabboni, that I may receive my sight. And Jesus said unto him, Go thy way; thy faith hath made thee whole. And straightway he received his sight, and followed him in the way.

JAMES' REPORT.
Luke xviii. 35-43.

And it came to pass, as he drew nigh unto Jericho, a certain blind man sat by the way side begging: and hearing a multitude going by, he inquired what this meant. And they told him, that Jesus of Nazareth passeth by. And he cried, saying, Jesus, thou son of David, have mercy on me. And they that went before rebuked him, that he should hold his peace: but he cried out the more a great deal, Thou son of David, have mercy on me. And Jesus stood, and commanded him to be brought unto him: and when he was come near, he asked him, What wilt thou that I should do unto thee? And he said, Lord, that I may receive my sight. And Jesus said unto him, Receive thy sight: thy faith hath made thee whole. And immediately he received his sight, and followed him, glorifying God: and all the people, when they saw it, gave praise unto God.

reasons for which Jesus spake the parable of the Nobleman, a verbatim report of which he made a short time ago. These reasons have been told him by Jesus Himself, either just before or just after the delivery of the parable. Having written this passage and arranged his manuscripts in order, placing those containing the parable last, his work for the day is also completed.

In the foregoing sketch there is little that has been drawn from imagination. The outlines, at any rate, are strictly in accord with the Gospel narratives, and the local conditions which are known, or generally believed, to have existed at the time. The chief assumptions are those concerning the manner in which the portions were written which are quoted in the course of the last ten pages. Is there anything unreasonable or improbable in the supposition that they were written at the time or in the manner described? Do not the features of the three narratives when read side by side appear to be just such as might be expected if they were so written? Observe, that there is in them a general similarity, and many identical words and sentences, which show that the three are in some way related. Observe, again, that each has other words and sentences peculiar to itself, and characteristics of its own, which prove its independence of the other two. Then say whether such features as these could have been produced by any other cause than that to which I attribute them. My purpose, however, in this chapter, is illustration, not proof. My aim now is that the reader shall gain a clear idea of the Proposition which forms the subject of this Part; the evidence in support of the Proposition will come by-and-by.

Part V

THE THIRD SPECIAL KEY

THAT THE CHRONOLOGICAL DISORDER IN MATTHEW AND LUKE IS OWING TO THE NOTES USED IN THE COMPILATION OF THOSE GOSPELS HAVING BECOME DISARRANGED; AND IN THE CASE OF LUKE THROUGH THE ORIGINAL WRITER THEREOF BEING BY REASON OF DEATH, OR SOME OTHER CAUSE, UNABLE TO ASSIST IN THEIR REDACTION

Chapter I

THE NATURE OF THE CHRONOLOGICAL DISORDER

IT is hardly possible for any one to make a careful comparison of the Synoptic Gospels without coming to the conclusion that it is not in Mark but in Matthew and Luke that the greatest confusion exists. Papias, it is true, tells us that Mark's Gospel is not written in order, and it is impossible with certainty to contradict that assertion. But that Mark's sequence approaches chronological accuracy more closely than either Matthew's or Luke's is proved by this, that whereas in this respect Matthew and Mark frequently coincide as against Luke, and Mark and Luke sometimes coincide as against

Matthew, Matthew and Luke never coincide where they differ from Mark.

Mark

There is indeed no evidence that Mark ever differs from chronological order, except in the account of the Supper and Anointing at Bethany and the offer made by Judas to betray Jesus to the chief priests, which follows the account of events that happened subsequently. Curiously enough in this the only instance in which Mark certainly departs from the actual sequence of events he is supported in doing so by both the other Synoptics. With this one exception it will be found best in any attempt to construct a consecutive narrative of the life of Christ to accept the order of Mark implicitly.

Matthew

The disorder in Matthew is mostly in the earlier part of the book, where there is much confusion both as regards the sequence of events and the utterances of our Lord, some of which are evidently presented in a different connection from that in which they were spoken. Matthew's own call is related after the first Galilean circuit of Jesus and the Sermon on the Mount, both of which it must have preceded. The healing of Peter's wife's mother, and several other miracles, which, according to Mark and Luke, took place quite at the beginning of our Lord's ministry, occupy a later place in Matthew.

Luke

The greatest confusion of all is found in Luke, both incidents and sayings being frequently mixed up in a most extraordinary manner. It sometimes seems as if the author was governed by no principle whatever in the arrangement of his materials. An illustration of this appears in the account of our Lord's last journey from Galilee to Judea. The beginning of this journey is related Luke ix. 51–56, where it is said that He sent messengers before Him, who entered into a Samaritan village, but were not received there, and that in consequence they went to another village. The route He now took was the border line between Samaria and Galilee towards the river Jordan, His purpose being to continue His journey to Jerusalem through Perea. This is mentioned eight chapters later: Luke xvii. 11 (R.V., margin). About this time or soon after He sent out the seventy to give timely notice of His approach to the cities and places on His line of travel. For the account of this we have to go back to chap. x. 1. The continuation of this journey through the cities and villages of Perea is mentioned Luke xiii. 22. Finally His arrival at Bethany, a suburb of Jerusalem, is related Luke x. 38.

Not only is there great disregard of chronological order in the arrangement of Luke's facts; but in many cases it appears that sayings of our Lord are located quite out of their proper connection. One of the most noticeable instances of this is the insertion in the account of the last supper of a paragraph (xxii. 24–30) which belongs properly to the last journey to Jerusalem, being parallel with Matthew xx. 24–28 and Mark x. 41–45.

The confusion in Luke is the more puzzling since Luke is generally credited with being a man who loved the methodical and precise. And compared with the other New Testament writers such seems to have been really the case. He alone intentionally gives a date of any of the events which he records. He alone tells the age of Jesus when He began His ministry. How is it then that it is Luke's Gospel of all others that bears the least approach to chronological sequence?

John

In John there does not appear to be any want of chronological sequence, except perhaps in one place (John xii. 36a–43 with 44–50) where two connected portions seem to have been transposed.

Composition and Redaction

In order to a right understanding of the cause of the confusion here referred to, it is necessary to keep in mind the clear distinction between the composition of the records which form the substance of the Gospels, and the arrangement and redaction of those records into books for publication. I have already stated my concurrence with the general belief that the Gospels were not redacted until many years after the events which they relate; and in a former chapter I have called attention to the editorial notes which were interspersed among the original materials when that was done. But, as a right conception of this subject is essential to the whole purpose of this book, I propose here to devote a chapter to a consideration of the manner in which, some twenty or thirty years, and in the case of John perhaps forty or fifty years, after the time of Christ, the work of redacting the Gospels was accomplished.

Chapter II

THE WORK OF REDACTION

ALL histories, ancient and modern, are composed of materials previously in existence. In the works with which ordinary readers are most familiar, the facts are usually presented in the authors' own language, and the original materials are kept out of sight—except it be in footnotes; nevertheless in every case, in proportion to the accuracy of the work, has the author with more or less diligence sought out from older authorities the particulars of the story he narrates.

Herodotus, "the father of ancient history," travelled in many lands to collect the materials for his work, and from his time to the present every historian of repute has devoted much time and labour to obtain, when possible from contemporary sources, the exact truth concerning the events which form the subject of his book.

Even when a writer narrates events in which he himself was concerned, he does not depend entirely on memory. Xenophon doubtless made use of the journals kept by himself and other officers to compose the *Anabasis*. And although Kinglake was present at the war in the Crimea, his own unwritten recollections form probably no appreciable part of his *History of the Invasion*.

Sometimes historians, and especially biographers, present their facts almost without alteration as they appear in the original sources, recognising that the very words in which contemporaries have expressed themselves in journals and letters will often better convey a right impression to the reader than anything the author can say himself. Thus some of Froude's works consist largely of a literal transcription or translation of original letters and diplomatic reports.

In Oriental histories the practice of quoting earlier documents without alteration appears to be more generally in use than among ourselves. According to Robertson Smith: "If we take up the great Arabic historians we often find passages occurring almost word for word in each. All use directly or indirectly the same sources, and copy these sources verbally as far as is consistent with the scope and scale of their several works. Thus a comparatively modern book has often the freshness and full colour of a contemporary narrative, and we can still separate out the old sources from their modern setting." (*Old Testament in Jewish Church*, p. 328.)

Old Testament Histories

It was in such manner as this that the historical books of the Old Testament were composed. Their composite character is now generally admitted, as is also the distinction between the writing of the records which compose them, and their redaction. What has not been recognised is the great antiquity of the original materials. As with the Gospels, so with these, Naturalistic critics have fallen into an unfortunate habit of treating as "traditions" what are really authentic narratives, copied from documents written in the first instance contemporaneously with the events which they record.

Were it not for the prevailing bias against the supernatural element in Scripture it would be recognised that the lives of the Patriarchs in the book of Genesis are family records, written originally on clay tablets by the Patriarchs themselves, and handed down from generation to generation. Speaking of Chaldæa and inclusively of a time long anterior to the migration of Abraham from that country to Canaan, Maspero says: " Families had their private archives, to which additions were rapidly made by every generation; every household thus accumulated not only the evidences of its own history, but to some extent that of other families with whom they had formed alliances, or had business or friendly relations." (*Dawn of Civilization*, p. 732.)

There is nothing unreasonable in the supposition that when Terah, Abraham's father, left Ur of the Chaldees on his memorable journey, he, to avoid the inconvenience of carrying with him a great number of heavy clay documents, made condensed summaries of the family records of his ancestors, and took these with him instead of the originals. The more important histories however of the Creation and the Deluge, the former of which may have been written during the lifetime of Adam, and the latter during that of Noah, he probably carried with him entire. These documents would be brought by Abraham to Canaan and retained by his descendants, who would add to them as time went on. May it not be that Genesis is composed of records thus accumulated which, making allowances for translation, editorial emendations and mistakes in copying, are in the main accurately reproduced in that book?

Exodus, Leviticus, Numbers and Deuteronomy are composed of records written during the forty years' wanderings of Israel in the wilderness. These remain almost in their original integrity, but intermixed with many subsequent additions. The additions can often be distinguished by the ordinary reader, and some of them so manifestly interrupt the flow of the original story that the Revisers of the English Version have enclosed them with marks of parenthesis.

In Deuteronomy the distinction between the modern settings and the original Sermons is evident enough, and at the time of the Book's first publication could not have been misapprehended by any reader. One specimen of the former may here be cited (iv. 44–49) :—

"And this is the law which Moses set before the children of Israel: these are the testimonies, and the statutes and the judgments, which Moses spake unto the children of Israel, when they came forth out of Egypt; beyond Jordan in the valley over against Beth-peor, in the land of Sihon king of the Amorites, who dwelt at Heshbon, whom Moses and the children of Israel smote, when they came forth out of Egypt : and they took his land in possession, and the land of Og king of Bashan, the two kings of the Amorites, which were beyond Jordan toward the sunrising; from Aroer, which is on the edge of the valley of Arnon, even unto Mount Sion (the same is Hermon), and all the Arabah, beyond Jordan eastward, even unto the sea of the Arabah, under the slopes of Pisgah."

In this passage the standpoint of the writer declares itself without any attempt at concealment. Over and over again he uses the expression, "beyond Jordan," showing that he lived on the opposite side of the river to that occupied by those of whom he was speaking. Note too the full description which he gives of the localities referred to, proving that he wrote among and for those to whom the places named were distant and unfamiliar. The expression twice used, "when they came forth out of Egypt," but both times referring to events which happened nearly forty years after the Exodus, could only have been written after a lapse of time so great that a space of forty years would seem trifling in comparison. In such respects the Sermons of Deuteronomy present a complete contrast to the settings. True, a redactor's hand appears now and then even in the Sermons, nor is this to be wondered at. It is admitted that, during the centuries which followed the conquest of Canaan, considerable modifications took place in the language of the Hebrews. This together with the copying, in the modern Phœnician alphabetic characters, of manuscripts written in the old Egyptian syllabary, would necessitate what would be almost equivalent to the making of a translation from one language to another, and would excuse, if not justify, a transcriber in making such emendations as might seem to him desirable to make the work intelligible. It may be easily understood then how, in one instance, when copying the name of a place situated East of the Jordan, he came to insert the words "beyond Jordan" (iii. 8), forgetting for the moment that he resided on the opposite side of the river to that on which the speaker resided. But, on the other hand, it is incredible that an author, who, if the Sermons were a concoction of later times, displays such consummate skill in self-suppression, and in placing himself in the standpoint of the supposed speaker, should be guilty of such an egregious blunder as to make Moses use the expression "beyond Jordan" in two contradictory senses. (See ii. 29, iii. 20, 25, 27, iv. 26, xi. 30, etc. etc.)

Undoubtedly, however, there are in the Old Testament writings many interpolations of comparatively recent date, and the words "beyond Jordan," in iii. 8, may be one of them. The phrase "when ye came forth out of Egypt," in xxiii. 4, is probably an interpolation, being a repetition from other places where it is legitimately used.

The real standpoint of the author of the Sermons appears in the familiar way in which he speaks of places well known to the Israelites prior to their entrance into Canaan : Horeb, the hill-country of the Amorites, Kadesh-Barnea, the Red Sea, Seir, Hormah, Elath, Ezion-geber, the brook Zered, Ar the border of Moab, and many others. Contrast his minute description of Mounts Gerizim and Ebal (xi. 30), places about which Israel at that time knew nothing, but which would not need careful identification at the date at which Naturalistic critics assume the words were first written. Contrast again the equally minute descriptions of places East of the Jordan in the passage quoted above, and in another portion of which Moses was obviously not the author (i. 1, 2).

The subsequent historical books were all composed in a more or less similar manner. Records were made of the more important events at the time they took place. These were written, sometimes by prophets or priests, sometimes by scribes officially appointed for the purpose. They were most probably written on parchment and the documents were carefully preserved until a time came when some one undertook the task of redacting them for publication. The redactor would copy out the documents, as nearly as he was able in their chronological order, and form of them a connected history such as we find in the books referred to. Some redactors would do little else than make a copy of the materials; others would allow themselves more freedom; they would make such changes in the text as they deemed desirable to make the narrative more understandable, and would insert additional information from other sources, and explanatory comments of their own. Thus the old and the new would become blended together, so as to make it difficult to distinguish one from the other. It is a great mistake however to infer that all was new—a mere modern work based partly on oral tradition and folk-lore, and partly on the imagination of the composer.

Daniel

The book of Daniel affords an excellent example of the simpler mode in which works of a historical character were sometimes composed.

The process of manufacture of Daniel is betrayed by the curious circumstance, noted in the margin of the Revised Version, that the language changes from Hebrew to Aramaic at ii. 4, and back again from Aramaic to Hebrew at viii. 1. (The Aramaic of Daniel however is shown by Pusey to be of an earlier and more eastern type than the Aramaic of Palestine in New Testament times. See Pusey's *Lectures on Daniel*.) These singular changes of language have been in their degree as great a puzzle to critics as the questions concerning the origin of the Gospels. So far as I am aware no explanation of the fact has yet been suggested that has even the semblance of probability. The following hypothesis seems to afford an adequate solution of the problem.

When Daniel was brought before Nebuchadnezzar, in the second year of his reign, to tell the King his dream of the great image and to interpret its meaning, the shorthand writers in attendance, in accordance with the custom of the time, made a verbatim report of his speech. Afterwards a narrative of the facts, including the speech so reported, was duly entered in the official records of the Empire, the historical part being dictated by Daniel himself.

THE WORK OF REDACTION 171

A narrative of the deliverance of Shadrach, Meshach and Abednego was also dictated by Daniel and similarly recorded.

The same was done with the circular letter of Nebuchadnezzar relating the story of his insanity—the letter itself being doubtless the composition of Daniel approved by the King.

The accounts of Belshazzar's feast, and of Daniel's deliverance from the den of lions were also inserted in the records.

Daniel's vision in chapter vii. was likewise recorded in the public chronicles. Unlike the dreams in the subsequent chapters it is said of this: " He told the sum of the matters." Doubtless the King was one of those to whom he told it, and the King, being deeply interested, ordered the report that had been taken to be deposited in the State archives.

' These reports were written in Aramaic, which so to speak, was the French of that time, the international language that every man of education understood in that vast conglomerate of peoples that composed the Babylonian Empire.

The other visions with which Daniel was favoured (chap. viii.-xii.) all related specially to the future of Israel and the Kingdom of God in distant ages. These were hardly matters that would interest a heathen king and court, and Daniel did not "tell" them. He wrote a record of them however, naturally in Hebrew, his own native tongue and the proper language of the nation whose destiny they foretold.

Now my theory is that when Daniel was advanced in life he set himself to write, for the instruction and encouragement of his countrymen when re-established in their own land (and therefore of course in Hebrew), a history of God's dealings with him in Babylon, and of the revelations concerning the future that had been vouchsafed. He did not however attempt to compose the whole narrative afresh. To do so by his own unaided memory would have been impossible. So he availed himself of the materials already in existence. First of all he wrote by way of introduction the account of the bringing up of himself and his companions. Then he began the story of his first appearance at court. But from this point

(ii. 3), the State records suited his purpose and, instead of translating what he required of them from Aramaic to Hebrew, being a busy man, he ordered a clerk simply to copy out the portions into his Book. This brought him to vii. 28, and he thereto affixed the document previously written by himself in Hebrew, consisting of viii. 1 to the end of the Book.

The Gospels

It has seemed to me desirable to deal thus fully with the manner in which the historical books of the Old Testament were composed, in order that readers, especially those who had not hitherto devoted much attention to the subject, might clearly realise the distinction in such books between the work of the original writers and of the redactors. For, making due allowance for differing circumstances, the four Gospels were, I believe, composed in a manner very similar to that in which the older books were composed that we have spoken of. Like the Old Testament redactors, Matthew, Mark, Luke and John made up their treatises of manuscripts written long before, and which they transferred, as nearly as possible in their original form, into their works.

Chapter III

DISARRANGEMENT OF MANUSCRIPTS

NOW it is obvious that a composer of history in the manner described in the last chapter would often have difficulty in discovering the proper chronological order in which his materials should be arranged. Even in modern times biographers are often puzzled as to the location of undated letters. In the case of the historical books of the Old Testament the contents of the manuscripts would usually give some indication of their date, and hence those books are in the main, though not invariably, arranged in chronological order. But many of the Gospel manuscripts would contain no clue to their date, and hence, unless they rested undisturbed from the time they were written until their redaction, it was hardly possible that no displacement should occur.

It is probable that the original writers of the Gospel narratives wrote on slips of papyrus, which, for convenience of handling, usually in the open air, were no larger than the sheets of paper used by modern reporters. Their number therefore would be great, and, if they were after Christ's Ascension frequently referred to, they would inevitably become mixed up to such a degree that it would not be easy to rearrange them.

An important fact should here be observed, a fact which is of itself sufficient to prove that a long time elapsed between the writing of the manuscripts and the redaction of the Synoptic Gospels; namely, that no two Gospels ever agree in an order differing from the probable chronological order of events, except in one place in which there is good reason to believe that the original documents were themselves written out of chronological order (Matt. xxvi. 6-16 ; Mark xiv. 3-11 ; Luke xxii. 3-6).

Mark

It is possible that Peter may have numbered the pages written by him; if not his excellent memory may have enabled him, supposing they had become disarranged, to restore them to their original order before handing them over to Mark.

John

John probably never allowed his manuscripts to pass out of his own possession, and hence had little difficulty in keeping them in their original order.

Matthew

The belief that Matthew redacted the manuscripts which he had himself written is not inconsistent with the fact that his Gospel is not always arranged in strict chronological order. If Papias can be trusted the primitive Church would appear to have had the general run of his papers, and in such case they would be sure to get mixed, and there is no cause for wonder if, after twenty or thirty years (and such years !), his recollection was so far dimmed that he failed in some instances to rearrange them in exact accordance with the relative date of every saying and event.

In arranging the manuscripts Matthew seems to have been influenced by the order in which he wrote, as well as by the order in which events happened. It will be seen when we come to examine the narratives in detail that the first thing he wrote was his report of the Sermon on the Mount. He therefore located this almost at the beginning of Christ's ministerial work. His own call took place a few days before the Sermon was preached; but he did not write the record of it until after; therefore he located it after. He also wrote a brief account of other incidents which took place prior to the delivery of the Sermon; but as he probably had not been himself an eye-witness of these earlier incidents, but gained his information from some of the Twelve who were in attendance upon Jesus before he was, it is not surprising that, not only are they mostly located after the Sermon, but that their order differs from that in which the incidents themselves happened. He seems in short to have remembered fairly well the sequence of events which came under his own personal observation; but not that of events which he knew of only from information supplied by his colleagues.

Luke

The confusion in Luke is much greater than in Matthew. It is continued right through the book and meets us in circumstances where we should least expect it. What for instance should seem more unlikely than that in the account of our Lord's three temptations two of them would be transposed? Or, that in the narrative of the Last Supper an incident should be inserted quite out of harmony with that solemn season, and which occurred a week before?

The mere fact that Luke was not himself an eye-witness of the facts he relates, or that the papers he edited were not his own composition, would not be sufficient to account for this disorder if, like Mark in the redaction of Peter's notes, the original writer were at hand to consult with and seek direction from. We are forced therefore to the conclusion that such was not the case; that, in the twenty-eight years that had probably elapsed since the manuscripts were written, their author had died or through removal to a distance become inaccessible, and that Luke found himself in the position of being required to translate and edit without assistance a confused mass of documents, undated, and written in a language, which it is true he well understood, but which he was not accustomed usually to employ.

But the question will now be asked, Who was the writer of the papers referred to—the papers of which the greater part of Luke's Gospel is composed? Before proceeding further it may be well to see if we can find an answer to this question.

Chapter IV

THE WRITER OF THE MANUSCRIPTS USED BY LUKE

THE writer of the records of which the Gospel of Luke (with the exception of the first two chapters and the genealogy in the third chapter) is composed was manifestly one who was in close attendance on Christ during the course of His ministry; therefore he must have been one of the Apostles. But which one? Not Peter, John or Matthew, for the notes written by them are embodied respectively in the other Gospels. There are thus left eight to choose from; namely, James the son of Zebedee, Andrew, Philip, Bartholomew, Thomas, James the Son of Alphæus, Thaddæus, and Simon the Cananæan.

One has but to glance at this list to see the name of James the son of Zebedee stand out in relief above all the others. He was one of the three who were honoured by Jesus with surnames, the other two being his brother John and Simon Peter. This was a distinction in itself; besides which the name given—Son of Thunder—implies that he was a man of exceptional ability and force of character. He was one of the three—the same three—whom Jesus specially favoured by taking them with Him to scenes to which the others were not invited, such as the raising of Jairus' daughter, the Transfiguration, and the Agony in the Garden. As John's brother, we may well suppose him to have been a man of considerable talent and fair education. The prominent part that he took in the affairs of the Church after the Ascension is indicated by his being the first that Herod singled out to slay, Peter being the second. For all which reasons it may be inferred that James was a man whose abilities entitled him to be placed on a par with Peter and John, and on a higher level than the remaining nine, and was therefore more competent than most for the duty of reporting our Lord's words and actions. It seems probable therefore, it being admitted that notes were taken by Matthew, Peter and John, that notes were also taken by James.

There is one circumstance that tends strongly to confirm this view. It has already been shown that Luke's narrative of the birth and childhood of Jesus must have been written by Mary the Mother of our Lord, and that this manuscript was in all probability handed to Luke either by Mary herself (who in that case was then residing with John), or by John if she was no longer living. Now it is almost certain that on James' decease his belongings would fall into the possession of his brother John, and amongst them the notes (if he made any) of the events of Christ's ministry. It is reasonable therefore to conclude that, when Luke obtained Mary's manuscripts, he also obtained from John the papers written by James. What indeed can be more feasible than that Luke, whose reputation was at that time thoroughly established, on his arrival in Jerusalem with the honoured Apostle of the Gentiles, should be entrusted by those possessing them with the duty of redacting the records written by the Mother of the Lord and by the faithful disciple who so early sealed his testimony with his blood?

Internal Indications

But are there any features in the Gospel itself that support the theory that James was the original author of the material of which the greater part of it is composed? In trying to find an answer to this question, it should be remembered, that the personality of the writers rarely appears in any of the Gospels; and that therefore it is not fair to expect very much in that direction. Nevertheless there are indications—slight it is true, and of themselves insufficient to form the basis of a theory—but which, taken in conjunction with what has been said already, make the case very strong.

In every place in Matthew and Mark where James and John are mentioned together, James' name comes first, showing that, either as the elder brother, or for some other reason, he was generally considered the more important of the two. The relative estimation in which they were held, during the earlier portion of the ministry, may be inferred from Peter's account, preserved in Mark, of the calling of the Apostles, and of the raising of Jairus' daughter, in both which places, not only does James' name come first, but John is described as the brother of James. Even towards the end of the ministry (Matt. xvii. 1) John is also described by Matthew as James' brother—although no other John is mentioned in the New Testament as taking an active part in the early Church—perhaps to distinguish James from others of that name, which, if he were the elder, it would hardly at that time be seemly to do by describing him as the brother of John.

In Luke however we find exceptions to the rule of priority so consistently observed in Matthew and Mark. In the story of the miraculous draught of fishes, where the two sons of Zebedee are first introduced to us by Luke, engaged at their occupation, James' name comes first. This is just what should be expected, even if James himself were the writer, presuming that he was the elder of the two, and that he wrote the story very shortly after the event. But later on, in the account of the healing of Jairus' daughter (Luke viii. 51, Revised Version), and of the Transfiguration (Luke ix. 28), John's name is placed before James'. If James was the writer this can be understood as the result of his now beginning modestly to recognise the fact of his brother's closer intimacy with their Master, and his growing influence among the Twelve. Otherwise these reversals of the order always observed in Matthew and Mark, as well as in the earlier part of Luke itself, are puzzling.

In another place, however, where the circumstance related

is not to the credit of the two brothers (Luke ix. 54), James name again takes first place :—

> "And it came to pass, when the days were well-nigh come that he should be received up, he steadfastly set his face to go to Jerusalem, and sent messengers before his face; and they went, and entered into a village of the Samaritans, to make ready for him. And they did not receive him, because his face was as though he were going to Jerusalem. And when his disciples James and John saw this, they said, Lord, wilt thou that we bid fire to come down from heaven, and consume them? But he turned, and rebuked them. And they went to another village."

This once more suggests that James is himself the narrator and that he accepts, as the older, the larger share of blame for the vindictive proposal they made on that occasion. The incident is not related in either Matthew or Mark, which may be accounted for, either by the absence of the rest of the disciples when it happened, or by their unwillingness to record a speech so uncharacteristic of those who made it.

The request of Salome and her two sons is related in Matthew (xx. 20) and Mark (x. 35) but not in Luke. This certainly presents a difficulty, that is, if the request was looked upon by the narrators as discreditable to the two brethren, for it was not the manner of any of the New Testament writers to suppress their own faults and emphasise those of others. But, although it caused indignation at the time, there is nothing to show that the desire of James and John to sit on the right and left of Jesus sprang from an unworthy motive, or from anything but their affection for their Master. There is no hint that our Lord was displeased with James and John. It was not the two but the other ten that He called to Him and addressed in terms of mild reproof. It must at least be admitted that their faith was great, and He who knew men's hearts may have been aware that their petition was not the result of any wish for undue pre-eminence.

Supposing then that the disciples when relating the incident began to see that they had been too hasty in their judgment of James and John, and that the circumstance was really more honourable to the two than to the ten, we may easily understand that Matthew and Peter would record it while James would modestly refrain from doing so.

If the manuscripts used by Luke in composing his Gospel were written by James, it is probable that Luke was also indebted to him for some of the materials he used in preparing the earlier chapters of the Acts. Accordingly we find in the enumeration of the Eleven assembled in the upper room in Jerusalem, immediately after the Ascension, John's name preceding that of James (Acts i. 13, Revised Version). The wording in Acts xii. 2 has no bearing on the argument either way. James is there described as the brother of John simply to distinguish him from others of the same name.

Although not carrying much weight in itself, it may also be mentioned as a slight confirmation of the argument, both for Peter's authorship of the materials used by Mark, and James' authorship of those used by Luke, that the raising of Jairus' daughter, at which only Peter, James and John were present is related in Mark and Luke and not in Matthew.

Luke's Introductory Statement

But it will be asked, If Luke composed his Gospel of manuscripts written by the Mother of Jesus and by a leading Apostle, why does he not say so in the statement which he makes at the beginning of the book? Such a statement would have added vastly to its authority and weight, and it might almost be said that its readers were entitled to be made acquainted with such an important fact.

There is no more reason, however, why this question should be asked with reference to the view we maintain than with reference to any other opinion. Such a question may just as pertinently be asked in respect to the theory that Luke listened to the oral tradition of the Apostles and himself reported their testimony, or to the theory that he collected and redacted a number of scattered writings in which that testimony had already been reported by others. The information given is very vague; but is certainly not inconsistent with the opinion here maintained. The only thing clearly intimated is that the sources from which the work is derived were perfectly trustworthy, being the testimony of those who " from the beginning were eye-witnesses and ministers of the word," and that the writer had himself "traced the course of all things accurately from the first." There is no denying that, from any point of view, it is remarkable that, being the only one to say anything at all on such a subject, Luke yet says so little.

On our hypothesis, however, the reason of this vagueness is not far to seek. It is almost certain that Luke accepted the task of composing the third Gospel at the time of, or soon after, his visit to Jerusalem in company with Paul in the year 58. Now, at that very time, the Jews were displaying a bitter hostility towards the Christians. They had risen in tumultuous riot against Paul, and nearly slain him, in the very precincts of the Temple. They were now following this up by persistent attempts to induce the Roman authorities, either to kill him themselves, or to give them an opportunity of doing so. There can be little doubt that all believers residing in Jerusalem felt themselves at that time to be in peril of their lives. It would therefore be far too serious a risk for Luke to call specific attention, in the book he was about to publish, to the family from whom he derived the substance of his narrative, the relatives of the martyred James, who were probably living in Jerusalem.

Especially if Mary was still living would it be most imprudent to mention names in this Introduction. It is not at all unlikely that she was still living. Supposing that she was 20 at the date of our Lord's birth, she would only be 81 at this time. That her name is not mentioned in the Acts, subsequently to the day of Pentecost, goes far to confirm the opinion that she was still alive; the absence of all later allusions to her being doubtless dictated by the same prudential motive as that which led Luke to word his Introduction so discreetly.

It needs some such explanation as this to account for the curiously mysterious terms in which the Introduction is composed:—

"Forasmuch as many have taken in hand to draw up a narrative concerning those matters which have been fulfilled among us, even as they delivered them unto us, which from the beginning were eye-witnesses and ministers of the word, it seemed good to me also, having traced the course of all things accurately from the first, to write unto thee in order, most excellent Theophilus; that thou mightest know the certainty concerning the things wherein thou wast instructed."

This seems to have been most carefully prepared so as to assure the reader of the absolute reliability of the writer's authorities and yet at the same time to conceal their nature. And why is the name of Theophilus brought in, unless it be to divert the attention of any enemy, into whose hand the book might fall, from the persons of real importance whom the author had in his mind? In fact the light of day shines on the whole of this puzzling passage, if it be understood that Luke was most desirous to impress Christian believers with the perfect accuracy of his narrative; yet dare not speak in plain terms for fear of directing attention to a household wherein resided one for whom was felt the deepest reverence and tenderest solicitude, and who, if her existence should become known to the enemies of Christ, might well become to them an object of cruel persecution.

Does not favour the Oral Tradition Theory

In any case it must be admitted that the Introduction does not lend any countenance to the Oral Tradition theory. It does not contain one word that suggests that Luke had been in the habit of attending catechumens' classes or other meetings and reporting the addresses of Apostles or other eye-witnesses of the facts about which he writes. And yet if he gained his information in so singular a way; if his mode of collecting materials was so unlike that of every other person who ever wrote history (excepting of course the other Evangelists); it is surely strange that he gives no intimation that such

WRITER OF THE MANUSCRIPTS USED BY LUKE 183

was the case. If however like other historians he used written documents in the composition of his work, his not saying so is not surprising, for he would naturally expect that to be taken for granted.

So far as his words throw any light on the subject at all they favour the idea that his materials were in writing. The use of the term ἀνατάξασθαι ("to set forth in order") is certainly much more appropriate to the arranging in order of paper manuscripts than to the reporting and writing out of spoken statements. The word παρέδοσαν ("they delivered"), again, is used in its more strictly accurate meaning if it was written documents that the eye-witnesses and ministers of the word delivered. The object of the verb is wanting in the Greek and is supplied in the English version by the pronoun "them." To discover what is implied by this pronoun we must be guided by the usage of the verb that governs it, and that leads to the choice of a real material article such as a collection of papers, rather than information conveyed in the shape of addresses or oral narrations. The instances in which the word is used in the latter sense are rare and hardly to the point; and, considering how accurate Luke usually is, and with what care this Introduction is composed, it seems right to take it in its literal and ordinary signification.

It is true that the two words just noticed relate, not to Luke's own work, but to that of the many who before him had taken in hand to draw up a narrative; but the conjunction κἀμοὶ in the third verse implies that his method was not different from theirs. Further the word παρηκολουθηκότι ("having traced the course") which Luke uses of himself indicates something very different from attending meetings and reporting speeches. Taken with the adverb ἀκριβῶς ("accurately") it is difficult to see how he can mean anything else by it but close personal investigation; and it seems to describe well the work of scrutinizing, translating and arranging a number of manuscript reports.

The passage apparently alludes to the fact asserted by

184 THE GOSPEL PROBLEMS AND THEIR SOLUTION

Papias : " Matthew composed the utterances in the Hebrew dialect, and everyone translated them as he was able " (Ματθαῖος μὲν οὖν Ἑβραΐδι διαλέκτῳ τὰ λόγια συνετάξατο ἡρμήνευσε δ' αὐτὰ ὡς ἐδυνάτο ἕκαστος). Luke in effect intimates that, many persons having undertaken to compose a redaction in Greek of the Aramaic manuscripts in circulation, it seemed good to him also, after a thorough investigation of the facts, to write out, from the similar materials he had acquired, a consecutive narrative for the use of his pupil or friend Theophilus. Theophilus, whose Greek name should be observed, must be understood to represent the numerous Greek-speaking converts who had been brought to Christ as the result of Paul's preaching, and who needed an authentic narrative in that language of the facts forming the foundation upon which their faith was built.

I take it then as a conclusion to which all must come who look the subject fairly in the face, that Luke used written documents in the composition of his Gospel. It is not essential to my argument to insist that James was the author of the greater part of them ; but the probability that such was the case is so strong that I feel justified in assuming it provisionally and until a better claimant for the honour appears. If however the reader prefers, where I use the name of James, to substitute that of Andrew or Philip or any other, it need not affect the main lines of reasoning as to the solution of the Gospel problems. The point, in this place, to be kept steadily in view is, that Luke was not himself an eye or ear-witness of the facts and sayings which he related, and that many years had passed away between the time when the original notes thereof were written, and the time when he redacted the notes, and arranged them in the form of a book. And, supposing the writer of the original notes to have died in the interim, the want of chronological order which is so frequently observable in the book is fully accounted for.

As a matter of convenience then, the name of James will still be used when speaking of the author of the notes in question.

Chapter V

LUKE'S DIFFICULT TASK

JUDGING by the length of many of the displaced portions, it seems that the sheets of papyrus on which James wrote his notes contained, as a rule, when filled up, as much as, translated into Greek, would amount to not less than forty or more than seventy words each, the most usual number being between fifty and sixty. In some cases however as when a single short incident was recorded, or at the conclusion of a narrative or discourse, the contents might be less even than the equivalent of forty Greek words.

These papers were probably left in order by James; but after his death they would be frequently referred to, and, it may be, copied. Hence they gradually became more and more disarranged, until at length, when they were handed to Luke, he found it necessary to sort and re-arrange them as well as to translate them from Aramaic to Greek. If in doing this he had had the Gospel of Matthew or of Mark before him his work would have been easy enough; but these works, if already published, had not come in his way. He doubtless obtained all the information and help he could from Apostles and other persons living and accessible; but after a lapse of twenty-eight years their recollection would avail him little, especially in regard to the sequence and connection of events and utterances. Accordingly (not to mention the supernatural aid of the Holy Spirit, but treating the subject from a purely literary standpoint) he was thrown almost entirely on his own resources.

We may almost imagine we see Luke sitting at a table on

which are spread out a great number of small slips of paper. He is trying to find the right place for each, and to fit them together in their proper sequence. Sometimes the order in which some of them still remain, or the continuation of a subject from one page to another, gives him a clue. Sometimes their connection with some well-known leading event is obvious and thus he is enabled to fix their place. But in many there is nothing whatever to guide him, and he can only locate these where in his own judgment seems most suitable. In such cases some displacements are inevitable.

As a whole, that is as regards the principal facts, the arrangement is chronologically correct. If in a considerable number of instances the details are not in order of time, or in the connection in which the facts recorded actually occurred, no student has thereby been misled on any vital matter. The question of divine inspiration is not affected, as the Gospel makes no claim to being composed in chronological order. The worst results that have followed have been the perplexity of critics and the despair of harmonists.

Part VI

THE WRITERS AND REDACTORS

BEFORE proceeding to examine the Gospels in detail, it is necessary to say something about the persons who took part in their composition, either as original reporters, or redactors, or both.

Mary and Joseph

Nothing whatever is known about Mary and her husband beyond what is recorded in the New Testament. The stories in the Apocryphal books and other traditions are all absolutely worthless.

The honourable position held by women is one of the most striking proofs of the civilization of the period. Their high social standing both among Jews and Gentiles is well known to all students of Scripture and of the Greek and Latin classics. There is no reason to doubt that in Palestine girls as well as boys went to school and were taught to read and write.

It may be assumed that she who was chosen to be the Mother of our Lord was above the average in intelligence and had received a fair education. That such was the case is confirmed by the Song of praise attributed to her. True it contains very little that is original; but the sentences selected show that she had a large acquaintance with Scripture, and the few phrases she composed herself, with the arrangement of the whole, evince a gifted and cultured intellect.

I have already given reasons for holding that the narratives in Matthew and Luke relating to the birth, infancy and early life of Christ were written by Mary and Joseph, and I propose to state the arguments more fully later on. Assuming this, the following is a recital of facts either directly asserted in the Gospels and Acts or which may be inferred from statements therein made.

Both Joseph and Mary were living in Galilee at the time of their espousal. Immediately after the Annunciation Mary went from Nazareth to the hill country of Judea to visit her relative Elisabeth. Mary belonged to a poetic race, being a lineal descendant of the "Sweet Singer of Israel." After her interview with Elisabeth she took pen and paper and expressed the overflowings of her heart in the "Magnificat."

After the birth of John the Baptist, his father Zacharias expressed his feelings also in a Hymn of praise which he likewise committed to writing.

After the return of the Holy Family to Nazareth, Mary, impressed with the importance of the facts connected with the miraculous birth of her Son, wrote a narrative thereof; and included her own Song and that of Zacharias, as also the Nunc Dimittis and the Blessing of Simeon. The utterance of Anna, the aged prophetess was not reported. Those were in the nature of literary compositions; this was not.

When Mary had written her narratives, Joseph wrote also a supplementary statement of the facts in which he was himself more directly concerned.

With each of these compositions they placed a copy of their respective genealogies.

Only one other incident in the early life of Christ seemed sufficiently important to be recorded, namely, the visit to the Temple when He was twelve years old. Mary, some little time after, wrote an account of this and put the manuscript with the papers relating to the Birth and Infancy.

From the fact that no mention is made of Joseph in the Gospels it is inferred that his death took place before our Lord's ministry began. The papers he had written with his other effects would thereupon, according to Jewish law, become the property of his eldest son, if of age, or as soon as he attained his majority, and he no doubt retained them until Matthew began the redaction of the papers comprised in the Gospel named after him.

Mary, of course, retained her own manuscripts.

Immediately after the Crucifixion Mary went to reside with John who appears to have had a home in Jerusalem. Nothing further is recorded of her, except that she was one of those who continued steadfastly in prayer in the upper chamber in Jerusalem from the day of our Lord's Ascension until Pentecost. There is no reason why she may not have lived to old age in that city along with the family of John.

The Apostles

According to the view we maintain, all the Apostles were participants in the work of composing the Gospel narratives. Accordingly it was to the whole Eleven that our Lord addressed the words: " Whose soever sins ye forgive, they are forgiven unto them; whose soever sins ye retain, they are retained"; the condition of forgiveness being faith in the records made by them of Christ's incarnation, life, death and resurrection, and of the truths which He taught (John xx. 23).

The chosen Apostles of Jesus are sometimes spoken of as "illiterate fishermen." It is true that several of them were fishermen; but it is an injustice to call them illiterate, if by that term it is meant that they had not received the equivalent of what would now be called a fair English education. Josephus (*Against Apion*, i. 12), says, "Our principal care of all is this, to educate our children well." The Apostles, or at least all of them about whom we have any information on the subject, could read and write, and we have seen that they had a knowledge of Greek, as well as of their native Aramaic. Too much stress should not be laid on the remark of the rulers and elders that Peter and John "were unlearned and ignorant men" (Acts iv. 13). The Priests and Pharisees were accustomed thus to speak of those who had not been instructed in the learning of the Rabbinical schools; that is, in what our Lord describes as "the tradition of the elders." Like certain superior people of our own age they were wont to extinguish with mild disdain any who, not having passed through their curriculum, ventured to trespass on their monopoly of theologic thought.

In truth the popular estimate of the men who were chosen to form the Apostolic band is far too low. Both intellectually and morally they were worthy—if it were possible for any men to be worthy—of the high office to which they were called.

Matthew

It is generally agreed that Matthew was identical with the Levi, son of Alphæus, mentioned Mark ii. 14 and Luke v. 27. Men bearing a name in common use, like Levi, usually had a surname given them to prevent confusion and mistake. He belonged to the unpopular class called in the Synoptic Gospels "publicans"; that is, he was a collector of taxes as subordinate agent for the representative of a capitalist or syndicate at Rome which had purchased from the Imperial Government the right to the revenues of the province of Galilee.

Plumptre, in *Smith's Dictionary of the Bible* (vol. ii., p. 968) thus describes the system by which the Government obtained its income:

"The Roman Senate had found it convenient at a period as early as, if not earlier than, the second Punic war, to farm the *vectigalia* (direct taxes) and the *portoria* (customs, including the *octroi* on goods carried into or out of cities) to capitalists who undertook to pay a given sum into the treasury (*in publicum*), and so received the name of *publicani* (Liv. xxxii. 7). Contracts of this kind fell naturally into the hands of the *equites*, as the richest class of the Romans. Not unfrequently they went beyond the means of any individual capitalist, and a joint-stock company (*societas*) was formed, with one of the partners, or an agent appointed by them, acting as managing director (*magister*; Cic. *ad Div.* xiii. 9). Under this officer, who resided commonly at Rome, transacting the business of the company, paying profits to the partners and the like, were the *sub-magistri*, living in the provinces. Under them, in like manner, were the *portitores*, the actual custom-house officers (douaniers), who examined each bale of goods exported or imported, assessed its value more or less arbitrarily, wrote out the ticket, and enforced payment. The latter were commonly natives of the province in which they were stationed, as being brought daily into contact with all classes of the population. The word τελῶναι which etymologically might have been used of the *publicani* properly so called (τέλη, ὠνέομαι), was used popularly, and in the N. T. exclusively, of the *portitores*."

Matthew's occupation then would be to sit at the entrance gate of Capernaum and exact payment of the duty on all goods passing into or out of the town. As he would be required to keep a strict account of all his takings he would need to have writing materials ready at hand. On market days and at other busy times he would have as much as he could do to keep pace with his work, and his accounts would consist of brief memoranda hastily jotted down; a fair copy of which he would afterwards make at his leisure and render to his superior officer. An occupation of this kind would both require and promote a habit of fast writing and accurate business-like ways.

As the greater part of the carriers passing to and fro would belong to the humbler classes, their language would usually be Aramaic, and it would doubtless be in that language that he would keep his original accounts. The returns which he would render to his superior would probably be in the same tongue, as the "chief among the publicans" to whom he was responsible was most likely, like himself, a Galilean, speaking the vernacular of the country. But a man in his position would certainly not be ignorant of Greek. Matthew was a diligent student of the Scriptures; but as his own quotations from the Old Testament approach the Hebrew more closely than the Septuagint it may be inferred that he was not, like our Lord, accustomed to read the Greek version.

Matthew a man of the city, accustomed to commercial life and to dealings with men, does not seem to have been so acute as some in observing minute details of fact. That is a quality that an employment such as his would not tend to develop. Nor does it appear that his memory was exceptionally good. But constant argument with men anxious to defraud the revenue which it was his duty to protect, would make him a keen judge of character, quick to note spoken words and even to read men's thoughts.

It was while engaged in the course of his daily business that a momentous change took place in the current of Matthew's life. One day, as he sat at the place of toll, Jesus passed by and said to him, "Follow Me." Already he had felt deeply interested in the Great Rabbi, and recognised the validity of His claims. When called therefore there was on his part no hesitation, no delay for the purpose of settling up his accounts. Leaving his table, his cash and his books to his assistants he at once arose and followed Christ. His pen, ink and paper; his talent for fast writing; his business-like methodical ways; were henceforth to be applied to a very different purpose than that for which they had been acquired.

It is plain from some of our Lord's expressions, and especially from one recorded only by Matthew himself (xviii. 17), that the business of a publican was not compatible with discipleship of Christ. Matthew, therefore, did not, like the fishermen, return once and again to his secular engagements after he had joined the number of our Lord's followers. That there might be no mistake about his determination to begin a new chapter in his life he at once gave a great farewell feast to his old associates. At that feast Jesus Himself was present.

It was not long before Matthew turned his talents to

account in the service of his new Master. He reported in full the Sermon on the Mount and many other of our Lord's addresses, and, with the help of his fellow-Apostles, he recorded many of the more noteworthy events of their daily experience and observation. Thus he wrote, in the Aramaic tongue, those precious notes, or *logia* as Papias calls them, which copied and handed from one to another, gained a wide circulation, and became the sustenance of the early church.

Matthew is mentioned in the New Testament for the last time as one of those who were present at the meetings held in Jerusalem just before Pentecost. There is nothing but internal evidence to guide us as to whether he himself translated and redacted his notes into the existing Greek form of his Gospel. It is most probable that he did so. The editor was very fond of quoting from the Old Testament, and the original writer appears also to have had a thorough knowledge of the Scriptures. The natural inference is that writer and editor were one and the same person.

Peter and Andrew; James and John

The four men named above were probably intimate companions from infancy. Their fathers were doubtless both fishermen, neighbours and perhaps partners. It may be that the youthful Jesus was among the number of their friends. The readiness with which they left their all to follow Him at His bidding implies a degree of confidence which could only have been the result of long acquaintance. To the same cause also, and not alone to His divine intuition, must be attributed that perception of their characters which led Him to describe the true-hearted, strong-willed, clear-headed, cultured young brothers James and John, by the name Boanerges—sons of thunder. Nazareth was not much more than twenty miles from Capernaum, and it is probable that Jesus often visited the latter town, and that sometimes, when the sons of Zebedee and Jonas went for a sail on the lake, the son of Mary made one of the party. That trait of our Lord's humanity, so conspicuous in the Gospel narratives—His fondness for the sea—was doubtless as keen in His youth as it was in His manhood.

When first these disciples appear in history, they are themselves engaged in the fishery business in partnership with Zebedee, making in all a firm of at least five persons. The Galilean lake abounded with fish and supplied the surrounding population with a large portion of its food. The firm was in prosperous circumstances. It had in its employ hired servants. It possessed a number of boats, some of which were large enough to carry a good sized party on a lake liable to severe tempests. It appears to have had a fair stock of nets and other necessary tackle. It must also have owned sheds for the boats and some sort of warehouse or store wherein to sell the fish, salt the surplus when the catch was heavy, and keep the fish so preserved for sale as required. It was therefore not without reason that the partners regarded their "all" as considerable when, at a later period, they reminded their Master that they had left all to follow Him.

To carry on a concern of that extent would involve, not merely the catching of fish and other labour requiring chiefly physical qualifications; but also a good deal of mercantile and clerical work. It would be needful to bear in mind the sorts of ware required by different classes of customers. Dealers who supplied poor neighbourhoods would take the commoner kinds of fish, whilst those who catered for the wealthy would purchase the choicer descriptions and pay a corresponding price. And accounts would have to be kept of the business done.

When after a night's toil on the sea the fishermen returned at early morning to the shore, they would find a motley crowd awaiting them—dealers from the neighbouring towns and villages, anxious to stock their barrows and baskets with the wares of the trade. The fish would be landed and taken to the warehouse where they would be sorted out on benches.

Then a busy time of cheapening and chaffering would ensue, with all the excitement and gesticulation that characterise buying and selling in Oriental markets. Time however would be precious both to sellers and buyers, and when the catch was a good one business would be brisk. As each sale was effected one of the firm would hastily note it down on paper, and when a dealer had completed his purchases, a reckoning would be made.

With some customers doubtless running accounts were kept and settlements made periodically.

All moneys received, whether for cash transactions or in settlement of accounts, would be taken charge of by one or two of the partners, who would disburse what was requisite for new nets and gear, wages and other expenses, and divide the remainder from time to time rateably amongst the proprietors. Thus Peter, James, John and Andrew became accustomed to accurate methods of business, and to making brief and hurried memoranda of their dealings.

The majority of dealers would be Hebrews using the Aramaic tongue, but there would also be a fair proportion from the Gentile city, Tiberias, whose language would be Greek. As the partners were all familiar with both Aramaic and Greek they would in bargaining with the dealers suit their speech to the convenience of the latter. But in noting down their sales and making out bills a division of labour would be necessary. Thus John acquired the habit of writing in Greek to enable him, whilst the other young men recorded the purchases and debts of Aramaic-speaking customers, to take account of sales made to traders from the Heathen town.

Dr. Farrar thinks it probable that John managed a branch of the business in Jerusalem, and Père Didon says, "there was a special market at Jerusalem where the boatmen from the lake went to sell their dried fish." If this were so it affords an additional reason why John should have acquired the habit of writing in Greek.

It must be admitted that the view here given of the four

disciples differs from that generally entertained. It is customary to think and speak of them simply as fishermen, it being usually overlooked that the fish caught had to be disposed of. But a little reflection should lead anyone to see that a partnership of five persons, with men in their employ, must really have constituted a large establishment, the commercial side of which was quite as important as the industrial. Mr. J. G. Griffin, who was engaged for some time in Turkey at his profession of Civil Engineer, informs me that he was well acquainted with what according to his description must have been a very similar fishery business on the Danube. There were several partners in the firm, they had a number of men in their service and they carried on an extensive trade, supplying the district around with fresh, salt and dried fish.

It will be seen that the occupation of Peter, James and John was just such as would cultivate the qualifications needed in the office they were soon to be called to fill. As regards the fish-catching part of their occupation this has often been noticed before. Thomson, in *The Land and the Book*, describes the different modes of fishing ;—with the hook and line, the hand-net, the drag-net, the bag-net and basket-net, and the spear—and points out the qualities—patience, perseverance, caution, skill, watchfulness, promptness—required and strengthened in their practice. "No one occupation of humble life," he says, "not even that of the shepherd, calls into exercise and developes so many of the elements necessary for the office of a religious teacher as this of fishing " (p. 403).

But their dealings with men were quite as useful a part of the Apostles' education as their dealings with fishes. One reason why men of great learning are often so deficient in the critical faculty, and therefore draw such wrong conclusions from ascertained facts, is that their close application to study has allowed them but few opportunities for mingling with their fellow men, and so acquiring the talent of clear discernment. There is nothing so effective as trade to make a man sharp and logical, quick to observe facts, to discriminate between truth and falsehood, and to arrive at correct results when the facts are known. Had Jesus been an impostor, the last men He would have succeeded in duping would have been those whose occupation every day was to baffle, like Matthew, the artful devices of those who tried to cheat the Romans of tribute, or to contend, like the Galilean fishermen, with shrewd Jew and pagan hawkers trying to get the best of a bargain.

Again, as to their book-keeping. There should be no question that they did keep books. A business of that magnitude could no more be carried on satisfactorily without books then than now. They need not to have been large or elaborate books. They may have consisted merely of scraps of paper—second-hand paper perhaps from which the former writing had been partially obliterated—and may have been used by themselves several times over. (When permanence was not desired a sort of ink was often used that could be easily washed off; thus heavy expense in the purchase of papyrus was avoided.) The discoveries to which we have referred in Part II abundantly prove that it was the custom in ancient times for small tradesmen and others to keep accounts, and it is most unlikely that the firm in which Zebedee seems to have been the senior partner neglected so necessary a duty. Thus it was that in noting down hurriedly the morning sales as they were made the younger men acquired the art of rapid writing.

Lastly, having to trade with men speaking two different languages led to their gaining a command of those languages for conversational purposes, and to their respectively acquiring the ability to write quickly therein, so that whilst Peter and James became fast writers in Aramaic, John became a fast writer in Greek.

Bear in mind that their rough toil on the sea would produce strong, healthy, vigorous frames, and that, as children of

pious parents, they had been trained up in the nurture and
admonition of the Lord, and it will be seen that, in Peter,
James and John, Jesus chose ideal persons for the duty of
witnessing and recording the essential facts and doctrines of
His manifestation to men.

It will be necessary to speak more particularly about Peter,
James and John in connection with the Gospels of which
they were respectively, either in whole or in part, the composers.

So far as can be learned, Andrew did not take an equally
prominent part in the composition of the Gospels. He merely
assisted, like the rest of the disciples, with his memory and
advice.

Peter

There is no need to repeat here the reasons which have
led the great majority of commentators to hold that Mark
derived the materials for his Gospel from Simon Peter. They
are well known to New Testament students, and I see no
reason to doubt their validity. The features of the narration
agree well with Peter's powerful but somewhat impulsive
character. I assume then that, in company with the other
disciples, he reported some of our Lord's utterances, and some
of the incidents of His ministry.

There are but few facts and sayings mentioned in Mark—
and those but briefly—which may not also be found in either
Matthew or Luke or both. The following are peculiar to
this Gospel: Our Lord's request that a little boat should
wait on Him (iii. 9); the intention of the friends of Jesus
to lay hold on Him in the belief that He was out of His
mind (iii. 21); the healing of a blind man at Bethsaida
(viii. 22-26); our Lord's injunction to His disciples to tell no
man about His transfiguration until after His resurrection
(ix. 9); and His entry into the temple and retirement to
Bethany on the evening of the first day of His last visit to
Jerusalem (xi. 11).

What is most striking in Mark is the perception of slight

details which seem to have escaped the notice of the other historians. For instance: Both Mark and Luke mention the people's astonishment at our Lord's authoritative manner in His teaching; but the former alone adds "not as the scribes" (i. 22). Mark is the only one who records the surname "Boanerges," given to the sons of Zebedee (iii. 17). In relating along with Matthew how the people of Gennesaret brought their sick friends to Jesus, Mark notices that they carried them on their beds (vi. 55.) In describing the case of the afflicted lad brought by his father to Jesus immediately after the Transfiguration, Mark's account is much fuller than that of either Matthew or Luke (ix. 14-29). Narrating the second cleansing of the Temple, Mark alone of the Synoptics observes that our Lord would not suffer that any man should carry a vessel through the Temple. (xi. 16). Matthew and Mark relate how a lawyer or scribe enquired of Jesus which was the greatest commandment; but the second Evangelist only records the scribe's answer to our Lord's reply and our Lord's approving rejoinder (xii. 32-34). It is Mark alone who gives the original Aramaic and Hebrew words used by Jesus when working two of His miracles : "Talitha cumi" (v. 41); and "Ephphatha" (vii. 34).

These features of Mark's Gospel are quite consistent with the view that it is composed of the notes of Christ's sayings made at the time by Peter, and of the united testimony of the Apostles to His doings recorded by him immediately after their occurrence. But they can hardly be reconciled with any one of the existing theories.

It was not because of an imperfect acquaintance with Greek that Peter handed over to Mark the task of translating and editing his notes. That he had a good command of that language is proved by his conversation with Cornelius, and by the foremost position he held in the Jerusalem Church. By the time the Gospel was redacted he would have almost discontinued the use of Aramaic. The Galileans, who at first formed so large a proportion of the Church, had long since been scattered abroad by persecution, and Peter himself had travelled and laboured in lands where Greek was the prevailing tongue. But although he spoke Greek with ease it is doubtful whether he ever did much writing in that language. There is no need to attach much weight to the old tradition that Peter employed an interpreter to write his Epistles. Apart from the improbability that when he indited them he was in the habit of speaking only in Aramaic, the style of their composition is adverse to the opinion that they are translations from another tongue. But it is not unlikely that, like Paul, he dictated his letters to an amanuensis, and this may be the basis of truth upon which the tradition was built. It is probable that Mark was the scribe in both cases, as it appears that he was with Peter at Babylon when the first Epistle was written, and there is no hint that he would accompany Silas, who was to carry the letter with him on his journey west (1 Peter v. 12, 13).

Fluent in speech, full of energy and vigour, burdened with numerous duties and responsibilities, Peter would have little time or inclination for the drudgery of literary work, and he would gladly place his papers in the hands of a competent man like Mark to translate into Greek and arrange for publication.

Mark

The proper name of this Evangelist was the Jewish name John; but the surname Marcus was given him, perhaps to distinguish him from John the son of Zebedee. He was a cousin of Barnabas, who was a Levite, but belonged to a Cyprus family, of which island he was probably himself a native. A number of words of Latin origin are found in his Gospel, these, taken along with his Latin surname, suggest that he had associated with people who spoke that language. It is not quite certain whether he was in Judea or Galilee during the time of our Lord's ministry or had any personal knowledge of the facts he relates. It is usually supposed, however, and with reason, that he was himself the young man mentioned Mark xiv. 51, 52. It is thought that he was then living with his mother at Jerusalem, as was certainly the case at the time of Peter's miraculous deliverance from prison (A.D. 44). From Peter's speaking of him as his son (1 Peter v. 13) it may be inferred that Mark was much younger than the Apostle.

Mark accompanied Paul and Barnabas on their first missionary journey as far as Perga in Pamphylia, whence, to the great annoyance of Paul, he returned to Jerusalem. About three years later he went with Barnabas on a second journey; about which the only information afforded is that they proceeded to Cyprus.

He was at Rome with Paul during the latter's first imprisonment (A.D. 61-63) and some time after appears to have been with Peter at Babylon (1 Peter v. 13). The latest mention of him in the New Testament is in Paul's second Epistle to Timothy (iv. 11) who was then at Ephesus, in which epistle the Apostle requests Timothy to bring Mark with him to Rome, giving as his reason that he was useful to him for ministering.

It is generally understood that Papias, in the extracts from his writings quoted elsewhere, intends to say that Mark recorded in his Gospel the substance of Peter's oral teaching. This is more definitely asserted by Justin Martyr, Irenæus, Origen, Clement, Tertullian and later writers. Papias' words however will quite as well bear the construction that Mark obtained his materials from Peter in the shape of written documents, and in all probability that is what he really meant. It does not much matter however, for when he wrote, thirty or forty years had elapsed since the Gospel was composed, and, although his statement is deserving of attention as to the general fact that Mark acquired his materials from the Apostle, he might easily have been mistaken as to the shape of the materials which he received. As to the statements of later writers on such a subject, they are not worth consideration.

If the tradition that Mark wrote at Rome be correct, or if he wrote at Babylon, which is far more likely, it cannot possibly be true that the Book is composed of the substance of Peter's oral teaching. For Peter's preaching either at Rome or Babylon, would certainly have been in Greek, and the Gospel of Mark is manifestly a translation from Aramaic.

It happens too that we have some specimens of Peter's oral teaching or preaching preserved in the Acts of the Apostles, and these do not bear the least resemblance to any part of Mark's Gospel.

The chronological order of Mark, if not quite exact, is far more so than either Matthew or Luke, and conveys the impression that the original writer, who was a man with an excellent memory, was readily accessible to the redactor, at the time he was engaged at his task.

Putting everything together the probability is that the redaction of the Gospel of Mark was in this wise: In the troublous times times preceding the siege of Jerusalem, Peter removed to Babylon. About the same time, Paul having been released from prison and started on his journey west, Mark left Rome and came to Jerusalem, whence he either accompanied or followed Peter to Babylon. The comparative leisure which they enjoyed in that city, afforded at last an opportunity for the preparation of Peter's notes for publication. This duty he deputed to Mark, and the latter translated and redacted the notes accordingly, availing himself of Peter's personal assistance, when necessary, in their arrangement.

James

I have elsewhere stated my reasons for believing that James was the writer of the greater part of the notes embodied in the Gospel of Luke. It is not strange that he did not himself undertake the task of translating and editing his manuscripts. Amongst all the followers of Jesus he is the only one about whom we have certain information as to the time and manner of his death. In the year 44 he was beheaded by Herod Agrippa I. During the interval of fourteen years between our Lord's resurrection and James' death, he was like Peter and

John charged with heavy cares and responsibilities in connection with the Church, and, more accustomed to writing in Aramaic than in Greek, he allowed his notes to remain in their original state. On his death, his parents having in all probability died at some former period, his effects naturally reverted to his brother John, and among them the manuscripts in question.

Although it is an opinion not largely entertained, I think it well worth considering whether this Apostle may not really have been the author of the Epistle of James. There can be little doubt that the Epistle was written at a very early date, and its contents bear many remarkable resemblances to the teachings of Christ recorded in the Gospel of Luke.

Luke

The belief that Luke was the composer of the third Gospel dates at any rate from the second century; nor, until recent years, has there ever been any doubt that such was the case.

Very little is known about Luke. It is not at all probable that he was, as supposed by many, a Gentile. Colossians iv. 11, 14 proves nothing in this respect, as it nowhere appears that Luke was a fellow-worker with Paul in the sense in which the latter here uses the word. He appears to have acted rather as medical attendant on Paul himself. It can hardly be doubted that the bulk of the Gospel is a translation from Aramaic, and no Gentile would have been likely to have acquired a sufficient knowledge of that language, as spoken in Palestine, to qualify him to translate into Greek manuscripts therein written. It is more likely that he was a Hellenistic Jew, though born it may be in a foreign land.

Paul several times mentions Luke in his Epistles, and from one of them we learn that he belonged to the medical profession. From this it is inferred that he was a man of superior education, an opinion that is confirmed by his literary style.

It appears that Luke accompanied Paul on some portions of his missionary tours. By the use of the first person plural in Acts xxi., and still more by the autoptic style of the narrative, we learn that he came to Jerusalem with Paul on the return of the latter from his last reported journey. Soon after their arrival Paul was arrested, and, a day or two later, was sent by the chief captain, Claudius Lysias, to Cæsarea. Judging by the full report that is given in Acts xxiv. of Paul's hearing before the Governor, Felix, there is little doubt that Luke followed him there. But all the proceedings which took place in the course of the next two years, during which Paul was kept at Cæsarea in bonds, are summed up in a single verse (Acts xxiv. 26), from which it would seem that Luke did not remain there with him throughout that time. It may therefore be reasonably inferred that Luke was during that period at Jerusalem, the more so as the full account given in Acts xxv. of what took place between Festus and the principal Jews, on the first visit of the new Governor to the capital of Judea, indicates Luke's presence there at that time.

Taking these facts into consideration, we conclude that it was in the course of that two years, say from A.D. 58 to 60, that Luke was engaged at Jerusalem in the redaction of the Gospel.

In quest of materials for the narrative he designed to write, it is assumed in this book that Luke had recourse to the Apostle John, who gave him all the assistance in his power. He did not, indeed, part with his own manuscripts in Greek, which he intended at a fitting season to edit and publish himself; but he handed to Luke the documents, left in his keeping, written by his deceased brother James. Luke also obtained from Mary, the Mother of Jesus, other documents of surpassing value, being the genealogy of Joseph as the son-in-law of Mary's father; and her own narrative of the circumstances surrounding the birth of our Lord, and of His visit to the Temple when twelve years old.

It has been observed that Luke gives fewer names of places than either of the other Evangelists. Considering how particular he is in the Acts in this respect, this would be surprising if he had the same opportunities as the others to supply such details. But he could not give more information than was contained in the papers at his disposal. Though he might ask the aid of others in arranging the order of the papers, he could not, on any man's authority, insert or alter a single word in the papers themselves. He knew too well how little men's memories are to be trusted, and had too solemn a sense of the responsibility which rested on him, as the editor of an Apostle's records of the Redeemer's life, to allow himself to take any liberties with the text. Even in translating, he studied accuracy before elegance, and allowed his style, usually so pure and classical, to betray the Aramaic of the original. The only additions he made were such as were necessary to form the various fragments into a connected story. He did not, like Matthew, insert appropriate quotations from the Old Testament; nor did he, like Mark, explain Jewish customs for the benefit of Gentile readers (Mark vii. 3, 4; xv. 6). Thus the Gospel of Luke contains scarcely anything but a faithful translation of original documents written at the time or immediately after the events they narrate.

John

It does not come within the scope of this work to discuss the question whether John was the author of the fourth Gospel. The burden of disproof rests with those who deny it, and these have never been able to produce an atom of evidence in support of their denial.

The only argument, other than the dogmatic objections springing from unwillingness to admit the truth of any fact which goes to prove the supernatural character of our Lord's life on earth, is that based upon the literary contrast between the Gospel of John and the Synoptics; and for this peculiarity we have found in our first Special Key a satisfactory explanation. But, even if that difficulty were still unaccounted for, it would require a marvellous amount of credulity to believe, either that such a work as the fourth Gospel could have been composed by anyone except an actual eye- and ear-witness of our Lord's ministry, or that such a work, if a forgery, could have found general acceptance among Christians in the second century as the genuine production of the beloved disciple.

John's education appears to have been stronger on the Hellenistic side than was that usually given to the boys of Galilee. It was doubtless felt by his parents to be desirable that one of their sons should receive such instruction as would make him fully competent, when he entered his father's business, to trade on equal terms with the Greek-speaking dealers who supplied the surrounding Gentile population with fish. So, whilst most of his companions learnt to write in the old Phœnician characters running from right to left, John's hand was trained to trace the letters of the Greek alphabet from left to right. Moreover, he was thoroughly instructed in the Hellenistic grammar and art of composition, so as to enable him to express himself in that tongue with lucidity and grace.

The effect of this teaching is reflected in his literary work. The Gospel and the First Epistle, which are the earliest of his writings, are couched in terms of purity, simplicity and elegance which have not been surpassed. But, with his advance in years, the diction of his native Aramaic becomes progressively intrusive, the Third Epistle being less pure than the Second, whilst, in the Apocalypse, which was written last of all, towards the end of his life, the Semitic idioms and Hebraistic style, to which he was accustomed in his childhood, continually recur. This agrees exactly with the experience of all persons who have been taught to speak or write in a language different from the one that was current among those with whom they passed the first twenty years of their life. They may for a long time be able to speak or write in the language they have learned even with greater purity than a native; but as age advances the earlier influence will assert itself, and, either in pronunciation or manner of expression, prove that though mastered it has never been effaced.

As was intended, John's Hellenistic education opened the way for easier business relations than he could otherwise have hoped for, both with foreigners and with Jews in the higher ranks of life. He alone of all the Evangelists mentions the town of Tiberias, and he alone calls the Sea of Galilee by its Gentile name, derived from that of the city re-built by Herod on its shore. Whether or not there be any truth in the surmise that he sometimes resided in Jerusalem, it is certain that he in some way made the acquaintance of the highest Jewish official in the Capital (John xvii. 15, 16). The High Priest at that time was a Sadducee and therefore a Hellenist, and whether the acquaintance was an accident of trade or otherwise, we may be sure that it was facilitated by John's familiarity with Greek.

It is sometimes said that there is great similarity in John's own style, both in the Gospel and in his First Epistle, with that of the discourses of Christ recorded in the Gospel, and also in a lesser degree with that of the sayings of John the Baptist. This is to some extent true, although the resemblance is not so great as Naturalistic writers would have us believe. But some degree of likeness was to be expected. Intimate friends insensibly copy one another's mode of expression, and especially do pupils follow the style of a master, just as clerks in an office often unconsciously imitate the handwriting of their chief. John was a disciple, first of John the Baptist and afterwards of Jesus, and he would have been but a poor scholar if in his work no trace were visible of instruction received from both those mighty teachers.

It is most likely that it was in the days of their boyhood that the attachment began between Jesus and the amiable but fiery John, and it is not surprising that the influence of the Greater on the less, which continued with growing strength until the Master was taken away, should show itself in the literary style of the disciple.

Like Matthew, John was both reporter and redactor; but unlike him he was not a translator. He reported in Greek the discourses spoken by Christ in that language; or rather the few of them that have been preserved: for, in accordance with the statement in the last chapter of John itself; it cannot be doubted that the recorded utterances of our Lord, in both the languages He used, form but a small proportion of the addresses He delivered.

The conditions at Jerusalem, after our Lord's departure, were not favourable to the publication of the Gospel; but it need not be assumed that the preparation of the work was wholly neglected until the late date at which it appears to have been given to the world. It is likely that John revised his manuscripts as soon as his onerous duties in the Church would permit; though probably he finally redacted them, when, in the comparative quiet of his Ephesian episcopacy, he found opportunity, in the industrial resources of that great commercial centre, to put the book in circulation. Even the Prologue (i. 1–18) was probably written long before the time of the Book's publication; that is, if the publication was really delayed as long as is commonly supposed. And, if its publication was so delayed, there is no reason for thinking that the Book itself lay hidden away from the light, or that copies were not made for private use.

It should be observed that Papias is silent with reference to John's Gospel; and the puerile tales about John told by Irenæus, Clement and others prove the utter worthlessness of the traditions. We have therefore nothing to guide us in forming our opinions on this subject but internal evidence and external probability.

Part VII

DETAILED APPLICATION OF THE FOREGOING PRINCIPLES TO THE NARRATIVES

HAVING described the manner in which, as I am convinced, the four Gospels came into being, and stated in general terms the reasons for the conclusions I have reached on this subject, the important question has now to be faced, Will these conclusions bear detailed application to the narratives themselves? It is one thing to propound a theory and to support it by argument: it is quite another thing to show that the theory coincides with facts. Many theories have already been put forth on the subject before us; the misfortune is that every one of them breaks down when it is attempted to fit it in to the literary works whose origin it claims to account for. Are the principles laid down in this book better able to bear the test?

To settle this question it is necessary to go right through the course of the Gospel history and to examine briefly, but honestly, each portion in its relation to the views herein maintained. The reader who takes the trouble to do this, with the Revised Version of the New Testament before him, will find it to be a work of absorbing interest, and will meet with new surprises almost on every page.

In the remaining part of this work I endeavour to give some assistance in the pursuit of this quest. I am however but a pioneer in this particular portion of the field, and hope that far richer results may be achieved when others turn their steps in the same direction.

I follow generally but not invariably the order of events observed in that most valuable work, *The Life of our Lord upon Earth* by S. J. Andrews.

PROVISO

It is necessary however to premise that, although in our view the manuscripts of which the Gospels are composed were for the most part written at the time or immediately after the events related, this is not strictly speaking the case with the earlier portions of the narratives of Christ's ministry. They were written during Christ's lifetime ; but not until after the lapse of a period varying from two years to a few weeks after the events recorded. The disciples did not any of them begin to make written notes until some time after the beginning of the Ministry, and it was not until after the choosing of the Twelve that the Apostles as a whole set themselves to the work of keeping records. And the records they first wrote were those of events happening at the time. Soon, however—perhaps after a month or two— they felt the necessity of writing some account of the ministry of John the Baptist, and of the earlier events of the public life of Jesus; and they taxed their memories to that end. Following the most approved chronology, the preaching of John began about July A.D. 26, the Apostles were chosen about June A.D. 28, and the recollections of what took place between those dates were written in July or August of the latter year. The recollections written at that time are comprised in the following portions: Matthew iii. 1–iv. 22, viii. 14–17 ; Mark i. 2–39 ; Luke iii. 2–22 ; iv. 1–15, 31–44; John i. 19–51, ii. 1–25.

IN THE BEGINNING

John i. 1–18

The Prologue to John's Gospel is remarkable for the manner in which the doctrinal gradually merges into the historical. It is difficult if not impossible to mark the exact place in these verses where the introduction ends and the narrative begins. Nevertheless, though the transition is so gradual there should be no doubt that the verses indicated above were written at a much later date than the rest of the book. This appears from the general style of their composition; from the manner in which John the Baptist is introduced to the reader in the sixth verse; and from the use of the messianic title as a proper name: "Grace and truth came by Jesus Christ." The use of this name here brings into clearer relief its non-use elsewhere; a sure proof that, like the other Gospels, its main portions were written long before any other New Testament book.

As showing how little use John made of his memory when writing history, notice that the only utterance of the Baptist quoted in the Prologue (verse 15) is copied from one of his old manuscripts (i. 30).

LUKE'S DEDICATION

Luke i. 1-4

Like John, Luke begins with a Prologue; but its style is very unlike that of John. It is written in classical Greek, and was evidently composed with the utmost care.

MATTHEW'S INTRODUCTIONS

Matthew i. 1 ; i. 18^a

The first verse in Matthew is not an introduction to the Book; but only to the Genealogy, which ends at verse 17, and doubtless formed a separate roll of itself.

The history therefore required its own introduction, which Matthew also wrote in his editorial capacity, and which is found in the first clause of verse 18.

MARK'S INTRODUCTION

Mark i. 1

Mark's introduction is the briefest of all, and it bears no resemblance to any of the others.

212 THE GOSPEL PROBLEMS AND THEIR SOLUTION

BIRTH OF JOHN THE BAPTIST;
THE GENEALOGIES; BIRTH, INFANCY AND CHILDHOOD OF
JESUS

Matthew i. 2-25; ii. 1-23; *Luke* i. 5-80; ii. 1-52;
iii. 23-38

In Part II. Chapter VII., I pointed out that neither Mark nor John supplies any information whatever with reference to the birth, infancy or early life of our Lord, and that the accounts in Matthew and Luke relate, in addition to the circumstances attending His birth and infancy, nothing except the visit to Jerusalem when He was twelve years old, and that He returned to Nazareth and resided there with His parents in subjection to them. I also presented the narratives in Luke and Matthew to the eye of the reader, so as to show at a glance that the two, while quite distinct, yet mutually supplement one another in a most remarkable manner, there being neither repetition of the same facts, nor yet one word of contradiction.

It should be obvious that these are peculiarities which cannot be made to harmonise with any existing theory as to the origin of the Gospels. It cannot be doubted that at the time when Mark and John composed their Gospels, the doctrine of the Incarnation of the Son of God was generally believed in the Church. Why do both refrain from mentioning so important an event? They must have desired to instruct their readers on this subject. Why do they totally ignore it?

Turning to the narratives of Matthew and Luke, we find a difficulty equally great. Here are two accounts, each of considerable length, and yet, excepting two or three essential particulars which could not be omitted, no fact is related in both. And yet there is no contradiction. Each narrative leaves room for the incidents told in the other, and the two can be fitted together so as to form a consecutive and intelligible story. Is it credible that the two Evangelists, each collecting the floating material, oral or written, of the time, could have composed two separate narratives such as we find before us, which in their details never clash, yet hardly ever coincide?

Let the reader reflect, and ask himself whether he can conceive of any way in which the peculiarities referred to could have come into existence, except that the Evangelists rigidly confined themselves to the use of trustworthy written materials in the composition of their works and that, as concerned the birth and early life of Christ, none such were available other than those that fell into the hands of Matthew and Luke respectively, which materials were written unitedly and virtually formed one narrative.

If this be conceded, there can hardly be any alternative but that the account in Luke was written by Mary, or by Joseph at her dictation, and that the account in Matthew is a supplementary statement written by Joseph, and that both were written not very long after the facts that they relate. In that case their history was probably as follows:—

The narrative beginning Luke i. 5 and ending ii. 39 was a single manuscript written by Mary, not long after her first return to Nazareth after Christ's birth. It contains no allusion to the Egyptian visit (which could have occupied but a short time), doubtless because Joseph was about to write a separate narrative which would include that incident.

The portion, Luke ii. 40–52, which includes the account of the twelve-year-old visit to the Temple, was also written by Mary soon after that event.

These two documents, together with the genealogy, Luke iii. 23–38, were retained by Mary and were eventually delivered into the hands of Luke.

The manuscripts written by Joseph, represented by Matthew i. and ii.; being a copy off his own proper genealogy, and his supplementary narrative of events connected with the birth of Jesus, were retained by him until his death, when they fell into the possession of his son, by whom they were ultimately handed to Matthew.

Both sets of papers were probably written in Aramaic, for Joseph and Mary resided in a small Galilean town where that language would be almost exclusively in use. But this is immaterial to our argument.

Mary's papers were literally copied or translated into Greek by Luke, who added very little derived from any other source. Verse 2 of Chapter ii. may perhaps be a parenthetical explanation inserted by Luke; and verses 39 and 40 of the same chapter may also be Luke's statement of facts which he had learned from Mary. But all through the Gospel Luke displays so much chariness of introducing any words of his own, that it seems more likely that at least the latter passage was in the original document. Doubtless, however, he obtained from Mary the particular as to Christ's age with which he introduces the Genealogy.

Matthew, perhaps, made freer use of the manuscripts written by Joseph, than Luke did with those of Mary. Most of the quotations from the Old Testament, together with the final words of i. 16 and the whole of i. 17, are probably editorial additions inserted by him. With these allowances the text of Matthew i. 2–ii. 23 is an accurate translation of the documents received by him from Joseph's eldest son.

We are now in a position to formulate the reasons for believing the foregoing to be a true statement of the origin of the portions specified at the head of this section. Amongst these are included some indications to which the reader's attention has not yet been called.

1. Its antecedent probability. It being, as we have seen in Part II. Chapters I., II., and III., the practice of the time to commit to writing matters of interest and importance, it is probable that intelligent persons like Mary and Joseph would feel the necessity of making a written record of facts of such supreme moment as those connected with the supernatural birth of Mary's Son, who, it had been revealed to them, was the Messiah.

2. The nature of the narratives themselves. The narratives

contain no hint of being reports at second-hand. They are positive statements of circumstances apparently within the direct personal knowledge of the authors. But these could have been known directly only to Mary and Joseph.

3. The mutually complementary character of the two narratives, and the absence from them either of contradiction or repetition of the same facts. This is inexplicable on the supposition : (*a*) That they are legend or fiction ; (*b*) That they are based on oral tradition ; (*c*) That they were derived from documents in circulation at the time the Gospels were composed, which documents were written subsequently to the time of Christ's ministry; (*d*) That one or both of the accounts was obtained by word of mouth from the Mother of our Lord or from Joseph; (*e*) Or, on any conceivable theory except that herein maintained.

4. The literary style of the narrative in Luke which differs from any other portion of the New Testament. It is highly poetic and may well have been written by the Authoress of the Magnificat. The narrative in Matthew is also poetic, indicating that Mary assisted in its composition likewise.

5. The poetical compositions included in Luke's narrative, and which, if genuine, must have been written at the time. The presumption is that they are genuine, and it is incumbent on those who question their being so to account for their origin in some more feasible way than that stated in Luke, to do which is impossible.

6. The use of the word "father" in Luke ii. 33. It was natural for Mary, writing during her Son's infancy, to apply this term to her husband ; but it is very unlikely that the author of a narrative which includes the explicit statement of i. 26–38, writing after the end of Christ's ministry and the establishment of the Church, would refer to Joseph thus.

7. The peculiar terms in which the birth of Jesus is mentioned in Matthew. It is not historically asserted at all ; it is referred to only in i. 25, and in ii. 1 as a fact already known, as if the author had in his mind, when writing this,

some other narrative, which, he took it for granted, the reader would be acquainted with. Taken together with the other considerations to which attention is here called, the importance of this can hardly be over-estimated.

8. The view here maintained harmonizes with the fact that the genealogies in Matthew and Luke are, on quite independent grounds, held by the majority of believing commentators to be the genealogies of Joseph and Mary respectively.

9. It likewise harmonizes with the common opinion, also based on independent grounds, that Joseph had died before the period of our Lord's public ministry.

10. It harmonizes further with the theory advanced in this book, that the materials used by Luke in the composition of the remaining part of his Gospel, were notes written by James' the son of Zebedee; inasmuch as such notes would, on James, martyrdom, naturally fall into the hands of his brother John, with whom Mary, in all probability, resided until her death; thus both sets of manuscripts would be handed to Luke at the same time.

11. The omission of Mark and John to give any account of the birth, infancy or early life of Christ. These Evangelists were probably aware that documents relating thereto were in existence; but, whether or no, they refrained from making in their Gospels any statement for which they had not undoubted written authority.

JOHN THE BAPTIST'S MINISTRY AND THE BAPTISM OF CHRIST

Matthew iii.; *Mark* i. 2–11; *Luke* iii. 1–22; *John* i. 19–36

As stated a few pages back these portions were not written contemporaneously with or immediately after the events narrated. Some of the Twelve were attendants, whether occasional or regular attendants is unknown, on John's preaching, and may have helped him to baptise. But there is nothing to show that such was the case with others. Matthew, for instance, and James do not appear at all in this connection. Our

Lord had not at that time chosen his little band of witnesses, and none of them could foresee how important an office they were soon to be called to fill. It is not likely therefore, that, prior to the beginning of Christ's ministry, any notes were taken of John's preaching.

At what subsequent period then were these accounts written?

Now, strange as it may seem, a careful examination will enable us to give a nearly exact answer to this question. These accounts of John's work were written just after the visit of the two messengers whom John, when in prison, sent to our Lord to enquire, "Art thou he that should come, or look we for another?" (Matt. xi. 2-19; Luke vii. 19-35), which is generally understood to have taken place about eighteen months after the baptism of Jesus.

Matthew and James, as we shall see later on, each noted this visit at the hour it occurred, and reported verbatim, as He spake, the chief part of our Lord's utterances with reference thereto. It should seem that soon after, the Twelve being assembled, they discussed as usual the circumstances of this the principal event which had recently happened, and from that they naturally went on to talk of John's mission in the wilderness, at which some of them had been present from eighteen months to two years previously. While thus engaged, it occurred to one of the party that it was desirable that there should be prefixed to each of the narratives that four of their number were writing a brief description of John and his work, and a statement of the testimony which he bore to the messiahship of Jesus. Thereupon, while one and another related what they remembered of the Baptist's manner of life, his baptising, and his message to the multitudes, Matthew, Peter and James wrote each his own report of what was thus narrated.

The conversation doubtless in this gathering was as usual carried on in Aramaic, and John, who wrote in Greek, probably did not begin writing his account until the party had broken up. His account describes a somewhat later portion of John's ministry than that described in the Synoptics. The accounts in the first three Gospels refer to the Baptist's work prior to the temptation of Jesus. The account in the fourth Gospel records the testimony delivered by the Baptist after our Lord's return from the wilderness. It is probable that several of the disciples were in attendance on John's preaching at the earlier period, and so, at the conference at which the accounts were written, the things then said and done were freely rehearsed. But it should seem from John i. 35, 40 that, at the later season, Andrew and John were the only disciples present. John always, if possible, avoided repeating what the others had written, and there seems, on this occasion, to have been a sort of understanding that the Aramaic-writing Apostles should record the earlier testimony which had been heard by several of the company, while the Greek-writing Apostle should record the later testimony which he had heard himself.

Bearing these facts in mind, let us see how we are enabled to fix so definitely the moment when the accounts were written.

In the first place it is evident that they were all written about the same time. For although there is more than sufficient dissimilarity in the accounts to prove that no one of them was borrowed from either of the others, and that no two of them were based upon any one earlier account, there are also many resemblances which indicate that all were affected by some common influence. This common influence, it will be seen, was the conversation of the twelve Apostles at the conference we have just described.

In this conversation all the writers were reminded of confessions, more than once made by the Baptist, of his unworthiness even to carry the shoes or unloose the sandal-strings of that Greater One who was to come. Accordingly when we compare the narratives we find that the four writers all recorded these confessions in similar though not quite identical terms (Matthew iii. 11; Mark i. 7; Luke iii. 16; John i. 27).

As only Matthew, Peter and James recorded the circumstances of the earlier part of the Baptist's ministry, they alone noted his announcement that One mightier than he was about to come (Matt. iii. 11; Mark i. 7; Luke iii. 16). John, though he did not record this announcement, did record the Baptist's reference to it made a few weeks later, and his direct application of it to Jesus (John i. 30). But it was doubtless due to the conversation that the four writers were all reminded of these words of the Baptist.

It must have been John who related at the conference how the Baptist in reply to the deputation sent to him from Jerusalem had applied to himself the words from Isaiah, " I am the voice of one crying in the wilderness, Make straight the way of the Lord" (John i. 23). All the other writers, without mentioning that the Baptist had said this—which indeed he had not done at the time about which they were writing—nevertheless quote the words, and more or less of the context, as appropriate to him (Matt. iii. 3; Mark i. 3; Luke iii. 4).

Some of the disciples remembered having been told by the Baptist, soon after the baptism of Jesus, that he had seen the Spirit of God descending as a dove and coming upon Jesus as He went up from the water. This also Matthew, Peter and James recorded (Matt. iii. 16; Mark i. 10; Luke iii. 22). John likewise, who probably was not present at the baptism, and who at any rate, recorded nothing in direct connection with that event, recollected that on the later occasion he had heard the Baptist make publicly a similar statement, and he included the testimony in his account (i. 32-34).

Thus we see, even in the diverse accounts of the Synoptics and John respectively, how the common influence of a conversation in which all took part, affected all the narratives. And by this we judge that Matthew, Peter and James wrote their accounts while the conversation was proceeding, and that John wrote his immediately after its conclusion.

It follows, then, that if we can find a clue to the date at which any one of the accounts was written we shall be able to determine the date of them all.

Well, in the account in Luke we have a partial clue, for it is there almost stated in so many words that the narrator was writing during the time of John's imprisonment and previously to his death. "But Herod the tetrarch, being reproved by him for Herodias, his brother's wife, and for all the evil things which Herod had done, added yet this above all, that he shut up John in prison" (iii. 19, 20). The absence here of any allusion to John's martyrdom proves that that event had not yet happened. The writer speaks of the imprisonment of John as Herod's crowning act of wickedness: he could not thus have spoken if Herod had already committed the still greater crime of putting John to death. Now, as it is generally agreed that John's imprisonment lasted something less than a year, and as the portion in Luke must certainly have been written during that time, it should on this ground alone seem probable that it was the visit of John's messengers which gave occasion for its composition.

But in Peter's account, which comes to us through Mark, there is a curious feature which settles the date to a certainty. Our Lord, when addressing the people after the departure of John's messengers, had quoted and applied to John the text (Malachi iii. 1), "Behold, I send my messenger, and he shall prepare the way before me." This was duly reported by both Matthew and James (Matt. xi. 10; Luke vii. 27). But Peter did not on this occasion take a report; for Mark's Gospel makes no mention of the visit of the Baptist's messengers, or of what our Lord then said. Nevertheless, Peter was present and listening, and when, shortly after, he wrote, in company with the others, the account before us of John's work in the wilderness, he made use of this very same text as a sort of introduction to his story. And thus we have what, without this explanation, is a most puzzling coincidence; namely, that an identical Old Testament text is quoted in all the Synoptic Gospels (Mark i. 2; Matt. xi. 10; Luke vii. 27), with the distinction that while in Mark it is applied directly to the Baptist by the Evangelist himself in narrating his work in

THE NARRATIVES AND THE THEORY 221

the wilderness; in Matthew and Luke it is given as a quotation made by our Lord, and applied by Him to the Baptist, in the course of an address delivered a year and a half after the wilderness work was done.

It is hardly necessary to repeat here that Luke iii. 1, 2 does not form part of James' original report, but is one of the very few editorial additions which Luke made in composing the work.

THE TEMPTATIONS

Matthew iv. 1-11; *Mark* i. 12, 13; *Luke* iv. 1-13

The temptations of Christ are narrated in detail in Matthew and Luke and briefly mentioned in Mark. From whom did the writers learn the facts? Doubtless from some two or more to whom our Lord had Himself related them; it may have been John the son of Zebedee, Andrew and Simon Peter, for they appear to have been the first who passed an evening in His company after His return from the wilderness. It is probable that, amazed and distressed by the agonizing experience through which He had passed, He sought the sympathy of loved and trusted friends, and gave them His confidence. What He then told them sank deeply into their memory, so that they were able after a lapse of fifteen or eighteen months to repeat with accuracy the story they had heard from their Master's lips.

For it should seem that the assembled companions of Jesus, after assisting four of their number in preparing an account of the work of John the Baptist to prefix to the narratives they were composing, felt further impelled to add some statement of those strange experiences which befell their Lord during his six weeks' absence from the busy scene of the Baptist's ministry on the banks of the Jordan. The two or three to whom He had told that story now proceeded to relate it to the others.

Peter condensed their statement into a few sentences; but Matthew and James recorded it fully. Accordingly we have in Matthew and Luke two narratives, which in substance are almost identical; but which, when placed side by side for verbal comparison, are found to be perfectly distinct.

It is in this place that we meet with the first instance of that confusion in Luke's narrative which is accounted for by our Third Special Key.

In Matthew the order of the temptations is placed as follows:

1. Jesus is told to command that the stones be made bread.
2. He is told to cast Himself from the pinnacle of the Temple.
3. He is told to fall down and worship Satan.

In Luke however the order is given thus:

1. He is told to command that a stone become bread.
2. He is told to worship Satan.
3. He is told to cast Himself from the pinnacle of the Temple.

This discrepancy is easily accounted for on the supposition that Luke transposed two of the sheets of papyrus upon which the account was written. The whole account was written by James on three pages: the first containing verses 1-4 and consisting of the equivalent of 67 Greek words; the second containing verses 9-12 being the equivalent of 63 Greek words; and the third containing verses 5-8 and equal to 62 Greek words. Luke however placed the third sheet before the second.

JOHN'S NARRATIVE CONTINUED

John i. 37 *to* ii. 25

We have seen that the four accounts of John the Baptist's work of preparation for the coming of Christ were written just after the visit of John's messengers to Jesus. That was in the summer of the year 28, at which time our Lord was fully engaged in His work. Having written this account, the four Apostles, it appears, continued to write up their narratives until the time at which they had begun to take notes. While Matthew, Peter and James recorded the experiences of Jesus in the wilderness, John wrote a narrative of some of the more important incidents that transpired subsequently. As however he had made no note of the incidents at the time they happened, but was still writing from memory, he recorded but little of what our Lord said—only an occasional sentence here and there, which had lodged in his mind and formed an essential part of the story.

The First Disciples: John, Andrew, Simon, i. 37-42.—There can be little doubt that John was himself the unnamed disciple, who, with Andrew, followed the new Rabbi to His abode. Hence it is that it is John who tells the story of that time about which he had a fuller knowledge than any other writer. Peter joined the party apparently the same afternoon; but Matthew and James were not then with them.

Philip and Nathanael: i. 43-51.—As John is writing from memory the events of the next few days are very much condensed, and no indications of time are given. The proceedings appear to have been as follows: Jesus, being at Bethany east of the Jordan, and purposing to return to Galilee, finds Philip and bids him follow Him. They start on their journey, and in the course of a few days arrive at Nazareth, a distance of from seventy to a hundred miles, the exact locality of Bethany being uncertain. Philip then proceeds to Bethsaida, some thirty miles away, finds Nathanael and brings him to Jesus at Nazareth.

Marriage at Cana: ii. 1-11.—On the third day after the return of Philip to Nazareth with Nathanael, Jesus proceeds with His mother and the five disciples to Cana, a few miles north from Nazareth, to be present at a wedding to which they have received invitations. Here He turns the water into wine and thus manifests His glory.

Removal to and short stay at Capernaum: ii. 12.—John's memory does not enable him to give an account of anything that happened during this visit to Capernaum.

Passover and First Cleansing of the Temple: ii. 13-25.— Though more than a year has elapsed, the exciting scene of our Lord's driving the traders out of the Temple is vividly described from memory. John does not recall much that was said on that occasion; but one saying of Jesus had often recurred to his mind, the more so from its enigmatical nature, and he now commits it to paper. It is the reply which our Lord gave to the Jews' demand that He should show them some sign in justification of His assumption of so much authority. He also remembers and records the scoffing incredulous answer of the Jews. Verses 21, 22, are not written now; they are inserted many years later when John is revising his papers for publication.

OBSERVATION

There is a marked difference between the character of the foregoing and that of the remaining chapters of John's Gospel. Up to this point no instance occurs of that which is the special feature of the Book. The rest of it—except the last four chapters which describe the closing facts of Christ's earthly career—consists mainly of full reports of discourses delivered by Jesus at various times. Very few facts are related, scarcely any but such as are necessary to explain or elucidate the utterances of which they were the occasion. The first two chapters are totally different. No discourse or address of any length is quoted, nothing indeed except here and there a few sentences spoken by John the Baptist, by Jesus, and by one or two other persons. They are sentences that would make a deep impression on the mind, and be permanently remembered, especially by men comparatively young. They are all sentences either of exceptional importance or that are essential to the historical facts related. In the first two chapters, the words recorded, with a few exceptions, hold a place subordinate to the facts narrated: in the next fifteen chapters, the facts narrated hold, for the most part, a subordinate place to the words recorded.

The reason for the difference manifestly is, that the portion forming the first two chapters of John was written from memory after a considerable lapse of time; whereas the remainder, up to the 17th chapter inclusive, consists chiefly of reports made at the very moment that our Lord was speaking.

FIRST TAUTOCHRONISTIC REPORT
CONVERSATION WITH NICODEMUS
John iii. 1-21

It appears that John had not long attached himself to Christ before the thought occurred to him that a report ought to be taken of some of the wonderful sayings of his Master. An opportunity soon offered itself for John to make a first trial, in this new direction, of his skill as a fast writer.

While our Lord was at Jerusalem, there came to His lodging in the city 'a man of the Pharisees,' 'a ruler of the Jews.' Although he came at night there is no reason to suppose that he did so from timidity. Our Lord was busily engaged during the day and could not be expected to put aside His public engagements for a quiet and lengthened interview with one individual.

Not that the interview was strictly of a private nature. Nicodemus seems to have considered that he approached our Lord in something like a representative capacity. The bitter hostility which the Pharisees afterwards displayed towards Jesus was not as yet fully developed. The Jewish leaders observed the influence which, by His miraculous works, He was gaining over the masses, and we may believe would gladly have acknowledged Him in some sort, if He would but have conformed to their ideas and worked in unison with them. Nicodemus probably misunderstood remarks to that effect which he had heard them make for a genuine desire, such as he had himself, to know the truth and do the right. He saw with regret that a breach was opening between his brother Pharisees and Christ; but never dreamed that its cause lay deep down in that enmity against God which is hidden in every unregenerate human heart. He thought that nothing was needed to heal the breach but a better understanding between the parties, and that a personal interview between

Q

Jesus and himself might prepare the way to smooth over difficulties and bring about a reconciliation. Accordingly, he comes to Christ, and venturing to speak for his colleagues of the Sanhedrin as well as for himself, he uses the pronoun in the plural and says: "WE know that thou art a teacher come from God." Nor does our Lord Himself ignore the representative character assumed by His visitor, but He also in His reply uses the plural: "YE must be born anew"; "YE receive not our witness;" "YE believe not"; "How shall YE believe"?

John was probably already acquainted with Nicodemus, and may have known beforehand of the intended visit. It was certainly with the latter's consent that he took a report of the interview; it is indeed not unlikely that it was Nicodemus' wish to have an exact report to show to his friends, and convince them that their prejudices against Jesus were without foundation. For he little expected the conversation to take the turn that it did. He may have requested John to write the report; if not, it must have been after seeking and obtaining his permission that John proceeded to do so.

Although a Pharisee, Nicodemus' Greek name indicates the Hellenistic tendencies of his father, and he had doubtless received some amount of Greek as well as Jewish instruction. Greek being, as we have seen, the language in vogue in Jerusalem, at least amongst the higher classes, it was that language which he usually spoke, and it was in that language that the conversation before us was carried on. Hence John, who had accustomed himself to write in Greek, had no difficulty in reporting what passed.

JOHN THE BAPTIST'S TESTIMONY
John iii. 22-36

John took an address of his namesake and former master for the subject of his second tautochronistic report.

Leaving Jerusalem, our Lord chose some unknown place in Judea for carrying on His mission. Doubtless it was a place having an ample supply of water, and therefore convenient for

the work of baptising the large numbers who flocked around Him and professed to believe in Him. John the Baptist also was still engaged in his work of baptising and preaching, for, as mentioned by the Evangelist, he was not yet cast into prison. The sentence (John iii. 24) stating this fact was probably inserted in John's manuscript a year later, after the visit of the Baptist's messengers to Jesus. We have seen that John at that time wrote the account of the forerunner's earlier testimony to the Christ, as recorded in John i., and probably also the remaining part of that chapter and the whole of chapter ii. He would naturally at the same time read again the notes he had previously made, and insert in them any needful explanatory remark. Occasional revisions, such as the one here supposed, are exactly what should be looked for in records written at the time the recorded events happened.

To return to the narrative: John the Apostle, being in the company of Jesus, and aware that his namesake was preaching and baptising at a place not far distant, took the opportunity to pay him a visit. We may well believe that it was not alone from a desire to greet once more his old friend and master that he did so. He had only a few days before made a beginning of taking notes of the utterances of Jesus, and it occurred to him that it was very desirable also to preserve a sample, taken down verbatim on the spot, of his namesake's testimony to Him, Who, he was quite convinced, was the promised Messiah. It was the Baptist's testimony that had led him a few months before to attach himself to Christ. Yet, although he remembered well the tenor of that teaching, he could not recall with literal accuracy more than a few sentences of what was then spoken. And now reports had reached the place where Jesus and His disciples were that John the Baptist was declaring in plainer terms than ever that their Lord was indeed He for Whom it had been his special mission to prepare the way. Considering what multitudes had 'gone out into the wilderness' to see and hear John the Baptist, and that the people were 'persuaded that John was a prophet,' a report, taken at the moment and which could be vouched for as exact, of his witness to Jesus, would be of the greatest value for future use. We may assume then that it was chiefly to obtain such a report that the disciple left his Master for a short time, and, going to Ænon, near to Salim, joined the crowd who were gathered at the scene of the Baptist's ministry.

The few recorded sentences spoken by John the Baptist, prior to the time which we are now considering, not having been committed to writing till some time after, give no clue to the language in which he actually addressed his congregations. The writers, dependent on the memory of themselves or others, would record John's message in the language in which they wrote, irrespective of that in which it was originally spoken. But there can be little doubt that John's usual language was Greek. His audience consisted of persons gathered to him from all parts of Judea and Galilee, who spoke Aramaic, when they spoke it at all, in two very diverse dialects; it included Pharisees and Sadducees from Jerusalem, whose ordinary language was Greek; and amongst those who asked him for directions and received his reply were soldiers, sent we may suppose by the Roman authorities to prevent disorder, and who certainly did not speak Aramaic. In such an assemblage Greek was the only language which all or nearly all could understand.

Soon after the arrival of the Apostle John at Ænon there arose, between the disciples of the Baptist and a Jew, an argument concerning which the only information given is that it was 'about purifying.' The question was referred to the preacher, but, being a matter of no permanent importance, the Apostle took no notes of what was said on either side concerning it. But when the people went on to speak of Christ and what He was doing, he began to write, and continued doing so until he had recorded the whole of that striking testimony given by John the Baptist to the Messiahship and Sonship of Jesus which forms the closing portion of this chapter.

Conversation with Samaritan Woman

John iv. 1-38

Reasons have been given in an earlier page for believing that Greek was greatly in use in the larger towns of Samaria. There can be little doubt that this would be the case at Sychar, which is supposed to have been either identical with the large and important city Sichem, or one of its suburbs. In any case Greek would be used in conversation between a Samaritan and a Jew or Galilean, communication in Aramaic being too difficult on account of the differences in the dialects. That the conversation between Jesus and the woman of Samaria was in Greek is evident from the woman's words (John iv. 25) 'I know that Messiah cometh which is called Christ' (οἶδα ὅτι Μεσσίας ἔρχεται ὃ λεγόμενος Χριστός). The words 'which is called Christ' (ὃ λεγόμενος Χριστός) are plainly not a parenthetical interpretation of John (as in i. 41, ὅ ἐστιν μεθερμηνευόμενον Χριστός); but are the woman's own translation of the Hebrew word Μεσσίας for the information of her Jewish Auditor.

This conversation would doubtless have been lost, as was many another wayside discourse of our Lord, but for the circumstance that He and His disciples remained in that place two days, thus affording an opportunity for John to write his report. The woman, who would easily remember every word of Christ's short but impressive utterances, rehearsed to him, as he wrote, all that transpired during the absence of the disciples.

The few sentences which Jesus spoke to His disciples on their return from the city were doubtless spoken, as usual in His familiar intercourse with them, in Aramaic. Writing, not at the moment, but a day or two after, the language used by the Speaker would be immaterial; John would not report the very words, but would express, in whatever language he was writing in, the sense of what was said.

Arrival in Galilee

John iv. 39–45

There has been much perplexity with reference to the applicability in this place of our Lord's saying, 'that a prophet hath no honour in his own country'; and many explanations have been attempted, most of which are unsatisfactory. Some time later, He made a similar remark with reference to His rejection at Nazareth, and hence it is inferred that in this instance He also referred to Nazareth, or to the province of Galilee in which Nazareth was situated. But He could not here have referred to Nazareth, for that town is nowhere mentioned in this connection. He did not now proceed to Nazareth but to Cana some ten miles further north. For the idea that he referred to the entire province of Galilee as His own country there is no justification whatever. The saying quoted in the Synoptics was uttered in connection with a direct contrast between the behaviour of the men of Nazareth and that of the inhabitants of the rest of Galilee, and specially of the not distant town of Capernaum.

It should be noted that there is a very important distinction between the saying recorded in John and that in the Synoptics (Matthew xiii. 57; Mark vi. 4; Luke iv. 24). In the former our Lord speaks of the prophet's 'own country' ($\tau\hat{\eta}$ $\iota\delta\iota\alpha$ $\pi\alpha\tau\rho\iota\delta\iota$). In the latter the emphatic word $\iota\delta\iota\alpha$ is omitted and, in addition to the prophet's country, He speaks, according to Mark, of his family connections and his home. Such words could allude only to Nazareth, where He had been brought up, and where Mary and her family had until recently resided. But Christ's own country in the truest and deepest sense was Judea, and especially Jerusalem and its vicinity. He was born in David's city, Bethlehem. The Temple at Jerusalem was His Father's house. For Jerusalem he had the most tender regard, as witness His weeping over the city at the time of His final visit. At the time he uttered the words recorded John iv. 44, He had not been rejected by the people of Nazareth;

it is evident however that he had found but little reverence in Judea. For although it is said that 'many believed on His name beholding His miracles which He did,' it is significantly added that 'Jesus did not trust Himself to them because He knew all men.' And, although we learn incidentally that great numbers came to His baptism, yet the fact that John makes no direct mention of this, and the smallness of the number of Judean followers which He appears to have had at a subsequent period, are proof that there were not many who heartily accepted Him. Those who did really believe on Him were in all likelihood Galileans who had come to Jerusalem to the Feast (John iv. 45).

It should seem then that Jesus' reason for leaving Judea and proceeding to Galilee was not merely, as at first sight appears from John iv. 1, His desire to avoid any appearance of competition with John the Baptist; but also the indifference with which His first assertion in Judea, and especially at Jerusalem, of His regal claims had been received. For the indifference of the Jewish authorities and their unwillingness to receive Him were now placed beyond all doubt; continuing as they did in spite of their knowledge of His increasing success in the making and baptizing of disciples. To quote from Andrews, "The Lord knew that He had thus been brought sufficiently into prominence to make it plain that they refused to come to His baptism, and so rejected Him with full knowledge. Any further presentation of His baptismal work could, therefore, be of no profit . . . since it was not now the gathering of a body of disciples around Him at which He aimed, but the repentance of the priests and leaders of the people." (*Life of our Lord*, p. 181.)

But it will naturally be asked, Why is this reason for His leaving Judea and returning to Galilee stated at the latter part of this chapter rather than at the beginning? Why is one apparent cause for this journey given in the first verse, and another more important—in fact the real—cause reserved for the 44th verse? The answer is: Because Jesus had not Himself uttered this saying at the time when the first 38 verses of the chapter were written. John wrote that portion during the two days' sojourn in Sychar. It was after that, on the way from Sychar to Galilee, that our Lord, conversing with His disciples, expressed Himself as recorded in the 44th verse. The remark was we may assume suggested by the contrast between the conduct of the Jews and that of the Samaritans. In Samaria, which was in no sense His own country—not even on friendly terms with His own country—He did find honour. Verses 39-45 were not written until after their arrival in Galilee. When John was writing at Sychar all he knew about Christ's reason for leaving Judea was that he himself on his return from his visit to Ænon, narrating to his Master what had been going on there, told how the Pharisees had been twitting the disciples of John the Baptist with the growing popularity of Jesus; and that thereupon his Lord had decided to go away to Galilee. But now when he writes in Galilee he has learned explicitly from our Lord's own lips the principal motive which has led Him to make that journey. And this reason he thereupon records.

CANA: HEALING OF NOBLEMAN'S SON AT CAPERNAUM

John iv. 46-54

The fulness of this report proves that it was written not long after the miracle was wrought; but the words in verse 46 " again " and " where He made the water wine," must have been inserted later, if, as I suppose, the account of the first miracle at Cana was not written until the time when John was writing up his narrative after the visit of the messengers from John the Baptist. The same applies to verse 54, " This is again the second sign that Jesus did, having come out of Judea into Galilee." The additions may have been made either at the time referred to above, or when John was finally revising his work for publication.

It is most probable that the nobleman or king's officer here spoken of addressed our Lord in Greek, and was answered in

THE NARRATIVES AND THE THEORY 233

that language. But whether such was the case or not is immaterial, and would not affect John's writing a report of the miracle, the few sentences that were exchanged not being recorded at the moment of utterance but shortly after.

JERUSALEM : HEALING OF MAN AT POOL OF BETHESDA
AND DISCOURSE TO THE JEWS
John v

"Now there is at Jerusalem by the sheep market a pool, which is called in the Hebrew tongue Bethesda, having five porches. In these lay a great multitude of impotent folk, of blind, halt, withered, waiting for the moving of the water. For an angel went down at a certain season into the pool, and troubled the water; whosoever then first after the troubling of the water stepped in was made whole of whatsoever disease he had. And a certain man was there which had an infirmity thirty and eight years. When Jesus saw him lie, and knew that he had now been a long time in that case, he saith unto him, Wilt thou be made whole? The impotent man answered him, Sir, I have no man, when the water is troubled, to put me into the pool: but while I am coming, another steppeth down before me."

Unlike most of the quotations in this book the above is taken from the Authorised Version. The passage is plain enough and might have been written in Ephesus at the end of the first century, or, for that matter, in England at the end of the nineteenth century. But it is now generally agreed that a considerable part of this was not written by John at all; and in the Revised Version the lines beginning, "waiting for the moving of the water," and ending, "whatsoever disease he had," are eliminated, and placed in the margin.

Without these lines however the narrative is rather puzzling, and suggests the questions: Why did a multitude of afflicted people crowd into the porches of the pool? and, What did the paralysed man mean by his complaint, that he had no man, when the water was troubled, to put him into the pool, and that while he was coming, another stepped down before him?

These questions in fact suggested themselves in very early times, and it was to meet them that some well-meaning person interpolated in a copy of the Gospel, between the sentences that form in the Revised Version the third and the fifth verse, an explanation based either on tradition or imagination. The copies made from this copy repeated the interpolation, and so carried it into many manuscripts, amongst others into those from which the original text of the Old Version was derived.

But, in the place and time in which John, as we believe, first wrote, no explanation was needed. He wrote in Jerusalem within a few days after the miracle took place. Everybody there and then knew all about the intermittent spring which was credited with the power of effecting miraculous cures. It did not occur to John that the story he was writing might some day be a source of perplexity to the reader. If he had first written the story at Ephesus after the lapse of many years he would not have left it in so imperfect a shape.

That the narrative was written while the facts were fresh in the writer's memory is shown by the exactness of the statement as to the duration of the man's infirmity. It would surely be a superfluous miracle for the Apostle, through more than half a lifetime, to recollect in such a connection a precise period like thirty-eight years. It is still more unlikely that anyone writing a fictitious or semi-fictitious story should exhibit such minuteness. His doing so would detract from, not add to, the credibility of his narration.

The portion of this chapter which John first wrote was the latter part beginning at the 17th verse. He had reported our Lord's discourse to Nicodemus and a short address of John the Baptist. He had also taken down, at the Samaritan woman's dictation, an account of Christ's conversation with her at the well. He was now emboldened to practise his talent as a fast writer in the midst of less friendly auditors than were present at his previous essays. He was anxious to preserve some specimens of the manner in which Jesus was wont, in the Temple, to assert to the Jewish rulers His authority and claims. An opportunity presented itself when our Lord was summoned before the Sanhedrin, to answer for His breach of Sabbath observance, by healing an impotent man and directing him to carry his mattress on that day. John was present with pen, ink and paper, and, paying little regard to the proceedings of the court, which were not what he had come to report, he wrote down rapidly our Lord's answer to the charge; first the words, " My Father worketh even until now, and I work," and, after a short interval caused by the interruption of the Jews, the whole discourse from verse 19 to the end of the chapter.

At John's earliest leisure moment, probably the same evening, he wrote the introductory part comprised in the first sixteen verses. He also inserted the statement in verse 18, and probably made a fair copy of his report of our Lord's discourse.

It is not unlikely, however, that, as first written, this narrative began in some such terms as these: " There lay in the porches of Bethesda a multitude," etc. The statement in verse 2 appears to be an editorial explanation of later date. So also is verse 1, in which "a feast of the Jews" is mentioned without specifying which; probably for the simple reason that, when John was redacting his work and wrote this, he was unable to remember what feast it was that our Lord attended on that occasion.

Observation

The first five chapters of John cover a period which is estimated to have lasted fully twelve months. During that time our Lord made two journeys from Judea to Galilee and twice returned from Galilee to Judea. In the Synoptic Gospels there is no notice whatever of anything that occurred in the course of that period. In all three the narrative proceeds without a break from the Temptations of Christ in the wilderness to His journey to Galilee after the imprisonment of John the Baptist; nor is the least intimation given that there was over a year's interval between the two events.

We know from John that some of the disciples were in the company of Jesus during some parts of the interval referred to. The Twelve however had not yet been set aside to the Apostolic office, and several had not yet been called to follow Christ. No disciple except John had at this time begun to take notes, and, of those who afterwards did so, Peter alone, so far as we know, was in attendance on Him, and even his attendance may not have been continuous. John however appears to have been with Jesus all the time, and it was therefore but natural that the others should leave to him the task of narrating this portion of the history.

RETURN TO GALILEE AND MISSION THERE

Matt. iv. 12-17; *Mark* i. 14, 15; *Luke* iv. 14, 15

In these short passages the Synoptics summarise a residence and mission in Galilee which must have lasted some little time. The brevity of the accounts shows that they were not written at the time to which they relate, and it may be concluded that they were written shortly after the visit of John the Baptist's messengers to Jesus, at which time the Apostles engaged themselves in writing up the earlier and unreported portion of Christ's ministry.

On comparing the three accounts, it will be seen that they bear very plainly those features which can be explained only by the fact that they were respectively written in company and conference by three individuals.

Matthew's quotation from Isaiah is of course an editorial addition of much later date than the rest of the passage.

CALLING OF FOUR DISCIPLES

Matt. iv. 18-22; *Mark* i. 16-20

While Jesus was in Galilee, Peter, Andrew and John returned to their business as fishermen, and, while they were so employed, our Lord, walking on the beach, called them and

James to follow Him. The accounts of this calling were also written shortly after the visit to Christ of the Baptist's deputation. The calling was at that time comparatively recent, and, being an event in which several of the Apostles were personally interested, it was related by them, when assembled in conference, with some degree of detail, and was in like manner recorded by Matthew and Peter.

It does not seem that these four disciples even now finally left their business and their homes; for not long after they are again found at the lake washing their nets.

HEALING OF DEMONIAC AT CAPERNAUM
Mark i. 21–28 ; *Luke* iv. 31–37

The narratives gradually become more detailed, and it might at first sight be supposed that the story of this miracle was written immediately after it was wrought. But the statement (Mark i. 28 ; Luke iv. 37) that the fame of Jesus spread in consequence throughout the country, shows that some time must have elapsed ere this was recorded. The period that passed was probably about three or four months, if, as I suppose, these, like the portions we have considered above, were written just after the visit of John's messengers. An interval of that length would harmonise well with the wording of the story.

HEALING OF PETER'S WIFE'S MOTHER AND MANY OTHERS
Matt. viii. 14–17 ; *Mark* i. 29–39 ; *Luke* iv. 38–44

The Aramaic writers are still writing up their back narratives.

In this instance it is Matthew's, not Luke's, account that has been placed out of its chronological order. Matthew was a careful and methodical man, and did his best to ensure accuracy in this as in other respects: still it is not surprising that, when after a number of years he redacted his manuscripts, he should in some instances have found himself unable to place them exactly in their original sequence.

The First Miraculous Draught of Fishes
Luke v. 1-11

This incident is recorded only in Luke. The story consists of a manuscript written by James soon after the event occurred. It is apparently the first Gospel narrative that this Apostle wrote and he probably was prompted by his brother John to make the record. Its style is quite different from those portions of Luke which we have already considered, and which were not written contemporaneously with the events related, nor until many months after. This portion bears upon its face the vividness of a story related at a time when the mind of the narrator is still strongly impressed with the facts.

Healing of a Leper
Matt. viii. 2-4; Mark i. 40-45; Luke v. 12-16

Healing of One Sick of the Palsy; Calling of Matthew; Feast at his House; Question about Fasting
Matt. ix. 2-17; Mark ii. 1-22; Luke v. 17-39

Disciples Pluck Corn on Sabbath; Jesus Heals Man with Withered Hand; Jesus Withdraws to the Sea, and Ascends a Mountain, where He Spends the Night in Prayer. In the Morning He Appoints the Twelve Apostles, and Great Multitudes Gather round Him
Matt. xii. 1-21; iv. 23-v. 1; Mark ii. 23-iii. 19; Luke vi. 1-19

We now reach the time when, if my judgment be correct, the three Aramaic-writing disciples unitedly began to make contemporaneous notes. This they did as soon as the Twelve were chosen and set aside to the Apostolic office. On the very same day two of their number reported, with more or less completeness, the Sermon on the Mount. It requires no great stretch of imagination to suppose that at the first leisure moment thereafter, they held a meeting among themselves to consider their future course of action. At that meeting it was, we may assume, agreed that it was above all things essential that records should be made of the wonderful things that the Great Rabbi was doing and saying. It was known to them that John had already written reports of some of His works and discourses; and that James, not long before, assisted perhaps by John, Peter and Andrew, had written the account of the miraculous draught of fishes. They had also, it may be on the morning of that very day, seen Matthew and James reporting our Lord's Sermon as He delivered it. And now doubtless it was unanimously resolved that Matthew, Peter and James should henceforth as often as practicable record the utterances and actions of Jesus when He spoke in Aramaic; and that John should do likewise when He spoke in Greek; also that the other eight should render these four all the help in their power in their performance of this duty.

We may be sure that they lost no time in putting their resolve into practice. They would be full of enthusiasm and eager to begin. Pens, ink and paper were provided forthwith, and Matthew, Peter and James at once sat down to write.

What was the first thing they wrote? This is a question that cannot be answered off hand. Whatever was now written was revised later by themselves—not to mention the final revision by the redactors—and the parts were fitted together so as to form a continuous history. It is not easy therefore to find the exact place where the part written on this occasion is joined on to the part, written afterwards, but narrating an earlier part of the history.

All things considered, I am of opinion that the passages specified above are those which were written at this first meeting of the newly appointed Apostles. It appears, from their position in Mark and Luke, that the cleansing of the leper and the healing of the man sick of the palsy; the calling of Matthew, the feast in his house and our Lord's reply to the question about fasting; the plucking of corn on the Sabbath and the healing of the withered hand; all occurred just previously to the appointment of the Twelve. These incidents are related with more fulness and minuteness than any that had happened previously, showing that when the accounts were written they were fresh in the minds of the disciples. And they all lead up naturally to the delivery of that great discourse, of which two reports had been taken, and which had so deeply impressed them and the multitude a few hours before.

I must leave it to the reader's own imagination to see the twelve disciples, gathered in a room in the evening of that day, discussing the incidents referred to. One and another gives each his version, while the three whose task it is to write are busy with their pens. The stories told by all are substantially alike, but there is much diversity in the manner of telling. And hence the three reports bear those striking features of likeness and unlikeness, of dependent independence, which more or less characterise all the parallel passages in the Synoptic Gospels, and which have so much puzzled students. When however they deal with the utterances of Jesus Himself, they are very careful to quote His words exactly, and in this respect the three accounts are in consequence almost identical.

It was doubtless Peter who carried out the Lord's wish that a boat should be provided for His use: hence he alone recorded the request (Mark iii. 9).

The appointment of twelve disciples to be the Lord's Apostles is related only in Mark and Luke; though their names are given in Matthew x. 1-4. Note that Luke's account, written by James, mentions the names merely of James and John; while Mark's account, written by Peter, describes them as the sons of Zebedee, and states that Jesus surnamed them Boanerges, Sons of Thunder. Yet Luke's account, as well as Mark's, does not fail to say that Simon was surnamed Peter.

THE SERMON ON THE MOUNT

Matt. v. 1–viii. 1; *Luke* vi. 20–49; xi. 1–13, 33–36; xii. 22–34, 58, 59; xvi. 10-18

This Sermon appears to be the first of Christ's Aramaic utterances that was tautochronistically reported. No part of it is contained in Mark: this goes a long way to prove that the Sermon, as reported in Matthew, is not a collection made by him of sayings spoken at various times, but a continuous discourse as it is therein represented to be; notwithstanding that in Luke it is found only in fragments distributed through different parts of the book.

Matthew had but a short time previously been called to follow Jesus. The business he had abandoned was one that made it necessary for him almost invariably to carry writing materials about him, and he had them with him now as heretofore. James had a few days before made a beginning at literary work, and had now also come prepared to take notes of the sayings of Christ. Peter however had probably not yet reached the reporting stage, and did not attempt, like his two friends, to take down the Master's utterances.

On comparing the reports in Matthew and Luke it will be seen that in this, their first attempt to make a verbatim report, James was less expert than Matthew. This is not to be wondered at. It is obvious that, in their prior occupations, Matthew would have had more practice in writing than probably any other of the disciples, and in circumstances too that would be more likely to accustom him to the distractions of noisy surroundings. After a few months' practice James became quite the equal of Matthew in this respect; but at this time he was hardly able to keep pace with the Speaker, and while completing one sentence would sometimes allow a subsequent one to escape him. Sometimes also for causes unknown to us he omitted passages of considerable length. Nevertheless there are in Luke a few sentences which were missed by Matthew.

R

The differences in the wording of those portions which are preserved in both Gospels are doubtless for the most part variations in the translations separately made from Aramaic to Greek of the two reports, by Matthew and Luke respectively.

Luke xi. 1 I take to be an editorial addition, the result of Luke's personal enquiry as to the circumstances in which the Lord's Prayer was given. If so, the "praying in a certain place" refers to Christ's prayer on the mountain all the previous night, as stated Luke vi. 12. The grammatical construction in the Greek will bear this interpretation. No doubt there were many interruptions and intervals in the course of the delivery of the Sermon, and it must have been in one of the intervals that a disciple approached Christ with the request here recorded.

If the reader will cut out from Matthew and Luke the portions above cited, and place them side by side, he will be struck with the disagreement in the order of the two reports; and it will at first sight appear that the disagreement is of a nature that does not seem capable of explanation by our Third Special Key. In Part V. Chap. 5, it is said that James appears to have written on small sheets of papyrus, containing in Aramaic as much as when translated would amount to not less than 40 nor more than 70 Greek words. But to make the order of Luke's report of the Sermon agree with Matthew's the former must sometimes be broken up into much smaller fragments than that. For instance, if Luke vi. 27–36 be placed beside Matthew v. 38–48, it will be seen that verses 29, 30 of the former are parallel with 39–42 of the latter, while 27, 28, 32–36 in Luke are parallel with the subsequent verses in Matthew. But verses 27, 28, which are thus broken off from 32–36, contain only 23 Greek words, and 29, 30 only 34 Greek words, each section therefore being insufficient to fill up a page. There are many similar examples which the reader may if he chooses find for himself.

It is antecedently probable that the other disciples who took

THE NARRATIVES AND THE THEORY 243

notes used slips of paper similar to those used by James, that is to say, about $5\frac{1}{2}$ inches by $3\frac{1}{2}$, the size by the way of the recently discovered papyrus containing the so-called New Sayings of Christ, and which may perhaps be a page of a catechumen's report of a Christian teacher's lecture. It is therefore probable that disorder in the arrangement of the Sermon is not confined to Luke's report, the more so as there certainly are many instances of transposition in other parts of Matthew. Indeed it seems hardly possible that Matthew, when arranging the numerous papers containing the Sermon, would be able always to remember the exact sequence in which each portion was spoken.

Is it possible to rearrange each of the reports in sections of about the required length so as to bring about a harmony between the two? This is the question that occurred to me when making a final revision of this Work. To my delight, I found that it was possible to do so, and that without marring the symmetry or continuity of the Sermon in whole or in part.

I submit the following tentatively as probably the original order of the pages in Matthew:

v.	1–16	213 Greek words	4	pages
vi.	19–23	94 ,, ,,	2	,,
v.	43–45	50 ,, ,,	1	,,
	38–42	69 ,, ,,	1	,,
	46–48	45 ,, ,,	1	,,
vii.	1–6	108 ,, ,,	2	,,
vi.	24–34	213 ,, ,,	4	,,
v.	17–20	101 ,, ,,	2	,,
	27–37	206 ,, ,,	4	,,
	21–26	139 ,, ,,	3	,,
vi.	1–18		several	,,
vii.	7–27		,,	,,

And the following as the order of the pages in Luke:

vi.	19–26	142 Greek words	3	pages
xi.	33–36	83 ,, ,,	2	,,
vi.	27–42		several	,,
xvi.	10–15	112 ,, ,,	2	,,
xii.	22–34	212 ,, ,,	4	,,
xvi.	16–18	51 ,, ,,	1	,,
xii.	58, 59	59 ,, ,,	1	,,
xi.	2–13	201 ,, ,,	4	,,
vi.	43–49	157 ,, ,,	3	,,

244 THE GOSPEL PROBLEMS AND THEIR SOLUTION

It will be seen that, according to these arrangements, the matter on each page amounted with but few exceptions to the equivalent of from 50 to 60 Greek words, and that of the exceptions the smallest amounted to not less than 40 and the largest to not more than 70. In English the number of words is on the average about one-fourth larger, but there is more variation. Possibly in the original Aramaic there may have been less variation than there is in the Greek.

On the above basis the two reports compare side by side as follows, parallel texts being placed on the same line, and a blank being left where a text has no parallel:

MATTHEW.		LUKE.	
v.	1–3	vi.	20
	4, 5		
	6		21
	7–9		
	10–12		22, 23
			24–26
	13, 14		
	15	xi.	33
	16		
vi.	19–21		
	22, 23		34–36
v.	43		
	44	vi.	27, 28
	45		
	38		
	39, 40		29
	41		
	42		30
			31
	46, 47		32, 33
			34, 35
	48		36
vii.	1, 2		37, 38
			39, 40
	3–5		41, 42
	6		
		xvi.	10–12

THE NARRATIVES AND THE THEORY 245

MATTHEW.	LUKE.
vi. 24	xvi. 13
	14, 15
25-33	xii. 22-31
34	
	32-34
	xvi. 16
v. 17	
18	17
19, 20	
27-31	
32	18
33-37	
21-24	
25, 26	xii. 58, 59
vi. 1-8	
9-13	xi. 2-4
14, 15	
	5-8
16-18	
vii. 7-11	9-13
12-16	
17, 18	vi. 43
	44, 45
19, 20	
21-23	46
24-27	47-49

HEALING OF CENTURION'S SERVANT

Matt. viii. 5-13 ; *Luke* vii. 1-10

5 And when he was entered into Capernaum, there came unto him a centurion, beseeching
6 him, and saying, Lord, my servant lieth in the house sick of the palsy, grievously tormented.
7 And he saith unto him, I will
8 come and heal him. And the centurion answered and said, Lord, I am not worthy that thou shouldest come under my roof: but only say the word, and my

After he had ended all his sayings in the ears of the people, he entered into Capernaum.
2 And a certain centurion's servant, who was dear unto him, was sick and at the point of
3 death. And when he heard concerning Jesus, he sent unto him elders of the Jews, asking him that he would come and
4 save his servant. And they,

9 servant shall be healed. For I also am a man under authority, having under myself soldiers: and I say to this one, Go, and he goeth; and to another, Come, and he cometh; and to my servant, Do this, and he
10 doeth it. And when Jesus heard it, he marvelled, and said to them that followed, Verily I say unto you, I have not found so great faith, no, not in Israel.
11 And I say unto you, that many shall come from the east and the west, and shall sit down with Abraham, and Isaac, and Jacob,
12 in the kingdom of heaven: but the sons of the kingdom shall be cast forth into the outer darkness: there shall be the weeping
13 and gnashing of teeth. And Jesus said unto the centurion, Go thy way; as thou hast believed, *so* be it done unto thee. And the servant was healed in that hour.

when they came to Jesus, besought him earnestly, saying, He is worthy that thou shouldest
5 do this for him: for he loveth our nation, and himself built us
6 our synagogue. And Jesus went with them. And when he was now not far from the house, the centurion sent friends to him, saying unto him, Lord, trouble not thyself: for I am not worthy that thou shouldest come under
7 my roof: wherefore neither thought I myself worthy to come unto thee: but say the word, and my servant shall be healed.
8 For I also am a man set under authority, having under myself soldiers: and I say to this one, Go, and he goeth; and to another, Come, and he cometh; and to my servant, Do this, and
9 he doeth it. And when Jesus heard these things, he marvelled at him, 'and turned and said unto the multitude that followed him, I say unto you, I have not found so great faith, no, not in
10 Israel. And they that were sent, returning to the house, found the servant whole.

It cannot be doubted that one and the same incident is narrated in both these passages. The words in Matthew (8, 9) said to have been spoken by the centurion, and in Luke (6-8) by friends on his behalf, are for the most part identical. So are the words spoken by Jesus in Matthew 10, and Luke 9. And yet in some respects the story is very differently told. According to Matthew the centurion came in person, while according to Luke he sent friends to intercede for him. Alford truly remarks that this difference does not affect the accuracy of the reports. But, that the two narratives should in one respect differ so widely, and in others agree so closely, is utterly incompatible with the oral teaching theory which Alford holds. All difficulties vanish, however, if we recognise that both accounts were written immediately after the event, and in the company of a number of men who assisted the writers by rehearsing and discussing the facts.

It will be seen that, during the earlier period of the ministry, Matthew aimed rather at reporting the words of Christ, while James was more acute at observing and reporting facts. This will be apparent to any reader who will take the trouble to compare parallel passages in the two Gospels; for instance, the following :—

Matt. viii. 2-4 with Luke v. 12-16.
,, ix. 2-8 ,, ,, v. 17-26.
,, xii. 1-8 ,, ,, vi. 1-5.
,, xii. 9-14 ,, ,, vi. 6-11.

Accordingly, in reporting the story, as told by his fellow disciples and remembered by himself, of the Healing of the Centurion's Servant, Matthew condensed the facts as far as possible, relating only what was requisite as a setting to the solemn words spoken by our Lord, and which he recorded at length. James, on the contrary, omitted the greater and more important part of what Christ said, recording only just as much as was essential to the facts; but related the facts in detail.

It is not unlikely that Matthew took a report of the words of Jesus, at the time He uttered them, and supplied James afterwards with so much as he required to complete his story. For, although the centurion must himself have spoken in Greek, it is probable that his Jewish friends, being at Capernaum, where Aramaic appears to have prevailed, interpreted his message into Aramaic when delivering it to Christ.

NAIN : RESTORING WIDOW'S SON TO LIFE
Luke vii. 11-17

It is remarkable that although this is one of only three recorded instances in which Jesus restored a dead person to life, it is related in Luke only. Its omission by Matthew however is quite consistent with the usual manner of that Evangelist, to concern himself less about the things which our Lord did than the words He spake.

Visit of Messengers from John the Baptist, and Christ's Discourse Occasioned Thereby

Matt. xi. 2–30 ; *Luke* vii. 18–35, x. 13–15, 21–24

These portions afford an excellent example of independent reports of the same utterances.

The incident which gave rise to the utterances occurred in Galilee, probably at or near Capernaum, some eighteen months after the beginning of Christ's ministry, and about four or five months after John the Baptist had been put in prison. The proceedings seem to have been as follows :—

On the morning when the messengers arrived, Jesus was busily engaged at His usual occupation of preaching the glad tidings and healing those who had infirmities. After they had delivered their message, they remained in the place awaiting a reply ; and saw the wonderful works that Jesus wrought. During the time they were there, our Lord's apostles entered into conversation with them and learned from them fully the circumstances of John's imprisonment, and how it was they came to be sent on their present errand.

At length the time came for the messengers to return, and then it was that our Lord spoke the words that are reported almost verbatim in the portions we are about to consider. Our Lord called John's messengers to Him, and Matthew and James, inferring from His manner that He was about to deliver an utterance of special importance, also approached, and arranging each a sheet of papyrus on a thin piece of board, which, being used with the left hand, as a tablet, enabled a reed or quill to be held by the right hand, prepared to write. Then, as our Lord addressed the messengers, and afterwards as He discoursed to the people, they quickly noted down the words that He spake.

THE NARRATIVES AND THE THEORY 249

Nothing else was written then. The explanatory sentences at the beginning, and elsewhere inserted in the reports, were added later; probably in the evening of the same day.

It is by these explanatory sentences, which are subjoined here in parallel columns, that we know, beyond all question, that the two reports were independently written.

MATTHEW'S REPORT	JAMES' REPORT
MATT. xi.	LUKE vii.
2 Now when John heard in the prison the works of the Christ, he sent by his disciples, and 3 said unto him, Art thou he that cometh, or look we for another?	18 And the disciples of John told 19 him of all these things. And John calling unto him two of his disciples sent them to the Lord, saying, Art thou he that cometh, or look we for another? 20 And when the men were come unto him, they said, John the Baptist hath sent us unto thee, saying, Art thou he that cometh, 21 or look we for another? In that hour he cured many of diseases and plagues and evil spirits; and on many that were blind he 22 bestowed sight. And he answered and said unto them,
4 And Jesus answered and said unto them,	

It will be seen that, while there is not in these passages the slightest disagreement as to the facts, there is a decided contrast in the manner of stating them. The only parts that are similar are John's question, and this is identical in both. (In some manuscripts they are not quite alike in the Greek; but doubtless they were alike in the original Aramaic).

Now compare the reports of our Lord's answer:

Go your way and tell John the things which ye do hear and 5 see: the blind receive their sight, and the lame walk, the lepers are cleansed, and the deaf hear, and the dead are raised up, and the poor have good	Go your way, and tell John what things ye have seen and heard; the blind receive their sight, the lame walk, the lepers are cleansed, and the deaf hear, the dead are raised up, the poor have good tidings preached to

6 tidings preached to them. And blessed is he, whosoever shall find none occasion of stumbling in me.	23 them. And blessed is he, whosoever shall find none occasion of stumbling in me.

It will be seen that these are almost identical: in the original Aramaic doubtless they were quite identical, what differences exist are simply the result of their being separately translated from Aramaic into Greek.

The next sentence is the connecting link between the foregoing and our Lord's address to the multitude which followed.

7 And as these went their way, Jesus began to say unto the multitudes concerning John,	24 And when the messengers of John were departed, he began to say unto the multitudes concerning John,

Here there is sufficient similarity to suggest—taken together with the identity in John's question noted above—that the two reports were written in company, and that the subject was a matter of conversation amongst those present.

Now comes the discourse to the people. Allowing for the omission of a word here and there by one or other of the reporters, and for diversities which are the result of translation, the two reports, down to a certain point, are virtually identical.

What went ye out into the wilderness to behold? a reed 8 shaken with the wind? But what went ye out to see? a man clothed in soft (raiment)? Behold they that wear soft (raiment) 9 are in kings' houses. But wherefore went ye out? to see a prophet? Yea, I say unto you, and much more than a prophet. 10 This is he, of whom it is written, Behold, I send my messenger before thy face, Who shall prepare thy way before thee.	What went ye out into the wilderness to behold? a reed 25 shaken with the wind? But what went ye out to see? a man clothed in soft raiment? Behold, they which are gorgeously apparelled and live delicately, are 26 in kings' courts. But what went ye out to see? a prophet? Yea, I say unto you, and much more 27 than a prophet. This is he of whom it is written, Behold, I send my messenger before thy face, Who shall prepare thy way before thee.

11 Verily I say unto you, Among them that are born of women there hath not arisen a greater than John the Baptist: yet he that is but little in the kingdom of heaven is greater than he.	28 I say unto you, Among them that are born of women there is none greater than John: yet he that is but little in the kingdom of God is greater than he.

So far our two reporters have got on about equally well. The people have been listening in silence and there has been nothing to distract the attention of the writers. But now there is something like an altercation in the crowd. This assertion of John's greatness gives much satisfaction to the people and the publicans, who " verily hold John to be a prophet," and were amongst those who went to be baptised by him; and they express their approval aloud. But the Pharisees and the lawyers, who have held themselves coldly aloof from John, are not so well pleased, and they reply to the others in terms of dissent. This little controversy for the moment diverts James' attention, and, in consequence, he misses some sentences of our Lord's address. Matthew, on the other hand, who has been accustomed in his business calmly to go on with his writing in the midst of hostile and angry declamation, is not so easily moved, but, carefully following the Speaker, continues his report.

Accordingly, the next four verses in Matthew are a continuation of Christ's discourse, while the next two in Luke are a description, written by James in the evening, of the effect of His words on the audience.

12 And from the days of John the Baptist until now the kingdom of heaven suffereth violence, and men of violence take it by 13 force. For all the prophets and the law prophesied until John. 14 And if ye are willing to receive *it*, this is Elijah, which is to 15 come. He that hath ears to hear, let him hear.	29 And all the people when they heard, and the publicans, justified God, being baptized with 30 the baptism of John. But the Pharisees and the lawyers rejected for themselves the counsel of God, being not baptized of him.

The rest of the discourse is for the most part nearly identical in both Gospels. The closing invitation and one or two other sentences are omitted in Luke. Here and there a word is missed in Matthew, but not so as to affect the meaning. The other slight differences (which by the way are rather more numerous in the Greek than in our English Revised Version) are the natural result of the two reports having been independently translated from the Aramaic originals.

In Luke, however, the latter part of the discourse has been transposed, in two sections, to the tenth chapter. That they properly belong to this place is evident, although it is easy to see why Luke placed them where he did.

Anointing by Woman in Pharisee's House
Luke vii. 36–50

This incident is related only by Luke. It is not stated where it happened: probably it was at Capernaum or some neighbouring Galilean town. The party described does not appear to have been a large one, like that described in Luke xiv. There is nothing to indicate that the disciples were present: indeed it may be inferred from verse 49 that they were not. It is pretty certain at any rate that Matthew, the ex-publican, was not invited. Possibly the two sons of Zebedee may have been in the company, and, if so, James wrote this account from his own observation soon after the party broke up. It is more likely however that James obtained his information from Simon himself.

Most expositors express a harsher opinion of the Pharisee and his conduct than the narrative seems to warrant. Those who take the more lenient view of Alford, and regard the Pharisee as a sincere believer on Jesus, but one who had not as yet attained to a very high level of piety or love, may be able to understand how he, amazed and humbled at the revelation which Christ's rebuke made to him of his own unworthiness and cowardice, did not forbear, on meeting James soon after, to furnish him with details of the story to enter in his notes.

HEALING OF MAN POSSESSED WITH DUMB DEVIL; BLASPHEMY OF SCRIBES; DISCOURSE OF JESUS

Matt. xii. 22–50; Mark iii. 20–35; Luke xi. 14–23, 27–30, 32, 31, 24–26, viii. 19–21

MATTHEW	MARK	LUKE
xii. 22 Then was brought unto him one possessed with a devil, blind and dumb: and he healed him, insomuch that the dumb man spake and saw. And all the multitudes were amazed, and said, Is this the son of David?	iii. 20 And he cometh into a house. And the multitude cometh together again, so that they could not so much as eat bread. 21 And when his friends heard it, they went out to lay hold on him: for they said, He is beside himself. 22 And the scribes which came down from Jerusalem said, He hath Beelzebub, and, By the prince of the devils casteth he out devils.	xi. 14 And he was casting out a devil which was dumb. And it came to pass, when the devil was gone out, the dumb man spake; and the multitudes marvelled. 15 But some of them said, By Beelzebub the prince of the devils 16 casteth he out devils. And others, tempting *him*, sought of him a 17 sign from heaven. But he, knowing their thoughts, said unto them, Every kingdom divided against itself is brought to desolation; and a house *divided* against a house 18 falleth. And if Satan also is divided against himself, how shall
24 But when the Pharisees heard it, they said, This man doth not cast out devils, but by Beelzebub the prince of the devils. 25 And knowing their thoughts he said unto them, Every kingdom divided against itself is brought to desolation; and every city or house divided against itself shall 26 not stand: and if Satan casteth	23 And he called them unto him, and said unto them in parables, How can Satan cast out Satan? 24 And if a kingdom be divided against itself, that kingdom cannot 25 stand. And if a house be divided	

19 his kingdom stand? because ye say that I cast out devils by Beelzebub. And if I by Beelzebub cast out devils, by whom do your sons cast them out? therefore shall
20 they be your judges. But if I by the finger of God cast out devils, then is the kingdom of God come
21 upon you. When the strong *man* fully armed guardeth his own
22 court, his goods are in peace: but when a stronger than he shall come upon him, and overcome him, he taketh from him his whole armour wherein he trusted,
23 and divideth his spoils. He that is not with me is against me; and he that gathereth not with me scattereth.

out Satan, he is divided against himself; how then shall his king-
27 dom stand? And if I by Beelzebub cast out devils, by whom do your sons cast them out? therefore shall
28 they be your judges. But if I by the Spirit of God cast out devils, then is the kingdom of
29 God come upon you. Or how can one enter into the house of the strong *man*, and spoil his goods, except he first bind the strong *man*? and then he will
30 spoil his house. He that is not with me is against me; and he that gathereth not with me scat-
31 tereth. Therefore I say unto you, Every sin and blasphemy shall be forgiven unto men; but the blasphemy against the Spirit shall not
32 be forgiven. And whosoever shall speak a word against the Son of man, it shall be forgiven him; but whosoever shall speak against the Holy Spirit, it shall not be forgiven him, neither in this world, nor in that which is to come.

against itself, that house will not
26 be able to stand. And if Satan hath risen up against himself, and is divided, he cannot stand, but hath an end.
27 But no one can enter into the house of the strong *man*, and spoil his goods, except he first bind the strong *man*; and then he will spoil his house.
28 Verily I say unto you, All their sins shall be forgiven unto the sons of men, and their blasphemies wherewith soever they shall
29 blaspheme: but whosoever shall blaspheme against the Holy Spirit hath never forgiveness, but is guilty of an eternal sin: because
30 they said, He hath an unclean spirit.

33 Either make the tree good, and its fruit good; or make the tree corrupt, and its fruit corrupt: for the tree is known by its fruit.
34 Ye offspring of vipers, how can ye, being evil, speak good things? for out of the abundance of the heart the mouth speaketh. The good man out of his good treasure bringeth forth good things: and the evil man out of his evil treasure bringeth forth evil things.
36 And I say unto you, that every idle word that men shall speak, they shall give account thereof in the day of judgement. For by thy words thou shalt be justified, and by thy words thou shalt be condemned.
38 Then certain of the scribes and Pharisees answered him, saying, Master, we would see a sign from

27 And it came to pass, as he said these things, a certain woman out of the multitude lifted up her voice, and said unto him, Blessed is the womb that bare thee, and the breasts which thou didst suck.
28 But he said, Yea rather, blessed are they that hear the word of God, and keep it.

39. thee. But he answered and said unto them, An evil and adulterous generation seeketh after a sign; and there shall no sign be given to it but the sign of Jonah the
40. prophet: for as Jonah was three days and three nights in the belly of the whale; so shall the Son of man be three days and three nights
41. in the heart of the earth. The men of Nineveh shall stand up in the judgement with this generation, and shall condemn it: for they repented at the preaching of Jonah; and behold, a greater than Jonah is here.
42. The queen of the south shall rise up in the judgement with this generation, and shall condemn it: for she came from the ends of the earth to hear the wisdom of Solomon; and behold, a greater than Solomon is here.
43. But the unclean spirit, when he is gone out of the man, passeth through waterless places, seeking
44. rest, and findeth it not. Then he saith, I will return into my house

29. And when the multitudes were gathering together unto him, he began to say, This generation is an evil generation: it seeketh after a sign; and there shall no sign be given to it but the sign of
30. Jonah. For even as Jonah became a sign unto the Ninevites, so shall also the Son of man be to this generation.
32. The men of Nineveh shall stand up in the judgement with this generation, and shall condemn it: for they repented at the preaching of Jonah; and behold, a greater than Jonah is here.
31. The queen of the south shall rise up in the judgement with the men of this generation, and shall condemn them: for she came from the ends of the earth to hear the wisdom of Solomon; and behold, a greater than Solomon is here.
24. The unclean spirit when he is gone out of the man, passeth through waterless places, seeking rest; and finding none, he saith,

THE NARRATIVES AND THE THEORY

I will turn back unto my house
25 whence I came out. And when he is come, he findeth it swept and
26 garnished. Then goeth he, and taketh *to him* seven other spirits more evil than himself; and they enter in and dwell there: and the last state of that man becometh worse than the first.

viii. 19 And there came to him his mother and brethren, and they could not come at him for the
20 crowd. And it was told him, Thy mother and thy brethren stand
21 without, desiring to see thee. But he answered and said unto them, My mother and my brethren are these which hear the word of God, and do it.

whence I came out; and when he is come, he findeth it empty,
45 swept, and garnished. Then goeth he, and taketh with himself seven other spirits more evil than himself, and they enter in and dwell there: and the last state of that man becometh worse than the first. Even so shall it be also unto this evil generation.
46 While he was yet speaking to the multitudes, behold, his mother and his brethren stood without,
47 seeking to speak to him. And one said unto him, Behold, thy mother and thy brethren stand without, seeking to speak to thee.
48 But he answered and said unto him that told him, Who is my mother? and who are my bre-
49 thren? And he stretched forth his hand towards his disciples, and said, Behold, my mother and my
s. 50 brethren! For whosoever shall do the will of my Father which is in heaven, he is my brother, and sister, and mother.

31 And there come his mother and his brethren; and, standing without, they sent unto him, calling
32 him. And a multitude was sitting about him; and they say unto him, Behold, thy mother and thy brethren without seek for thee.
33 And he answereth them, and saith, Who is my mother and my bre-
34 thren? And looking round on them which sat round about him, he saith, Behold my mother and
35 my brethren! For whosoever shall do the will of God, the same is my brother, and sister, and mother.

258 THE GOSPEL PROBLEMS AND THEIR SOLUTION

The foregoing portions exhibit in a most interesting way several of the features which characterise the Synoptic Gospels.

The few sentences which form the narrative parts differ so greatly as to prove that they were written by three different persons. Mark alone mentions our Lord's entrance into a house and the gathering of the multitude. He is silent respecting the healing of the possessed man, which both Matthew and Luke relate, but in very dissimilar terms. Luke says that the man was dumb; Matthew that he was both blind and dumb. With reference to the slanderous report that was circulated respecting Christ, Matthew attributes it to the Pharisees; Luke simply says "some of them said"; while Mark, with the strict accuracy as to fact which is characteristic of the observant Peter, states that it was "the scribes which came down from Jerusalem" who set the slander afloat.

And yet there is such a manifest similarity in the ensemble of the three portions as proves that they were all in some way moulded by a common influence.

In Luke's report we see a result of the confusion in James' manuscripts with which the redactor had to contend. One passage (viii. 19-21—54 Greek words) is located in a different connection altogether. That it really belongs to the connection in which we have placed it above, is proved by the fact that the parallel passages in Matthew and Mark are so arranged. For it must be admitted that, in a matter of this kind, wherever two Gospels agree their testimony must be final as against the third. Within chapter xi. itself also, three verses (24 – 26, — 56 Greek words) are transposed. The transposition of verse 31 (31 Greek words) with verse 32 (24 Greek words) seems less consistent with our theory. But we cannot tell what accidental circumstances may have shortened the contents of a page. In these instances we have not the double evidence of Matthew and Mark to prove that Luke's order is wrong; but, as Matthew's order is confirmed by Mark in the case first mentioned, it is fair to infer that it is right in these cases also.

The spoken words of Christ in Matthew and Luke differ from one another rather more than is usual with reports taken at the moment of utterance. Though essentially alike, each report contains words, phrases and even sentences which are absent from the other. One section (33–37) in Matthew is entirely wanting in Luke. Nevertheless, there should be little doubt that the utterances were taken down by Matthew and James as they were spoken.

At first sight it looks as if Mark's is not a tautochronistic report; but one made from memory very soon after our Lord spoke. Peter certainly had a good memory, and we know from other examples that he and some of the other Apostles were able to recall spoken words with great accuracy. It seems on closer examination, however, more probable that like the others, it was written while Jesus was speaking. If so, it is the first tautochronistic report that Peter made, and its meagre and fragmentary character may be owing to his want of experience in that kind of work. Even he however secured some words and phrases which both the others missed.

It may be that our Lord on this occasion, stung by the infamous accusation which had been made against Him, spoke warmly and more rapidly than usual, and that for this reason, neither of the writers was quite able to keep pace with Him. Possibly however they may purposely have condensed His utterances to some extent. In public speaking a certain diffuseness is often necessary to enable an audience, always more or less inattentive, to grasp the ideas which the speaker desires to convey. Our Lord was a perfect Master of oratory, and if there were in some of His speeches, and not in others, a certain amount of redundancy and repetition, it only shows how well He knew how to adjust His deliverances to the capacity and mood of His hearers. On the other hand the omission of such superfluous words in the written record, is a proof of the ability and good sense of the reporters.

260 THE GOSPEL PROBLEMS AND THEIR SOLUTION

The conclusion to which these observations leads us is, that the reported utterances of Jesus were taken down respectively by Matthew, Peter and James as He spake, and that the narrative parts were written, probably in the evening of the same day, by the same men, in conference with the rest of the Apostles.

It may here be noticed that Luke mentions the request for a sign at the beginning of his report (verse 16), whereas Matthew records it immediately before our Lord's reference to it (verse 38). This seems to have been a frequent demand of the Pharisees and scribes (Matt. xvi. 1, John vi. 30, 1 Cor. i. 22), and was doubtless repeated several times during the course of what is here related.

The final words of Jesus (Matt. xii. 49, 50; Mark iii. 34, 35; Luke viii. 21) were probably not written at the moment but from memory when the rest of the portions were completed.

In this connection a difficulty appears for which I am unable to offer any solution. In Matthew ix. 32–34 there is an account of the healing of a dumb possessed man, that agrees so exactly with that above referred to in Luke xi. 14, 15, that it is impossible to doubt that the two passages were written in concert and relate to the same incident. If, in choosing a parallel for Luke xi. 14, 15, we had nothing outside the passages themselves to guide us, we should certainly select Matthew ix. 32–34 in preference to Matthew xii. 22–24, which appears in the example above.

MATT. ix. 32-34	MATT. xii. 22-24	LUKE xi. 14, 15
And as they went forth, behold, there was brought to him a dumb man possessed with a devil. And when the devil was cast out, the dumb man spake: and the multitudes marvelled, saying,	Then was brought unto him one possessed with a devil, blind and dumb: and he healed him, insomuch that the dumb man spake and saw. And all the multitudes were amazed, and said, Is this the	And he was casting out a devil *which was* dumb. And it came to pass, when the devil was gone out, the dumb man spake; and the multitudes marvelled. But some of them said, By Beelzebub the prince

It was never so seen in Israel. But the Pharisees said, By the prince of the devils casteth he out devils.	son of David? But when the Pharisees heard it, they said, This man doth not cast out devils, but by Beelzebub the prince of the devils.	of the devils casteth he out devils.

But then the succeeding portion in Matthew xii. agrees so closely with Luke that we are obliged to admit the parallel here also. However the matter is to be explained, it is difficult to avoid the conviction that both the passages in Matthew, as well as that in Luke, refer to one and the same incident.

THE DISCIPLES EXHORTED TO BOLDNESS

Matt. x. 24-33; *Luke* xii. 1-12

I locate the above portions here because I cannot find any other equally suitable place. These utterances may very well have been spoken in continuation of those we have just been considering.

THE PARABLE OF THE SOWER AND MANY OTHER PARABLES

Matt. xiii. 1-52; *Mark* iv. 1-35; *Luke* viii. 4-18; xiii. 18-21

It would seem that our Lord delivered the parable of the Sower, of the Tares, and some others to the multitude, from a boat on the sea of Tiberias, on the morning of the day the proceedings of which are related in the above portions. In the middle of the day He retired to a house for rest and refreshment, and while there the disciples asked and obtained from Him an explanation of the parables of the Sower and the Tares. After some further time, during which some of the disciples were engaged in writing, they again went down to the beach, and Jesus, re-entering the boat, continued for a short while His address to the people. He then with His disciples set sail for the opposite side of the lake.

These portions are interesting as affording an illustration of three sorts of reporting.

First, there is narrative reporting: that is to say the statement of fact as observed by different men and recorded by different writers.

Next, there is tautochronistic reporting: the report of our Lord's utterances made at the very moment He was speaking.

Lastly, there is memory reporting: the report of our Lord's utterances, not written down at the moment, but recorded from memory immediately or very soon after.

It is probable that, while Jesus was addressing the people from the boat, Matthew, Peter and James were sitting in a boat also, either the same one or another moored near it, writing down His utterances.

The memory reports were written probably in the house immediately after the private conversation between Jesus and the disciples which followed their mid-day meal.

The narrative portions up to that point may have been written at the same time, or they may have been added later, after their return from the trip across the lake.

To enable us to form a clearer idea of the manner in which the Apostles performed their literary work, let us compare at length a section of each of the above portions, namely the parts that contain the parable of the Sower and its interpretation.

MATTHEW'S ACCOUNT.	PETER'S ACCOUNT.	JAMES' ACCOUNT.
Matt. xiii.	Mark iv.	Luke viii.
On that day went Jesus out of the house, and sat by the sea side. And there were gathered unto him great multitudes, so that he entered into a boat, and sat; and all the multitude stood on the beach. And he spake to them many things in parables, saying,	And again he began to teach by the sea side. And there is gathered unto him a very great multitude, so that he entered into a boat, and sat in the sea; and all the multitude were by the sea on the land. And he taught them many things in parables, and said unto them in his teaching:	And when a great multitude came together, and they of every city resorted unto him, he spake by a parable:

It is evident that these three passages were separately written, and yet there are expressions in all three to suggest that they were governed by some common influence. The first two, especially, show much similarity; but the fact of a great multitude being gathered is mentioned by all, and the word "parables" or "parable" is found near the end of each. All the passages in fact reflect the conversation that was going on amongst the assembled Apostles at the time they were being written. Still there is in them nothing like the similarity we shall now see in the reports that were made of Christ's own utterances at the moment of His speaking.

Behold, the sower went forth to sow; and as he sowed, some (seeds) fell by the wayside	Hearken, Behold, the sower went forth to sow; and it came to pass, as he sowed, some (seed) fell by the wayside	The sower went forth to sow his seed ; and as he sowed, some (seed) fell by the wayside; and it was trodden under foot,
and the birds came and devoured them. And others fell upon the rocky places, where they had not much earth: and straightway they sprang up, because they had no deepness of earth; and when the sun was risen they were scorched; and, because they had no root, they withered away. And others fell upon the thorns; and the thorns grew up, and choked them. And others fell upon the good	and the birds came and devoured it. And other fell on the rocky (ground); where it had not much earth; and straightway it sprang up, because it had no deepness of earth; and when the sun was risen it was scorched; and because it had no root, it withered away. And other fell among the thorns; and the thorns grew up, and choked it, and it yielded no fruit. And others fell into the good	and the birds of the heaven devoured it. And other fell on the rock; and as soon as it grew it withered away, because it had no moisture. And other fell amidst the thorns; and the thorns grew with it, and choked it. And other fell into the good

ground,	ground,	ground, and grew
and yielded	and yielded	and brought forth
fruit,	fruit, growing up	fruit.
	and increasing;	
	and brought forth,	
some a hundred fold,	thirty fold, and sixty	a hundred fold.
some sixty, some	fold, and a hundred	
thirty. He that hath	fold. Who hath	He that hath
ears, let	ears to hear, let	ears to hear, let
him hear.	him hear.	him hear.

In the foregoing reports the harmony is very close. The few slight variations may be accounted for (1) by the omission by each of the reporters of a word or phrase here and there; and (2) by changes made by independent translators from the Aramaic originals into Greek. Samples of the first will strike the reader's eye in the various blank spaces above. As an instance of the second, note that Matthew, following doubtless the original Aramaic, translates the pronouns which stand for 'seeds' in the plural (ἅ; ἄλλα); while Mark and Luke render them, more classically, in the singular (ὅ; ἄλλο—ἕτερον). In this respect however, Mark is not quite consistent, for in verse 8 he falls back into the plural (ἄλλα) in conformity with the manuscript before him.

The diversities in these reports are just such as might be expected in reports, which were intended to be verbatim, made separately by three individuals, and which have since severally passed through the hands of three distinct translators. It is scarcely possible to conceive of any other way by which such close correspondence together with such occasional diversity could have arisen.

In the narrative parts there is no such close correspondence, because these are the several work of the writers themselves. As illustrating this, observe the different ways in which the three present the final sentence of the discourse: "He that hath ears, let him hear." Doubtless our Lord paused for a moment before speaking these words, and uttered them in a louder tone and in an impressive manner. In Matthew there is no indication of this: the words follow immediately on to the parable. In Mark they are preceded by the expression, "And he said" (καὶ ἔλεγεν); and in Luke by, "As he said these things, he cried" (ταῦτα λέγων ἐφώνει).

Again, compare the terms in which they describe the application of the Twelve for an explanation of the parable :

| And the disciples came, and said unto him, Why speakest thou unto them in parables? And he answered and said unto them, | And when he was alone, they that were with him with the twelve asked of him the parables. And he said unto them, | And his disciples asked him what this parable might be. And he said, |

A statement of fact could hardly be so concisely expressed by three persons in more diverse terms.

Although the interpretation of the parable of the Sower ollows the parable itself in all three Gospels, it is most likely that the parable of the Tares and some of the other parables recorded in Matthew were spoken in the interval. After reporting the parable of the Sower, Peter and James left off writing; perhaps because they were tired and desirous of listening for their own edification. It may be inferred that towards noon our Lord closed His discourse and the crowd dispersed to their homes for lunch. Jesus, with the Twelve and some others, entered a house at Capernaum for the same purpose. After their repast they asked Him why He spake in parables and what the parables meant, and He thereupon expounded to them the parables of the Sower and the Tares, and added several other short parables for their own instruction. They did not at the moment make any report of this conversation, but, after Jesus had finished speaking and retired from their midst, talking among themselves they felt the need of keeping a record of the interpretation which He had given them of the parables, without which indeed the reports of the parables themselves would be incomplete.

Thereupon one and another proceeded to rehearse what our

Lord had just before said, while Matthew, Peter and James wrote, partly from their own recollection and partly by the aid thus afforded by the rest, the report of Christ's recent communication. Their three reports of the explanation of the parable of the sower are presented on pages 267 and 268.

Matthew's report contains a quotation, with which he was no doubt familiar, from the book of Isaiah, and two or three other sentences, which are not included in the others. But as regards the rest of the reports the intrinsic resemblance in the three is sufficiently great to prove that some of the disciples had very faithful memories. Nevertheless the verbal variation is considerable enough to show, by contrast, that in the case of the parable itself, as well as in other cases where the wording for the most part exactly coincides, the reports could not have been like these written from memory.

One clause in Matthew's report (verse 12) is given before the interpretation of the parable but comes after it in the reports of the others. This is one of those proverbial sayings which Christ seems to have been accustomed to use, for we find it again in Matthew xxv. 29 and its parallel, Luke xix. 26.

As Matthew alone had reported the parable of the Tares, he only recorded the interpretation.

Luke xiii. 18–21 is parallel with Matthew xiii. 31–33. The former consists of 64 Greek words, and probably filled a page which was misplaced by Luke. The passage in Matthew consists of 73 Greek words.

THE HESITATING DISCIPLES

Matt. viii. 18–22; *Luke* ix. 57–62

In these passages Matthew relates two, and Luke three instances of disciples who expressed a wish or were called upon to follow Jesus but hesitated to make the sacrifice that would result from their doing so. It is evident that the two instances in Matthew are identical with the similar two in Luke. Both accounts were written at the same time by Matthew and James, in the company of the other disciples,

| Unto you it is given to know the mysteries of the kingdom of heaven, but to them it is not given. For whosoever hath, to him shall be given, and he shall have abundance: but whosoever hath not, from him shall be taken away even that which he hath. Therefore speak I to them in parables; because seeing they see not, and hearing they hear not, neither do they understand. And unto them is fulfilled the prophecy of Isaiah, which saith, | Unto you is given the mystery of the kingdom of God: but unto them that are without, all things are done in parables: that seeing they may see, and not perceive; and hearing they may hear, and not understand; lest haply they should turn again, and it should be forgiven them. And he saith unto them, Know ye not this parable? and how shall ye know all the parables? | Unto you it is given to know the mysteries of the kingdom of God: but to the rest in parables; that seeing they may not see, and hearing they may not understand. |

By hearing ye shall hear, and shall
    in no wise understand;
And seeing ye shall see, and shall
    in no wise perceive:
For this people's heart is waxed
    gross,
And their ears are dull of hearing,
And their eyes they have closed;
Lest haply they should perceive
    with their eyes,
And hear with their ears,
And understand with their heart,
And should turn again,
And I should heal them.

But blessed are your eyes, for they see; and your ears, for they hear.

For verily I say unto you, that many prophets and righteous men desired to see the things which ye see, and saw them not; and to hear the things which ye hear, and heard them not.

Hear then ye the parable of the sower. When any one heareth the word of the kingdom, and understandeth it not, *then* cometh the evil one, and snatcheth away that which hath been sown in his heart. This is he that was sown by the way side. And he that was sown upon the rocky places, this is he that heareth the word, and straightway with joy receiveth it; yet hath he not root in himself, but endureth for a while; and when tribulation or persecution ariseth because of the word, straightway he stumbleth. And he that was sown among the thorns, this is he that heareth the word; and the care of the world, and the deceitfulness of riches, choke the word, and he becometh unfruitful. And he that was sown upon the good ground, this is he that heareth the word, and understandeth it; who verily beareth fruit, and bringeth forth, some a hundredfold, some sixty, some thirty.

The sower soweth the word. And these are they by the way side, where the word is sown; and when they have heard, straightway cometh Satan, and taketh away the word which hath been sown in them. And these in like manner are they that are sown upon the rocky *places*, who, when they have heard the word, straightway receive it with joy; and they have no root in themselves, but endure for a while; then, when tribulation or persecution ariseth because of the word, straightway they stumble. And others are they; these are they that have heard the word, and the cares of the world, and the lusts of other things entering in, choke the word, and it becometh unfruitful. And those are they that were sown upon the good ground; such as hear the word, and accept it, and bear fruit, thirtyfold, and sixtyfold, and a hundredfold.

Now the parable is this: The seed is the word of God. And those by the way side are they that have heard; then cometh the devil, and taketh away the word from their heart, that they may not believe and be saved. And those on the rock *are* they which, when they have heard, receive the word with joy; and these have no root, which for a while believe, and in time of temptation fall away. And that which fell among the thorns, these are they that have heard, and as they go on their way they are choked with cares and riches and pleasures of *this* life, and bring no fruit to perfection. And that in the good ground, these are such as in an honest and good heart, having heard the word, hold it fast, and bring forth fruit with patience.

amongst whom the facts were rehearsed by those who had observed the incidents.

It seems unlikely that two, and still more unlikely that three incidents, bearing as these do a certain likeness one to another, should have happened on the same day. It is more probable that they happened at different times during this period of our Lord's growing popularity in Galilee. As the writers were engaged, in the company of the other Apostles, recording the first related of these incidents soon after it occurred, the other two would naturally recur to the memory of some present, and, at their dictation, Matthew recorded one and James both of them also.

CROSSING THE SEA AND CALMING THE STORM

Matt. viii. 23–27 ; *Mark* iv. 36–41 ; *Luke* viii. 22–25

(See page 270.)

These three accounts agree exactly as to the facts, and yet no two of them are told in similar terms. From beginning almost to end the wording of each differs from that of the others, including even the few sentences spoken by our Lord. They are beautiful specimens of nearly independent narration, and may serve to give an idea of how little resemblance there would be to one another in the entire histories, if the different narrators had written from memory alone and without conferring together. In this case there was little need for conference. Every detail was vividly impressed on each man's mind, and each could write his own story.

And yet even here we are sensible of a certain kinship in the structure of the stories; and, by the closing sentence describing the effect of the miracle on the disciples and recording their expression of surprise, we learn to a certainty that the three narratives were written in company and not quite in silence.

And when he was entered into a boat, his disciples followed him. And behold, there arose a great tempest in the sea, insomuch that the boat was covered with the waves: but he was asleep. And they came to him, and awoke him, saying, Save, Lord; we perish. And he saith unto them, Why are ye fearful, O ye of little faith? Then he arose, and rebuked the winds and the sea; and there was a great calm. And the men marvelled, saying, What manner of man is this, that even the winds and the sea obey him?

And leaving the multitude, they take him with them, even as he was, in the boat. And other boats were with him. And there ariseth a great storm of wind, and the waves beat into the boat, insomuch that the boat was now filling. And he himself was in the stern, asleep on the cushion: and they awake him, and say unto him, Master, carest thou not that we perish? And he awoke, and rebuked the wind, and said unto the sea, Peace, be still. And the wind ceased, and there was a great calm. And he said unto them, Why are ye fearful? have ye not yet faith? And they feared exceedingly, and said one to another, Who then is this, that even the wind and the sea obey him?

Now it came to pass on one of those days, that he entered into a boat, himself and his disciples; and he said unto them, Let us go over unto the other side of the lake: and they launched forth. But as they sailed he fell asleep: and there came down a storm of wind on the lake; and they were filling *with water*, and were in jeopardy. And they came to him, and awoke him, saying, Master, master, we perish. And he awoke, and rebuked the wind and the raging of the water: and they ceased, and there was a calm. And he said unto them, Where is your faith? And being afraid they marvelled, saying one to another, Who then is this, that he commandeth even the winds and the water, and they obey him?

CASTING OUT OF DEVILS AND DESTRUCTION OF SWINE

Matt. viii. 28–ix. 1; *Mark* v. 1–20; *Luke* viii. 26–39

When Matthew, Peter and James had finished writing the story of the tempest, they proceeded to write an account of the exciting event that had happened on their arrival at Gergesa. But now the conversation was general and the three writers wove in, with their own recollection of the facts, details recounted by the others, each of whom in different words dwelt on some phase of the incident. The narratives which have resulted are most remarkable. Read the three accounts one after the other, and, with one exception, they seem to be almost exactly alike. But analyse and compare them, sentence by sentence and word by word, and they present all through most striking diversities—not in fact but in diction.

The difference in fact alluded to above is of course the statement of Matthew that there were two demoniacs whereas Mark and Luke mention only one. Doubtless there were two, but one of them played a subordinate part and left all the talking to the other. Hence he attracted little attention. But Matthew's love of accuracy led him to mention both. In like manner, on a later occasion, it is Matthew who tells us that there were two blind men to whom Jesus gave sight at Jericho, the other Synoptics mentioning only one.

The concluding statement in Mark (18–20) and Luke (38, 39) which is wanting in Matthew, was probably not written at the same time as the rest of the story but added later when the report of the man's subsequent proceedings and their effects reached the disciples.

RAISING OF DAUGHTER OF JAIRUS AND HEALING OF WOMAN

Matt. ix. 18–26; *Mark* v. 21–43; *Luke* viii. 40–56

According to Mark, confirmed by Luke, the raising to life of the daughter of Jairus, and the healing of a woman, took place immediately after the return from Gergesa. Although this does not agree with the sequence in Matthew, it must be accepted as correct, and the introductory clause in the last-named (verse 18), "While he spake these things unto them," must be regarded as a mere editorial link.

In these accounts there is not the least diversity as to matters of fact. They were all written by eye-witnesses, except that Matthew was not permitted to be present at the final scene—the actual raising of the maiden—and accordingly his story is at that point very brief. Peter's account in Mark is all through much fuller than the others. In the Greek, Matthew's story consists of 249 words; Luke's of 288 words; Mark's of 352 words. The diction differs greatly, showing that each writer depended largely upon his own memory. And yet there is sufficient similarity in the general structure of the three accounts, and in occasional sentences and expressions, to prove that they were all written at one time and under some common influence. It is impossible to conceive of any adequate cause for the features of the narratives in question, except that the narrators were themselves personally acquainted with the facts, that they recorded them soon after they happened, and that they did so in conference with one another, and with others who had also observed more or less of what took place.

The statement that the fame of the miracle went forth into all that land is peculiar to Matthew (verse 26) and must have been added later—probably at the same time that Peter and James added the somewhat similar statement to their accounts of the last preceding miracle.

HEALING OF TWO BLIND MEN AND DUMB MAN POSSESSED WITH DEVIL

Matt. ix. 27–34

The healing of these blind men is related only by Matthew, and the account of the healing of the dumb possessed man is also peculiar to him unless as already suggested it is to be identified with Luke xi. 14, 15.

REJECTION BY MEN OF NAZARETH

Matt. xiii. 53–58; Mark vi. 1–6a; Luke iv 16–30

And it came to pass, when Jesus had finished these parables, he departed thence. And coming into his own country he taught them in their synagogue, insomuch that they were astonished, and said, Whence hath this man this wisdom, and these mighty works? Is not this the carpenter's son? is not his mother called Mary? and his brethren, James, and Joseph, and Simon, and Judas? And his sisters, are they not all with us? Whence then hath this man all these things? And they were offended in him. But Jesus said unto them, A prophet is not without honour, save in his own country, and in his own house. And he did not many mighty works there because of their unbelief.

And he went out from thence; and he cometh into his own country; and his disciples follow him. And when the sabbath was come, he began to teach in the synagogue: and many hearing him were astonished, saying, Whence hath this man these things? and, What is the wisdom that is given unto this man, and *what mean* such mighty works wrought by his hands? Is not this the carpenter, the son of Mary, and brother of James, and Joses, and Judas, and Simon? and are not his sisters here with us? And they were offended in him. And Jesus said unto them, A prophet is not without honour, save in his own country, and among his own kin, and in his own house. And he could there do no mighty work, save that he laid his hands upon a few sick folk, and healed them. And he marvelled because of their unbelief.

And he came to Nazareth, where he had been brought up; and he entered, as his custom was, into the synagogue on the sabbath day, and stood up to read. And there was delivered unto him the book of the prophet Isaiah. And he opened the book, and found the place where it was written,

The Spirit of the Lord is upon me,
Because he anointed me to preach good tidings to the poor:
He hath sent me to proclaim release to the captives,
And recovering of sight to the blind,
To set at liberty them that are bruised,
To proclaim the acceptable year of the Lord.

And he closed the book, and gave it back to the attendant, and sat down: and the eyes of all in the synagogue were fastened on him. And he began to say unto them, To-day hath this scripture been fulfilled in your ears. And all bare him witness, and wondered at the words of grace which proceeded out of his mouth: and they said, Is not this Joseph's son? And he said unto them, Doubtless ye will say unto me this parable, Physician, heal thyself: whatsoever we have heard done at Capernaum, do also here in thine own country. And he said, Verily I say unto you, No prophet is acceptable in his own country. But of a truth I say unto you, There were many widows in Israel in the days of Elijah, when the heaven was shut up three years and six months, when there came a great famine over all the land; and unto none of them was Elijah sent, but only to Zarephath, in the land of Sidon, unto a woman that was a widow. And there were many lepers in Israel in the time of Elisha the prophet; and none of them was cleansed, but only Naaman the Syrian. And they were all filled with wrath in the synagogue, as they heard these things; and they rose up, and cast him forth out of the city, and led him unto the brow of the hill whereon their city was built, that they might throw him down headlong. But he passing through the midst of them went his way.

The question has been much discussed, whether the rejection of our Lord at Nazareth related by Luke is identical with that recorded in Matthew and Mark. In other words: Did He visit Nazareth twice or only once?

It seems to me that the probabilities are decidedly in favour of a single visit.

No inference to the contrary can be drawn from the early position which Luke's account occupies in that Gospel. We have seen that, except as regards a few leading events, the third Gospel is not arranged in any sort of chronological order; for the simple reason that Luke had no means of fixing the dates or sequence of the collection of papers which he arranged and edited. Certainly the portion before us is not placed in its chronological order. It is separated by only two verses from the story of the Temptations; and comes at the beginning of the first Galilean mission. But that the visit did not take place so early as that is proved by verse 23 where a prior work at Capernaum is referred to, a work that had resounded through all the land.

Besides, it is unlikely that, after the strong animosity displayed, and the attempt on the life of Jesus that was made on the occasion described in Luke, He would soon after re-visit Nazareth, and again enter the synagogue and teach.

The main objection to the view of a single visit is the dissimilarity between the accounts in Matthew and Mark and that in Luke. This dissimilarity however may be owing simply to Luke's account being totally independent of the other two. If so, we have here almost the only instance in the Synoptics, prior to the Resurrection, in which more than one Gospel relates the same incident, and in which one of the stories was written entirely apart from the others. The stories in Matthew and Mark were written in conference, as usual, and show the usual features of dependent independence, of general resemblance and individual diversity. They are the separate reports made by Matthew and Peter of the united testimony of the Apostles to the incident. But the story in Luke is a narrative written by James alone, and recording the facts that passed under his own observation.

The truth probably is that, in the tumult described in Luke, most of the disciples had to flee for their lives. They thus became separated, and, while a number of them were soon reunited at Capernaum, 28 miles distant, James did not rejoin the party until all the narratives were written — those of Matthew and Peter in conference, and his own separately.

It appears from Mark and Luke, and may be inferred from Matthew, that our Lord arrived at Nazareth some time during the week. It was while staying in the town prior to the Sabbath that the coldness and indifference were displayed by His old acquaintance which caused Him so much surprise. It was then also that He performed His few mighty works—the healing of a few sick folk—recorded in Matthew and Mark, and alluded to by the people in the synagogue. On the Sabbath He entered the synagogue, but the pressure of the crowd was probably so great that scarcely any of the disciples were able to obtain good places. James however succeeded in getting near his Master and thus was able to report the substance of His sermon. Matthew and Peter, on the other hand, heard more of what was said by the people on the outskirts of the congregation. When the disturbance took place, and the mob led Christ out of the building and conducted Him towards the brow of the hill, James still kept near Him while the others fled. Hence he was able to write the account of the attempt to kill Jesus, while the others, who were always scrupulous to record nothing for which they had not trustworthy evidence, not having seen themselves, nor as yet learned from James, what happened, said nothing about it.

MINISTRY IN GALILEE AND MISSION OF THE TWELVE

Matt. ix. 35–x. 16; x. 34–xi. 1; *Mark* vi. 6^b–13; *Luke* viii. 1–3; ix. 1–6; xii. 49–53

It is impossible to avoid the conviction that Matthew x. includes utterances of Christ that were spoken in a different connection from that in which the Redactor of the Gospel has placed them. The portion 17–23 is certainly out of its original connection, as its parallels, both in Mark and Luke, are found in the address delivered to the disciples, on the Mount of Olives, just before the Passion (Mark xiii. 9–13; Luke xxi. 12–19). This double testimony is conclusive as to the time at which it was spoken and renders its exclusion from this place imperative. Again, the parallel in Luke to 24–33 begins with a statement that hardly seems to fit in with this occasion.

It is possible however that 34–42 with xi. 1 (173 Greek words) may have formed the last three or four pages of Matthew's original account of the sending forth of the Twelve.

The Reports in Matthew and Luke of the directions to the Twelve were taken down by Matthew and James as our Lord spoke. But the narrative portions in these two Gospels, and the whole of Mark's account, appear to have been written after the return of the Twelve. At first sight it might be thought that these narrative parts were written quite independently by different Apostles, while out on their respective journeys, and so separated one from another. But on closer examination it will be seen that there are certain phrases and expressions common to the three which prove them to have been written in company. Thus, it is stated in each that He went about the villages teaching, cities as well as villages being mentioned in Matthew and Luke. Matthew x. 1, Mark vi. 7 and Luke ix. 1 bear too close a resemblance to allow of the supposition that they were quite independently written. It must be remarked, however, that the diversity is very great, so great indeed as completely to exclude the idea that two of them are derived from the third or that they are all variations of one original account.

The portions next following were written about the same time as these, probably at the same sitting.

HEROD HEARS OF JESUS; DEATH OF JOHN THE BAPTIST; RETURN OF THE TWELVE

Matt. xiv. 1-12; *Mark* vi. 14-30; *Luke* ix. 7-10¹

As both Mark and Luke agree in placing these portions immediately after the account of the mission journey of the Twelve, we accept their order as correct. Matthew himself confirms this order in the portion following this.

On the return of the Twelve to Capernaum they found the disciples of John the Baptist who, during their absence, had arrived from Machærus with the news of their master's death. They also learned from Joanna (Luke viii. 3), who had received the information from her husband, Chuza, Herod's steward, that the tetrarch had been much disturbed by the tidings which had reached him concerning the works and fame of Jesus. By the same channel they learned, what Josephus at a later date was unable to learn, the exact circumstances which led Herod to slay John.

Matthew, Peter and James thereupon took the first opportunity to write down the substance of the guilty ruler's comments concerning Christ. Matthew and Peter added to this an account of the circumstances under which the forerunner finished his course. James had some time before noted the fact of John's imprisonment and its cause: he makes no allusion to it now, nor does he make any mention of his death other than the fact of Herod's reference thereto.

It should be noted that Matthew and Peter are careful not to mention the names of their informants, Chuza and Joanna, doubtless for fear of compromising them.

On the other hand Peter and James, not Matthew, record the return of the Twelve and their making a report to our Lord of their proceedings while away on their missionary tour.

CROSSING LAKE TIBERIAS AND FEEDING THE FIVE
THOUSAND

Matt. xiv. 13-21; *Mark* vi. 31-44; *Luke* ix. 10^b-17; *John* vi. 1-13

RECROSSING THE LAKE, WALKING ON THE SEA, AND
WORKS AT GENNESARET

Matt. xiv. 22-36; *Mark* vi. 45-56; *John* vi. 14-21

DISCOURSE IN CAPERNAUM

John vi. 22-71

For a period of something like twelve months John has taken no share in the task of reporting the sayings and doings of Christ. During all this time our Lord's teachings and work have been carried on in Galilee. If any visits have been made to Jerusalem no record thereof has been kept. In Galilee His labours have been chiefly among the rural population, whose ordinary speech is Aramaic. It is true that scribes and Pharisees from Jerusalem, despatched by the Sanhedrin, have dogged His steps. But He has not concerned Himself much about them; having addressed His words rather to the more simple-minded people of the country. Therefore, Aramaic has been the language used during all this time. Three of the disciples write quickly in Aramaic, and there has been no need for John's assistance, even if it were not the case that he is able to write fast only in Greek. But now we shall see that, although they are still in Galilee, John for once takes part in the work of reporting; and it will behove us to scrutinise the narratives with care, and discover, if possible, why he thus departs from his usual custom; why he relates incidents which his colleagues relate also, and why he reports this, the only Galilean discourse contained in his Gospel.

There can be no denying that the recital by John of the facts and discourse recorded in his sixth chapter is the most difficult question with which we have to deal. At first sight it seems incompatible with our theory. It is however certainly incompatible with any other theory, and it at any rate proves that the Evangelists were not governed by mere local considerations in the choice of materials for their works. Finally, on close investigation it will be found fully to harmonise with and confirm the principles we maintain.

The feeding of the five thousand, and the walking on the sea, are the only miracles which John relates in common with the other Evangelists. It is an obvious remark, and one that has often been made, that his purpose in relating these is to introduce the discussion which occupies the latter part of the chapter, and to make its allusions clear to the reader. The insertion of these introductory incidents is a proof of the accuracy of the report of our Lord's discourse. If John were in the habit of taking liberties with Christ's addresses, he might easily, by one or two slight alterations, have made the introductory part unnecessary, and yet left the essential teaching of the discourse intact. But John was far too reverent of his Master's sayings to omit or alter a single word as written in his original manuscript.

The narrative part of this chapter, though in no point contradictory to or inconsistent with the Synoptics, yet differs so much from them in detail as to prove it to be an independent story. No allusion is made to any other account and it is hardly conceivable that the author had the other narratives before him at the time of writing. This however is a very different thing from saying that the Evangelist had not seen the Synoptic narratives when he prepared the book for publication. This he may have done, but if so he was too conscientious to try to harmonise the original written records which he embodied in his work with other accounts; nor did he deem it needful to offer any explanation of seeming disagreement.

It is said by John that the Passover, the feast of the Jews, was nigh. The bearing of this on the story is not at once apparent. Père Didon, following Godet, finely remarks that our Lord, being debarred from attending the Passover at Jerusalem, provided His own feast in the wilderness; but it is certain that John had no such idea as this in his mind when he wrote. From his use of the word 'therefore' in the next verse, it is evident that John makes the statement to account for the great concourse of people who gathered themselves to Jesus in a desert place. We shall see presently that the nearness of the Passover explains not only the largeness of the congregation, but the presence of women and children as mentioned by Matthew, and some other things besides.

But if John had been writing this narrative years after in another country he would have explained more fully. The lucidity of John's style of composition cannot be surpassed, and he would not have left the matter thus obscure were it not that, writing at the time in Palestine, among people who knew well the topography of the country, and the customs of the nation, it never occurred to him that the reader would find any difficulty in understanding what he meant.

After the return of the Twelve from the mission recorded in the Synoptic Gospels they had a busy time. Immense crowds of people gathered round Jesus and His disciples. They were not the ordinary Galilean multitude. Capernaum was situated on the high road to Jerusalem from the countries north of Palestine, and numerous bands of pilgrims were passing through the town on their way to the Passover. These were naturally desirous of learning all they could about the new Prophet, whose fame may have reached them in their own lands, and about whom, since they entered Galilee, they had heard most amazing reports. Finding that He was at Capernaum, they lingered on their journey, and crowded round the place where He was, in the hope of seeing and hearing Him. They may all have succeeded in obtaining at least a glimpse of Jesus ; but their numbers were so great that it was impossible for them all to get near enough to Him to hear much of His very words ; consequently many gathered round the Apostles to learn from them who and what manner of Man He was. The Twelve had not a moment's rest, for, as fast as some pilgrims left to continue their journey, others arrived and took their places. " There were many coming and going and they had no leisure so much as to eat" (Mark vi. 31). Of course under such circumstances the disciples could take no notes of any of our Lord's utterances or even of His works, and the narratives therefore are silent with reference thereto.

Seeing how fatigued they all were, Jesus, early one morning, proposed to the Apostles to come apart into a desert place, and rest awhile. Accordingly they walked down to the lake, and embarked in one of the fishermen's boats. But the people saw them going, and 'many knew them' (Mark vi. 33). If all the people had been Galileans they would all have known them ; but the majority being strangers these only learned from others who the boating party were.

Perhaps our Lord had intended in the first instance to cross over to the eastern side of the sea where they might be free from the intrusion of any large assembly. But the wind may have been adverse. At any rate the boatmen steered in a north-easterly direction, towards Bethsaida-Julias, two miles past the place where the Jordan enters the sea of Tiberias in the north.

The men on the shore, seeing whither they were bound, 'ran there together on foot from all the cities and outwent them.' The distance they had to travel was some six or eight miles. Part of this was along the main northern road already alluded to, and which skirted the sea on the north-west. As they hurried on they encountered successive bands of pilgrims moving in the opposite direction, many of whom, learning that there was now a chance of seeing and hearing the great Jesus of Nazareth, turned back and went with the stream, which thus kept increasing in volume as it proceeded.

When Jesus and His companions arrived at their destination, some of those who had started by land at the time they embarked were already approaching the landing place; and, by the time they reached the mountain, a good number surrounded them (Mark vi. 33, 34). But the pilgrims to Jerusalem, encumbered with their luggage, and many of them with their families, could not walk so fast, and it was not until our Lord was seated, with His disciples, on the mountain, that 'lifting up His eyes' He saw a great multitude approaching from the direction of the Jerusalem road (John vi. 5). Thereupon, Jesus asked the question of Philip: "Whence are we to buy bread that these may eat?" (John vi. 5). This was really a serious matter; for the pilgrims, among whom were many women and children, having nearly reached Capernaum, where they expected to obtain all they needed, had not provided themselves with food, and would suffer greatly if, at the close of the day, they had to make a journey of several miles before finding a meal. Later on in the day the disciples themselves became anxious and requested the Master to send the people away that they might go into the villages and country round about and lodge and get victuals (Luke ix. 12). There was nothing absurd in this suggestion. As the time approached for the great feasts, the people dwelling on or near to the roads leading to the Holy City would always lay in a stock of provisions, and prepare to accommodate pilgrims, and by this means add somewhat to their ordinary earnings.

During the day our Lord forgets His weariness, and, having compassion on the multitude, heals their sick and teaches them many things. But the disciples in the morning came away hurriedly for rest, and brought no writing materials with them; therefore no word of His teaching is reported.

At length the five thousand are fed, the disciples embark for their homeward journey, our Lord dismisses the multitude and retires to the mountain to pray. This the disciples learn afterwards from some who have been the last to leave the place. Walking on the water He overtakes the Twelve, and arrives with them at Gennesaret in the early morning. Here He is at once recognised, and sick people from all the district round are brought to Him to be healed. He makes His way to Capernaum, arriving there it may be at night, and the next morning He enters the synagogue.

Thus far we are brought by following, first the united testimony of the four Evangelists, then that of Matthew, Mark and John, and finally that of John only. Luke's narrative terminates with the feeding of the five thousand, and Matthew's and Mark's with the cordial reception of Christ by the people of Gennesaret. It is from John that we learn that He came to Capernaum and there met some of the people whom He had fed in the wilderness a day or two before. It is John also who reports the discussion and discourse that ensued in the synagogue, and concerning which the Synoptics are perfectly silent.

Now comes the question which it is incumbent upon us to answer; Why is it that John and John only reports this discussion and discourse? Our first Special Key requires the reply; Because our Lord and the people on this occasion carried on their conversation in Greek. Have we then reason to apprehend that Greek was used in this instance seeing that at other times our Lord when in Galilee usually spoke in Aramaic? It should be seen that there is very strong reason for coming to this conclusion.

It is by no means unlikely that Greek was the language always used in the Capernaum synagogue. Capernaum was an important town situated on a main highway of commerce. A Roman garrison was stationed there. It is probable that the place of worship in which this discussion took place was the large and handsome building erected by the centurion and of which remains are still extant. In such a place Greek would probably prevail and the Sabbath services be conducted in that tongue.

But even if Aramaic were commonly employed in the synagogue, it is nearly certain that in this instance, which did not occur on a Sabbath, Greek was the language used; simply because the congregation was differently composed than the multitudes who usually attended Christ's ministry in Galilee.

In the first place: We have seen already that the multitudes who were present at the miracle of the loaves and fishes consisted partly of pilgrims on their way to the Feast at Jerusalem. Many of these came from countries outside Palestine and were therefore speakers of Greek. There were probably a good sprinkling of such among those who came to Capernaum seeking for Jesus. For many of the multitude had crossed the lake in ferry boats, which had come over from the western shore, to earn a few denarii by conveying such of the people to the town, as preferred the payment of a fare to a lengthy walk (John vi. 23, 24).

There is also good reason to think that a very prominent part in the discussion was taken by the emissaries from Jerusalem who appear so often about this time (Matt. xv. 1; Mark vii. 1). John designates the persons 'Jews,' who, as the argument proceeded, took the lead in disputing with Christ.

The term Jew is used far more often by John than by either of the other Evangelists, and he uses it in a somewhat different sense. The word had a twofold meaning, just as the word 'Englishman' has a twofold meaning. In foreign countries, every man from the United Kingdom is called an Englishman, although he may really be a native of Scotland, Ireland or Wales. Indeed a native of Canada, South Africa or Australia is so designated if of English parentage. But in Ireland or Scotland the term Englishman is taken to imply that the person spoken of comes from the other side of the Channel or the Tweed. So with the term 'Jew.' In a broader sense, all the faithful descendants of Israel were so named; though they may have been Galileans, or even born in a distant land and separated for generations from the home of their fathers. But in Palestine itself the term was often used in a narrower sense to distinguish those belonging to the province of Judea—the territory of the ancient kingdom of Judah—from the people of Galilee or Perea. It is in this sense that the word always seems to be employed in the fourth Gospel. At any rate it is certainly used in this narrower sense in the first verse of the very next chapter to that we are now considering. "After these things, Jesus walked in Galilee, for He would not walk in Judea, because the Jews sought to kill Him." In the Greek, these words are even more striking than in our translation : οὐ γὰρ ἤθελεν ἐν τῇ Ἰουδαίᾳ περιπατεῖν ὅτι ἐζήτουν αὐτὸν οἱ Ἰουδαῖοι ἀποκτεῖναι, " He would not walk in Judea because the Judeans sought to kill Him." It is worth noting that Dr. Farrar uses the word in the same sense when he says, that Judas was "perhaps the only 'Jew' in the Apostolic band" (*Life of Christ*, p. 118). If it be objected that verse 42 implies a more intimate acquaintance on the part of the speakers with the family connections of Jesus than citizens of Jerusalem are likely to have had, I reply in the words of Alford (*in loco*), "surely the verb (οἴδαμεν) will bear the sense of knowing as matter of fact who they were, and need not be confined to personal knowledge." It may be taken for granted that every one who was interested in our Lord's doings would make enquiry as to Who He was and the names and circumstances of His reputed parents.

Now, although these emissaries from Jerusalem were well able to speak Aramaic, and did so when it suited their purpose, perhaps even in the Galilean dialect, yet Greek was more familiar to them, and in the synagogue at this time, where, it being a week day, probably but few of the townspeople were present, they would certainly prefer it.

Taking all these considerations into account, does it not seem highly probable that the discussion and discourse reported in this sixth chapter of John were spoken in Greek ; and, if so, have we not here a sufficient answer to the question, Why does John and not either of the Synoptics report these utterances?

We assume then that John reported this discourse of Jesus,

together with the interjections of His hearers, verbatim, whilst He was speaking. Afterwards he wrote from memory the preliminary part forming the first twenty-five verses of the chapter thus forming a complete story. He wrote apart and quite independently of the others.

The three Aramaic-writing disciples wrote their reports as usual in conference. These accordingly bear the features of similarity and dissimilarity so frequently observed in the Synoptic records.

OBSERVATION

It has been remarked that Luke's narrative does not proceed beyond the feeding of the five thousand. It gives no account of the return trip to Gennesaret, and it will be seen as we proceed that Luke does not again take up the story of our Lord's life until after His return from His visit to Jerusalem to attend the feast of Tabernacles. There is therefore an interval of half a year or more during which Luke is silent. Possibly James was for some reason not with the other disciples in attendance on Jesus during that time. He may, soon after his return from Bethsaida, have hurried off to Jerusalem to be present at the Passover. Be that as it may, this hiatus in the narrative is one proof among several that the materials of Luke's Gospel were quite distinct from those of which the others were composed.

ENMITY OF THE JEWS

John vii. 1

Knowing that the Jewish leaders were desirous to take His life, our Lord did not go up to Jerusalem to attend this year's Passover. The bitterness of their enmity is shown by their sending scribes and Pharisees to watch Him and to take every opportunity to prejudice the people against Him.

Although John tells us Christ's reason for remaining in Galilee, he gives no further account of His doings or sayings at this time, doubtless because He usually spake in Aramaic.

It will be observed by the narrative in Matthew and Mark

THE NARRATIVES AND THE THEORY 287

which we have next to consider, that Jesus is no longer surrounded or followed by immense crowds of people. The pilgrims to the Passover have now arrived at the Temple, and only the residential population remains. With them the novelty of our Lord's works and teachings is beginning to wear off, and so, although He is never without a large audience, there is not the excitement of earlier days.

ABOUT ABLUTIONS
Matt. xv. 1-20; *Mark* vii. 1-23

It is probable that after the discussion in the Capernaum synagogue the emissaries from Jerusalem hastened back to that city to attend the Passover. They have now returned or else others have taken their places.

They accost our Lord in Aramaic. Had it been to gain instruction themselves that they enquired concerning the disciples' disregard of the tradition of the elders they would have addressed Him in Greek, the language with which they were most familiar. But their purpose was very different. They desired to discredit Jesus through His disciples with the multitude; therefore they spoke in the popular dialect. Our Lord well understood this, and calling the people together He exposed to them the sophistry and shallowness of the rabbinical tradition.

In the passages before us we have Matthew's and Peter's reports of the united testimony of the Apostles to the facts and the words spoken. The words of Christ were apparently not written at the moment of utterance and therefore differ considerably, though not essentially, in the two accounts. To this cause probably is due what at first looks like a transposition of either Matthew iii. 9, or Mark vi. 33.

Mark, when redacting, added some explanatory notes to Peter's manuscript—perhaps by the Apostle's direction. Thus, in verse 2 we find three words inserted ("τοῦτ' ἔστιν ἀνίπτοις"; "that is unwashen"). The whole of verses 3 and 4 are of a similar character. There are also four words in verse 19 ("καθαρίζων πάντα τὰ βρώματα"; "making all meats clean") which the revisers of the English version understand to be, not a part of our Lord's utterance, but a parenthetical remark of the Evangelist pointing out the effect of His teaching. The insertion of these four words by Peter, or by Mark under Peter's instruction, is worthy of special note in view of the lesson which Peter learned through the vision recorded in Acts x.

TOUR THROUGH NORTHERN GALILEE AND PHŒNICIAN BORDER; DETOUR TO THE EAST; AND RETURN BY WAY OF DECAPOLIS AND SEA OF GALILEE

Matt. xv. 21–xvi. 12 ; *Mark* vii. 24–viii. 21

These portions in Matthew and Mark are exactly parallel, the same course of events being narrated in each and in the same order. It is impossible therefore to doubt that they are in some way nearly related one to the other. But although the general resemblance is so great there is in parts a dissimilarity so remarkable as to prove that neither account can by any possibility have been copied from the other and that they cannot both be variations of one original. There is in fact no conceivable way in which they could have originated except that one in which, as we contend, so much of the Synoptic Gospels was written.

Whether these portions were written in sections as the disciples proceeded on the journey, or whether they were written as a whole on its completion, is uncertain; but there should be no doubt that they were written by two different men at the same time, in conference with one another and other disciples whose united testimony to the facts they record.

The Gospels tell us very little of what our Lord said on this tour. He seems to have desired privacy, and though he performed many miracles He probably did little in the way of public speaking. Consequently there was nothing that could very well be tautochronistically reported. Wherever His words are given however they agree very closely in both Gospels, showing what care was exercised in this respect.

Note for instance that both in Matthew and Mark the word translated "dogs" is not κύνες, but the diminutive κυνάρια—tame or domestic dogs. Alford says, " Our Lord, in the use of the familiar diminutive, has expressed, not the uncleanness of the dog so much as his attachment to and dependence on the human family."

The interpretation of the word "ephphatha" (Mark vii. 34, ὅ ἐστιν Διανοίχθητι) is doubtless an editorial addition.

The sections which relate the feeding of the four thousand agree more closely than the other sections of the portions before us. A large part of this section however consists of the quoted words of Jesus and others, and we have repeatedly seen that in such cases the agreement is always very close. Still, in the strictly narrative parts, there is here more similarity in the diction than usual.

The two accounts are subjoined for comparison :—

Matt. xv. 32-39	*Mark* viii. 1-10
	(In those days when there was again a great multitude, and they had nothing to eat)
And Jesus called unto him his disciples, and said,	he called unto him his disciples and saith unto
I have compassion on the multitude, because they continue with me now three days and have nothing to eat : and I would not send them away fasting lest haply they faint in their way.	them, I have compassion on the multitude, because they continue with me now three days and have nothing to eat : and if I send them away fasting to their home, they will faint in the way ; and some of them are come from far.
And the disciples say unto him, Whence should we have so many loaves in a desert place, as to fill so great a multitude? And Jesus saith unto them, How many loaves have ye? And they said, Seven, and a few small	And his disciples answered him, Whence shall one be able to fill these men with bread here in a desert place? And he asked them, How many loaves have ye? And they said, Seven.

U

fishes. And he commanded
the multitude to sit down
on the ground ; and he took
the seven loaves, and the
fishes ; and he gave thanks
and brake, and gave to the
disciples,
and the disciples to the
multitude.

And they did all eat, and
were filled : and they took
up, that which remained
over of the broken pieces,
seven baskets full. And
they that did eat were
four thousand men, beside
women and children. And
he sent away the multitudes,
and entered into the boat

and came into
the borders of Magadan.

And he commandeth
the multitude to sit down
on the ground ; and he took
the seven loaves,
and having given thanks
he brake, and gave to his
disciples, to set before them ;
and they set them before the
multitude. And they had a
few small fishes ; and having
blessed them, he commanded
to set these also before them.
And they did eat, and
were filled : and they took
up, of broken pieces that
remained over,
seven baskets. And
they were about
four thousand.
            And
he sent them away.
And straightway he entered into the
boat
with his disciples, and came into
the parts of Dalmanutha.

It will be seen that, except that a sentence or two is omitted by Matthew, the two accounts, in so far as they report the words of Jesus, are word for word the same.

Omitting the first clause in Mark which may have been written by the redactor the variation in other respects also is very slight. It would seem that in writing their reports both Matthew and Peter followed very closely the recital of one of the Apostolic party among whom the events of the day were rehearsed.

Those parts that refer to the fishes are very curious. Did Peter forget these until reminded by the conversation when he had nearly finished his story ; or was it that Jesus did not bless and break them until after the bread was in course of distribution, and that Peter stated this more exactly ? At any rate I am unable to imagine a way in which this variation of the

account in Mark from that in Matthew could have arisen—
the two being so much alike in other respects—except on the
principle that they are separate reports of united testimony.

It should be observed that on this occasion seven baskets
(σφυρίδας: large travelling baskets) of fragments were collected;
whereas after the feeding of the five thousand twelve baskets
(κοφίνους) were filled. This would seem to imply that only
seven disciples accompanied Jesus on this tour; and it is not
too much to infer that James was one of the absent five, and
that Luke's long silence is thus accounted for. It is worth
noting that during this tour the disciples are never spoken of
as 'the Twelve.'

HEALING OF BLIND MAN AT BETHSAIDA

Mark viii. 22-26

The account of this miracle seems to form a continuation of
and the conclusion to Peter's narrative of our Lord's circuit
in the north. The miracle is not recorded in Matthew. Perhaps on the arrival of Jesus and His disciples at Bethsaida
"the city of Andrew and Peter," Matthew went on and returned
to his own city, Capernaum, while our Lord remained for a
day or two with Peter at Bethsaida.

ATTENDANCE AT THE FEAST OF TABERNACLES

John vii. 2-52

It is now John's turn to continue the history. After His
long absence Jesus is about once more to go up to Jerusalem.
There Greek will be spoken, and the reporting must be done
by the Apostle who has made it his practice to write fast in
that language.

It must be admitted that this portion of John's Gospel was
not completed in its present shape until some time after the
termination of our Lord's ministry. Its final revision may
have been made at any time from a few months after Pentecost
until the redaction of the Gospel many years later; nearer than
this it is impossible to fix the date even approximately. In-

dications of its late revision are found in such sentences as these: "For even his brethren did not believe on him" (vs. 6); "Because his hour was not yet come" (vs. 30); "But this spake he of the Spirit, which they that believed on him were to receive; for the Spirit was not yet given; because Jesus was not yet glorified" (vs. 39). These texts are explanatory notes such as one might expect to find inserted in a narrative that was prepared for publication many years after it was originally written. It is indeed the very office of an editor to make such additions and comments as are needed to render a work more intelligible to its readers. In dealing with any historical book it would be absurd to infer the date of the original materials which compose it from that of editorial additions such as these. In the composition before us there is abundant evidence that the original manuscript which forms its chief part was written at the very time the events occurred, and remains embodied here without essential alteration. The only thing to wonder at is that such later additions are so few.

Preliminary, John vii. 2-9

Although quoted by John, there is no need to suppose that the conversation between our Lord and His brothers was conducted in Greek. These few sentences were not reported at the moment: John heard them spoken, and soon after, perhaps at Jerusalem when writing up his account of what was done at the Feast, he recorded, not the very words, but the sense of what was said. Hence the language in which it was first written need not have been that in which the conversation was spoken. John's object in recording it was to throw light on the circumstances attending this visit to the Temple. It is John's manner, by a short preliminary statement, thus to introduce each new section of his story.

But though this conversation took place in Aramaic and was reported in Greek its sense has been accurately retained. This is proved by the 'undesigned co-incidence' between what our Lord's brothers said to Him, and the course of events just preceding, as we have seen it narrated by Matthew and Mark. " Depart hence and go into Judea, that thy disciples also may behold thy works which thou doest. For no man doeth anything in secret, and himself seeketh to be known openly. If thou doest these things manifest thyself to the world." These words imply that Jesus had been secluding Himself and avoiding publicity; and that, although He had been doing works, His numerous Galilean disciples had not seen them but had known about them only by report. Now we have just learned from the other Gospels that this had been exactly the case for the greater part of six months. He had been on a circuit through Northern Galilee and the coasts of Tyre and Sidon, had crossed the upper Jordan into Gaulanitis, and turning southward had travelled through Gaulanitis to Decapolis; had made two trips in a boat along the lake, and finally had returned by way of Bethsaida to Galilee. The districts He had visited were largely inhabited by heathen, and He had done His best to preserve secrecy : it was only toward the latter part of the tour, that He entirely failed to do so. Then indeed His fame was spread abroad, and great crowds, collected from all parts of the districts through which He passed, gathered around Him. Thereupon He wrought the miracles about which reports soon found their way to Galilee. Now that He had returned His relatives thought the time was come when He ought again to make a more prominent appearance. They demanded, therefore, that He should go up to Jerusalem, there to present His claims to the highest authorities in the land, and at the same time encourage His many Galilean disciples whom He would meet there at the Feast.

This conversation then is accurately reported, and that being so the report must have been written within a reasonably short time after the conversation occurred.

In the Temple, John vii. 10–36

This remarkable composition vividly reflects the circumstances under which it was written. John is trying to report our Lord's utterances as He speaks ; but, in the noise and confusion, he is able only now and then to secure some detached sentences. Sometimes he is separated for a while from his Master, and then he listens to and carries in his mind the opinions expressed by various elements which go to form the crowd. After a while he observes the Chief Priests and the Pharisees instructing officers to apprehend Him; or perhaps he learns from Nicodemus the fact that they have done so. Notwithstanding which he observes that Jesus remains unmolested.

If there were any truth in the idea that John wrote the fourth Gospel from memory, years after the events took place, it would indeed be surprising to find, here in its midst, a piece of work so unlike the rest. The discourses of Christ recorded by John, are pieces of logical and finished composition. They prove the Author, whoever he was, to be a master, not only of Hellenistic Greek, but of the literary art. But this portion is far from being a perfect specimen of literary art. The sentences spoken by our Lord are disconnected, and sometimes seem to have no bearing on anything that was then being said or done. In short the original manuscript remains in all its crudeness and ruggedness, just as it was finished in the evening of the day on which these stirring incidents were witnessed by the writer. The picture it presents is all the more graphic for that very reason.

Could any attempt at description bring the scene in the Temple so clearly before the imagination : the people moving about in curious expectancy asking for Jesus; His unannounced appearance when half the week of the Feast had elapsed, and they had ceased to expect Him ; the Jews' surprise at His superior knowledge ; our Lord's calm dignified boldness; the insolence of His enemies; the timid hesitating attitude of some who were inclined to be His friends; the murmurings and disputings of the multitude concerning Him?

The words spoken by Jesus and perhaps a few other notes must have been taken down by John on the spot and were copied into the paper which he wrote in the evening at his home.

The question asked by the Jews (vs. 35), "Will he go unto the Dispersion among the Greeks and teach the Greeks?" seems to show that our Lord had been seen conversing with foreigners. There were usually during the great feasts a number of Gentiles in the outer court of the Temple, observing the ceremonials which could be seen over the barrier that shut them out from the more elevated courts within. In passing in and out it is not unlikely that Jesus may have been accosted by some of the strangers, desirous as they doubtless were to learn something of Him who was then the general theme of conversation. With that gentle courtesy by which He was always distinguished He would certainly reply, and His kindly bearing and friendly answers to their questions may well have excited attention.

The Last Day of the Feast, 37-52

John tells us nothing of what Christ taught on this last great day of the Feast, except when He stood and cried, saying, " If any man thirst, let him come unto me and drink. He that believeth on me, as the scripture hath said, out of his belly shall flow rivers of living water." Perhaps he was unable in the throng to come near Jesus, and so heard but that one announcement, which, uttered in a loud voice, rang across the spaces of the Temple. Perhaps too the bustle and noise were such serious obstacles to the taking of notes, that, disappointed and dissatisfied with his seeming want of success so far, he made no further attempt to do so while the Feast continued.

That our Lord had much to say on this day, and that He spake with power, is apparent from the officers' excuse to the Sanhedrin for not arresting Him. "Never man so spake."

But John heard the comments of the people; and later on he learned from Nicodemus what passed in the Sanhedrin. Thus he was enabled to supply this account of the closing day of that eventful week.

THE WOMAN BROUGHT BEFORE CHRIST IN THE TEMPLE
John viii. 1-11

In the Revised Version this portion, including the last sentence of vii. 53, is enclosed in brackets. In Westcott and Hort it is omitted here and placed at the end of the Gospel. In some ancient manuscripts it is found at the end of Luke xxi.; in the majority it is omitted altogether; and in those that contain it there is great diversity in the readings. Under these circumstances it hardly comes within the scope of this work to discuss its origin.

DISCOURSES AND MIRACLES IN JERUSALEM
John viii. 12-x. 21

The Feast being now over the visitors to Jerusalem had left; and the Temple was no longer thronged. The usual worshippers residing in the city, together with the chief priests and elders, attended as usual. Our Lord remained some days in the city, and went into the Temple to teach, thus giving the representative men of the nation another opportunity of calmly considering His claims.

In this comparative quiet John had no difficulty in reporting. Jesus spake in Greek, and we have here, as elsewhere in this Gospel, the very words He used taken down at the moment of utterance.

But His stay in Jerusalem does not last long, in a few days more we shall find Him back in Galilee.

JOURNEY THROUGH GAULANITIS AND ITUREA, AND RETURN VIA MOUNT TABOR TO CAPERNAUM
Matt. xvi. 13-xvii. 23; *Mark* viii. 27-ix. 32; *Luke* ix. 18-45

Jesus having now returned to Galilee the task of reporting again falls to the Aramaic-writing disciples. James has rejoined the party, and shares the duty with Matthew and Peter.

Our Lord however does not stay in Galilee. The period is fast approaching when He must leave the world, and He desires to employ a portion of the time remaining in the instruction of His disciples, and in preparing them for the great events impending. So He takes them to the parts of Cæsarea Philippi, in the extreme north of Palestine. He will there escape the persecutions of the scribes and Pharisees, and will not be disturbed by the presence of such large crowds of people.

The time occupied in the tour is probably about three weeks.

With one exception the disciples do not report at the time of speaking any of the addresses delivered during this journey, either to themselves in private, or to the people who in some places gather about Him. (Mark viii. 34; ix. 14.) Most of what is recorded is written from memory, perhaps on their return to Capernaum. The three accounts agree in substance, and exhibit beyond all question the effect of a common governing influence. And yet the phraseology differs so greatly that their independence is equally certain. They have clearly defined all the indications of being separate reports of the united testimony of the Apostles to the facts.

The resemblance is very close between the three reports of the one short address of which notes were taken at the time it was spoken. (Matt. xvi. 24-28; Mark viii. 34-ix. 1; Luke ix. 23-27.)

During the week following the delivery of this address the Lord and His disciples made their way southward through Gaulanitis, and, crossing the Jordan below the Sea of Galilee, arrived at Mount Tabor. This mountain, according to ancient tradition, was the scene of the Transfiguration. The presence of scribes, immediately after the manifestation of Christ's glory, shows that it did not take place at Mount Hermon, as some modern travellers have thought. Besides, the length of time allowed by the narrative will hardly permit of its happening so far from Capernaum.

Although John does not give any account of the Transfiguration in his Gospel, it is perhaps alluded to in the Prologue, when he says, "We beheld his glory." If so, is not this an indication that the Prologue was written at a much later date than the rest of the Book?

It is stated in Matthew and Mark, and the statement is confirmed in Luke, that our Lord directed the three disciples who witnessed His Transfiguration to tell the vision to no man until after the Son of man should have risen again from the dead. But it is highly improbable that this interdict was either intended or understood to apply to the rest of the Twelve. Such a reservation towards them would be altogether out of keeping with that friendly candour and confidence He ever showed towards them. Not long after, when all the Apostles except Judas were present, He said to them, 'All things that I heard from my Father I have made known unto you.'

It may be interesting to compare the closing statements in this fragment of the history, as presented in the three Gospels. Our Lord has been all through the journey preparing His disciples for the disappointment of their temporal hopes, and for the terrible humiliation and death He is soon to undergo. As they are returning and approach Capernaum, He recurs again to the subject, and tries yet more earnestly to impress it on their minds.

Matt. xvii. 22, 23. "And while they abode in Galilee, Jesus said unto them, The Son of man shall be delivered up into the hands of men; and they shall kill him, and the third day he shall be raised up. And they were exceeding sorry."

Mark ix. 30-32. "And they went forth from thence, and passed through Galilee; and he would not that any man should know it. For he taught his disciples and said unto them, The Son of man is delivered up into the hands of men, and they shall kill him; and when he is killed, after three days he shall rise again. But they understood not the saying, and were afraid to ask him."

Luke ix. 43-45. "But while all were marvelling at all the things which he did, he said unto his disciples, Let these words sink into your ears: for the Son of man shall be delivered up into the hands of men. But they understood not this saying, and it was concealed from them, that they should not perceive it: and they were afraid to ask him about this saying."

It will be seen that there is not in either of the three the slightest hint that at the time of writing they had learned the purport of the warning that so perplexed them.

THE TEMPLE TRIBUTE

Matt. xvii. 24-27

This incident is related only by Matthew. Doubtless it occurred in Matthew's presence and was recorded by him immediately after, while Peter was absent on his errand. This explains why, contrary to his usual practice, Matthew does not state the result; it was unknown to him at the moment of writing, though he could not doubt what the result would be.

DISPUTE AMONG DISCIPLES: DISCOURSE

Matt. xviii. 1-35; *Mark* ix. 33-50; *Luke* ix. 46-50

It will be noticed that much fuller reports are given by Matthew of the utterances of Jesus at and near Capernaum than elsewhere. The greater part of Matthew xviii. appears to be a tautochronistic report of an address delivered to the disciples soon after their return from their tour in the north. The reports in Mark and Luke are not tautochronistic; but were written from memory immediately after the address was spoken.

The verbal exactness which is characteristic of Matthew's reports is illustrated in the use of the word 'then' ($ἄρα$) in verse 1, "Who then is greatest in the kingdom of heaven?" It is from Mark that we learn what was referred to. His account begins as follows:—

And they came to Capernaum: and when he was in the house he asked them, What were ye reasoning in the way? But they held their peace: for they had disputed one with another in the way, who *was* the greatest.

And he sat down, and called the twelve ; and he saith unto them, If any man would be first, he shall be last of all, and minister of all.

At this point Matthew begins to take verbatim notes :—

In that hour came the disciples unto Jesus, saying, Who then is greatest in the kingdom of heaven? And he called to him a little child, and set him in the midst of them, and said,

It is obvious that Matthew's retention of the particle can be accounted for only on the theory that he wrote his report when the words were fresh in his memory. Little points like this—insignificant as they may seem, or rather, because of their seeming insignificance—should carry incalculable weight in an argument such as ours.

FINAL DEPARTURE FROM GALILEE

Matt. xix. 1	*Mark* xi¹	*Luke* ix. 51
And it came to pass when Jesus had finished these words, he departed from Galilee, and came into the borders of Judæa beyond Jordan.	And he arose from thence, and cometh into the borders of Judæa and beyond Jordan.	And it came to pass, when the days were well-nigh come that he should be received up, he stedfastly set his face to go to Jerusalem.

Both from the positions they hold in the Gospels, and from the subsequent course of each narrative, it is manifest that the above verses in Matthew and Mark refer to our Lord's last departure from Galilee, previous to His crucifixion. From the wording of the text itself, it is equally manifest that the verse in Luke refers to the same event.

While there is nothing specially striking in the terms in which the fact is stated in Matthew and Mark, we cannot read the verse in Luke without asking the question, How is this to be reconciled with the view maintained in this book, that the materials of which the Gospels are composed were written at the time the events occurred which they narrate? For obviously this could not have been written at the time or immediately after the event it records ; it could not, in fact, have been written until after the ascension of Christ to heaven.

If the parallel text in Matthew or Mark at all resembled this verse in Luke, I confess it would present a difficulty not easily to be overcome; but conversely the absence from these of any similar sign of late composition adds not a little to the strength of our case. The verse in Luke is, in truth, a unique example of a class of passages of which there ought to be a great number in all the Gospels, if the opinion were true that no part of them was written until after the termination of our Lord's ministry. In that case, the late standpoint of the writer would be continually apparent, whereas no late standpoint ever appears in the narrative parts except in this one instance. For the editorial notes and additions which we have so often observed, and shall hereafter observe, in our study of the Gospels, though interspersed through the narratives, never form an essential part of them, and may always be distinguished from them. It is in this one place only that we find a historical fact of our Lord's life recorded in terms that prove themselves to have been written after the termination of His earthly career. That there are not many or any similar texts, is strong negative proof of the truth of our contention that the bulk of the narrative portions of the Gospels was written while the events recorded were in progress.

The terms in which Luke mentions this last removal from Galilee to Judea throws into stronger relief the simplicity of Matthew's and Mark's statements of the same event. Can any one believe that when these were written the writers knew that they were recording an event of surpassing interest, and that the Lord would never return to Galilee again until after His death and resurrection?

The strength of our case is further increased when we come to consider the question: By whom was this verse first written? It is not likely on our hypothesis that it originated with James. There is no indication that he ever made any revision of his manuscripts. After the Ascension he at once took a most prominent part in the affairs of the Church, and from that time until his death he could have had but little leisure for literary

302 THE GOSPEL PROBLEMS AND THEIR SOLUTION

work. Everything goes to show that his papers were handed to Luke in their original imperfect and unarranged condition. The verse then must have been written by Luke. Although Luke is most chary about inserting editorial notes or comments, it is not without precedent for him to supply chronological data, the result of his own personal enquiry. (Luke i. 5; ii. 1, 2; iii. 1, 2; iii. 23.) He alone of the New Testament writers seems to have had some faint idea of the usefulness of dates. When redacting the Gospel therefore, he appears in these few instances to have taken some trouble to furnish indications of time.

Now, when we examine the verse itself we find strong internal evidence that it was not written by the original author of the notes of which the third Gospel was composed. But we do find that it bears a very striking resemblance to the style of Luke.

No expression similar to the phrase 'when the days were well-nigh come' (ἐν τῷ συμπληροῦσθαι τὰς ἡμέρας) is to be found elsewhere in Luke or in any of the Gospels. But in Acts ii. 1 there is an almost identical phrase (ἐν τῷ συμπληροῦσθαι τὴν ἡμέραν) rendered in the Revised Version 'When the day (of Pentecost) was now come.' The verb (συμπληρόω) is used in but one other place in the New Testament, namely Luke viii. 23.

Again the noun, ἀνάληψις, is found in this place only, and the verb from which it is derived, ἀναλαμβάνω, is nowhere used in the Gospels except in the added portion of Mark (xvi. 19). It is used however in a very similar connection in Acts i. 2, ἧς ἡμέρας ἀνελήφθη 'the day in which he was received up,' and is used again in Acts i. 11.

Lastly the expression 'he stedfastly set his face' (τὸ πρόσωπον ἐστήρισεν) is peculiar to this place, and the verb στηρίζω is found in no Gospel except Luke.

THE NARRATIVES AND THE THEORY 303

PRÉCIS OF SUBSEQUENT PROCEEDINGS.

According to the opinion most largely entertained, and which has the most appearance of probability, our Lord's proceedings from this time forward were somewhat as follows :—

It was now late in November, and His death was to take place in the following April. Leaving Capernaum, He proceeded southward, apparently with the intention of going through Samaria (Luke ix. 51, 52). Being rejected by the first Samaritan village at which His messengers arrived (verses 53, 56), He turned eastward and journeyed along the border line between Galilee and Samaria (Luke xvii. 11), towards the Jordan, which He crossed. About this time he sent out the seventy disciples (Luke x. 1) to announce His coming to the various towns and villages along His intended route through Perea towards Jerusalem. Travelling in pairs they would visit at least thirty-five places; but, as most of the couples would go to more than one place, His approach would be well advertised. The result was that large multitudes gathered round Him whom He frequently addressed, as He passed southward through Perea (Luke xiii. 22). Arriving at the Jordan, opposite Jericho, He made a quiet journey to Bethany, where He stayed for a short time at the house of Lazarus, Martha and Mary (Luke x. 38). It was now the end of December, and the feast of the Dedication was being held at the Temple (John x. 22). This He attended; but, as the Jews again sought His life, He soon returned to the eastern side of the Jordan (John x. 40). While He was there Lazarus fell sick and died (John xi.), and Jesus came again to Bethany and raised him to life. The Jews again conspiring to put Jesus to death, He retired to Ephraim (John xi. 54), where He remained until the near approach of the Passover, when He for the last time entered Judea and proceeded to Jerusalem to die.

REJECTION IN SAMARIA; INDIGNATION OF JAMES AND JOHN.
HEALING OF TEN LEPERS. MISSION OF THE SEVENTY
AND THEIR RETURN. INCIDENTS AND PARABLES
DELIVERED DURING THE JOURNEY THROUGH PEREA.
VISIT TO BETHANY AND COMMENDATION OF MARY.

Luke ix. 52–56; xvii. 11–37; x. 1–12, 16–20, 25–37; xi. 37–41; xii. 13–21, 54–57; xiii. 1–17, 22–33; xiv. 1–35; xv. 1–32; xvi. 1–9, 19–31; xvii. 1–10; xviii. 1–14; x. 38–42

Both Matthew and Mark skip the whole of the events and discourses recorded in the above portions. It is probably not until after Christ's return to Perea from the feast of Dedication that they resume writing. The reason of their silence may be thus accounted for: At the beginning of His journey from Galilee, Jesus 'sent messengers before His face' to prepare the people for His coming (Luke ix. 52), and He probably continued to do this until He recrossed the Jordan and entered Judea. The seventy went out first, made a preliminary announcement of His coming, and, returning, reported to Him at what places He might expect a friendly reception. To those places He proceeded as He travelled south, sending messengers in advance to notify that He was about to arrive. These messengers were doubtless chosen from the Apostles, and Matthew and Peter were probably among them. Thus they were very little in their Master's company. As soon as He rejoined them at any town or village He would send them on to another. Hence James, who was not one of those thus sent in advance, was the only reporter writing Aramaic who was in a position to take notes during this progress. By this time he had had sufficient practice in tautochronistic reporting to make him quite expert and able to keep pace with our Lord's utterance.

The chronological disorder which characterises Luke's Gospel is very pronounced in chapters x. to xviii. Luke seems to have found it hopeless to attempt to arrange in systematic sequence the papers of which these chapters are composed, so he simply translated and copied them as they came. Some of the fragments it is generally agreed belong to this Perean journey, an opinion that is confirmed by the nature of the portions themselves.

The sending forward of the Seventy seems to fit in with this time better than any other. Our Lord could hardly have had at an earlier period a following large and well-instructed enough to supply so many men competent for such a mission. On former occasions too He seems rather to have avoided publicity; but now, as His earthly course came near its termination, He showed more disposition to assert openly His regal authority and claims.

The parables of the Good Samaritan, the Barren Fig Tree, the Great Supper, the Lost Sheep, the Missing Money, the Prodigal Son, the Dishonest Steward, the Rich Man and Lazarus, and the Pharisee and Publican, show an advanced stage of doctrinal teaching which suits this later period of Christ's ministry. Their aim was, if possible, to pierce through the infatuated confidence of Pharisaic self-righteousness, and convince the Jews of the worthlessness of the legal and ceremonial observances in which they were trusting for salvation. The great lesson which they teach is that it is not by works of righteousness which men can do themselves, but by the substitutionary sacrifice and imputed righteousness of God's incarnate Son, that peace with God and eternal life are to be secured.

Thus, in the parable of the Good Samaritan, looking below the surface we see the indifference of the ritual and moral law to the sinner's fate, contrasted with the saving grace and power of the Gospel. The parable of the Great Supper, although in some respects resembling the parable of the Marriage of the King's Son (Matt. xxii. 2–13), delivered on a later occasion in the Temple, is in others quite different. The point specially brought out in the parable in Luke is the satisfaction which those bidden felt in their own acquirements. The first has just come into possession of a landed property he has bought

x

himself—whether he has paid for it he does not say—he does not stand in need of a meal, and he politely declines the invitation. The second has hitherto been an idle improvident man, and, it may be inferred, has come down low enough in the world, but he has determined to reform, he has already made a start, he has bought (doubtless on credit), not one yoke, but five yoke of oxen. He is too well satisfied with his own good resolutions to see the need of accepting the hospitality offered by another. The third has married a wife, which according to Oriental custom would mean the giving of a feast himself. He implies therefore by his answer that he has enough and to spare, and has no need to place himself under any obligation to him who has called him to the feast. All these are types of those who think their spiritual needs can be met by their own virtues and efforts, and reject the bounteous provision of the Gospel. So likewise in the three parables of the Strayed Sheep, the Lost Money and the Prodigal Son, the respectable but self-righteous Pharisee is unfavourably contrasted with the sinful but penitent publican and outcast.

The parable of the Strayed Sheep bears indications of having been spoken, not in a city or town, but in a pastoral district, such as Perea was. 'What man *of you* . . . doth not leave the ninety and nine *in the wilderness?*'

Mixed up with the portions in Luke which belong to this journey from Galilee to Jerusalem are others, some of which have their parallels in Matthew and Mark, and which for various reasons seem to belong to other periods of the Ministry. The section x. 13-15, which is nearly identical with Matthew xi. 20-24, was probably located here by Luke as apparently harmonising with the reference to Sodom in verse 12. In like manner, section x. 21-24, which corresponds with Matthew xi. 25-30, may have seemed to Luke to suit the connection in this place. He probably had no special reason for choosing the position in which he placed the sections composing chapter xi. and the first 12 verses of chapter xii., but, having nothing to guide him as to the time or circumstances to which they actually belonged, he thought they would come in here as well as anywhere else. The same applies to a number of other passages in these chapters which we have not included in the list of portions above. Of many of them it may be said that Luke would not have placed them where they are if he had had either Matthew's or Mark's Gospel before him when he composed his. The whole of chapters x. to xviii. exhibit the difficulty of the task which Luke had undertaken, namely, to arrange in order, with little or no external aid, a great number of detached papers, written some thirty years previously, and relating events about which he was, though very well informed, without personal knowledge.

It is not surprising that the instructions to the Seventy, when being despatched on their mission, bear some resemblance to those addressed on a former similar occasion to the Twelve. They are, however, sufficiently unlike to show that the two addresses were distinct.

There are also other passages, included in the list of portions assigned by me to this Perean journey, bearing more or less resemblance to passages in Matthew and Mark, but which latter belong to other connections. Amongst them may be noted the following :—

xiii. 28, 29 comparing with Matt. viii. 11, 12,
xiv. 1–6 ,, ,, ,, xii. 9–13,
xvii. 1, 2 ,, ,, ,, xviii. 6, 7,
and Mark ix. 42.

Also, xiv. 11, which is repeated almost word for word xviii. 14, and is found again in a third connection Matt. xxiii. 12.

> For every one that exalteth himself shall be humbled ; and he that humbleth himself shall be exalted.

Although it is improbable that our Lord would repeat an address of moderate length, it is not at all unlikely that He would sometimes in similar circumstances use similar expressions, or that He would make frequent use of an aphorism like that we have just quoted. We must beware of the modern mania for tracing to a common origin all passages of Scripture which bear to one another the slightest resemblance.

The conversation between Jesus and Martha, which took place at the latter's home, was doubtless spoken in Greek. Of course it was not reported at the moment. It was recorded by James soon afterwards from memory and rendered by him into Aramaic, the language in which he always wrote.

It may seem strange that the narrative does not give the name of the village at which our Lord had this conversation with the sisters. But James had good reason for his silence on that point. As we shall see directly; the Jews, probably at the very moment when James was writing, were making renewed efforts to put Jesus to death; and if this manuscript had fallen into their hands, and they had learned that He had attached disciples living at Bethany close to Jerusalem, their lives also would have been endangered. Within a very short time, however, such caution ceased to be useful. The name of Lazarus became famous, and no additional risk would be occasioned by its mention; therefore John did not show similar reticence.

FEAST OF THE DEDICATION; DISCOURSE TO THE JEWS; THEY ATTEMPT TO KILL JESUS; HE RETURNS TO PEREA

John x. 22-42

The portions in Luke which we have just been considering bring us from Galilee, through Perea, into Judea as far as Bethany, and there stop short. Into Jerusalem itself Luke never leads us until that last visit of all, the account of which stands forth so prominently in every one of the Gospels. True, in this latter respect, Luke does not differ from the other Synoptics. But then both Matthew and Mark always keep outside the borders of Judea, whereas Luke, in this instance, comes into the heart of the province, within two miles of the capital itself. How is it to be accounted for that

Luke should tell so much of what Jesus did from the time He left Galilee until He reached the very outskirts of Jerusalem, and yet preserve perfect silence as to what happened in the city itself?

There is but one conceivable answer to this question; namely, that an understanding, tacit or otherwise, existed among the Apostles, that the task of reporting the occurrences in Jerusalem should be left in the hands of John. But the existence of such understanding implies that the reports were written at the time the events happened. And the only adequate reason which one can suggest why such an understanding was come to is the linguistic one for which we contend. All becomes plain when we recognise that, while in other places our Lord usually spake in Aramaic, in Jerusalem He generally spake in Greek, and that, while Matthew, Peter and James were competent to report in the former language, John alone could write fast in the latter.

It is quite possible that the Apostles did not all accompany Jesus on His visit to Jerusalem at the feast of Dedication. All that our view makes it necessary to assume is that James was with Him at Bethany and that John was taking notes in the Temple. The others may have remained behind in Perea. That they were not all with Him now may perhaps be inferred from Thomas' words, John xi. 16: "Let us also go, that we may die with Him."

We have certainly in this place an exact, and therefore, we maintain, a tautochronistic report of the words spoken by Christ to the Jews. Those persons must be gifted with a large measure of credulity who can believe that these utterances were invented at some later time for controversial purposes. Even if it be granted that the strong assertion of His deity expressed in this portion accords with such a theory, the seeming (but only seeming, not real) qualification of that assertion in verses 34, 35 is altogether at variance with it.

The story bears the stamp of reality in every detail. This was the last opportunity our Lord would have of declaring to the highest representatives of God's chosen people His divine authority and claims; and it was His purpose to do so in clear and unmistakable terms. It was perhaps for this reason that He had come to Jerusalem during the celebration of this minor feast. But He did not thrust Himself upon them. He knew that they would come to Him, and waited. Usually, when teaching in the Temple, He sat surrounded by His audience, in one of the unroofed inner spaces. But now, to gain shelter from the wintry weather, He walked to and fro in the long colonnade running beside the outer eastern wall which rose from the face of the cliff that overhung the valley of Jehoshaphat. The feast of Dedication was not like the three great feasts which were celebrated only at Jerusalem. It was kept up all over the country; hence the Temple was not thronged with visitors, as at Passover, Pentecost and Tabernacles.

The Jewish rulers had evidently been discussing the situation. They were well aware of the immense popularity of Jesus in Galilee, and, more recently, in Perea. Even now, if He would conform to their ideal; if He would be willing as their secular champion to head a revolt against the hated yoke of Rome, and re-establish their nation's independence, it might be well to come to terms with Him and hail Him as their Prince. Might they infer from His attending this feast, which was held in commemoration of the deliverance wrought by Judas Maccabeus from the tyranny of Antiochus two centuries before, that He was prepared to perform a similar service? They agreed to form themselves into a deputation and find out definitely what He claimed to be and what His intentions were.

We are here reminded of the deputation that three or four years before waited on John the Baptist to ask him, "Who art thou?" Only the deputation to the Messenger consisted of messengers. "The Jews sent unto him from Jerusalem priests and Levites." But now, to interview the Master, they come themselves. Leaving then the chamber where they held their meeting, near to the central sacred edifice, they made their way across the wide open spaces to Solomon's Porch, where probably from their elevated room they may have seen Him walking. Gathering round about Him, they put the question bluntly, " How long dost thou hold us in suspense? If thou be the Christ tell us plainly." But to this enquiry Jesus did not give a direct reply. Why? Because a simple affirmative would have carried a false impression to their minds. He meant them to understand that He was One infinitely greater than what they thought of when they spoke of the Christ—a mere carnal worldly deliverer. So He appealed first to His works, evidences which were too numerous and distinct for them to gainsay. With a few more sentences He led them on, and then declared in plainest terms, "I and the Father are one." There was no mistaking this. Either they must accept Him as God made manifest in human form, or reject Him altogether.

They chose the latter; and took up stones from the roughly paved court to stone Him. But He had not yet finished and it was His will that they should hear Him out, and hear Him calmly. They should not, as later when about to stone Stephen, cry out with deafening noise and stop their ears. " Many good works have I showed you from the Father; for which of those works do ye stone me? " They saw at once the need to justify the deed they were threatening to do. " For a good work we stone thee not, but for blasphemy; and because that thou, being a man, makest thyself God." The moment's pause gave Him the opportunity He required. Quoting a familiar phrase from the 82nd Psalm, it seemed for an instant as if He were about to explain away His utterance. Thus with consummate wisdom He once more gained their attention, while He asserted His Godhead in yet more forceful terms, declaring Himself to be He whom the Father had sanctified and sent into the world, and appealing to His works as convincing proof that the Father was in Him and He in the Father.

All this time John, who had doubtless been walking in the

colonnade with Jesus before the Jews approached Him, was busy taking notes of what was said on either side.

Our Lord having now fully and finally delivered His testimony, His mission to Jerusalem at this time was fulfilled, and, as the Jews sought again to take Him, He again left Judea.

It seems to have been John's way to write up and finish off his stenographic notes at the first convenient opportunity after he had taken them. This explains the abrupt manner with which so many of his sections close. Thus, following his report of the allegory of the Shepherd and His Sheep, in the earlier part of this chapter, are three verses (19-21) describing its effect upon the Jews. Then follows the portion we have just been considering, without a single word to indicate that in the meantime Jesus left Jerusalem and passed a long interval in other parts of Palestine. John finished off the portion ending vs. 21, in or near Jerusalem probably on the evening of the day on which the allegory of the Shepherd was spoken. He did not resume his pen until, after two months, he found himself again in Jerusalem at the feast of Dedication.

But now he cannot revise and finish off his notes directly they are written. He has to hasten from the city with his Master, whose life the Jews are seeking. Nor can they delay until they are safe once more in the domain of Herod Antipas, who, still remembering with shame and remorse his murder of John the Baptist, has no wish to be a party to another similar crime. Arrived at the place where "John was at the first baptizing," the Apostle takes an early opportunity to put his notes in shape. Having done this it now becomes the Aramaic-writers' turn to carry on the story.

IN PEREA: ABOUT DIVORCE; BLESSING THE CHILDREN; THE RICH YOUNG MAN; ABOUT RICHES; PARABLE OF THE HOUSEHOLDER AND HIRED SERVANTS

Matt. xix. 1-xx. 16; *Mark* x. 1-31; *Luke* xviii. 15-30

As already noticed, Matthew and Mark omit all reference

to the incidents and speeches recorded in Luke and John, between the departure from Galilee and the arrival in Perea after Dedication. It was not, indeed, until this arrival in Perea that Matthew and Peter recorded the fact of the departure from Galilee. Bearing in mind their manner of skipping long spaces of time without remark, the statements in Matthew xix. 1 and Mark x. 1 are not inconsistent with the lapse of an interval between the departure from the one place and the arrival in the other.

Mark's statement is rather more definite than Matthew's: "And he arose from thence, and cometh into the borders of Judea and beyond Jordan." This certainly implies that He arrived beyond Jordan, that is, in Perea, after visiting Judea. Owing, however, to this not being understood, the text in some ancient manuscripts was altered from καὶ πέραν to διὰ τοῦ πέραν, which reading is followed in the old version: "into the coasts of Judea by the farther side of Jordan."

The Parable of the Householder and the Hired Servants, which is peculiar to Matthew, is a tautochronistic report made by that Apostle. With that exception, the whole of the above portions are reports written from memory very shortly after the events. It would not require any unusual power of memory to retain for a short time a faithful impression of what was then done, and the few short and simple but incisive sentences that were spoken by our Lord. Amongst the disciples who assisted in the composition of these reports some must in the nature of things have had good memories, and that, with a conscientious desire to tell the exact truth, was all that was necessary.

There was nothing now to take Matthew and Peter away from the company of Jesus and their fellow Apostles and they therefore resumed their task of narrating the course of events. Hence we have now three synoptic accounts; that of Luke however beginning somewhat later than the other two; while the parable mentioned above, having been taken down verbatim by Matthew as it was delivered, is entirely omitted by both Mark and Luke.

But with this last exception, a comparison of the three portions shows unmistakably that they were all written under a common influence. Let us look first at the order of the relation:

MATTHEW	MARK	LUKE
Chap. xix.	Chap. x.	Chap. xviii.
1. Jesus leaves Galilee and comes to borders of Judea and beyond Jordan.	1. Jesus leaves Galilee and comes to borders of Judea and beyond Jordan.	
2. Multitudes follow and He heals them.	Multitudes follow and He teaches them.	
3–9. Pharisees enquire about divorce and He replies.	2–9. Pharisees enquire about divorce and He replies.	
10–12. Conversation with disciples on same subject.	10–12. Conversation with disciples on same subject.	
13–15. Children brought to Him and He lays His hands on them.	13–16. Children brought to Him and He blesses them.	15–17. Children brought to Him.
16–22. Rich young man comes to Him.	17–22. Rich young man comes to Him.	18–23. Rich young man comes to Him.
23–27. He speaks to His disciples about riches.	23–27. He speaks to His disciples about riches.	24–27. He speaks to His disciples about riches.
28–30. Of the reward to those who forsake all for Him.	28–31. Of the reward to those who forsake all for Him.	28–30. Of the reward to those who forsake all for Him.
Chap. xx.		
1–16. Parable of the Householder and the Hired Servants.		

THE NARRATIVES AND THE THEORY 315

Observe next the identity of terms which sometimes appears in the narrative portions of the several accounts:

MATT. xix.	MARK x.	LUKE xviii.
13. And the disciples rebuked them.	13 And the disciples rebuked those who brought them.	15. But when the disciples saw it, they rebuked them.
22. He went away sorrowful; for he was one that had great possessions.	22. He went away sorrowful; for he was one that had great possessions.	23. He became exceeding sorrowful; for he was very rich.

When we compare quotations of spoken words, not only of our Lord, but also of those who addressed Him, we find here as elsewhere in the Gospels, very close agreement.

MATT. xix.	MARK x.	LUKE xviii.
3. Is it lawful for a man to put away his wife for every cause?	2. Is it lawful for a man to put away his wife?	
7. Why then did Moses command to give a bill of divorcement, and to put her away?	4. Moses suffered to write a bill of divorcement, and to put her away.	
16. Master, what good thing shall I do, that I may have eternal life?	17. Good Master, what shall I do, that I may inherit eternal life?	18. Good Master, what shall I do to inherit eternal life?
20. All these things have I observed;($\dot{\epsilon}\phi\nu\lambda\acute{a}\xi a$) what lack I yet?	20. Master, all these things have I observed from my youth ($\dot{\epsilon}\phi\nu\lambda a\xi\acute{a}\mu\eta\nu$ $\dot{\epsilon}\kappa$ $\nu\epsilon\acute{o}\tau\eta\tau os$ μov).	21. All these things have I observed from (my) youth ($\dot{\epsilon}\phi\acute{\nu}\lambda a\xi a$ $\dot{\epsilon}\kappa$ $\nu\epsilon\acute{o}\tau\eta\tau os$).
25. Who then ($\check{a}\rho a$) can be saved?	26. Then ($\kappa a\acute{\iota}$) who can be saved?	26. Then ($\kappa a\acute{\iota}$) who can be saved?
27. Lo, we have left all, and followed thee? what then shall we have?	28. Lo, we have left all, and followed thee.	28. Lo, we have left our own and followed thee.

The quoted sayings of our Lord are not word for word the same, as in places where the report is tautochronistic, but the agreement is close enough to show the extreme care which the writers took to obtain as nearly as possible His exact words from those of their fellow disciples whose memories were most reliable.

When however we turn from the points of resemblance to those of dissimilarity the latter are found to be quite as striking as the former.

Thus it sometimes happens that in strictly narrative parts each Evangelist employs quite different diction to describe the same fact:

Matt. xix. 1. And it came to pass when Jesus had finished these words, he departed from Galilee, and came into the borders of Judea beyond Jordan; and great multitudes followed him, and he healed them there.

Mark x. 1. And he arose from thence, and cometh into the borders of Judea and beyond Jordan: and multitudes came together unto him again; and, as he was wont, he taught them again.

Matt. xix. 16. And behold one came to him and said.

Mark x. 17. And as he was going forth into the way, there ran one to him, and kneeled to him, and asked him.

Luke xviii. 18. And a certain ruler asked him saying.

Matt. xix. 21. Jesus said unto him.

Mark x. 21. And Jesus looking upon him loved him, and said unto him.

Luke xviii. 22. And when Jesus heard it, he said unto him.

In one place the likeness between Mark and Luke is so close as to make it almost certain that in the original Aramaic they were identical, while Matthew states the same fact in quite a different form:

Mark x. 13. And they brought unto him little children, that he should touch them. (Καὶ προσέφερον αὐτῷ παιδία, ἵνα αὐτῶν ἅπτηται.)

Luke xviii. 15. And they brought unto him also their babes, that he should touch them. (Προσέφερον δὲ αὐτῷ καὶ τὰ βρέφη, ἵνα αὐτῶν ἅπτηται.)

Matthew xix. 13. Then were brought unto him little children, that he should lay his hands on them and pray.

Finally there is the curious circumstance, already noticed,

that the parable which, according to Matthew, followed immediately after, and in continuation of, the promise of abundant reward to those who forsook their worldly interests for Christ's sake, and which Matthew reports in full, is not even alluded to by either Mark or Luke although they both record the promise which led up to it.

The more these features are studied the more plainly will it be seen that it is utterly impossible to make them tally with any of the existing theories as to the origin of the Gospels. But they all fall naturally into place when once it is seen that these are distinct reports made by three separate men of the united testimony of the twelve Apostles as to the facts; testimony given when met together in one place soon after the incidents happened, and recorded by the writers at the time they were speaking. It is easy to understand why, under such circumstances, the several resemblances and diversities to which attention has been called should come into existence. And it is easy also to understand why, one of the number having taken at the time of its delivery a verbatim report of the parable, the other two should deem it superfluous to attempt to report it at second hand.

THE RAISING OF LAZARUS
John xi. 1-44

While our Lord was engaged in Perea, teaching with acceptance the crowds who were beginning to gather round Him, a message came to Him from Bethany that one whom He loved was sick. Two days later He informed the disciples of Lazarus' death, and announced His intention to go into Judea again. This is related by John, who further proceeds to narrate His arrival at Bethany, and the bringing back of Lazarus to life. In all probability he wrote the narrative in Lazarus' house, immediately after his resurrection, obtaining of Martha and Mary such information as he required from them to complete the story.

Verse 18, like verse 2, is probably an editorial addition.

A careful examination leads to the belief that the narrative written by John at this time ends with verse 44. Again Jesus and the disciples had to hasten from Judea, thus once more abruptly terminating the story John was writing.

RESOLUTION OF THE SANHEDRIN. JESUS AGAIN LEAVES
JUDEA. ARRIVES AT EPHRAIM

John xi. 45-54

Here begins a new division of John's Gospel, the historical parts of which were evidently not written until after our Lord's death and resurrection. From the time he left Bethany, after the raising of Lazarus, until after the Passion, John wrote nothing except the tautochronistic reports of Christ's utterances contained in xii. 23-36, 44-50, and chaps. xiv., xv., xvi., xvii. The information supplied in the above passage as to the proceedings in the Sanhedrin was in all likelihood obtained, immediately after the Resurrection, from Nicodemus and Joseph of Arimathea, who came into close contact with the disciples at the burial of the body of Jesus, and, we may be sure, were much in their company from that time forward.

His life being again threatened, "Jesus no more walked openly among the Jews, but departed thence into the country near to the wilderness, into a city called Ephraim." This city is nowhere else mentioned in the Bible, and its site has not, I think, been identified. It is very unlikely that it was in Judea, as our Lord invariably absented Himself from that province when desirous of avoiding the plottings of the Jews against His life. In 2 Samuel xviii. 6, a "forest of Ephraim" is spoken of as the scene of the battle between Joab and Absalom. This forest was situated on the east of and near the Jordan, opposite to the territory of the tribe of Ephraim on the other side of the river. This locality would exactly suit the requirements of the narrative as to the place to which Jesus now retired. The wilderness to which it was near may well have been the ancient forest from which the town in that case derived its name. The low level at which it lay would accord with the expression "going up to Jerusalem," which is found in all the Gospels (Matt. xx. 17, 18; Mark x. 33; Luke xviii. 31; John xi. 55).

Aramaic being the language spoken in this rural district in Perea, John has now another rest from reporting.

JOURNEY FROM EPHRAIM TO JERICHO: INCIDENTS
AND ADDRESSES

Matthew xx. 17–34; *Mark* x. 32–52; *Luke* xviii. 31–34;
xxii. 24–30; xviii. 35–43; xix. 1–27

As these portions have been dealt with pretty fully in Part IV., in illustrating the subject of our Second Special Key, only one observation is here necessary.

The incident of the application of the mother of Zebedee's children, with her two sons, is related only in Matthew and Mark. This is certainly remarkable, if the conjecture be correct that James wrote the original notes which form the substance of the Gospel of Luke. It was not James' way, any more than it was Peter's, to ignore events that showed himself in an unfavourable light. It was he alone who recorded the vindictive suggestion concerning the Samaritan village, in that instance, contrary to his usual practice, putting his own name first. His omission of this incident therefore suggests the thought that he felt it was not one that he and his brother need be ashamed of.

Does it not seem probable, considering the special favour which our Lord showed on several occasions towards Peter, James and John, that they may have attained to some clearer conception than the other Apostles had reached of the spiritual nature of Christ's kingdom? May it not be that the repeated intimations which the Saviour had given of His approaching sufferings and death were at length leading James and John and their mother Salome to form some vague, indistinct idea that the pathway to His glory lay through humiliation and distress? And is it not possible that their application to Him at that time was intended modestly to assure Him of their stedfast devotion, and their readiness to drink with Him the cup of bitterness and shame? That they had some such purpose seems to be confirmed by their close attendance on Jesus a few days later, during His bitter experience in the Chief Priest's judgment hall, at a time when one of their number had just before basely betrayed Him, when others had fled, and when Peter himself denied Him.

They certainly were not unaware of the dangers of the position which they craved. Just before the last preceding visit to Jerusalem, Thomas had expressed the general feeling when he said, "Let us also go, that we may die with Him" (John xi. 16). The risk was even greater now, and those who were nearest the Master would incur the most peril.

FOREVIEW OF THE FINAL PORTIONS OF THE GOSPELS

In the final portions of the Gospels, the portions which remain to be considered, John is synoptic like the others.

MATT.	MARK.
xxvi. 11.	xiv. 7.
For ye have the poor always with you; but me ye have not always.	For ye have the poor always with you, and whensoever ye will ye can do them good: but me ye have not always.
xxvi. 21.	xiv. 18.
Verily I say unto you, that one of you shall betray me.	Verily I say unto you, one of you shall betray me.
xxvi. 34.	xiv. 30.
Verily I say unto thee, that this night, before the cock crow, thou shalt deny me thrice.	Verily I say unto thee, that thou to-day, even this night, before the cock crow twice, shalt deny me thrice.

It deals generally with the same series of events, and may be placed side by side and compared with them.

But it still preserves its distinctive character. Whilst Matthew, Mark and Luke continue to show the effect of a common influence, John remains generally independent. This narrative was written apart in Greek; those were written in company in Aramaic. Hence there sometimes seems at first sight to be a real discrepancy between the accounts in the first three Gospels and that in the fourth. But the discrepancies disappear when the circumstances in which the original reports were written come to be understood.

In several instances the narratives in the first three Gospels and that in the fourth touch one another, and consequently in some cases the quoted words of our Lord in John are also found in one or more of the other three. The following are the cases referred to:

LUKE.	JOHN.
	xii. 8.
	For the poor ye have always with you; but me ye have not always.
xxii. 21.	xiii. 21.
But, behold, the hand of him that betrayeth me is with me on the table.	Verily, verily, I say unto you, that one of you shall betray me.
xxii. 34.	xiii. 38.
I tell thee, Peter, the cock shall not crow this day until thou shalt thrice deny that thou knowest me.	Verily, verily I say unto thee, The cock shall not crow till thou hast denied me thrice.
xxiv. 36.	xx. 19.
Peace be unto you.	Peace be unto you.

V

There are also similar cases of agreement with respect to

MATT.	MARK.
xxi. 9.	xi. 9, 10.
Hosanna to the son of David: Blessed is he that cometh in the name of the Lord ; Hosanna in the highest.	Hosanna ; Blessed is he that cometh in the name of the Lord : Blessed is the kingdom that cometh, the kingdom of our father David : Hosanna in the highest.
xxvii. 11.	xv. 2.
Art thou the King of the Jews?	Art thou the King of the Jews?
xxvii. 22.	xv. 13.
Let him be crucified.	Crucify him.

Now it must be remembered that the foregoing were spoken under circumstances that, even on our hypothesis, preclude the possibility of their having been reported at the moment of utterance. They were reported from memory, and after a lapse of several days. And yet there is great similarity among all the reports, and in every instance the words quoted in John are nearly, if not quite, identical with the words in the parallel quotation in either Matthew, Mark or Luke.

That there should be similarity among the quotations in Matthew, Mark and Luke is not specially remarkable, for such similarities are a leading feature of the first three Gospels ; but the similarity between their quotations and John's is of great importance, for it proves the accuracy of all. For it is impossible, on a comparison of the four narratives, to suppose either that the author of any one of the first three borrowed from the fourth, or that the author of the fourth borrowed from any one of the first three, or that the first three, or either of them, and the fourth are based on a common original; the general unlikeness of the first three narratives to the fourth being too great to allow of any connection whatever between the former and the last. This is generally admitted, and will plainly appear as we proceed. It the quoted words of persons other than Jesus:

LUKE.	JOHN.
xix. 38.	xii. 13.
Blessed is the King that cometh in the name of the Lord: peace in heaven, and glory in the highest.	Hosanna; Blessed is he that cometh in the name of the Lord, even the King of Israel.

xxiii. 3.	xviii. 33.
Art thou the King of the Jews?	Art thou the King of the Jews?
xxiii. 21.	xix. 6.
Crucify him, crucify him.	Crucify him, crucify him.

follows, therefore, that we have two quite independent testimonies agreeing as to certain sentences that were spoken on seven distinct occasions.

The accuracy of these quotations then is beyond dispute, and their accuracy proves inferentially the accuracy of all quotations in the four narratives, and consequently of the narratives themselves.

But there are a number of longer utterances—addresses and discourses—that could not, except by means of a miracle, have been accurately reported unless they were taken down at the very time they were being spoken. Some of these longer utterances are found in Matthew, Mark and Luke, or in one or two of them; others are found in John. In no instance is one of the longer utterances found in either Matthew, Mark or Luke, and also in John. Thus it seems that even at this time when John joined in writing an account of events concerning which Matthew, Peter and James were also writing, he never wrote a tautochronistic report of an address when one of them was doing so, and neither Matthew, Peter or James ever wrote a tautochronistic report when John was doing so. We know the reason for this. When Jesus delivered a discourse in Aramaic, John did not attempt to report it; when He delivered one in Greek, no disciple except John attempted to report it.

But now we have to face the fact that in these final portions of the first three Gospels are reports of addresses spoken in the Temple at Jerusalem. Up to this time the reported utterances of Christ in the Temple are to be found only in John, a circumstance which we have accounted for on the ground that he spake in that place in Greek—the language most in use in the metropolis, and especially the ordinary language of the Jewish leaders. How are we to explain the act that the practice is now reversed, and that both the sayings and doings of Jesus in the Temple during this last attendance are reported at length by Matthew, Mark and Luke, while John reports only one incident and the words spoken by Jesus in connection therewith?

The explanation is that it was not the Jewish leaders whom on this occasion our Lord addressed, but the multitudes who came to the feast from Galilee and Perea, and whose vernacular was Aramaic. Hence those disciples who were accustomed to write in Aramaic reported Him.

Contrasting the applause which signalised our Lord's entry into Jerusalem with the outcry against Him on the day of His crucifixion, a moral has often been drawn as to the fickleness of public opinion, and the ephemeral nature of popularity. "The multitude," it is said, "cry 'Hosanna' one day, and 'Crucify Him' the next." Undoubtedly the multitude is fickle, and popularity is shortlived. But so sudden and complete a change as it is supposed took place in this instance is without an example, and did not really occur. The fact is, there were two multitudes—a Galilean multitude, and a Jerusalem multitude. It was the Galilean multitude who cried "Hosanna"; it was the Jerusalem multitude who cried "Crucify Him." The distinction between the two crowds is clearly observed in the narratives. Thus, in John xii. 9, we read that while our Lord was at Bethany "the common people of the Jews learned that He was there, and they came, not for Jesus' sake only, but that they might see Lazarus also, whom He raised from the dead." These people belonged to the Jerusalem multitude; and the chief priests were so much incensed that they "took counsel that they might put Lazarus also to death, because that by reason of him many of the Jews went away and believed on Jesus." But we are informed immediately after (ver. 12) that "on the morrow a great multitude that had come to the feast, when they heard that Jesus was coming to Jerusalem, took the branches of the palm trees, and went forth to meet Him, and cried out Hosanna," etc. Observe the distinction, "They had come to the feast"; therefore they were not residents of Jerusalem. They are not called Jews. This multitude, then, consisted mostly of Galileans. A like contrast appears in verses 17 and 18. "The multitude therefore that was with Him when He called Lazarus out of the tomb, and raised him from the dead, bare witness." These formed part of the Jerusalem multitude; but although they had seen the miracle, and some of them had believed on Jesus, there is no intimation that they joined in the acclamations of those who brought Him into the city. Those who did this—the multitude that "went and met Him"—had not seen the miracle; they had only "heard that He had done this sign." These were the Galilean multitude.

The other Gospels are explicit in their statements that large numbers accompanied our Lord on His last journey to Jerusalem. Great multitudes were with Him as He passed through Jericho (Matt. xx. 29; Mark x. 46; Luke xviii. 36). They doubtless accompanied Him to Bethany where He stayed over the Sabbath, whilst they went on to Jerusalem. When they returned on the Sunday morning to Bethany to bring Christ triumphantly to the city, so far from the citizens taking any part in the procession, we read that 'all the city was stirred, saying, Who is this?' Their question was answered by the multitude—the Galilean multitude who followed

Him—'This is the prophet, Jesus, from Nazareth of Galilee' (Matt. xxi. 10, 11). "Their answer, as remarked by Meyer, seems to show a kind of local pride in Him, as from Galilee, their own prophet. But this very answer was peculiarly adapted to set the people of Judea against Him" (Andrews, p. 435).

His popularity with the Galilean multitude did not cease. It was a serious fact to be considered by the Jewish authorities and they agreed not to arrest Him on the Feast-day for fear there should be an uproar of the people. However, when He had been arrested and was brought before Pilate, the Galileans appear to have been panic-struck and to have kept out of view, leaving the multitude of Jerusalem, who had been stirred up by the priests, to have their way without their interference.

Whilst our Lord was teaching in the Temple the Galileans gathered round Him, and it was to them that He addressed Himself. The time was past for trying to convince the official representatives of the Jewish nation that He was the Messiah. He had on His previous visits to Jerusalem asserted His claims and presented His credentials to them and they had rejected Him. They would no longer listen to Him or debate with Him; their hatred had reached a point beyond that; they had already decreed His death and were now plotting how they might bring it about. Twice only they appear upon the scene. On the first occasion they express their indignation at the Hosannas of the children. On the second, anxious to entrap Him into saying something upon which they may found an accusation, or, failing that, embarrass Him before the crowd, they demand His authority for His proceedings. Foiled in their purpose, they retire into the background, and henceforth content themselves with sending a number of Pharisees, Herodians and Sadducees and a lawyer to ensnare Him in His talk. These emissaries were probably some of the very men similarly described who had so often attacked Him in Galilee. As they desired to discredit Him with the Galilean crowd surrounding Him, they would address Him in Aramaic. As for our Lord Himself, it is clearly implied that His teaching at this period, though sometimes nominally addressed to priests, scribes, Pharisees and others, was really intended for the much larger audience of friendly Galileans. Hence He spoke in their familiar Aramaic, while Matthew, Peter and James, standing or sitting near Him, took notes more or less comprehensive of what He said. It is their reports that are preserved in the Synoptic Gospels.

GATHERING AT JERUSALEM FOR THE PASSOVER: ARRIVAL OF JESUS AT BETHANY: SUPPER AND ANOINTING: PLOTTING OF SANHEDRIN: TREACHERY OF JUDAS

John xi. 55-57; *Luke* xix. 28; *Matthew* xxvi. 6-16; *Mark* xiv. 3-11; *Luke* xxii. 3-6; *John* xii. 1-11

Assuming that our Lord's death took place in the year 30, He left the house of Zacchaeus on the morning of Friday, March 31, and arrived at Bethany the same evening. There He remained over the Sabbath, and on Saturday evening, April 1, after sunset, when the Sabbath was past, a supper was given in His honour at the house of Simon the leper. The next morning, Sunday, April 2, He made His triumphal entry into Jerusalem.

On comparing the accounts of the Supper and Anointing in Matthew, Mark and John, it will be seen that, while the first two show the usual indications of having been written by separate individuals under one common influence, the last appears to have been written quite independently. Not only is John's account in its general structure unlike those of Matthew and Mark, but there are several seeming differences, of fact so remarkable as to have caused doubt whether the same incident is referred to. It is however highly improbable that two incidents—or rather two pairs of incidents—the main features of which were identical, should have occurred within a few days of one another and under such similar circumstances. We shall now see that, examined in the light of our discovery as to the origin of the Gospel histories, the differences are easily explained.

The first and most important discrepancy is in the position which the Supper and Anointing hold in the order of events. According to John they took place soon after our Lord's arrival at Bethany on His way from Jericho to Jerusalem. This order is accepted by most commentators, and rightly so, for John's chronological arrangement is less open to question than any. But Mark's chronology is also as a rule correct, and he, as well as Matthew, relates the incident subsequently to the public ministry in the Temple and the private discourse to the disciples on the Mount of Olives. How is this to be explained? Simply thus, that the accounts of the Supper in Matthew and Mark were not written exactly at the time it took place but several days later.

The narratives which Matthew, Peter and James wrote prior to the Crucifixion end respectively with Matthew xxv. 46, Mark xiii. 37, and Luke xxi. 38. It was not until after the Resurrection, and therefore at the earliest not before Monday, April 10, that they with some of the other Apostles again assembled to continue their history. Meanwhile they had learned from their friends among the Jewish rulers how Judas had appeared before the Sanhedrin and offered to betray his Master. They had learned too that this had happened directly after the Supper at Bethany, and although they could not positively assert that the vexation of Judas at the use which Mary had made of the ointment was the immediate motive that prompted him to his treachery, they could not but feel that there was a connection between the two facts. So, to make all clear, it seemed needful now to two of the writers to relate the incident, although it had occurred some days before the final events narrated in the portions they had written before the Passover.

In each of the Synoptic Gospels the portion written after the Resurrection begins with a sentence or two that stand as a connecting link between it and the portion next preceding.

These connecting sentences mention first the near approach of the Passover. The plotting of the chief priests and the scribes or elders is next asserted, and then the narratives go back a few days to relate, in Matthew and Mark the story of the Supper, and, in all three, the first infamous overtures of Judas. So that, in short, Matthew xxi. 1–xxv. 46 overlaps xxvi. 6–16, Mark xi. 1–xiii. 37 overlaps xiv. 3–11, and Luke xix. 29–xxi. 38 overlaps xxii. 3–6.

It seems curious that, notwithstanding the obvious connection in Matthew and Mark between the murmuring of the disciples at the use made of the ointment and the treachery of Judas, neither of those Evangelists mentions Judas' name in the account of the Supper. It is from John that we learn that he it was who took the leading part in expressing disapproval. Considering John's intense love for Jesus, to say nothing of his intimacy with Lazarus and the sisters, it is hardly conceivable that he himself joined in the murmuring. Probably he already felt some vague distrust of Iscariot, although he could hardly at that time have suspected him to be a thief. John's quick eye and ear observed that Judas was the first to complain, and that those who concurred with him did so, not from an evil motive, but from the mere force of example. And the malice of Judas was so pronounced, and his disapproval of Mary's lavishness was expressed in such unkind and insulting terms, that John, in his pain and disgust, scarcely observed the faint echo of his remarks by others, and thought only of him who was the origin of the discontent. On the other hand the disciples who, when assembled after the Resurrection, recalled the facts, and whose testimony is recorded in Matthew and Mark, felt themselves compromised somewhat in that they or some of them had supported the protest of Judas, and weakly sympathised with his indignation. That being the case they could not single him out for blame, and the two historians therefore leave his name unmentioned. As John however was not one of those who murmured there was no reason why he should feel any such scruple.

Another thing that seems strange is that neither Matthew nor Mark mentions that it was Mary, the sister of Lazarus and Martha, who poured the precious ointment on Jesus' head. But it should be noted that no mention of any member of this Bethany family is elsewhere made in these two Gospels. Probably Matthew and Peter had but a slight acquaintance with them. It has been noticed already that there is no ground for supposing that any of the disciples besides James and John accompanied Jesus on His journey to Jerusalem to attend the Feast of Dedication, in the course of which journey the Bethany family is first introduced to us (Luke x. 38-42). And, although our Lord and His disciples passed the first four nights of Passion Week at the Mount of Olives (Luke xxi. 37), it is very unlikely that the entire party stayed at the house of Lazarus. Some of them may have lodged at the house of Simon where the Supper was given; and if so it is not surprising that Matthew and Peter should have recorded his name, and related Mary's action without mentioning her name. On the other hand it is natural that John, to whom we are indebted for the story of the raising of Lazarus and so much that concerns the two sisters, but who perhaps knew little of Simon, should mention the names of the three former and not that of the last.

The closer intimacy of James and John with Lazarus and his sisters would itself be a good reason why they should not have joined in finding fault with her costly display of affection for the Master. This may explain why Luke has no account of the Supper and the Anointing. At the time it was recorded it must have caused painful reflections to those of the Apostles who had thoughtlessly endorsed the animadversions of Judas. But James, who had not shared in their mistake, would naturally feel averse to recording an incident which reflected—not on himself—but on his brother Apostles.

TRIUMPHAL ENTRY INTO JERUSALEM. SECOND CLEANSING OF
THE TEMPLE. WITHERING OF FIG-TREE. LAST MINISTRY
IN THE TEMPLE. INTERVIEW WITH GREEKS. ATTEMPT TO
PROVOKE JESUS. FINAL DEPARTURE FROM TEMPLE

Matthew xxi. 1–xxiii. 39 ; *Mark* xi. 1–xii. 44 ; *Luke* xix.
29–48 ; xxi. 37, 38 ; xx. 1–xxi. 4 ; xi. 42–52 ; xiii. 34, 35
xi. 53, 54 ; *John* xii. 12–36ᵃ ; 44–50 ; 36ᵇ–43

There is considerable variation in the parallel parts of the tautochronistic reports contained in the portions before us. Probably there was a good deal of confusion and interruption at this time owing to the crowded condition of the place in which Christ was speaking, and to the opposition of the elders, and thus the writers may have been unable to do more than secure the substance of what He said. Matthew's reports are as usual the most complete, but even he sometimes let a word or a sentence escape him. The others sometimes condensed two or three sentences into one, besides omitting portions of considerable length.

The portions in Matthew, Mark and Luke which are not tautochronistic show great similarity in the parallel parts ; not only in the quoted utterances of our Lord and others, but in the statements of fact also.

Nevertheless the diversities are very great also. One of the most striking is the difference between Matthew and Mark in the manner of relating the incident of the barren fig-tree, and which is of itself proof positive that, similar as the two accounts are, they were originally written by separate persons.

With reference to the mention of "Zachariah son of Barachiah," in Matthew xxiii. 35, Alford remarks, "υἱοῦ Βαραχίου does not occur in Luke xi. 51, and perhaps was not uttered by the Lord Himself, but may have been inserted by mistake, as Zechariah the prophet was son of Barachiah, see Zech. i. 1." The omission of these words in the Codex Sinaiticus is a strong argument in favour of this suggestion.

For several chapters past the Gospel of Matthew has followed the order in which the notes were originally arranged. The same order is observed here, except with one incident. According to Matthew the second cleansing of the Temple took place on the Sunday evening, immediately after the Triumphal Entry. Mark however states that the cleansing took place on the Monday morning, and his narrative is so explicit that its accuracy cannot be doubted. The apparent discrepancy is easily explained on the supposition that Matthew xxi. 12-16 was transposed in the redacting. The section contains 106 Greek words, and would just make two pages of the original notes. In the sequence of events it should come between 19 and 20; but it is most likely that its original place was between 22 and 23, the story of the cursing and the withering of the fig-tree having evidently been related continuously by Matthew in the first instance.

There is still some confusion in Luke.

Part of the report of our Lord's denunciation of the scribes, Pharisees and lawyers is located in a different connection (xi. 42-52). This section consists of 209 Greek words, and may have been written on four slips of papyrus. As they bore no indication of the time at which the words were spoken, Luke took them to be a continuation of Christ's utterances at the Pharisee's dinner, with which they seemed to harmonise fairly well.

The Lamentation for Jerusalem (xiii. 34, 35) is appended to Christ's reply to the Pharisees who warned Him to escape from the alleged menaces of Herod. The reference to Jerusalem in xiii. 33 was probably the reason why Luke located it there. The passage consists in the Greek of 51 words and doubtless in James' original report occupied one page of papyrus.

The statement (xi. 53, 54), that when Jesus was gone out the scribes and Pharisees tried to provoke Him into saying something which they could use for His destruction, was, I believe, originally divided from the passage which now next precedes it by the Lament for Jerusalem. The passage consists of 24 words, but, as it formed the termination of his account of the Temple ministry, James did not fill up the page upon which he wrote it.

Mark xii. 38-40, and Luke xx. 45-47 are not, I think, tautochronistic reports, but summaries, written in the evening, of the earlier part of Christ's discourse, a tautochronistic report of which is found Matthew xxiii. 2-12. The close verbal agreement between these two summaries, together with the agreement in the report of Christ's utterance in the sections which follow (Mark xii. 41-44, and Luke xxi. 1-4) show that they were written in company. They were doubtless the reports of the united testimony of the Apostles assembled in conference as usual.

The incident of the widow's mite, which is not reported in Matthew, probably belongs in order of time to between verses 12 and 13 in the last named Gospel.

John's account of the triumphal entry into Jerusalem does not appear to have been written until after the Resurrection.

I find it impossible to avoid the conviction that there is in this 12th chapter of John a departure from that strict order which elsewhere invariably characterises the fourth Gospel and that the manuscripts of which the latter part of the chapter consists were at some time transposed. Verses 44-50 seem properly to follow the first half of verse 36, and verses 36^b-43, which were not written until after the Resurrection, to follow verse 50. If John's original notes were copied on to parchment, each of these sections—they are of about equal length—may have occupied one sheet, and the two sheets may easily have become transposed at some time prior to the book's publication.

The subjoined synoptical table (page 334) shows what I take to be the actual order of events during these three days. It does not however agree always with the order in which the portions were written.

I propose to make a brief statement in narrative form of the events presented in the aforesaid table. But before doing so

Day	Proceedings	Matthew	Mark	Luke	John
Sunday	Triumphal entry into Jerusalem	xxi. 1–11	xi. 1–10	xix. 29–40	xii. 12–19
	Weeping over the city			41–44	
	Visit to Temple and return to Bethany		11		
Monday	Walk from Bethany to Jerusalem				
	Cursing and withering of fig-tree	18, 19	12–14		
	Cleansing of the Temple; Hosannas of the children	12–16	15–18	45–48	
	Return to Bethany in the evening	17	19	xxi. 37, 38	
Tuesday	Walk from Bethany to Jerusalem; Disciples see withered fig-tree; exhorted to have faith	20–22	20–25		
	In the temple; Court of the Women; Chief priests and elders challenge Christ's authority	23–27	27–33	xx. 1–8	
	Christ speaks parables	28–xxii. 14	xii. 1–12	9–18	
	Attempts to ensnare Christ in His talk	15–33	13–27	19–40	
	Question about greatest commandment	34–40	28–34		
	Christ questions Pharisees	41–46	35–37	41–44	
	Denunciation of scribes and Pharisees	xxiii. 1–12	38–40	45–47	
	The widow's mite		41–44	xxi. 1–4	
	Denunciation continued	13–36		xi. 42–52	
	Lamentation for Jerusalem	37–39		xiii. 34, 35	
	Greeks seek to see Jesus; Discourse in Court of the Gentiles				20–36a
	Scribes and Pharisees follow Jesus into Court of Gentiles and try to provoke Him				44–50
	Jesus departs and hides Himself			xi. 53, 54	36b–43

it may not be amiss to say something about the sacred locality in which they for the most part occurred.

Situated on the rocky eminence of Mount Moriah, the entire Temple area occupied a space of rather more than eight acres. It is said by Josephus to have been one stadium (606 feet 9 inches English) square. The site was not a level plateau, but rose in slopes and terraces towards the centre. The highest part was not quite in the middle, but nearer to the north-west corner, and upon it rose the Sanctuary (ὁ ναός), the sacred edifice itself—facing the east. In front of the Sanctuary was the Court of the Priests, in which was the Altar of Sacrifice. This court was surrounded on the north, east and south by a wall one cubit (18 inches) high, to keep back the worshippers, who were not allowed to enter this enclosure. Outside the wall was the Court of the People into which Jewish males alone were admitted. This court could be entered by gates on its north and south sides from the outer court—the Court of the Gentiles. Along its eastern side was a wall which separated it from an oblong space known as the Court of the Women, so called because it was open to Jews of both sexes, women not being permitted to pass beyond its limits in the direction of the Sanctuary. Surrounding the whole of these enclosures was the Court of the Gentiles, which was free to all nationalities, but bore on its inner walls notices in Greek and Latin forbidding foreigners from proceeding further on pain of death. The outer walls of all surrounded this court. In three of these were the entrances from the city, while inside and adjoining the fourth, which overlooked the deep valley on the east, was the long colonnade called Solomon's Porch.

The question now arises: In which of the three courts—the Court of the People, the Court of the Women, or the Court of the Gentiles—was our Lord wont to carry on His work of controversy with the Jewish rulers, or of instructing the people? There are not many texts which help us to answer this question; still the difficulty in coming to a conclusion is not great. We may at once decide against the Court of the People, for the reason that on two occasions a woman was present in the place where Christ was teaching—the woman taken in adultery, and the widow with the mite. On a third occasion too He is said to have been speaking in the Treasury (John viii. 20) which we know from the incident of the widow's mite could be approached by women. Our choice then lies between the Court of the Women and the Court of the Gentiles. In John x. 23 He is said to have been walking in Solomon's Porch which was attached to the latter court, but as His doing so is accounted for on the ground that it was winter we may infer that that was not His usual place of resort. From the fact that the Treasury is twice mentioned it seems highly probable that His customary place of teaching was in its vicinity. Now the general belief is that the Treasury was situated in the Court of the Women—some say in the south-east angle of that court. It is very unlikely that it was situated in the Gentiles' Court, a position that would obviously be too distant from the Sanctuary and the building occupied by the priests. As it was intended for the receipt of the offerings of Hebrew worshippers of both sexes and no others the Women's Court was the only suitable place for it. We are thus led to the conclusion that it was in the Court of the Women that Jesus usually taught.

The Court of the Women was entered from the Court of the Gentiles by a flight of steps, at the top of which were porches, on its eastern side. Running the full width of the inner enclosures its length must have been at least 200 feet and its width was probably 60 or 70 feet. The wall on the western side which separated it from the Court of the People was most likely a low one, and, as the sacred innermost area rose slopingly towards the Altar and the Sanctuary, persons in the Women's Court could see the ritual service as it proceeded. It should seem that this court itself was not a single level, but ascended from east to west by a series of steps, running probably its full length or in a semicircle from south to north. Thus it was well adapted for the purpose of addressing an audience. It afforded ample room for a large congregation, who would stand or sit as in a theatre on the steps rising in front of the speaker; and by raising his voice the speaker might make himself heard in the People's Court on the other side of the low western wall (John vii. 37).

NARRATIVE

On the morning of Sunday, April 2, Jesus left Bethany, and after proceeding a short distance sent two of His disciples to a village for an ass and colt. On their return He rode triumphantly into Jerusalem, amidst the acclamations of the crowd of Galileans who had come out from the city to welcome and accompany Him. On the way as He came into full view of the city He wept over it. He arrived at the Temple late in the day and after looking round upon all things He returned with the Twelve to Bethany.

Next morning, Monday, Jesus again left Bethany and walked with His disciples to the city. On the way He pronounced the doom of the barren fig-tree which in the course of the day perished accordingly. Entering the Temple He expelled the traders who occupied the Court of the Gentiles. After that He healed the blind and the lame who came to Him, and preached to the people who were astonished at His teaching. The children sang hosannas in His praise and the rulers were filled with indignation. He replied to their remonstrances and in the evening again returned to Bethany.

On the morning of Tuesday He once more walked into Jerusalem. On the way the disciples saw the withered fig-tree and expressed their surprise. Our Lord used the incident as an encouragement to His disciples to have faith.

On arriving at the Temple He entered the Court of the Women and engaged in teaching and preaching. Presently some of the chief priests and elders approached Him and demanded to know by what authority He did these things. As He was surrounded by Galileans in whose minds they

z

desired to create an impression unfavourable to Jesus, they addressed Him in Aramaic; He replied in the same tongue by questioning them concerning John the Baptist. He then spake the parable of the Two Sons, of the Husbandmen, and of the Marriage of the King's Son. These were taken down by Matthew as He spoke, and the second parable was taken down by Peter and James also. Attempts were now made to ensnare Jesus in His talk. A Pharisee questioned Him about tribute; and a Sadducee submitted a case concerning the Resurrection. Next a lawyer or scribe asked Him which was the greatest commandment. He then asked the Pharisees a question concerning the Christ. Jesus now addressed to the multitudes and His disciples—His friends and followers from Galilee—His severe denunciation of the scribes and Pharisees. He spake in Aramaic, and His words were reported at the time by Matthew. Peter and James took no report, but in the evening they wrote, doubtless with the help of the other disciples, a short summary from memory, and also an account of the incident of the widow's mite.

This incident appears to have taken place during an interruption in Christ's address caused by the influx, at the usual hour, of worshippers, who, before proceeding to engage in their devotions, approached the treasury and cast their offerings into the chest. While this was going on our Lord sat down on the steps opposite the treasury and watched, and after a while observed the widow with the mites.

When the stream of worshippers ceased to arrive, and quiet was restored in the Court of the Women, He resumed His denunciation of the scribes and Pharisees. Tautochronistic reports of this, including the Lamentation for Jerusalem with which it ended, were taken by both Matthew and James.

It was probably just after the termination of this discourse, that is to say in the afternoon of Tuesday, April 4th, and as our Lord was on the point of leaving, that the circumstance happened which is the only event of this last ministry in the Temple recorded by John. Certain Greeks—Heathen visitors from abroad—having heard the fame of the Galilean Teacher, and being desirous of seeing Him, entered the Court of the Gentiles and made their wishes known to some of the people there. Philip, who was well-known to be one of our Lord's disciples, happening to pass at the time was pointed out to them. Approaching, they 'asked him saying, Sir, we would see Jesus.' Philip thereupon walked up the steps and through the gate into the Women's Court, and made his way through the crowd to the spot where the Lord stood with His disciples, and told Andrew, whereupon the two came together to Jesus Himself and told Him. John's narrative then proceeds: "And Jesus answered them saying, etc." Now it has been supposed by some that these words imply that our Lord took no notice of the request of the strangers; but proceeded to address at considerable length the two disciples and perhaps a few other bystanders. Following which, according to verse 36, He departed and hid Himself. But to have acted thus would have been quite alien from that perfect courtesy and consideration for the feelings of others which invariably appear in the character of Christ. We may therefore be sure that the pronoun 'them,' in verse 23, representing the persons to whom Christ addressed Himself, describes, not Andrew and Philip, but the Greek visitors. As soon as our Lord heard from the two disciples the desire of the strangers to see Him, He left the spot where He was, and, threading His way through the throng, passed out and down to the Gentiles' Court, and, guided by Philip, approached the waiting Greeks. A few words of greeting and perhaps some other unrecorded sentences were exchanged. This conversation naturally took place in Greek, and John, who had followed his Master from the Court of the Women, and whose pen had been idle during the delivery there of Christ's addresses in Aramaic, now drew it with tablet and paper from his wallet, and, adjusting the inkhorn at his girdle began to write. Just then Jesus, still speaking in Greek, uttered these words: "The hour is come, that the Son of man should be glorified," and went on to speak the subsequent sentences recorded in John xii. of which John took down a report as He was speaking.

It must have been at this moment, as Jesus finished speaking, that the scene took place described Luke xi. 53, 54. The scribes and Pharisees had never before heard Him express Himself so strongly as in His denunciation this day of their wickedness and hypocrisy, and, thinking that His wrathful mood might afford them an opportunity to effect by insult what they had failed to accomplish in a guise of friendliness, they determined once more to try and entrap Him into saying something that might furnish a pretext for an accusation. It was while they were arranging their plans that He had left the Women's Court to interview the Greek visitors, and they now followed Him into the Court of the Gentiles. Here is Luke's statement of what then took place: "And when he was come out from thence, the scribes and the Pharisees began to press upon *him* vehemently, and to provoke him to speak of many things; laying wait for him, to catch something out of His mouth."

Our Lord perceived that the time had now come for Him to withdraw. He had preached the Gospel to representatives of the Gentile world, and in doing so had completed the delivery of His message to mankind. He purposed to spend the remainder of this day with His disciples to instruct them and through them the rest of His people concerning the destruction of Jerusalem and His own Second Coming. And He desired for the morrow a season of communion with His Father to prepare for that dread hour that was now so fast approaching. So, in the words of John, 'He departed and hid Himself from them,' or, as the margin reads, 'was hidden from them.' But there was no secrecy in His immediate movements. The elders had no intention of arresting Him publicly in the crowded Temple. He passed out conversing with His disciples who lovingly tried to divert His thoughts from His late painful experiences by calling His attention to the Temple buildings.

Discourse to Disciples Foretelling Destruction of Jerusalem and End of the World

Matt. xxiv. 1–9; x. 17–23; xxiv. 10–xxv. 46; *Mark* xiii. 1–37; *Luke* xxi. 5–36; xii. 35–48

That these are the reports of three different persons is proved by the difference in the settings. Here are the introductory sentences placed side by side.

MATTHEW.	MARK.	LUKE.
And Jesus went out from the temple, and was going on his way; and his disciples came to him to shew him the buildings of the temple. But he answered and said unto them, See ye not all these things? verily I say unto you, There shall not be left here one stone upon another, that shall not be thrown down. And as he sat on the mount of Olives, the disciples came unto him privately, saying, Tell us, when shall these things be? and what *shall be* the sign of thy coming, and of the end of the world? And Jesus answered and said unto them,	And as he went forth out of the temple, one of his disciples saith unto him, Master, behold, what manner of stones and what manner of buildings! And Jesus said unto him, Seest thou these great buildings? there shall not be left here one stone upon another, which shall not be thrown down. And as he sat on the mount of Olives over against the temple, Peter and James and John and Andrew asked him privately, Tell us, when shall these things be? and what *shall be* the sign when these things are all about to be accomplished? And Jesus began to say unto them,	And as some spake of the temple, how it was adorned with goodly stones and offerings, he said, As for these things which ye behold, the days will come, in which there shall not be left here one stone upon another, that shall not be thrown down. And they asked him, saying, Master, when therefore shall these things be: and what *shall be* the sign when these things are about to come to pass? And he said,

There are it is true sufficient points of resemblance amongst the above to prove that they were written in company as usual; but it is impossible to suppose that they are all variations of a common original.

When we come to examine the reports of the discourse itself we find the agreement very close among those parts of it which are contained in more than one Gospel. A good deal of the earlier part is word for word alike in all three, and where variations occur they are evidently in many cases the result of distinct translations of matter that was alike in the originals. Sometimes a word or a sentence is missing in one or other of the three. This may be owing either to the reporters being sometimes unable to keep pace with the Speaker's utterance, or to their intense interest in what He was saying causing them now and then to suspend for the moment the use of their pen.

It is not to be inferred from Mark's statement that 'Peter and James and John and Andrew asked Him privately' that only those four were present when our Lord delivered the discourse. All that is implied by the expression 'privately' (κατ' ἰδίαν) is that the application was not made in the presence of the multitude—thus distinguishing the address from those just before delivered publicly in the Temple. The names of Peter, James, John and Andrew are specially mentioned because they made the request as spokesmen for the Twelve.

Our Lord spoke in Aramaic. He was addressing His own disciples who were even now more familiar with that language than with Greek. The subject of His discourse not being a doctrinal one He could speak on it plainly and forcibly in the Semitic tongue. Accordingly the discourse is recorded, not in John, but in Matthew, Mark and Luke.

The portion Matt. x. 17-23 compares so closely with Mark xiii. 9-13 and Luke xxi. 12-19, that it cannot be doubted that all three are reports of the same utterance. According to Matthew it forms part of the charge which Jesus delivered to the Twelve when He sent them forth on their mission through the villages, preaching the Gospel. As however Mark and Luke agree in omitting it from that connection and in locating it here we are bound to accept their united testimony as correct. It would seem that in this instance Matthew was not quite satisfied with his choice of a place for the portion in question, for in the place which it ought

THE NARRATIVES AND THE THEORY 343

to occupy in chap. xxiv. are two verses (9, 10) of similar purport to some of the sentences in x. 17–23. Further, Matthew omits in chap. x. the sentence which forms verse 10 in Mark's report, "And the Gospel must first be preached unto all the nations"; but retains a similar sentence in his report of the Mount of Olives discourse (xxiv. 14), "And this Gospel of the Kingdom shall be preached in the whole world for a testimony unto all the nations." One sentence corresponding to Mark ver. 13 and (probably) Luke ver. 19 is found in both the earlier and the later report of Matthew, "But he that endureth to the end the same shall be saved" (x. 22^b; xxiv. 13). It thus appears that Matthew in his uncertainty as to the proper location of the sheet of papyrus containing this portion made a sort of compromise, copying the greater part of it into his account of the Mission address, but repeating the substance of part in the Mount of Olives address, in which he also included one sentence omitted, and the duplicate of another sentence retained, in the former.

TWO DAYS BEFORE THE PASSOVER. DECIDED MEASURES OF
JEWISH RULERS

Matt. xxvi. 1–5 ; *Mark* xiv. 1, 2 ; *Luke* xxii. 1, 2

These passages form the beginnings of the portions written by Matthew, Peter and James after our Lord's Resurrection, and about which we shall have something more to say later on.

WEDNESDAY, APRIL 5

No account is given of the manner in which the day was occupied which followed the one we have just been considering; but it may be inferred from John xii. 36 that Jesus spent the day in retirement and alone. It was in all probability on this day, Wednesday, April 5, that Matthew, Peter and James, in conference with the other disciples, wrote up their narratives from the date of their leaving Jericho until now; in which narratives they included in their proper places the tautochronistic reports they had taken. No account of the supper at Bethany was written at this time however.

THE PASSOVER SUPPER

Matt. xxvi. 17–29; *Mark* xiv. 12–25; *Luke* xxii. 7–23; *John* xiii. 1–35

It is impossible to say for certain in what language the various utterances of Christ and His disciples recorded in these passages were spoken. Hitherto all conversation among themselves appears to have taken place in the dialect of Galilee. But the disciples had been gradually acquiring a greater familiarity with Greek; so much so that soon after the Ascension of Jesus their use of it seems to have quite superseded Aramaic. It may be therefore that Greek was spoken at this meal, and there are some slight indications that such was the case. The use in John xiii. 10 of the synonyms rendered in the Revised Version 'bathed' and 'wash' is a case in point: ὁ λελουμένος οὐκ ἔχει χρείαν εἰ μὴ τοὺς πόδας νίψασθαι. Still there were corresponding synonyms in Aramaic that these may have represented; and on the whole it seems more probable that, in the earlier part of the evening, when the conversation was general and colloquial, Aramaic was employed. As all the reports were written from memory, they give no reliable clue on this question. The identical words used would no longer remain in the minds of those who heard, however accurately the thoughts expressed thereby might be retained.

The common influence as usual appears plainly in Matthew, Mark and Luke, showing that their accounts were written in conference. It is especially striking in the two former; whole sentences sometimes showing only such differences as would follow from the independent translation of the original manuscripts from Aramaic to Greek. There is less verbal resemblance in Luke; the variations arising partly from greater independence in James' original report, and partly from greater freedom exercised by Luke in his Greek rendering.

to occupy in chap. xxiv. are two verses (9, 10) of similar purport to some of the sentences in x. 17-23. Further, Matthew omits in chap. x. the sentence which forms verse 10 in Mark's report, "And the Gospel must first be preached unto all the nations"; but retains a similar sentence in his report of the Mount of Olives discourse (xxiv. 14), "And this Gospel of the Kingdom shall be preached in the whole world for a testimony unto all the nations." One sentence corresponding to Mark ver. 13 and (probably) Luke ver. 19 is found in both the earlier and the later report of Matthew, "But he that endureth to the end the same shall be saved" (x. 22ᵇ; xxiv. 13). It thus appears that Matthew in his uncertainty as to the proper location of the sheet of papyrus containing this portion made a sort of compromise, copying the greater part of it into his account of the Mission address, but repeating the substance of part in the Mount of Olives address, in which he also included one sentence omitted, and the duplicate of another sentence retained, in the former.

TWO DAYS BEFORE THE PASSOVER. DECIDED MEASURES OF JEWISH RULERS

Matt. xxvi. 1-5; *Mark* xiv. 1, 2; *Luke* xxii. 1, 2

These passages form the beginnings of the portions written by Matthew, Peter and James after our Lord's Resurrection, and about which we shall have something more to say later on.

WEDNESDAY, APRIL 5

No account is given of the manner in which the day was occupied which followed the one we have just been considering; but it may be inferred from John xii. 36 that Jesus spent the day in retirement and alone. It was in all probability on this day, Wednesday, April 5, that Matthew, Peter and James, in conference with the other disciples, wrote up their narratives from the date of their leaving Jericho until now; in which narratives they included in their proper places the tautochronistic reports they had taken. No account of the supper at Bethany was written at this time however.

THE PASSOVER SUPPER

Matt. xxvi. 17–29; *Mark* xiv. 12–25; *Luke* xxii. 7–23; *John* xiii. 1–35

It is impossible to say for certain in what language the various utterances of Christ and His disciples recorded in these passages were spoken. Hitherto all conversation among themselves appears to have taken place in the dialect of Galilee. But the disciples had been gradually acquiring a greater familiarity with Greek; so much so that soon after the Ascension of Jesus their use of it seems to have quite superseded Aramaic. It may be therefore that Greek was spoken at this meal, and there are some slight indications that such was the case. The use in John xiii. 10 of the synonyms rendered in the Revised Version 'bathed' and 'wash' is a case in point: ὁ λελουμένος οὐκ ἔχει χρείαν εἰ μὴ τοὺς πόδας νίψασθαι. Still there were corresponding synonyms in Aramaic that these may have represented; and on the whole it seems more probable that, in the earlier part of the evening, when the conversation was general and colloquial, Aramaic was employed. As all the reports were written from memory, they give no reliable clue on this question. The identical words used would no longer remain in the minds of those who heard, however accurately the thoughts expressed thereby might be retained.

The common influence as usual appears plainly in Matthew, Mark and Luke, showing that their accounts were written in conference. It is especially striking in the two former; whole sentences sometimes showing only such differences as would follow from the independent translation of the original manuscripts from Aramaic to Greek. There is less verbal resemblance in Luke; the variations arising partly from greater independence in James' original report, and partly from greater freedom exercised by Luke in his Greek rendering.

Luke xxii. 21-23 (containing in the Greek 46 words) represents a page of James' notes that was transposed. We learn from Matthew and Mark that this portion should follow verse 16 and precede the report of the institution of the Lord's Supper.

John's account was written quite independently, yet with some general knowledge of the nature of the record the others were making. This is proved by his omission of any mention of the institution of the Lord's Supper, an event which, the others having recorded it, he did not deem it needful to repeat.

This omission however is utterly inexplicable if the Gospel originated at the late date usually assigned. For the observance of the Lord's Supper was general in the Church, and its institution was a subject of interest to all; so much so that even Paul deemed it right to place an account of it on record. The supplementary theory will not explain John's silence, as it will be seen when we come to consider John xviii. that John could not have had the other Gospels before him when he wrote the history of the closing events of Christ's earthly life, or even have had a clear recollection of their narratives of those events in his mind.

Not only is the omission referred to fatal to every theory except that for which I contend, and especially to the theories which post-date the composition of the fourth Gospel to any part of the second century, it even proves that John when redacting his work avoided adding any fact from memory. He added many elucidatory remarks but no new fact—otherwise he would certainly have inserted an account of the origin of this ordinance.

What makes the omission more striking is that John records some occurrences which are also found in the other Gospels. Thus he records our Lord's announcement of His betrayal by Judas; also the warning that was given to Peter, and Peter's assertive self-confidence thereafter. For a time such occurrences as these would more vividly impress the Apostles than the institution of the Supper. But after the lapse of years the latter event would far transcend them in its apparent importance.

CHRIST'S LAST DISCOURSE AND HIS PRAYER FOR HIS DISCIPLES

John xiv. 1–xvii. 26

This discourse and prayer were spoken in the room where the Supper was held; previously therefore to the prediction of Peter's denial recorded in the last three verses of the preceding chapter. They seem to have been placed here and not between verses 35 and 36 of chapter xiii. so as not to break the symmetry of the account of the Supper which was written from memory after the Resurrection. Chapters xiv., xv., xvi., xvii. are a verbatim report made at the time Jesus was speaking.

It is quite without example for an address of such length to be accurately recorded from memory, and there is not the least reason for supposing that it was miraculously communicated to the mind of the writer at a later time. That it is an exact report of the very words of Christ should be beyond question, and could never have been questioned with any show of plausibility but for the difficulties which this book claims to have removed.

By this time all the Apostles had become thoroughly accustomed to the use of Greek, so our Lord, in delivering this last address—an address designed to instruct the Church in all ages in the profoundest truths of theology—chose for His purpose the classic tongue which has ever been recognised as the most perfect vehicle for the expression of scientific and philosophic thought. Consequently John was able to take of it a full report.

The party had finished their sad repast, and, in accordance with Jewish custom, had washed their hands. When they had resumed their reclining attitude our Lord intimated to John His intention to speak at length, whereupon the disciple produced his writing materials and proceeded to write. After a while (xiv. 31) they all rose to their feet, and Jesus continued His discourse standing, John still writing. Not until the prayer (chap xviii.) was finished did the party leave the upper room and make their way across the Kidron to the Mount of Olives.

Peter's Fall Foretold

Matt. xxvi. 30–35 ; *Mark* xiv. 26–31 ; *Luke* xxii. 31–38 ; *John* xiii. 36–38

The passage Luke xxii. 24–30 is entirely out of its connection here. It belongs, as stated elsewhere, to the narrative of the last journey to Jerusalem and is parallel with Matt. xx. 20–28 and Mark x. 35–45. It contains in Greek 110 words and consisted doubtless of two pages of James' manuscript which Luke, having no guidance as to its real connection, placed here. His reason for placing it here is obvious. But even if the words quoted verse 27 had been spoken at the Supper they could not have been intended as an allusion to the circumstances of the moment. For our Lord certainly did not then act the part of an attendant; He was one of those who reclined at the table. The words had a purely spiritual signification ; they referred to the feast of salvation, and should be read in close connection with the words recorded Matt. xx. 28.

The words which in the Authorised Version stand at the beginning of Luke xxii. 31, 'And the Lord said' (εἶπε δὲ ὁ Κύριος), are, I think, wrongly omitted in the Revised Version, the weight of manuscript authority being decidedly in favour of their retention. They are found in the Codices Sinaiticus, Alexandrinus and Bezæ. Their omission by the Codex Vaticanus is owing doubtless to a transcriber thinking them superfluous, which they certainly seem to be according to Luke's arrangement. It can only be for the same subjective reason that Westcott and Hort omit the words against the weight of documentary evidence. But they are not superfluous according to the original arrangement intended by James, by which verse 31 would have immediately followed 20. (Verses 21-23 it will be remembered belong to between verses 16 and 17.)

Comparing the four narratives it appears that the warning to Peter was spoken by Christ on the way to the Mount of Olives just after leaving the house where the Supper was held in Jerusalem.

The resemblance between Matthew and Mark is here very close, Matt. ver. 30 and Mark ver. 26 being identical, and Matt. vs. 31-33, Mark vs. 27-29 showing but little difference except such as might result from their being independent translations of the same Aramaic original. Matt. vs. 34, 35 and Mark vs. 30, 31 show a greater divergence, the Lord's prediction in the latter being more detailed, and Peter's protestation more emphatic.

Luke bears less resemblance to the others than usual, ver. 34 being the only text that exhibits the common influence.

John's account is quite independent, and supplies a part of the conversation which is not recorded by either of the others.

GETHSEMANE

Matthew xxvi. 36-46; *Mark* xiv. 32-42; *Luke* xxii. 39-46; *John* xviii. 1, 2

The words spoken by Jesus in His prayer in the Garden of Gethsemane were heard only by Peter, James and John. He was parted from the other eight disciples 'about a stone's cast' (Luke); He 'went forward a little' only from the three (Matthew, Mark).

The accounts in Matthew, Mark and Luke were written in conference as usual; but that of Matthew, who was among the eight and did not hear the prayer, was gathered by him from Peter whose own account is preserved in Mark. Hence the accounts in Matthew and Mark are almost word for word alike. James, on the other hand, heard for himself; his account therefore, though in substance the same, is somewhat differently worded. It should be noted that verses 43, 44 in

Luke, which have no parallel in the other Gospels, are of doubtful authenticity.

John records the arrival at the Garden but does not mention the Agony or the Prayer. Although John's narrative was not, like the others, written in conference with the rest of the Apostles, and hence shows none of the indications of the common influence which dominates them, it is probable that John was aware that the Aramaic writers were recording the Prayer, which was doubtless spoken in that language.

THE ARREST

Matt. xxvi. 47–56; *Mark* xiv. 43–52; *Luke* xxii. 47–53; *John* xviii. 3–11

The common influence is here very apparent in Matthew, Mark and Luke, the resemblance between the two former being specially striking. But it should be observed that, whereas in the previous section, wherein Matthew was indebted to Peter for most of his information, Mark's account is fuller than Matthew's, in this one Matthew's account is fuller than Mark's.

There is one incident related in Mark that is not mentioned in either of the others. It is that of the young man who was seized by the officers, and who left his garment in their hands and fled (vs. 51, 52). In all probability this was Mark himself, and these two verses were inserted by him when redacting Peter's notes, doubtless with the Apostle's permission.

350 THE GOSPEL PROBLEMS AND THEIR SOLUTION

BEFORE ANNAS AND CAIAPHAS
Matt. xxvi. 57–xxvii. 1 ; *Mark* xiv. 53–xv. 1[a]

As stated in John ver. 24 Annas sent Jesus bound to

MATT. xxvi.
57 And they that had taken Jesus led him away to *the house of* Caiaphas the high priest, where the scribes and the elders were gathered together. But
58 Peter followed him afar off,

MARK xiv.
53 And they led Jesus away to the high priest : and there come together with him all the chief priests and the elders and the
54 scribes. And Peter had followed him afar off,

unto the court of the high priest, and entered in, and sat with the officers, to see the end.

even within, into the court of the high priest ; and he was sitting with the officers, and warming himself in the light *of the fire*.

PETER'S DENIALS

Luke xxii. 54–71; *John* xviii. 12–27

Caiaphas the high priest.

JOHN xviii.

12 So the band and the chief captain, and the officers of the Jews, seized Jesus and bound
13 him, and led him to Annas first: for he was father-in-law to Caiaphas, which was high
14 priest that year. Now Caiaphas was he which gave counsel to the Jews, that it was expedient that one man should die for the people.

LUKE xxii.

54 And they seized him, and led him *away*, and brought him into the high priest's house. But Peter followed afar off.

15 And Simon Peter followed Jesus, and *so did* another disciple. Now that disciple was known unto the high priest, and entered in with Jesus into the court of the high priest; but
16 Peter was standing at the door without. So the other disciple, which was known unto the high priest, went out and spake to her that kept the door, and
17 brought in Peter. The maid therefore that kept the door saith unto Peter, Art thou also *one* of this man's disciples? He
18 saith, I am not. Now the servants and the officers were standing *there*, having made a fire of coals; for it was cold; and they were warming themselves: and Peter also was with them, standing and warming himself.

55 And when they had kindled a fire in the midst of the court, and had sat down together, Peter sat in the midst of them.

59 Now the chief priests and the whole council sought false witness against Jesus, that they might put him to death; and 60 they found it not, though many false witnesses came. But 61 afterward came two, and said, This man said, I am able to destroy the temple of God, and to build it in three days.	55 Now the chief priests and the whole council sought witness against Jesus to put him to 56 death; and found it not. For many bare false witness against him, and their witness agreed 57 not together. And there stood up certain, and bare false wit-58 ness against him, saying, We heard him say, I will destroy this temple that is made with hands, and in three days I will build another made without 59 hands. And not even so did their witness agree together.
62 And the high priest stood up, and said unto him, Answerest	60 And the high priest stood up in the midst, and asked Jesus

THE NARRATIVES AND THE THEORY 353

19 The high priest therefore asked Jesus of his disciples, and
20 of his teaching. Jesus answered him, I have spoken openly to the world; I ever taught in synagogues, and in the temple, where all the Jews come together; and in secret spake I
21 nothing. Why askest thou me? ask them that have heard *me*, what I spake unto them: behold, these know the things
22 which I said. And when he had said this, one of the officers standing by struck Jesus with his hand, saying, Answerest
23 thou the high priest so? Jesus answered him, If I have spoken evil, bear witness of the evil; but if well, why smitest thou
24 me? Annas therefore sent him bound unto Caiaphas the high priest.

v. 24 is parenthetical, see above between vs. 14 and 15.

thou nothing? what is it which
63 these witness against thee? But
Jesus held his peace. And the
high priest said unto him, I
adjure thee by the living God,
that thou tell us whether thou
64 be the Christ, the Son of God.
Jesus saith unto him, Thou hast
said : nevertheless I say unto
you, Henceforth ye shall see the
Son of man sitting at the right
hand of power, and coming on
the clouds of heaven.
65 Then the high priest rent his garments, saying, He has spoken
blasphemy: what further need
have we of witnesses? behold,
now ye have heard the blas-
66 phemy: what think ye? They
answered and said, He is worthy
67 of death. Then did they spit
in his face and buffet him: and
some smote him with the palms
68 of their hands saying, Prophesy
unto us, thou Christ: who is
he that struck thee?

saying, Answerest thou nothing?
what is it which these witness
61 against thee? But he held his
peace, and answered nothing.
Again the high priest asked
him, and saith unto him, Art
thou the Christ, the Son of the
62 Blessed? And Jesus said, I
am : and ye shall see the Son
of man sitting at the right hand
of power, and coming with the
clouds of heaven.
63 And the high priest rent his
clothes, and saith, What further
need have we of witnesses? Ye
64 have heard the blasphemy :
what think ye? And they all
condemned him to be worthy of
65 death. And some began to spit
on him, and to cover his face,
and to buffet him, and to say
unto him, Prophesy : and the
officers received him with blows
of their hands.

While this was going on James gained admittance to the

69 Now Peter was sitting without
in the court : and a maid came
unto him, saying, Thou also
wast with Jesus the Galilæan.
70 But he denied before them all,
saying, I know not what thou
sayest.

71 And when he was gone out
into the porch, another *maid*
saw him, and saith unto them
that were there, This man also

66 And as Peter was beneath in
the court, there cometh one of
the maids of the high priest ;
67 and seeing Peter warming himself, she looked upon him, and
saith, Thou also wast with the
68 Nazarene, *even* Jesus. But he
denied, saying, I neither know,
nor understand what thou sayest : and he went out into the
porch ; and the cock crew.
69 And the maid saw him, and
began again to say to them that
stood by, This is *one* of them.
70 But he again denied it.

court of the high priest.

56 And a certain maid seeing him as he sat in the light *of the fire*, and looking steadfastly upon him, said, This man also
57 was with him. But he denied, saying, Woman, I know him not.

25 Now Simon Peter was standing and warming himself. They said therefore unto him, Art thou also *one* of his disciples? He denied, and said, I am not.

58 And after a little while another saw him, and said, Thou also art *one* of them. But Peter said, Man, I am not.

was with Jesus the Nazarene.
72 And again he denied with an oath, I know not the man.
73 And after a little while they that stood by came and said to Peter, Of a truth thou also art *one* of them; for thy speech bewrayeth
74 thee. Then began he to curse and to swear, I know not the man. And straightway the cock
75 crew. And Peter remembered the word which Jesus had said, Before the cock crow, thou shalt deny me thrice. And he went out, and wept bitterly.

And after a little while again they that stood by said to Peter, Of a truth thou art *one* of them;
71 for thou art a Galilæan. But he began to curse, and to swear, I know not this man of whom
72 ye speak. And straightway the second time the cock crew. And Peter called to mind the word, how that Jesus said unto him, Before the cock crow twice, thou shalt deny me thrice. And when he thought thereon, he wept.

xxvii. Now when morning was come, all the chief priests and the elders of the people took counsel against Jesus to put him to death.

xv. And straightway in the morning the chief priests with the elders and scribes, and the whole council, held a consultation.

59 And after the space of about one hour another confidently affirmed, saying, Of a truth this man also was with him: for he
60 is a Galilæan. But Peter said, Man, I know not what thou sayest. And immediately, while he yet spake, the cock crew.
61 And the Lord turned, and looked upon Peter. And Peter remembered the word of the Lord, how that he said unto him, Before the cock crow this day, thou shalt deny me thrice.
62 And he went out and wept bitterly.
63 And the men that held *Jesus* mocked him, and beat him.
64 And they blindfolded him, and asked him, saying, Prophesy: who is he that struck thee?
65 And many other things spake they against him, reviling him.
66 And as soon as it was day, the assembly of the elders of the people was gathered together, both chief priests and scribes; and they led him away
67 into their council, saying, If thou art the Christ, tell us. But he said unto them, If I tell you, ye will not believe:
68 and if I ask *you*, ye will not
69 answer. But from henceforth shall the Son of man be seated at the right hand of the power
70 of God. And they all said, Art thou then the Son of God? And he said unto them, Ye say
71 that I am. And they said, What further need have we of witness? for we ourselves have heard from his own mouth.

26 One of the servants of the high priest, being a kinsman of him whose ear Peter cut off, saith, Did not I see thee in the
27 garden with him? Peter therefore denied again: and straightway the cock crew.

A comparison of these four narratives discloses the following facts :

The original reports which constitute the first three, that is to say the reports of Matthew, Peter and James, were written by them in conference. But there is no indication that any one else was with them at the time they were so engaged.

John's report was written independently. It is moreover evident that he had not seen their narratives when he wrote his, and they had not seen his narrative when they wrote theirs.

Peter as we know was present for a time in the court of the high priest, and was the chief actor in one part of the story; and his account is a relation of what he himself saw and did.

James was also present, at least during the latter part of the night, and his account is a report almost entirely of what he himself observed.

Matthew was not present, and his account is composed of facts learned by him from the other two—chiefly from Peter.

John's account is composed entirely of the results of his own observation and recollection.

Apart from the internal evidence it should seem highly probable that James entered the high priest's house. His strong attachment to Christ would impel a man of his determined character to make an effort to be near his Master at such a time. He was one of the three whom our Lord had several times taken apart into a closer confidence, and it is not likely that after the Arrest he would let the whole night pass without making some attempt to rejoin Him. Like his brother he may have been known to the high priest, and if not he could, as Peter did, gain admittance to the house through John's influence. If, as supposed by Farrar, a branch of the Zebedee fishery business was carried on in Jerusalem, it is not unlikely that both John and James were well-known to the high priest's household, and known too to be disciples of Christ. The use of the word 'also' (καὶ) by those who challenged Peter with being one of Jesus' disciples implies that others who were present were known to be disciples. But it does not follow that James entered the house at the same time as John or Peter. He is not mentioned in John's narrative, and it is reasonable to suppose that, after he and the other disciples left the Lord and fled, some little time elapsed before he regained his self-possession and followed Him to the city.

It is not probable that Matthew was one of those who entered the high priest's house. His former occupation would generally be a bar to his admittance to places not open to all, and that the public were not freely admitted to the residence of Caiaphas is shown by John's deeming it needful to account for the admittance of himself and Peter (xviii. 15).

That the accounts contained in Matthew, Mark and Luke were written in conference is proved by their general resemblance and by their all using in the parallel texts identical or very similar expressions. For instance, they all say that, as Jesus was taken to the high priest's house, " Peter followed afar off." Peter's sitting with the officers and servants is mentioned by the three, and both Mark and Luke speak of the fire in the hall. It appears from all three that, when Peter was challenged the third time, his Galilean dialect was alluded to. All say that Peter on hearing the cock crow remembered our Lord's warning and wept. And all state that a session of the Council was held in the morning.

Nevertheless the diversity between Mark and Luke is very considerable, and sufficient to show that Peter and James was each too busy writing his own account to pay very close attention to what the other said. Mark relates first a trial and condemnation of Christ by the Council, then their insulting treatment of Him and His reception by the officers with blows, and lastly the denials of Peter. Luke here takes up the narrative, beginning with his version of Peter's fall, then describing the mockery of the guard, and next relating a second trial before the Council. In the accounts of Peter's denials there is marked variation both in the wording and the details of fact. According to Mark it was a maid, according to Luke it was a man, who challenged Peter previously to the second denial. Mark says that the third denial followed the second 'after a little while'; Luke says there was 'the space of about one hour' between them. Luke alone says that 'the Lord turned and looked upon Peter.'

That Matthew derived his report from the original writers of Mark's and Luke's reports is proved by his telling us almost nothing that is not related by one or both of the others. The only noticeable exceptions are the adjuration of the high priest and the statement that Peter's second denial was accompanied by an oath, facts which he doubtless learned orally at the time of writing from either Peter or James—most probably Peter—though not recorded by either of the latter.

That it was chiefly from Peter that Matthew obtained his information is shown by the general similarity of Matthew and Mark not only in the wording but in the substance and structure of the narratives. Yet Matthew's account is by no means identical with Mark's. He omits some details related by the latter, and it is to James that he was indebted for the last clause of verse 75.

Matt. 75 }
Luke 62 } "And he went out and wept bitterly,"

the corresponding clause in Mark being

(72) "And when he thought thereon he wept."

When we turn to John we see that we have a quite independent narrative. This is so manifest even to the most cursory reader that there is no need here to contrast his story with the other three. The essential fact to be remembered is that Matthew, Peter and James wrote in conference the accounts in Matthew, Mark and Luke respectively, and that while doing so they conversed in Aramaic, in which language they also wrote; whereas John wrote the account in the fourth Gospel separately and wrote it in Greek.

It is quite possible however that the others may have given John some idea of what they had written, so that he might make his narrative, in some measure, of a supplementary character.

John is the only one who mentions that our Lord was in the first instance taken to the house of Annas. No other disciple followed closely enough to observe this. The proceedings related in the verses following that statement manifestly took place in the house, not of Annas, but of the high priest, Caiaphas, although it is not until verse 24 that John says that Annas sent Him bound to Caiaphas. Peter's denial of Jesus to the maid that kept the door as he entered with John does not coincide with either of the denials recorded by the other Evangelists. It was made in the presence of only the maid and John, and, it would seem, is not to be reckoned as one of the three public denials foretold by our Lord. The preliminary examination by the high priest (verses 19-23) appears to have been heard by John only. He probably approached near enough to the hall of justice to see and hear what passed, while Peter remained with the servants warming himself at the fire. The proceedings that followed the questioning of Jesus were of a more formal character, and, while they were going on, silence would be preserved in the court; hence what was spoken would be heard by all. Mark accordingly records these. Peter's second denial is not mentioned by John, perhaps because it took place in the porch where John did not follow Peter.

It is recognised by many that the trial and condemnation recorded in Luke (66-71) is a different and later one than that recorded in Matthew (59-68) and Mark (55-65). The trial in Matthew and Mark took place soon after the arrival at the high priest's house, whereas that in Luke was not held until daylight. The Jewish law forbade the trial of capital cases at night; consequently the condemnation of Jesus as related in Matthew and Mark was invalid, and, in order to obtain a conviction which should not be too flagrantly illegal, it was necessary when the morning was come to re-enact the proceedings which had been already rehearsed. Andrews says, "This meeting was then a morning session convened to ratify formally what had been done before with haste and informality. The circumstances under which its members had been earlier convened at the palace of Caiaphas sufficiently show that the legal forms, which they were so scrupulous in observing, had not been complied with. The law forbidding capital trials in the night had been broken; the place of session was unusual, if not illegal; perhaps the attendance, so early after midnight, had not been full. On these accounts it was expedient that a more regular and legal sitting should be held as early in the morning as possible. At this nothing need be done but to hear the confession of Jesus, to pronounce sentence and to consult in what manner it could best be carried into effect; for although they had condemned Him, they had no power to execute the sentence" (p. 524).

There is no intimation however in any of the accounts that the morning session was held in a different place than that used for the night proceedings, and it is hardly possible that they should have taken our Lord away from the high priest's house to some other place without its being recorded that they had done so.

The probable reason why Mark and Matthew record the earlier trial while Luke does not is that Peter was present while those proceedings were in progress, whereas James did not come in until just after they were finished.

On the other hand Luke, and not Matthew and Mark, gives an account of the formal trial that took place in the morning, because he remained in the high priest's court, whereas Peter went out immediately after his last denial.

But why does John give no account of this morning trial and condemnation? Like Mark, and Matthew who follows Mark, John breaks off suddenly with Peter's third denial. How is this to be explained? Is it not that John, taking pity on Peter, followed him out to help him in his time of deep abasement, and remained with him in the street during the rest of the night? It is for this reason doubtless that John tells nothing of what passed from the time when Peter went out, until Christ was seen to be taken from the house of Caiaphas to the court of Pilate. He does not so much even as allude to the morning session which both Matthew and Peter, writing in company with James, briefly recorded in their notes.

It is evident from the attention that was called to Peter by his Galilean accent that the conversation among the underlings in the high priest's house was carried on in Aramaic. This quite accords with the views we maintain. These male and female servants and subordinates (ὑπηρέται, δοῦλοι, θυρωροί, παιδίσκαι) would be drawn from the lower orders, mostly of the country parts of Judea, and Aramaic would be the language they would employ among themselves. The elision of the deeper gutturals which was characteristic of Galileans would betray Peter's northern origin as soon as he spoke. The remark of the servants is of special interest as showing how well it was understood that, whilst the Judeans had rejected Jesus, the Galileans as a community, had, in a popular sense at least, acknowledged His claims.

To enable us to see in clearer light how exactly the features of the several narratives accord with the views we hold as to their origin, let us try to combine the four accounts into something like a consecutive story of what took place from the time of Christ's arrest until He was led away from the high priest to the Roman governor.

Our Lord, as soon as He was arrested, was led to Annas, the father-in-law of Caiaphas. John followed close after the crowd, but was not admitted to Annas' house; therefore no account is given of what took place there. After a while, John, who was watching outside, saw Jesus brought out bound, and followed Him to the house of Caiaphas the high priest, whither the officers conducted Him. As they were going in, John saw Peter, who had followed at a distance, coming towards the place. John went into the high priest's house immediately after the party in charge of Christ. After he had been there a few moments he noticed that Peter had not come in; going to the door he saw him standing without and, speaking to the porteress, brought him in. As he did so, the porteress, knowing that John was a disciple of Jesus, and inferring that his friend was one likewise, asked the latter, " Art thou also one of this man's disciples?" Peter answered, " I am not." This denial was heard by no one except the porteress and John, and is not recorded in any Gospel except the fourth.

The door by which they entered opened into a porch or vestibule, beyond which was an unroofed rectangular courtyard occupying the centre of the block of buildings devoted to the use of the high priest as his personal residence, and for the exercise of his official functions. At the further end of the courtyard, and at a slightly higher level, was the hall of justice which was reached by two or three steps running along its entire width. There was no wall to divide the hall from the court-yard, only pillars to support the roof. It was of moderate size, not so large but that the judicial proceedings transacted there might usually be heard in the court-yard. It was on this night well lighted, while the court-yard was nearly in darkness.

As John and Peter passed through the porch into the courtyard, the officers and servants there were about making a charcoal fire, the April night being cold. As the fire burnt up, Peter at first stood and afterwards sat with the others, whilst John approaching, perhaps entering, the hall of justice, where Jesus now stood before the high priest, listened to the proceedings. As this was an informal preliminary examination, the speaking was in a conversational tone, and was not heard by Peter at the fire. The object of this examination was to elicit from our Lord some statement or confession that might be used in evidence against Him; but He refused to answer the questions put to Him concerning His disciples and His teaching, and suggested to the high priest that he should obtain the information required in a legitimate manner, namely from those who had heard Him teach. One of the officers thereupon struck Jesus, who meekly protested against this unrighteous action.

Failing in their attempt to obtain from our Lord evidence against Himself, the chief priests and Council next endeavoured to work up a case with the aid of a number of hired witnesses. These proceedings were more in the nature of a trial, the speaking was louder, and silence was kept in the court; therefore Peter, who retained his place by the fire, was able to hear all that was said. The evidence produced was self-contradictory and insufficient to form a colourable ground for the condemnation of the Accused. At length therefore the high priest, determined to secure a conviction and unable to do so in any other way, administered the oath to Jesus Himself, and drew from Him a distinct declaration of His Divine majesty and power. This answered their purpose and the Council thereupon pronounced Him to be worthy of death. Some members of the Council at once proceeded to display their long pent up malice towards Him who had so often exposed their hypocrisy to the people. "And some began to spit on him, and to cover his face, and to buffet him, and to say unto him, Prophesy." The form of a trial being over He was once more given into the custody of the officers, who 'received Him with blows of their hands.' All this was observed by Peter, and his account, afterwards committed to writing both by himself and Matthew, is before us in the Gospels of Mark and Matthew.

Meanwhile, James the son of Zebedee, having recovered from the panic which had seized the Apostles on the arrest of their Master, had come into the city, and, making his way to the high priest's house, had gained admittance and entered the court-yard. There he saw Peter sitting before the fire.

The insulting treatment to which our Lord was now being

subjected, naturally led some to taunt John and the new arrival James, both of whom were known to be His disciples. Attention was next directed to Peter. One of the maid servants of the high priest accused him also of having been with Jesus. He at once denied it: "Woman, I know him not," and, on the charge being repeated by others, he rose to his feet and persisted in his denial. He then went out into the porch and the cock crew. Shortly after, either the same or another maid saw him in the porch and said, "Thou also art one of them," and addressing those around added, "This man also was with Jesus the Nazarene": the charge was repeated by a male bystander, and Peter again denied his Master. This second public denial was observed by James but not by John. About an hour later, Peter having again joined the group in the court-yard, and taken part in the conversation, was once more recognised as a disciple of Jesus. The belief that such was the case was confirmed by his Galilean accent, and attention having been called to him, a kinsman of Malchus whose ear Peter had cut off remembered having seen him in the garden at the time of the arrest. Peter now denied his Lord with oaths and curses, and a second time the cock was heard to crow. Some impulse caused Peter to look towards Jesus who stood amongst the officers in the lighted hall of justice, and James following the direction of his eye, saw Christ turn Himself and look upon Peter as he stood in the glow of the fire in the midst of the court-yard. That look brought Peter to himself, and, overwhelmed with shame and grief, he went outside the building to weep.

This last denial was witnessed by John as well as James, nor did the remorse which followed it escape his notice. John's desire was to remain near his Master to the last; but he now felt that duty to one who was both a brother Apostle and a life-long friend called him away. Broken-hearted as he knew Peter would be, he could not suffer him to roam the streets at night alone. He may have remembered the words that our Lord spake a few short hours before to Peter, "And do thou, when once thou hast turned again, stablish thy brethren." It was Peter himself who now needed strengthening, and who so well able to help him in this the darkest hour of his life as the Apostle of love? John therefore followed Peter out and remained with him until in the morning they saw Jesus led away to the house of the Roman governor.

James was now the only follower of our Lord in the house of Caiaphas, and it is from his narrative contained in Luke that we learn the subsequent proceedings there.

While Peter was denying his Master in the court-yard, the ill treatment which Jesus in the hall of justice had at first received from members of the Council was being continued by the guard. Peter himself had seen the latter receive Him with blows, and now James observes them imitate the insults and mockery of their superiors. They also, like the rulers, blindfolded Him, and asked Him, saying, "Prophesy: who is he that struck thee?"

In the morning, as soon as it was day our Lord was arraigned before a session of the Sanhedrin, formally convened in order to comply with the letter of the law which forbade a trial on a capital charge at night. They now repeated the question they had asked at the night session, and obtained from Him a repetition of the avowal upon which they relied for His condemnation. Although these proceedings are only reported in Luke, the fact that a session was held in the morning is mentioned in both Matthew and Mark.

THE PROCEEDINGS BEFORE PILATE AND HEROD
THE CONDEMNATION; CRUCIFIXION; DEATH AND BURIAL
OF CHRIST

Matt. xxvii. 2–61; *Mark* xv. 1^b–47; *Luke* xxiii. 1–56;
John xviii. 28–xix. 42

There are here two passages peculiar to Matthew; namely, verses 3–10, relating the fate of Judas, and the purchase of the potter's field; and verse 19, recording the dream of Pilate's wife. Just as John, owing probably to previous business relations, was acquainted with the high priest and his servants, so Matthew, as a result of his former occupation, may have had friends among the household of the Roman governor. Thus he was enabled to learn the fact of the message sent to Pilate by his wife. It is not likely however that either this, or the circumstances of Judas' death, and the disposal of the money which he returned to the Sanhedrin, were known either to Matthew or any other of the disciples until some considerable time after the Resurrection—hence these events are not recorded in either of the other Gospels, and the passages relating them in Matthew may be regarded as having been added by him at a later date.

Omitting the passages just referred to, Matthew's narrative now shows more individuality than in the latter part of the previous chapter. The proceedings before the Roman governor were public, and Matthew was there and saw for himself what took place; he was therefore no longer dependent on Peter and James for his information, as he was when narrating the trial in the high priest's house. His narrative it is true is still very similar to Mark's, in several places word for word the same, still there are numerous variations in the diction, and some additional details of matters of fact.

Matthew's account of the appeals of Pilate to the multitude is rather fuller than Mark's; and he alone relates the public washing of Pilate's hands in protest of his innocence of 'the blood of this righteous man,' and the people's answer, 'His blood be on us and on our children.' His account of the insults of the Roman soldiers after the condemnation of Jesus, and of the mockery of the chief priests and others as He hung on the cross, are also somewhat fuller.

It should further be noted that Matthew alone mentions the quaking of the earth and the rending of the rocks. The rising from the dead of many of the saints and their appearance to many persons in the holy city, which is also peculiar to Matthew, was probably added later, being only known to him

MATT. xxvii.		MARK xv.		LUKE xxiii.
11 And the governor asked him saying, Art thou the King of the Jews? And Jesus said unto him, Thou sayest.	2	And Pilate asked Him Art thou the King of the Jews? And He answering saith unto Him, Thou sayest.	2	And Pilate asked Him saying, Art thou the King of the Jews? And He answered him and said, Thou sayest.
22 They all say, Let him be crucified.	13	And they cried out again, Crucify him.	21	But they shouted, saying, Crucify him, Crucify him,
23 And he said, Why, what evil hath he done?	14	And Pilate said unto them, Why, what evil hath he done?	22	And he said unto them the third time, Why, what evil hath this man done?
32 They found a man of Cyrene, Simon by name.	21	And they compel one passing by, Simon of Cyrene, coming from the country.	26	They laid hold upon one Simon of Cyrene, coming from the country.
35 they parted his garments among them, casting lots.	24	part his garments among them casting lots upon them what each should take.	34	parting his garments among them they cast lots.
36 and they sat and watched him there			35	and the people stood beholding
45 Now from the sixth hour there was darkness over all the land until the ninth hour.	33	And when the sixth hour was come, there was darkness over the whole land until the ninth hour.	44	And it was now about the sixth hour, and a darkness came over the whole land until the ninth hour; the sun's light failing.

	40 And there were also women beholding from afar . . . who when he was in Galilee followed him and ministered unto him.	49 And all his acquaintance and the women that followed with him from Galilee, stood afar off, seeing these things.
55 And many women were there beholding from afar, which had followed Jesus from Galilee, ministering unto him.	41	
	43 there came Joseph of Arimathea, a councillor,	50 And behold, a man named Joseph, who was a councillor, a good man and a righteous
57 And when even was come, there came a rich man from Arimathea named Joseph, who also himself was Jesus' disciple:		51 . . . a man of Arimathea, a city of the Jews, who was looking for
58 this man went to Pilate, and asked for the body of Jesus.		52 the kingdom of God: this man went to Pilate, and asked for the body of Jesus.
59 And Joseph took the body, and wrapped it in a	46 and he went boldly in unto Pilate, and asked for the body of Jesus. And he bought a linen cloth and taking him down, wound him in the linen cloth, and laid him in a tomb which had been hewn out of a rock.	53 And he took it down, and wrapped it in a linen cloth, and laid him in a tomb that was hewn in stone, where never man had yet lain.
60 clean linen cloth, and laid it in his own new tomb, which he had hewn out in the rock.		

THE NARRATIVES AND THE THEORY 371

subsequently to the time at which he and the other Evangelists wrote their original narratives of the Crucifixion.

Peter's account, preserved by Mark, is also that of an eyewitness, containing as it does several details not found in the others.

The statement in Mark that Simon the Cyrenian was the father of Alexander and Rufus was doubtless inserted by Mark himself when redacting Peter's notes, Alexander and Rufus being, it may be assumed, at that time well known to the Christian community.

The narrative of Luke is far more independent than that either of Matthew or of Mark, showing that James, the original writer, profited little by the assistance of Matthew and Peter. He supplies a number of important facts—the reference to Herod amongst others—which are not found elsewhere, and omits some that are found in Matthew and Mark.

Nevertheless it is manifest that the three accounts were written in company, and that the writers during all the time they were engaged at their task, were constantly comparing their recollections. There are co-incidences of expression which are too numerous and unmistakable to admit of any other explanation. Those exhibited on pages 369, 370 are the most striking.

John's account is as usual quite distinct from the others. There are indeed co-incidences but they are not more numerous than would be inevitable in any independent report of the same facts.

John alone mentions the request made by the chief priests to Pilate that he should alter the wording of the title on the cross. Doubtless he was informed of this by his friend Nicodemus. John is the only one who tells of the assistance rendered by Nicodemus to Joseph of Arimathæa in the burial of the body of Jesus.

THE NAME GOLGOTHA. CALVARY

Matt. xxvii. 33. And when they were come unto a place called Golgotha, that is to say, The place of a skull.

Mark xv. 22. And they bring him unto the place Golgotha, which is, being interpreted, The place of a skull.
Luke xxiii. 33. And when they came unto the place which is called The skull.
John xix. 17. Unto the place called The place of a skull, which is called in Hebrew Golgotha.

It is probable that in their original Aramaic reports Matthew, Peter and James wrote simply the Hebrew name, Golgotha.

Matthew, when translating his report into Greek, added, ὅ ἐστιν Κρανίου τόπος λεγόμενος.

Mark, when translating Peter's report, added ὅ ἐστιν μεθερμηνευόμενος, Κρανίου τόπος.

Luke, when translating James' report, thought it needless to retain the Hebrew name and wrote only its Greek equivalent Κρανίου.

John wrote his report in Greek in the first instance and wrote as in the text giving the Greek name first and adding the Hebrew name τὸν λεγόμενον Κρανίου τόπον, ὃ λέγεται Ἑβραϊστὶ Γολγοθά.

THE TITLES ON THE CROSS

Matt. xxvii. 37. Οὗτός ἐστιν Ἰησοῦς ὁ βασιλεὺς τῶν Ἰουδαίων.
This is Jesus the King of the Jews.
Mark xv. 26. Ὁ βασιλεὺς τῶν Ἰουδαίων.
The King of the Jews.
Luke xxiii. 38. Ὁ βασιλεὺς τῶν Ἰουδαίων οὗτος.
This is the King of the Jews.
John xix. 19. Ἰησοῦς ὁ Ναζωραῖος ὁ βασιλεὺς τῶν Ἰουδαίων.
Jesus the Nazarene the King of the Jews.

"And it was written in Hebrew, and in Latin, and in Greek." John xix. 20.

The Latin inscription being of use only to the Roman soldiers and officials, who were not well informed on local matters, was probably "The King of the Jews," or "This is the King of the Jews," as given in Mark and Luke.

The Hebrew or Aramaic, intended for the people at large, would give the name and was probably written as rendered by Matthew, "This is Jesus the King of the Jews."

THE NARRATIVES AND THE THEORY 373

The Greek inscription, to be read by the Jewish rulers with whom Pilate was angry, and intended to mortify and humiliate them, set forth the name of the despised town after which His enemies were wont to designate Him. This inscription was recorded by John exactly as it was written.

DATE OF THE PASSOVER IN THE YEAR 30

There is apparently a discrepancy between the statements of Matthew, Mark and Luke and that of John as to the day upon which the Passover was kept at the time of our Lord's Passion. This has given rise to much discussion and the expression of many differing views. For a full and lucid summary of these and a review of the whole question the reader is referred to Andrews' *Life of our Lord*; but for the purpose of our argument the following may suffice.

Critics are now nearly unanimous as to the actual dates of the Last Supper, the Trial, the Crucifixion, and the Resurrection. They were as under:

Thursday Evening, April 6. The Supper.
Friday Morning, ,, 7. The Trial.
,, Afternoon, ,, ,, The Crucifixion.
Sunday Morning, ,, 9. The Resurrection.

The difficulty lies in fixing the day upon which the Passover was kept. It was ordained (Exodus xii.) that the paschal lamb should be slain on the afternoon of the 14th day of the month (Nisan), and eaten the same evening; that is, as the day was reckoned from sunset to sunset, on the evening with which the 15th day of the month began. But the day of the month was reckoned from the new moon; not however from the time at which astronomically the principal change of the moon really occurred, but from the day upon which the young moon was first seen by watchmen appointed for that purpose by the priests at Jerusalem. This would be sometimes on the second, sometimes on the third, and sometimes perhaps not until the fourth day. In cloudy weather the moon might not be seen at all and then the month would be considered to begin with the day after the 30th of the month just ended. It follows that it is impossible to say by calculation upon what day any day of a month fell in any given year; and in the case of the 15th of the Month Nisan, A.D. 30, the day upon which the Passover was celebrated which we are considering, we have no guidance except what is supplied by the Gospels themselves.

Now, so far as the first three Gospels are concerned there seems to be no room for doubt of their intention to say that the Supper of which our Lord partook was the Paschal Feast, and that it was eaten on the right day, which was the 15th of the month. They all say that on the day of unleavened bread, or the first day of unleavened bread, which could only be the 14th Nisan, the disciples received directions from Jesus as to the preparation of the Passover. And the only inference to be drawn from their several accounts of the supper that followed on the same evening—the evening which after sunset began the 15th—is that it was the recognised Passover Feast.

The same general impression is also produced by the narrative of John. The subject is introduced with the words "Now before the feast of the passover" (xiii. 1), and then in the next verse the account of the supper begins.

As no other supper is hinted at the natural inference is that the supper spoken of was that of the Passover.

Nor could there ever have been any doubt of John's meaning were it not for other passages which seem to contradict this inference. These passages are as follows:—

xiii. 29. "For some thought, because Judas had the bag, that Jesus said unto him, Buy what things we have need of for the feast," implying, it is said, that the feast had yet to come.

xviii. 28. "They lead Jesus therefore from Caiaphas into the palace; and it was early; and they themselves entered not into the palace, that they might not be defiled, but might eat the Passover." This text is held to exclude the supposition that the Jewish elders had eaten the Passover the previous night—the time at which Jesus and His disciples ate the supper.

xix. 14. "Now it was the Preparation of the Passover." This also seems at first sight to prove that the Passover had not yet been celebrated.

THE NARRATIVES AND THE THEORY 375

Nevertheless these texts are all capable of explanation.

With the first there need be little difficulty when it is remembered that the Feast was of seven days' duration and provision had to be made for subsequent days as well as the first, the day on which the lamb was eaten.

The same fact seems to explain the unwillingness of the Jews to associate with Gentiles in the prætorium. The whole seven days' feast was commonly included in the term Passover; and the Jews did not wish on the second day to disqualify themselves from further participation in it.

With regard to the text last quoted, it has been shown that the word 'Preparation' ($\pi\alpha\rho\alpha\sigma\kappa\epsilon\nu\dot{\eta}$) had a special signification, being the name commonly applied to the day preceding the Sabbath, and that there is no instance in the New Testament of its being used in any other sense. It was in fact the name of the sixth day of the week and simply meant 'Friday.' It is used in that sense by each of the other Evangelists and twice by John himself. (Matt. xxvii. 62; Mark xv. 42; Luke xxiii. 54; John xix. 31, 42.) Accordingly when John says, "It was the Preparation of the passover" ($\tilde{\eta}\nu$ $\delta\grave{\epsilon}$ $\pi\alpha\rho\alpha\sigma\kappa\epsilon\nu\grave{\eta}$ $\tau o\hat{\upsilon}$ $\pi\acute{\alpha}\sigma\chi\alpha$) he does not mean that it was the time for preparing the Passover; he intends to say that it was the Friday of Passover week, the day preceding the Sabbath and a day of the paschal celebration, in other words the day preceding a very important Sabbath (ver. 31). He mentions this, together with the fact that it was about the sixth hour, to explain the impatience and urgency with which the Jews cried, "Away with him, Away with him" ($^*\!A\rho o\nu$, $\mathring{a}\rho o\nu$), when Pilate brought Jesus out and sat down on the judgment seat. The revisers of the English Version recognise this as the true meaning of the word as is shown by their spelling it with a capital.

These passages being thus understood the fourth Gospel is seen to be consistent with itself and with the other three.

Now, the point that concerns us is this. It cannot be denied that, in the particular referred to, John's narrative shows some ambiguity. The difficulties we have noticed were just as apparent in very ancient times as they are to-day. They would be a cause of perplexity to the Christians of Ephesus at the end of the first century at which place and time the Gospel is supposed to have been originally published. But a chief characteristic of John's literary style being its lucidity, we may be sure that there was no obscurity or ambiguity in his account of the events concerning our Lord's Passion, as it would be understood by those among whom he was at the time of writing. The difficulty which has so much perplexed commentators arises from this, that, writing in Jerusalem soon after the events occurred, John uses terms in the sense in which they were currently employed at that time, and makes allusions about which there would then and there be no misunderstanding; but which, after the destruction of the Temple and the dispersion of the Jews, lost their acquired and special signification.

The Time of the Crucifixion

Mark xv. 25 And it was the third hour, and they crucified him.
John xix. 14 It was about the sixth hour.
16 Then therefore he delivered him unto them to be crucified.
Matt. xxvii. 45 Now from the sixth hour there was darkness over all the land until the ninth hour.
46 And about the ninth hour Jesus cried with a loud voice.
Mark xv. 33 And when the sixth hour was come, there was darkness over the whole land until the ninth hour.
34 And at the ninth hour Jesus cried with a loud voice.
Luke xxiii. 44 And it was now about the sixth hour, and a darkness came over the whole land until the ninth hour.

There is here apparently a contradiction between Matthew, Mark and Luke, on the one hand, and John on the other. Mark states that they crucified Jesus at the third hour, and this is confirmed by Matthew and Luke, which agree with Mark in saying that the darkness began at the sixth and lasted until the ninth hour.

John however says that it was about the sixth hour when Pilate delivered Jesus to be crucified.

Endeavours have been made to show that John reckoned

his time in a different way from the other Evangelists; but these have entirely failed, and the attempt to reconcile the two statements seems to have been given up. And yet the solution is simple enough. It is to be found in the inexactness which prevailed in that age with reference to the progress of the hours of the day. The principle of the pendulum not having been discovered, only very imperfect instruments for measuring time were in use even among the wealthy; and the bulk of the people had nothing at all to guide them in this respect except natural indications. Hence there was a want of precision, which we in modern times with our clocks and watches can hardly imagine.

Those who have lived in the East may find less difficulty in understanding this; the idea of exactness to a minute or even an hour being still quite foreign to the uncultivated Oriental mind. When railways were first opened in India natives intending to travel would arrive at a station hours late, and be surprised to find the train gone. Afterwards, to avoid being too late, they would come to the station at daylight in the morning and wait for hours till the train started.

The remarks of Cruden, the author of the Concordance, will here be useful:

"The ancient Hebrews did not divide the day by hours. The day was divided into four parts, morning, high-day or noon, the first evening, and the last evening; and the night was divided into three parts, night, midnight, and the morning watch. But afterward, when the Jews came to be under the Romans, they followed them in dividing the night into four parts, which they called watches, because they relieved their sentinels every three hours. Thus in Matthew xiv. 25 it is said that in the fourth watch of the night, Jesus went to His disciples, walking on the sea; that is about three hours before the rising of the sun. In the books of the New Testament we see clearly the day divided into twelve equal hours, after the manner of the Greeks and Romans.

"These hours were equal to each other, but unequal with

respect to the different seasons. The twelve hours of the longest days in summer were much longer than those of the shortest days in winter. The first hour was that which followed the rising of the sun, and was answerable to our six o'clock in the morning in the equinox; and to other times in proportion to the length or shortness of the days. The third hour was answerable to nine o'clock of the morning in the equinox; the sixth at all times to noon, and so on."

Now it must be apparent that with such a system there could be no approach to precision. Further, it will be found on referring to the passages in the New Testament which bear on the subject that in the time of Christ the day was, in practice, divided just as roughly as in more ancient times. People rarely mentioned any hours except the third, sixth and ninth, the recognised divisions of the day being in Spring and Autumn as follows :—

From daylight	to about 8	a.m. Morning
,, about 8 a.m.	,, ,, 10.30	,, the third hour
,, ,, 10.30 a.m.	,, ,, 1.30 p.m.	,, sixth hour
,, ,, 1.30 p.m.	,, ,, 4	,, ,, ninth hour
,, ,, 4	,, ,, dark	Evening

Thus, it 'was about the sixth hour' when Jesus sat by the well in Samaria (John iv. 6); it was the third hour when Peter addressed the multitude on the day of Pentecost (Acts ii. 15); it was the ninth hour when Peter and John went up into the Temple (Acts iii. 1); it was about the sixth hour that Cornelius saw His vision (Acts x. 3); it was about the sixth hour that Peter went up upon the housetop to pray (Acts x. 9).

The common usage is well illustrated in the parable of the Householder and the Hired Labourers (Matt. xx. 1–16). The householder went out first "early in the morning"; then 'about the third hour'; then 'about the sixth and the ninth hour.' Lastly, he went out at the eleventh hour, the point of the parable requiring that an exception should here be made to the usual practice of mentioning only hours divisible by three. For a similar reason, namely to intimate the near approach of nightfall, it is said (John i. 39) that 'it was about the tenth hour' when the disciples of John the Baptist came and saw where Jesus abode. The only other instance of an hour other than the third, sixth or ninth being mentioned is in the case of the healing of the nobleman's son at Capernaum whose fever left him at the seventh hour. The nobleman doubtless possessed the luxury of some sort of dial.

When it is remembered that, on the day of the Crucifixion, the disciples were lacerated with grief at the sufferings of their Lord, and overwhelmed with disappointment at what seemed to be the failure of all their hopes; and further that they were well nigh exhausted from want of sleep and anxiety, there is no need for wonder that it did not occur to them to make any unusual effort to note accurately the progress of time, and that in their several reports considerable divergence should appear. If our Lord was taken to Golgotha and nailed to the cross between 10 and 11 a.m. it is not surprising under the circumstances if by one observer this should be said to have occurred at 'about the third hour,' and by another at 'about the sixth hour.' The use of the word "about" (ὡς, ὡσεί, περί) shows that the writers did not profess to be exact.

On April 7, the probable date of our Lord's crucifixion, and in the latitude of Jerusalem, the sun rises at about 5.45 and the fowls fly down from their roosts about 15 minutes before that. The sun sets at about 6.20, and, twilight there being much shorter than in the higher latitudes of England, night follows quickly. Accordingly, following the indications supplied in the several narratives, the times at which certain of the events occurred may be approximately set down as under:

Luke	"As soon as it was day"	5.30 Formal Session of Council and Final Trial and Condemnation.
Matt.	"When Morning was come"	} 5.45 Council held Consultation.
Mark	"Straightway in the Morning"	
Matt.	After Consultation	} 6.0 They Lead Jesus to Pilate.
Mark	,, ,,	
Luke	,, Condemnation	
John	"It was early"	

John "About the sixth hour"	10.30	Pilate Delivers Him to be Crucified.
Mark "It was the third hour"	11.0	They Crucify Him.
Matt. ⎫ Mark ⎬ From the sixth hour Luke ⎭ until the ninth hour	12.30 to 3.0	Darkness over the Land.
Matt. ⎫ Mark ⎭ About the ninth hour.	3.0	Jesus cries out.
Matt. ⎫ Mark ⎭ When even was come	4.0	Joseph asks for the Body of Jesus.
Luke "Sabbath drew on"	4.30 to 6.0	Burial of the Body.

The Apostles resume Writing

Before proceeding further it may be well to devote a few pages to the consideration of the manner in which the Apostles after the Resurrection resumed their work of recording the events of which they were chosen to be the witnesses.

We have already observed that the portions written before the Crucifixion appear to terminate respectively with Matthew xxv. 46; Mark xiii. 37; Luke xxi. 38; and John xi. 44. John however took tautochronistic reports of certain discourses of Jesus which are included with the portion subsequently written.

Early in the week that began with the Resurrection, the Apostles, I believe, met to compose an account of the events which had happened since Matthew, Peter and James left off writing on the evening of our Lord's discourse on the Mount of Olives. Probably the greater part of the first day on which they thus met was occupied in talking over the events and recalling texts of Old Testament Scripture of which they were the fulfilment. There was doubtless also much deliberation as to the manner in which this closing portion should pick up the narrative and connect with the portion written some days before.

Not only had they to continue the story from that point, but they deemed it needful to mention some facts of a slightly earlier date which had only just come to their knowledge. They had learned from Joseph of Arimathea and Nicodemus something of what had transpired in the meetings of the chief priests and elders. From the same men they had also heard the particulars of the overtures made by Judas to the rulers, and the bargain which had resulted therefrom. And they now perceived a connection between the vexation displayed by Judas at the Bethany Supper and this his first overt act of treachery.

All these subjects were, we may be sure, long talked over, at this first meeting which the disciples held for the purpose of composing the beginning of the last chapter of the story of our Lord's sojourn among men.

At length they agreed that a note of time was desirable, and they recalled the words in which Jesus had reminded them that in two days the Passover would begin, when His death must be accomplished. So Matthew, Peter and James commenced to write and penned first the sentences which follow :—

MATT. xxvi. 1-5	MARK xiv. 1, 2	LUKE xxii. 1, 2
And it came to pass, when Jesus had finished all these words, he said unto his disciples, Ye know that after two days the passover cometh, and the Son of man is delivered up to be crucified. Then were gathered together the chief priests, and the elders of the people, unto the court of the high priest, who was called Caiaphas; and they took counsel together that they might take Jesus by subtilty, and kill him. But they said, Not during the feast, lest a tumult arise among the people.	Now after two days was *the feast of* the passover and the unleavened bread : and the chief priests and the scribes sought how they might take him with subtilty, and kill him : for they said, Not during the feast, lest haply there shall be a tumult of the people.	Now the feast of unleavened bread drew nigh, which is called the Passover. And the chief priests and the scribes sought how they might put him to death ; for they feared the people.

They continued writing the remaining portions of the narrative which we have been considering, in the composition of which they probably occupied the rest of the week.

John was present at least at the first of this week's meetings and heard the conversation (John xii. 16). But their talk was in Aramaic and he did not write any part of his narrative then. Afterwards however when alone he also proceeded to continue his history which he had not touched since the time he left Bethany after the raising of Lazarus.

In the narrative which he wrote now (beginning xi. 45) we see traces of the conversation which had taken place at the meeting referred to. He also gives a note of time in relation to the Passover : " Jesus therefore six days before the passover came to Bethany." He too gives an account—a much fuller one—of the consultations of the chief priests and Pharisees. He too writes from his own point of view an account of the supper at Bethany. And although he gives no account of the original contract between Judas and the Sanhedrin, knowing that this had already been recorded by his colleagues, he repeats at a later stage an expression which his brother James had also employed to denote that fearful state of spiritual ruin into which the traitor had fallen. (Luke xxii. 3; John xiii. 27.)

The Resurrection

As soon as we come to examine the concluding portions of the Gospels—the portions which narrate the Resurrection of Christ and the circumstances connected with and following that event—we find ourselves brought face to face with a singular and interesting fact. Hitherto as we followed the course of the narratives we observed that, wherever Matthew, Mark and Luke, or any two of them related the same event or saying, there was a common influence visible which more or less governed all or both the writers. Even where the details differed the presence of this common influence was unmistakable, affecting both the structure of the story and the language in which it was couched. Latterly, it is true, in narrating the Last Supper, the Arrest, and especially the Trial before Pilate and the Crucifixion, there has been a tendency in Luke's account to break away from the others and present an independent story. But even in those parts the common influence is manifest. We have cited in these pages some illustrations in proof of this, and many more can be found by the reader for himself. But after the account of the burial of Jesus a total change takes place in this respect; the common in-

MATT. xxviii. 1–10	MARK xvi. 1–8
Now late on the sabbath day, as it began to dawn toward the first *day* of the week, came Mary Magdalene and the other Mary to see the sepulchre. And behold, there was a great earthquake; for an angel of the Lord descended from heaven, and came and rolled away the stone, and sat upon it. His appearance was as lightning, and his raiment white as snow: and for fear of him the watchers did quake, and became as dead men. And the angel answered and said unto the women, Fear not ye: for I know that ye seek Jesus, which hath been crucified. He is not here; for he is risen, even as he said. Come, see the place where the Lord lay. And go quickly, and tell his disciples, He is risen from the dead; and lo, he goeth before you into Galilee; there shall ye see him: lo, I have told you. And they departed quickly from the tomb with fear and great joy, and ran to bring his disciples word. And behold, Jesus met them, saying, All hail. And they came and took hold of his feet, and worshipped him. Then saith Jesus unto them, Fear not: go tell my brethren that they depart into Galilee, and there shall they see me.	And when the sabbath was past, Mary Magdalene, and Mary the *mother* of James, and Salome, bought spices, that they might come and anoint him. And very early on the first day of the week, they come to the tomb when the sun was risen. And they were saying among themselves, Who shall roll us away the stone from the door of the tomb? and looking up, they see that the stone is rolled back: for it was exceeding great. And entering into the tomb, they saw a young man sitting on the right side, arrayed in a white robe; and they were amazed. And he saith unto them, Be not amazed: ye seek Jesus, the Nazarene, which hath been crucified: he is risen; he is not here: behold, the place where they laid him! But go, tell his disciples and Peter, He goeth before you into Galilee: there shall ye see him, as he said unto you. And they went out, and fled from the tomb; for trembling and astonishment had come upon them; and they said nothing to any one; for they were afraid.

fluence disappears, and we meet for the first and only time four perfectly distinct and independent stories of the same events.

The following synopsis of that part of the history of the Resurrection morning which is more or less common to all the Gospels shows at a glance how independent each of the accounts is from all the others :—

LUKE xxiv. 1–12	JOHN xx. 1–10
But on the first day of the week, at early dawn, they came unto the tomb, bringing the spices which they had prepared. And they found the stone rolled away from the tomb. And they entered in, and found not the body of the Lord Jesus. And it came to pass, while they were perplexed thereabout, behold, two men stood by them in dazzling apparel: and as they were affrighted, and bowed down their faces to the earth, they said unto them, Why seek ye the living among the dead? He is not here, but is risen: remember how he spake unto you when he was yet in Galilee, saying that the Son of man must be delivered up into the hands of sinful men, and be crucified, and the third day rise again. And they remembered his words, and returned from the tomb, and told all these things to the eleven, and to all the rest. Now they were Mary Magdalene, and Joanna, and Mary the *mother* of James : and the other women with them told these things unto the apostles. And these words appeared in their sight as idle talk ; and they disbelieved them. But Peter arose, and ran unto the tomb; and stooping and looking in, he seeth the linen cloths by themselves ; and he departed to his home, wondering at that which was come to pass.	Now on the first *day* of the week cometh Mary Magdalene early, while it was yet dark, unto the tomb, and seeth the stone taken away from the tomb. She runneth therefore, and cometh to Simon Peter, and to the other disciple, whom Jesus loved, and saith unto them, They have taken away the Lord out of the tomb, and we know not where they have laid him. Peter therefore went forth, and the other disciple, and they went toward the tomb. And they ran both together : and the other disciple outran Peter, and came first to the tomb ; and stooping and looking in, he seeth the linen cloths lying; yet entered he not in. Simon Peter therefore also cometh, following him, and entered into the tomb ; and he beholdeth the linen cloths lying, and the napkin, that was upon his head, not lying with the linen cloths, but rolled up in a place by itself. Then entered in therefore the other disciple also, which came first to the tomb, and he saw, and believed. For as yet they knew not the scripture, that he must rise again from the dead. So the disciples went away again unto their own home.

It will be seen that, with the exception of the words spoken by the angels to the women, which, being a quotation, are similarly (though not like most other quotations identically) reported, there is not a single phrase alike in the first three of the above columns.

This is the more singular because it is certain that the histories of the two days previous to and ending with the death and burial of Jesus were written after the Resurrection. It has been shown I think conclusively in these pages that the common influence so apparent in the three Synoptic Gospels is due to their having been composed in company, the writers rendering one another mutual assistance. It appears then that after the Resurrection—very soon after, as will be seen presently—Matthew, Peter and James met as usual with other of the Apostles to write their narratives, and that they continued so to write in company until they came to the interment of the body in the tomb. But when they had reached this point they dispersed and never met again to write; but each one by himself composed his own story.

This change in the conditions under which they wrote can hardly have been the result of accident; but was, we may fairly conclude, a matter of deliberate choice. They probably reasoned in some such way as this: "We have now to write a record of a startling and glorious event, an event within our own personal knowledge and of the truth of which we ourselves have not and cannot have the shadow of a doubt. But it is an event of so unique and marvellous a nature that men will not be inclined readily to believe it. There must therefore be no sign of collusion in our testimony. We must give no occasion for the charge that we have met in solemn conclave and concocted the story. Let each write separately and independently his own account of the facts."

It should be observed however that there is a remarkable likeness between verse 12 in Luke and verses 5, 6 and 10 in John.

386 THE GOSPEL PROBLEMS AND THEIR SOLUTION

LUKE xxiv.	JOHN xx.
12 But Peter arose, and ran unto the tomb; and stooping and looking in, he seeth the linen cloths by themselves; and he departed to his home, wondering at that which was come to pass.	5 And stooping and looking in, he seeth the linen cloths lying; 6 yet entered he not in. Simon Peter therefore also cometh, following him, and entered into the tomb; and he beholdeth the linen cloths lying. 10 So the disciples went away again unto their own home.

The verse in Luke is enclosed by Westcott and Hort in double brackets, and is held by them to be an interpolation. Alford says in his note on this verse, "The similarity in diction to John xx. 5, 10 (παρακαλύψας βλέπει τὰ ὀθόνια κείμενα and ἀπῆλθεν πρὸς ἑαυτὸν being common to the two passages) indicates a common origin, and, if I mistake not, one distinct from the rest of the narrative in this chapter." Supposing the verse to be genuine, the simple truth, I believe, is that both James and John wrote their narratives soon after an interview between them and Peter, at which the topic that filled their minds was discussed, and the experiences of the Resurrection morn were related, as doubtless they often were during that week. Both James and John, with the conversation still in their thoughts, unconsciously committed to paper words that had been used by either John or Peter on that occasion. Supposing that the conversation referred to took place in Aramaic, John of course wrote the Greek equivalents of the words, while James wrote the words themselves, which were afterwards turned into Greek by Luke.

The similar expressions compare in Greek as under :

LUKE xxiv.	JOHN xx.
12 καὶ παρακύψας βλέπει τὰ ὀθόνια μόνα.	5 καὶ παρακύψας βλέπει κείμενα τὰ ὀθόνια.
	Also
	6 καὶ θεωρεῖ τὰ ὀθόνια κείμενα
ἀπῆλθεν πρὸς αὐτόν.	10 ἀπῆλθον οὖν πάλιν πρὸς αὐτοὺς οἱ μαθηταί.

From the Resurrection to Pentecost.

The composition of the four narratives must be considered separately; but first of all it will be necessary to inquire how the Apostles filled up the time that elapsed between the Resurrection and the day of Pentecost.

The direct statements on this subject are meagre. On the day of the Resurrection, Sunday April 9, our Lord appeared at various times and places to Mary Magdalene, to two disciples going to Emmaus, and to all the Apostles except Thomas. The narratives are perfectly silent as to what took place during the ensuing six days. On the following Sunday He again appeared to the Eleven, Thomas this time included. After that, on dates not specified, He appeared to seven disciples fishing on the sea of Tiberias, and to the Eleven on a mountain in Galilee. Finally, at the end of forty days, He met the Apostles assembled in Jerusalem, and led them out to the mount of Olives, whence He was carried up into Heaven. From that time until Pentecost the Apostles were fully engaged in daily meetings for prayer.

It seems however that our Lord made many other appearances to His disciples besides those specially recorded. It is said (Acts i. 3) that He shewed Himself alive after His passion by many proofs, appearing unto the Apostles by the space of forty days, and speaking the things concerning the Kingdom of God. We also learn (1 Cor. xv. 6, 7) that He appeared to above five hundred brethren at once, and also to James (the Lord's brother).

It is evident however from the narrative of John that no manifestation took place during the first week except on the Sunday. He appeared to them again on the second Sunday, but after that it does not seem that He again appeared to them until they had gone from Jerusalem to Galilee. It must have been then during the latter part of the forty days that He made the frequent appearances mentioned in the Acts. These appearances are not recorded in the Gospels because the Apostles were from that time too busy with the duties and responsibilities newly devolved upon them to find leisure for writing. Most of what is recorded was written in Jerusalem before the later appearances took place.

Nothing is stated as to the way in which the Apostles spent in Jerusalem the week following the first Sunday. Doubtless it was then that they composed the narratives of what occurred during the few days preceding and ending with the death of Jesus. The narratives written at that time consist of Matthew xxvi. 1–xxvii. 61; Mark xiv. 1–xv. 47; Luke xxii. 1–xxiii. 56; John xi. 45–xii. 19, 36b–43, xiii. 1–38, xviii. 1–xix. 42. This duty would take up the greater part of the five days available. On the Saturday they doubtless attended the Temple services and rested as usual.

It was probably on the following Monday that they began to write the story of the Resurrection. It could not have been much later, for they must soon after have repaired to Galilee to keep the appointment made by Christ to meet them there. The following presumably are the portions that were written during the earlier part of the second week: Matthew xxvii. 62–xxviii. 15; Mark xvi. 1–8; Luke xxiv. 1–49; John xx. 1–29.

Having written the above, the disciples started on their journey to Galilee, where they arrived towards the end of the week. On the following Monday seven of their number, disappointed at not having again seen the Lord on the Sunday, returned to their old occupation of fishing on the sea of Galilee, and on the Tuesday morning Jesus appeared to them. The account of this appearance was written by John the same day.

Matthew was not one of the seven to whom our Lord appeared at the lake; but the whole Eleven shortly after went by appointment to meet Him at a certain mountain in Galilee. There they saw Him; and Matthew wrote his account of the interview immediately after (xxviii. 16–20).

Nothing more was written in the course of the seven weeks we are in this place considering.

The following table shews at a glance how this period was probably occupied:

April 9.	Sunday.	Christ rises from the dead: Appears to Mary Magdalene and other women, to disciples on the way to Emmaus, to Peter, and to all the Apostles except Thomas.
,, 10.	Monday. } to	The Apostles meet daily: Matthew writes xxvi. 1–xxvii. 61; Peter writes Mark xiv. and xv.;
,, 14.	Friday. }	James writes Luke xxii. and xxiii.; John writes and composes (separately) xi. 45–xix. 42, arranging in their places the tautochronistic reports already written.
,, 15.	Saturday.	The Sabbath observed as usual.
,, 16.	Sunday.	Christ appears to the Eleven, Thomas included.
,, 17.	Monday. }	Matthew, Peter, James and John write separ-
,, 18.	Tuesday. }	ately their accounts of the Resurrection, namely, Matthew xxvii. 62–xxviii. 15, Mark xvi. 1–8, Luke xxiv. 1–49, John xx. 1–29.
,, 19.	Wednesday.	The disciples start for Galilee.
,, 20.	Thursday.	On the journey.
,, 21.	Friday.	They arrive at Galilee.
,, 22.	Saturday.	They observe the Sabbath.
,, 23.	Sunday.	They hope to see Jesus, but are disappointed.
,, 24.	Monday.	Seven disciples resolve to go fishing: The day is spent preparing the boats and tackle: They set out in the evening and toil unsuccessfully all night.
,, 25.	Tuesday.	Christ appears to the seven disciples in the morning. Large draught of fish. After breakfast Peter and John leave the others to dispose of the fish and follow Jesus. John writes xxi. 1–22.
Some time this week. } Exact date uncertain. }		Christ meets the Eleven by appointment at a Mountain. Matthew writes xxviii. 16–20.
From this time until } May 14. Sunday. }		Frequent meetings between Christ and the disciples, in the course of which He instructs them in "the things concerning the Kingdom of God."
,, 15. Monday to } ,, 17. Wednesday. }		The Apostles return from Galilee to Jerusalem.
,, 18. Thursday.		Final interview at Jerusalem between Christ and the Apostles: He leads them out to near Bethany and ascends to Heaven.

May. 19. Friday ⎫ Daily meetings for prayer in "the upper cham-
         to   ⎬ ber": Election of Matthias to the vacant
,, 26. Friday. ⎭ apostleship: Frequent attendances at the
                    Temple for worship.
,, 27. Saturday.   Day of Pentecost.

MATTHEW'S NARRATIVE.
Matthew xxvii. 62–xxviii. 20.

For the same reason that Matthew relates the dream of Pilate's wife, he also is the one to inform us of the steps taken by the chief priests and Pharisees to secure the sepulchre, and the results of their precautions. Matthew doubtless learned from the women who were the first to arrive at the sepulchre, that they had seen Roman soldiers there. Accordingly he made inquiry amongst acquaintances in the Governor's offices and ascertained the facts stated in the last five verses of chap. xxvii. Not content with this, however, he appears to have sought out some member of the guard itself, and obtained from him the only description preserved to us of what took place at the very moment of the Resurrection. In the same way doubtless he learned how the chief priests and the elders bribed the soldiers to misreport the facts.

The latter clause of verse 15, "And this saying was spread abroad among the Jews, and continued until this day," it is needless to say is an editorial addition.

From the women he gathered the particulars of what they saw on their arrival at the sepulchre, and of their meeting with Christ as they ran to bring word of the Resurrection to the disciples.

All this Matthew wrote before leaving Jerusalem for Galilee.

The portion forming the five verses with which his Gospel concludes was written in Galilee after the interview with Christ at which he was himself present.

PETER'S NARRATIVE.
Mark xvi. 1–8.

This is but a mere fragment of the story which Peter intended to write. He obtained from the women an account of what they saw at the sepulchre, and proceeded to commit the same to paper; but owing to some unknown interruption left his task unfinished. The many duties which devolved upon him as the foremost of the Apostles left him no leisure afterwards to complete the story. The longer he delayed the work the less valuable would it be, and when at length he handed his papers to Mark to translate and redact he refused to weaken his testimony by the addition of a single word. Hence in this Gospel the fact of the Resurrection is not even asserted.

The section from verse 9 to verse 20 did not form part of the original Gospel of Mark, and therefore, whether composed by Ariston the Elder as asserted in the Armenian manuscript discovered by Dr. Conybeare or by some other early Christian, in order to complete the Gospel, does not come within the scope of our argument.

James' Narrative.

Luke xxiv. 1-53.

Like Matthew and Peter, James questioned the women who went first to the sepulchre and recorded the results of his inquiries. He also learned from Peter the fact of his running to the tomb after hearing the women's report, and recorded his statement in what constitutes a single verse.

At much greater length he narrated the experiences of the two travellers to Emmaus. The name of one of the travellers is given, Cleopas—who was the other? In all probability it was James himself, and the fulness of the story is thus explained.

The final section of Luke (verses 50-53) was added by James after the Ascension. Its extreme brevity is owing to the little time available to a leading Apostle as James was, and whose hands were full of the cares of the rapidly increasing Church.

John's Narrative and Closing Sentences.
John xx. 1–xxi. 25.

The first eighteen verses of John's story consist of the experiences related to him by Mary Magdalene and his own.

The remainder of his narrative was written entirely from his own personal knowledge. The statement in xxi. 11 of the exact number of fishes caught should have led students to recognise that the story was written very shortly after the catch was counted, it being inconceivable that such a detail would be remembered by John during the lapse of any considerable time.

Verses 30, 31 of chap. xx., and verses 24, 25 of chap. xxi., are of course editorial additions made by John at time of redaction.

CONCLUSION.

We have now reached the end of our survey and comparison of the Gospel narratives. We have examined every portion and have seen that the features in each are capable of being accounted for on the principles laid down in the earlier part of this book. We have seen that there is valid reason to believe, not only that the original materials of which the Gospels of Matthew, Mark and Luke were composed were written in Aramaic, but that the longer addresses recorded in those Gospels were spoken in that tongue. We have seen, on the other hand, that there is good ground for assuming that our Lord's discourses in John, whether delivered in Judea or Galilee, and to whomsoever addressed, were spoken in Greek. We have seen that the peculiarities which appear on comparing among themselves the parallel parts of the Synoptic Gospels may all be explained on the theory that they are separate reports of the same utterances, or of the united testimony of the Apostles to the facts narrated. And we have seen that the chronological confusion in Matthew, and the greater chronological confusion in Luke, may have been caused by the difficulty which editors may have experienced in rearranging, after a lapse of many years, the slips of papyrus on which the original notes were written—a difficulty increased probably in the case of Luke through his being unable to obtain the assistance of the writer thereof. And for this hypothesis we have found strong confirmation in the fact that in numerous instances the displaced portions are of nearly equal length and of dimensions about sufficient to fill a small page of paper.

The reader must now judge for himself whether the facts presented demonstrate the case which it is the aim of this work to prove. To me the argument seems so complete and consistent, that, if it fails to convince, it must be owing, not to any weakness in itself, but to the author's inability to do it justice. Nor can I escape the conviction that, when time enough has elapsed to allow adequate consideration of the evidence, the conclusion will be generally accepted, that we have, in the four Gospels, reports of sayings and records of events made at the very time the sayings were spoken and the events occurred, and that, with the exception of a few short editorial notes, no part of them was written subsequently to the Pentecost which followed the Ascension of our Lord.

Assured as I am of this ultimate result, let me, before parting from the reader, say a word or two with reference to its practical significance. The question is often asked : Is there such evidence for the Gospel miracles, and especially for the Resurrection of our Lord Jesus Christ, as would be admissible, and be deemed sufficient, in a court of justice? It may now be maintained that there is such evidence—evidence which cannot be gainsaid or impeached—the testimony of at least four witnesses, recorded at the very time, and in such circumstances as exclude the possibility of deception or mistake, and preserved in such a manner as to prove its authenticity beyond dispute.

There is one other point. All parts of the Bible are so closely related that any new light upon one portion cannot fail to assist in the elucidation of the rest. May it not be that the true solution of the problems of the Old Testament is to be attained on lines bearing some resemblance to those on which it is herein claimed that the solution of the Gospel problems has been reached? It cannot be pretended that, so far, any final results to command confidence have been arrived at with reference to such questions as the origin of those books of the Old Testament concerning which the old beliefs have of late years been impugned. To all whose judgment is free from the anti-supernatural bias, so conspicuous in much of the critical literature of the day, it must be apparent that even the negative results which have been announced, respecting the origin of the writings referred to, are curiously inconsistent, both with the ethical character of the writings themselves, and with the educational conditions of the times in which they are said to have made their appearance. There is plainly a fallacy somewhere. May it not consist in the striving to separate by an ever-widening interval the record from the fact, whereas the true path lies in the direction of bringing back the record closer to the fact? May it not be that the books in question require for a right understanding to be regarded as contemporary records, modernised perhaps in language, and arranged by the hands of redactors, but none the less in their essence faithful narratives, written at the time the events occurred, of God's dealings with the people whom He chose to be the channel for the communication of His will and purposes to men?

THE END.

Butler & Tanner, The Selwood Printing Works, Frome, and London.

VALUABLE AIDS TO WORKERS.

Crown 8vo, cloth, 220 pages, 3s. 6d. Abridged Edition, fcap. 8vo, 1s. net.

WHICH BIBLE TO READ?—Revised or Authorised.

By FRANK BALLARD, M.A., B.Sc., F.R.M.S., etc.

"An undisguised and unanswerable plea for the use of the Revised Version, in preference to the Authorised, in public and in private. It is an enlarged and much improved edition, altogether a more attractive and persuasive book. That the battle of the Versions will be won by the Revised, there are few who question. Mr. Ballard will share the honours of the victory. But apart from that, his book is instructive. It is scarcely possible that any one should read it, and not know even the Authorised Version better than before. Nor does Mr. Ballard desire that you should love the Authorised less that you love the Revised more."—*Expository Times.*

"Let me thank you for your book, which seems likely to be very useful. It is a very great advantage that you deal with the Old Testament."—*Rev. Dr. Westcott Bishop of Durham.*

"A vigorous plea addressed to the people."—*British Weekly.*
"It is an able book."—*Sunday School Chronicle.*

Handsome cloth, 5s.

WHAT SHALL I TELL THE CHILDREN?

By Rev. GEO. V. REICHEL, M.A.

A new volume of Object Sermons and Themes, with many illustrative anecdotes.

Handsome crown 8vo, 3s. 6d.

OBJECT SERMONS IN OUTLINE.

By Rev. C. H. TYNDALL.

A new edition has been prepared to meet the demands for this particular book, which can claim to be the first of its kind in pointing to truth by the means of the eye.

Fcap. 8vo, cloth, 1s. 6d.

DR. BOYD CARPENTER.

THOUGHTS ON PRAYER.

By the Right Rev. LORD BISHOP OF RIPON.

Contents:—Necessity of Prayer—Times Adverse to Prayer—Heartwork in Prayer—Reality of Answers to Prayer—Efficacy of Prayer, etc.

"It deals with many important questions. Cannot but prove helpful to all who may bestow any attention upon them. We accord this volume a most hearty welcome."—*Rock.*

Crown 8vo, cloth, 2s. 6d.

DR. BOYD CARPENTER.

FOOTPRINTS OF THE SAVIOUR.

Chapters on places visited by our Lord.

By the Right Rev. LORD BISHOP OF RIPON.

LONDON: H. R. ALLENSON, 30, PATERNOSTER ROW, E.C.

RECENT VOLUMES OF SERMONS.

Large Crown 8vo, 5s.

THE SPIRIT OF THE AGE.
Sermons.
By Rev. D. J. BURRELL, D.D., New York.
The subjects are brightly and vigorously treated.

New Edition. Crown 8vo, cloth, 6s.

SUNDAY MORNINGS AT NORWOOD.
With Four additional Sermons and Prayers.
By Rev. S. A. TIPPLE.

"There are more original ideas in Mr. Tipple's volume than in many which have rapidly run into nine or ten editions. Both the prayers and the sermons give evidence of a fresh, lucid, and forcible thinker. No connoisseur in sermons can fail to appreciate the fine quality of Mr. Tipple's work."—*British Weekly.*

"The first edition has long been out of print and many will be glad to know that they can obtain these rarely spiritual and suggestive sermons." —*Christian World.*

"The few added discourses of more recent date will increase the satisfaction of the old readers and of new."—*Congregational Magazine.*

Just ready. Crown 8vo, neat cloth, 5s.

THE SPIRIT OF TRUTH.
Sermons.
By JOSEPH HALSEY, Author of "The Beauty of the Lord."

"Original in the best sense,—genuine utterances of a true man's mind and conscience, full of straight thinking and strong conviction."—*Bradford Observer.*

"Mr. Halsey has something to say, and says it in a remarkably clear, simple and direct manner,—common sense utterances."—*Liverpool Mercury.*

Just ready. Crown 8vo, cloth, 384 pp., 5s.

REVIVAL SERMONS IN OUTLINE.
With Thoughts, Themes, and Plans, by eminent Pastors and Evangelists.
By Rev. C. H. PERREN, Ph.D., Author of "Seed Corn for the Sower."

Cloth Boards, 422 pp., 5s.

SEED CORN FOR THE SOWER.
A Book of Illustrations for the Pulpit and Platform. With Complete Indices to Subjects, Texts and Authors quoted.
By Rev. C. H. PERREN.

LONDON: H. R. ALLENSON, 30, PATERNOSTER ROW, E.C.

H. R. ALLENSON'S PUBLICATIONS.

Neat cloth, uniform with Phillips Brooks's Works, issued by Messrs. Macmillan. Crown 8vo, 5s.

LECTURES ON PREACHING.

By the Right Rev. PHILLIPS BROOKS.

"We have already had more than one edition in this country. But Mr. Allenson has done very well to let us have another, and to publish it in uniformity with the other books by Phillips Brooks which we possess. It is a book of permanent value."—*Expository Times.*

"They constitute a really great book."—*Baptist Magazine.*

"Simply impossible for a sensible man to read these lectures without gaining a new enthusiasm for preaching, and new power in it."—*Freeman.*

Uniform with "Lectures on Preaching."

Crown 8vo, cloth, 5s.

THE INFLUENCE OF JESUS ON THE MORAL, SOCIAL, EMOTIONAL, AND INTELLECTUAL LIFE OF MAN.

By the Right Rev. PHILLIPS BROOKS.

"'The Influence of Jesus' is theologically the most characteristic of all Bishop Brooks's works. So if one would understand the man, we must read this book."—*Expository Times.*

"Christianity is considered, not as a system of doctrines, but a personal force."—*British Weekly.*

"This volume gives us a kind of object-lesson to supplement 'The Lectures on Preaching.' Here, indeed, we see what the lecturer meant when he spoke of preaching Christ; here we have the whole range of man's possibilities illustrated in Christ's life."—*Saturday Review.*

Post 8vo, neat artistic wrapper, 28 pp., 6d. net ; post free, 7d.

THE LIFE WITH GOD.

Booklet address by the Right Rev. PHILLIPS BROOKS.

"The closing address of a series of mission services held in Boston, 1891. With unsurpassed eloquence the preacher emphasizes the great truth that the only natural and complete life is the religious life. Endeavourers will be particularly interested in what is told respecting prayer, Bible-reading, and seeking the Church."—*Christian Endeavour.*

"It is almost overwhelming in its power, eloquence, and tender pleading. It is also essentially human as is the religion which it sets forth. The preacher's great point is that the religious life is the only natural and complete life."—*Christian World.*

Strongly bound in cloth, round corners for the pocket, 2s. net.

THE PARISH DISTRICT VISITING BOOK,
AND
SICK AND COMMUNICANTS' LIST.

Compiled by JOHN PARRY, M.A.

LONDON: H. R. ALLENSON, 30, PATERNOSTER ROW, E.C.

MISSIONARY ENTERPRISE.

With Three Portraits. Second Edition. Large crown 8vo, 3s. 6d.

JOSEPH SIDNEY HILL (First Bishop in Western Equatorial Africa). By ROSE E. FAULKNER. With an Introduction by the Right Rev. BISHOP STUART.

"We wish specially and earnestly to recommend the Memoir of Bishop Hill. It is just the book to give away, particularly to young men and boys."—*C. M. Gleaner.*

"To a young man, the story it tells should be an inspiration."—Mr. EUGENE STOCK in the *C. M. Intelligencer.*

"Well written and full of interest."—*Literary World.*

With many Illustrations. Crown 8vo, cloth, 156 pp., 2s. 6d.

JOSEPH HARDY NEESIMA, LL.D., A Sketch of the Life of. The Runaway Boy who Founded the First Christian College in Japan. By REV. J. D. DAVIS, D.D.

"Few books of a biographical nature have ever fallen under my eyes which have so interested and delighted me. The riches of missionary literature more and more increases. No man or woman can read this book without a positive addition to heart-wealth."—Rev. A. T. PIERSON, D.D., in *The Missionary Review of the World.*

With Portrait Frontispiece. Second Edition. Handsome cloth, large crown 8vo, 3s. 6d.

FRED C. ROBERTS OF TIENTSIN; or, For Christ and China. By Mrs. BRYSON, Author of "Child Life in Chinese Homes," etc. With Preface by Rev. F. B. MEYER, B.A.

"It is clear his was a remarkably fine character. The Rev. F. B. Meyer describes him as 'glad and happy in spirit, courteous and sympathetic in manner, enthusiastic in devotion to his life-purpose, reverent and intense in his religious life.' We must add that Mrs. Bryson gives us many very interesting pictures and incidents from the Chinese and Mongolian life, in the midst of which Dr. Roberts spent his days."—*Times* (Weekly Edition).

"It is crowded with incident and interest."—*Christian.*

"A better tonic for doubting minds than the best and brightest discussion of difficulties."—*Sunday School Times.*

"His unsparing toil for the poor people among whom he lived cost him his life, and the price was paid cheerfully. The study of such careers as Dr. Roberts' is a good cure for the cheap pessimism of the age."—*Review of Churches.*

An artistic booklet. Narrow 8vo, 6d.

CHRISTIAN CHIVALRY. An Address to Young Men in the Cause of the Kingdom. By THOMAS PHILLIPS, B.A., Kettering.

An eloquent and stirring appeal to young men to follow Christ. Based on St. Paul's words, "I can do all things through Christ," etc.

"Friends of Missions might do well to distribute copies among young men."—*Christian.*

Narrow 8vo. Artistically printed and bound, 6d.

HEROIC ENDEAVOUR. A Word of Hope to Young Men. By W. ELSWORTH LAWSON.

"Among the books specially written for young men which claim attention, is one of very considerable merit, called *Heroic Endeavour.* It is able and strong, and full of suggestion."—*Young Man.*

LONDON: H. R. ALLENSON, 30, PATERNOSTER ROW, E.C.

H. R. ALLENSON'S CATALOGUE OF BOOKS FOR PREACHERS TEACHERS AND CHRISTIAN WORKERS

2 IVY LANE
PATERNOSTER ROW
LONDON E.C

COMPLETION OF A LIFE'S WORK.

Issue of the OLD TESTAMENT portion of the Emphasised Bible.

THE EMPHASISED BIBLE.

A New Translation, designed to set forth the Exact Meaning, the Proper Terminology, and the Graphic Style of the Sacred Originals; and Emphasised throughout after the Idioms of the Hebrew and Greek Tongues.

WITH EXPOSITORY INTRODUCTION, SELECT REFERENCES, AND APPENDICES OF NOTES.

This Version has been adjusted, in the Old Testament, to the Newly Revised "Massoretico-Critical" Text of Dr. Ginsburg.

By JOSEPH BRYANT ROTHERHAM.

Issued in 12 *small 4to Parts of* 64 *pages, price* 2s. *each; and in* 3 *Volumes, cloth,* 8s. *each, net. Uniform in size to the Emphasised* NEW *Testament.*

LONDON:
H. R. ALLENSON, 2, IVY LANE, PATERNOSTER ROW, E.C.

Important New Volume of Sermons.
Just out. Crown 8vo, cloth, 6s. post free.

CLARK (Rev. HENRY W.)—
MEANINGS AND METHODS OF THE SPIRITUAL LIFE.
By Rev. HENRY W. CLARK, Woking.

British Weekly.—"Very far above the average volume of sermons. Mr. Clark has so many qualities that, if he is a young man, we should expect him to develop into a really great and original preacher. We have not seen for a long time a volume of sermons which pleased us so much."

VIGOROUS SERMONS TO YOUNG MEN.
WELSH (Rev. R. E., M.A.)—
GOD'S GENTLEMEN.
By Rev. R. E. WELSH, M.A. Crown 8vo, cloth, 3s. 6d. post free.

Methodist Times.—"A good, wholesome, suggestive book."
British Weekly.—"A frank and manly book; brings a young man face to face with life."

WELSH (Rev. R. E., M.A.)—
THE PEOPLE AND THE PRIEST.
By Rev. R. E. WELSH, M.A. Crown 8vo, cloth, 2s. 6d. post free.

The Times.—"Mr. Welsh puts the Protestant point of view briefly and sensibly."
Samuel Smith, Esq., M.P.—"I have read with great interest your admirable book. It puts the whole question with wonderful brevity and lucidity. It is the question of the day for English people."

WELSH (Rev. R. E., M.A.)—
IN RELIEF OF DOUBT.
By Rev. R. E. WELSH, M.A. Crown 8vo, cloth, 2s. 6d. New Edition, with Introductory Note by the Right Rev. A. F. Winnington-Ingram, D.D., Bishop of London.

Dr. Ingram writes: "This little book deals with that vague atmosphere of doubt which is so common, and dispels it by its clear and pointed arguments; and it is written in so racy a style that none could put it down and call it dull."
Scotsman.—"A sensible and closely reasoned argument against scepticism."
Methodist Times.—"Nothing has appeared for years that is so well calculated to meet the average difficulties of the average man."

Just out. Fcap 8vo, cloth, 1s. 6d. net; 1s. 8d. post free.

GREGORY (ELEANOR C.)—
AN INTRODUCTION TO CHRISTIAN MYSTICISM.
By Miss GREGORY, of the Deanery, St. Paul's. With a Prefatory Letter by Dr. ALEXANDER WHYTE, of Edinburgh.

Dr. Whyte says: "I rejoice in the publication of anything that helps to turn the public mind to the study of the great spiritual writers; and this lecture will form an admirable introduction to that greatest and best of all studies."
The Christian.—"A welcome little volume."
The Rock.—"A delightful guide to the subject of which it treats."

New Book of Outline Addresses.
EDWARDS (Rev. CHARLES)—
PINS AND PIVOTS, FOR PREACHERS AND TEACHERS.
By Rev. CHARLES EDWARDS, Author of *A Box of Nails for Christian Workers*. Square 16mo, paper 6d., cloth 9d., each post free.

Methodist Sunday School Record.—"This is another choice little book for busy teachers. There are over forty outline addresses, all of them useful, and many of them adapted to evangelistic services and as addresses to the young."

Catalogue
OF PUBLICATIONS
AND
IMPORTATIONS OF
H. R. Allenson
2 IVY LANE
PATERNOSTER ROW
LONDON E.C.

Which may be had of all Booksellers, or will be sent post free to any part of the world, for the published price, except net books and where otherwise stated.

Information as to other Publishers' books supplied promptly from H. R. ALLENSON'S Retail Department, 2, Ivy Lane, Paternoster Row, E.C.

BALLARD (Rev. FRANK, M.A.)—

WHICH BIBLE TO READ—
REVISED OR AUTHORISED?

A Statement of Facts and an Appeal to the Modern Christian. By Rev. FRANK BALLARD, M.A., Minister of Wycliffe Church, Hull; Double Prizeman in Hebrew and New Testament Greek in the University of London. *Second Edition, revised and enlarged, crown 8vo, cloth,* **3s. 6d.**

The earlier edition may still be had, and makes a most suitable handbook for Bible classes. *Fcap. 8vo, neat cloth,* **1s.** *net; post free,* **1s. 2d.**

Rev. Dr. Westcott, Bishop of Durham says:—"Let me thank you for your book, which seems **likely to be very useful.** It is a very great advantage that you deal with the Old Testament."
British Weekly says:—" A vigorous plea addressed to the people."
Glasgow Herald says:—" His plea is vigorous and convincing, and his book should not only make converts, but will guide many who are already converted to the right use of the new Version."
Methodist Times says, referring to the first edition:—"This little volume condenses into its ninety-two pages an unanswerable argument for the superiority of the 'Revised' Version of the Bible of 1881 and 1885 over the 'Authorised' Version of 1611. . . . Every candid reader must, we think, admit that Mr Ballard has made out a good case. . . . We wish for its own sake that his admirable little book had been printed in larger type.* We **strongly recommend it** to all our readers, especially to Local Preachers and Sunday-school Teachers."

* This wish has been well met in the new and revised edition.

BANKS (LOUIS ALBERT, D.D.)—

THE UNEXPECTED CHRIST. By
LOUIS ALBERT BANKS, D.D. *Crown 8vo, cloth,* **6s.**

THE BIBLE STUDY UNION GRADED LESSONS.

Mr. Allenson has much pleasure in directing attention to these **admirable courses of Sunday School lesson or address material.**

Each grade contains **lessons for a year** and, from their being numbered, but undated, they can be used beginning at any time, and so no lesson be lost to the scholar by ordinary teaching being suspended for an anniversary address or other occasion.

The method of study lends itself also especially **to the private student** who desires a thorough introduction to the study of the Bible.

Six Series are now ready.

1. **STUDIES FROM THE GOSPELS.**
2. **STUDIES FROM THE ACTS, EPISTLES, AND REVELATION.**
3. **STUDIES FROM THE OLD TESTAMENT.**

BIOGRAPHICAL SERIES. FINELY ILLUSTRATED.

4. **THE GREAT MEN OF THE OLD TESTAMENT.**
5. **THE LIFE OF CHRIST.**
6. **THE THREE GREAT APOSTLES: PETER, PAUL, AND JOHN.**

Each of the above series are arranged to meet the capabilities of scholars of all ages, ranging from the Infants' Class to the Senior or Bible Class, and can be had as under. In most of the courses a very fine series of Illustrations are introduced.

FIRST COURSE of Three Grades for the JUNIOR SCHOOL of very young children.

First Grade, Infants' Pictorial Lessons. Fifty-two lessons for 1s. 8d.; post free, 1s. 10d.
Second Grade, Primary Lessons. Fifty-two lessons for 1s. 8d.; post free, 1s. 10d.
Third Grade, Children's Lessons. Fifty-two lessons for 1s. 8d.; post free, 1s. 10d.

SECOND COURSE of Three Grades for the MAIN SCHOOL.

Fourth Grade, Junior. Fifty-two lessons for 1s. 8d.; post free, 1s. 10d.
Fifth Grade, Intermediate. Fifty-two lessons for 1s. 8d.; post free, 1s. 10d.
Sixth Grade, Progressive. Fifty-two lessons for 1s. 8d.; post free, 1s. 10d.

THIRD or BIBLE CLASS COURSE.

Seventh Grade, Senior. Fifty-two lessons for 2s. 6d.; post free, 2s. 9d.

Teachers' Aids to the various series are supplied at **2s. 6d.** the year's course of lessons; post free, 2s. 9d.

Specimen lessons of Grades 1 to 6 sent post free for **6d.** each grade. Bible Class Course, **9d.** post free.

BATTERSHALL (Rev. W. W., D.D.)—

INTERPRETATIONS OF LIFE

AND RELIGION. Twenty Sermons. By Rev. WALTON W. BATTERSHALL, D.D., Rector of St. Peter's Church, Albany. *Crown 8vo, cloth*, **6s**.

The Church Standard.—"Twenty sermons, every one of which is brief, pointed, and in the true sense dogmatic."
The Outlook.—"All show spiritual insight, ardour of conviction, and uncommon literary gifts."
Boston Globe.—"Admirable in form, expressed with great fervour and sincerity, while abounding in many rhetoric beauties."
The Evangelist.—"If short sermons generally had as much clear, condensed thought as is here represented in a forcible and cultivated style, there would be good reason for the current prejudice in favour of sermonic brevity."

BIBLE READINGS, BOOKS OF.

(*See* Edwards, Ellis, Smith, and Wolfe.)

BOOK OF SERVICES FOR

PREACHERS. Baptismal, Communion, Marriage, and Burial.
(*See* "Nonconformist Minister's Ordinal.")
(*See* Marriage Service, Church of England.)

BRIANT (W. B.)—

PRAYERS AND PRAISES. A Series

of Responsive Services for use in Sunday Schools and at Christian Endeavour Meetings. Compiled by W. B. BRIANT. **40 pages**, *cloth*, 3d. ; *paper*, 2d. *Postage* ½d. *extra*.

Rev. W. J. Dawson, M.A.—"Admirable."
Rev. P. T. Forsyth, M.A., D.D.—"Serves its purpose well."
Rev. John Hunter, D.D.—"Excellent in every way."

BROCK (Rev. WILLIAM)—

A YOUNG CONGO MISSIONARY.

Memorials of Sidney Robert Webb, M.D. By Rev. WILLIAM BROCK. *Crown 8vo, cloth*, **1s. 6d.** *Second Edition*.

BROOKS (Right Rev. PHILLIPS)—

THE INFLUENCE OF JESUS ON

THE MORAL, SOCIAL, EMOTIONAL, AND INTELLECTUAL LIFE OF MAN. By the Right Rev. PHILLIPS BROOKS. Uniform with "Lectures on Preaching." *Crown 8vo*, **2s. 6d.** *net*. *Postage* 4d. *extra*.

Expository Times.—"'The Influence of Jesus' is theologically the most characteristic of all Bishop Brooks' works. If one would understand this man, one must read this book. Mr. Allenson has given us a new and attractive edition."
Baptist Magazine.—"A book which might well become popular. Bishop Brooks logic was always lighted up by imaginative power, and his strongest reasoning was tremulous with emotion. The purpose of the book is established with an irresistible force of logic and a wealth of choice illustration. **The re-issue of the book is altogether timely.**"

BROOKS (Right Rev. PHILLIPS)—
LECTURES ON PREACHING.
By the Right Rev. PHILLIPS BROOKS. Uniform with Phillips Brooks' Works, issued by Messrs. Macmillan. *Neat cloth, crown 8vo,* 2s. 6d. *net.* Postage 4d. *extra.*

Expository Times.—"Mr. Allenson has done very well to let us have it in uniformity with the other books by Phillips Brooks which we possess. It is **A BOOK OF PERMANENT VALUE.**"
The Baptist.—"These valuable lectures constitute **a really great book.**"
The Speaker.—"Readers of these noble and impassioned pages will be at no loss to discover wherein lay Dr. Phillips Brooks' secret of power."
Church Times.—"Well **worth reading and re-reading** by young clergy. They can hardly study the great preacher's methods without learning much, very much to help and strengthen them."
Methodist Times.—"We have more than once commended this delightful book. There is no preacher of the Gospel, there is hardly any public speaker on any subject, who can read any one of these lectures without learning something profitable. We only wish all our preachers could own, and make their own, the sterling truth of **this delightful and valuable book.**"
Independent.—"There is **no book** of Homiletics **more worthy** of earnest and prayerful study."

BROOKS (Right Rev. PHILLIPS)—
LETTERS OF TRAVEL (1865-1890).
By Right Rev. PHILLIPS BROOKS. *Large crown 8vo, cloth,* 5s.

These letters of travel cover a chapter of Phillips Brooks' life that was always of the greatest delight to him, and in which are represented many of his most striking personal characteristics. They convey not only an interesting story of travel, but also evidence of that personal charm, ready wit, and genial appreciation which those nearest to him loved so well.

Academy.—"Those who have not had the good fortune to hear Phillips Brooks will be surprised with this glimpse of what must have been a delightful character."
Spectator.—"The principal charm of the late Bishop Brooks' letters lies in their perfect unconsciousness."
Speaker.—"Any one who reads between the lines of these letters from abroad will see clearly enough that nothing in the nature of historical appeal, literary suggestiveness, or social comment was lost upon a genial observer who loved books and buildings only less than men and women."

BROOKS (Right Rev. PHILLIPS)—
ESSAYS AND ADDRESSES.
Religious, Literary, and Social. By the Right Rev. PHILLIPS BROOKS. Edited by the Rev. JOHN COTTON BROOKS. *Crown 8vo, cloth.* 2 *vols.* Sold separately. Vol. I.—Religious Topics; Vol. II.—Social and Literary. 5s. *each.*

BROOKS (Right Rev. PHILLIPS)—
THE LIFE WITH GOD.
By Right Rev. PHILLIPS BROOKS. A striking Address in booklet form. *Neat artistic wrapper,* 28 *pages,* 6d. *net ; post free,* 7d.

Christian World.—It is almost overwhelming in its power, eloquence, and tender pleading. It is also essentially human, as is the religion which it sets forth. The preacher's great point is that the religious is the only natural and complete life."

H. R. ALLENSON'S CATALOGUE 7

BROWN (CALVIN S.)—

THE LATER ENGLISH DRAMA.
Edited, with an Introduction and Notes, by CALVIN S. BROWN. *Small crown 8vo, cloth,* **6s. 6d.**

Extract from Preface.—"It is the object of this book to present in convenient and accessible form what has been done best in the English drama from the time of Goldsmith to the present. For this purpose six plays have been selected, and that the usefulness of the book might be increased, a number of notes have been added."

The texts are given complete, including dedications, prefaces, prologues, and epilogues. Only one expurgation has been made, and that is indicated in its proper place.

The six plays chosen are—

BROWN (Rev. CHARLES)—

THE MESSAGE OF THE GOSPEL.
Sermon preached at commencement of Simultaneous London Mission. 20 *pages, crown 8vo,* 1d.; *post free,* 1½d. (*Tracts for the Times,* No. 16.) "*A model Mission Address.*"

BROWN (Rev. CHARLES)—

FERME PARK MAGAZINE. Contains
Sermon by Rev. CHARLES BROWN each month. 1d.; *post free,* 1½d.; *Twelve months,* 1s. 6d., *post free.*

BROWN (RUTH MOWRY)—

Something Strikingly New for the Children.

THE BIBLE IN LESSON AND
STORY. By RUTH MOWRY BROWN. *Crown 8vo, cloth,* **5s.**

Forty chapters upon as many Bible truths, each chapter written in a manner that will especially interest the children. In connection with each lesson is a delightful illustrative story, together with a "Memory Gem" and an "Occupation," in which the children are given something to do that will help impress the truths that have been taught. There is a wealth of information and suggestion about this book that will delight all who have anything to do with the training of children. It is equally adapted to junior workers, primary teachers, or for use in the home.

BRYSON (Mrs.)—

FRED C. ROBERTS OF TIENT-
SIN; or, For Christ and China. By Mrs. BRYSON. With Preface by Rev. F. B. MEYER, B.A. *With Portrait Frontispiece. Second Edition. Handsome cloth, large crown 8vo,* **3s. 6d.**

Christian.—"It is crowded with incident and interest."

BURRELL (D. J., D.D.)—

FOR CHRIST'S CROWN. And other
Sermons. By DAVID JAMES BURRELL, D.D. *Crown 8vo, cloth,* **6s.**

BURRELL (D. J., D.D.)—
GOD AND THE PEOPLE. And other
Sermons. By David James Burrell, D.D. *Crown 8vo, cloth*, 6s.

BURRELL (D. J., D.D.)—
GOLDEN PASSIONAL. And other
Sermons. By David James Burrell, D.D. *Crown 8vo, cloth*, 6s.

BURRELL (D. J., D.D.)—
THE SPIRIT OF THE AGE. Thirty-
seven Sermons. By David James Burrell, D.D. *Crown 8vo, cloth*, 6s.

The subjects are brightly and vigorously treated.

BURRELL (D. J., D.D.)—
THE WONDERFUL CROSS. And
other Sermons. By David James Burrell, D.D. *Crown 8vo, cloth*, 6s.

CAMPBELL (Rev. J. M., D.D.)—
TEACHING OF THE BOOKS. By
Rev. J. M. Campbell, D.D. (*See* Willett & Campbell).

CARPENTER (Dr. BOYD—Right Rev. Lord Bishop of Ripon)—
THOUGHTS ON PRAYER. By Dr.
Boyd Carpenter. *Fcap. 8vo, cloth*, 1s. 6d.

Contents : Necessity of Prayer—Times Adverse to Prayer—Heartwork in Prayer—Reality of Answers to Prayer—Efficacy of Prayer, etc.

Rock.—" It deals with many important questions. Cannot but prove helpful to all who may bestow any attention upon them. We accord this volume a most hearty welcome."

CARPENTER (Dr. BOYD—Right Rev. Lord Bishop of Ripon)—
FOOTPRINTS OF THE SAVIOUR.
By Dr. Boyd Carpenter. *New Edition, with Thirteen Illustrations, printed on Art Studio paper. Crown 8vo, cloth*, 2s. 6d.

Chapters on places visited by our Lord : Bethlehem—Cana—Sychar—Nazareth—Capernaum—Gennesaret—Decapolis—Bethany—Gethsemane—Calvary—Emmaus—Olivet.

Expository Times.—"Great lessons from the Life of Christ grouped round the cities in which He did His mighty works. and illustrated by great artists, are told here simply for simple folks. It is a new edition of a **FOREMOST FAVOURITE** of the sick-room or prayer-meetings."

These Devotional Studies are attractively bound, and make a very handsome and acceptable gift book.

CAWS (LUTHER W.)—

THE UNRECOGNISED STRANGER. And other Sermons. By LUTHER WINTER CAWS.
Crown 8vo, neat cloth, 3s. 6d. *net; post free*, 3s. 10d.

Christian World.—"Not cast at all in the conventional sermon form, but throughout fresh and suggestive, the outcome of a thoughtful, earnest, and cultured mind."

Evangelical Magazine.—"To read them is to be held spellbound. Strong and spiritual sermons that stir and still."

CHILDREN'S SERMONS AND ADDRESSES TO YOUNG PEOPLE. (*See* Eames, Edwards, Ellis, James, Learmount, Mercer, Reichel, Snell, Thomas, and Tyndall.)

CLARK (Rev. R. W., D.D.)—

THE CHURCH IN THY HOUSE.
Daily Family Prayers, Morning and Evening, for a month. With selected Scripture Reading. By the Rev. R. W. CLARK, D.D. 12mo, *cloth*, 2s. 6d.

COMMON PRAYER, BOOK OF.
Revised, with some Additions. For use in Congregations of the Countess of Huntingdon's Connexion and other Free Churches. *Cloth*, 1s. *net; post free*, 1s. 2d. *Roan*, 1s. 6d. *net; post free*, 1s. 8d.

COOK (CHARLES, F.R.G.S.)—

ENTHRALLED! ENSNARED!! A
Tale of London Life. By CHARLES COOK, F.R.G.S. *Crown 8vo, cloth, gilt lettered title*, 1s. 6d.; *paper wrapper*, 1s.

COOK (CHARLES, F.R.G.S.)—

THY DEVIL SHALL BE MY DEVIL.
A Striking Evangelistic Address. By CHARLES COOK, F.R.G.S., Author of "The Prisons of the World," etc. *12 pages, narrow 8vo*, 1d.; *by post*, 1½d.

COSTER (Rev. G. T.)—

GLORIA CHRISTI. Verses by Rev.
G. T. COSTER. *Crown 8vo, buckram cloth*, 3s. 6d. *net; post free*, 3s. 9d.

DAVIS (Rev. J. D., D.D.)—

JOSEPH HARDY NEESIMA, LL.D.
A Sketch of the Life of. The Runaway Boy who founded the First Christian College in Japan. By Rev. J. D. DAVIS, D.D. *With many Illustrations. Crown 8vo, cloth*, 156 *pages*, 2s. 6d.

Rev. A. T. Pierson, D.D.—"Interested and delighted me. No man or woman can read this book without a positive addition to heart-wealth."

DAWSON (Rev. W. J., M.A.)—
HIGHBURY QUADRANT PULPIT
AND CHURCH MAGAZINE. Contains Sermon by Rev. W. J. Dawson each month. *Monthly*, 1d. ; *post free*, 2d.

DE KAY (CHARLES)—
BIRD GODS. By Charles De Kay.
With Decorations by George Wharton Edwards. 273 *pages*, 12*mo*, *cloth, gilt top*, 7s. 6d.

New York Times Saturday Review.—". . . Its manner is very charming and its matter is fruitful in suggestion. The most successful chapters are those that show how the cuckoo, the woodpecker, and the swan have entered into European mythology and given rise to such hero-gods as Cuchullaind and Pikker. It is indeed in the information gained of these and other mythical demigods of Northern Europe, and of their relations to the familiar names of classic mythology, that the interest and value of the book chiefly lie, and in this respect its interest and value are very great."

"The volume is sumptuously made. The value of the book as a work of reference is greatly enhanced by an unusually elaborate index.
"[Signed] Ernest Ingersoll."

DICKIE (Rev. JOHN)—
SOUTH AFRICA. Personal Experiences
and Impressions. By Rev. John Dickie. *Second Edition*. *Crown 8vo, cloth*, 1s. 6d.

South Africa.—"A pleasant, gossipy account of a visit to South Africa, and contains a number of useful hints to travellers."

DIX (Rev. MORGAN, D.D.)—
CHRIST AT THE DOOR OF THE
HEART. And other Sermons. By the Rev. Morgan Dix, D.D., Rector of Trinity Church, New York. *Crown 8vo, cloth*, 363 *pages*, 3s. 6d.

Contents. Twenty-seven Doctrinal and Practical Sermons : 1, Christ at the Door of the Heart (Advent)—2, The Light of Evening (Close of the Year)—3, God's Purpose Fulfilled (Epiphany)—4, The Parable of the Catacombs (Epiphany)—5, The Mystery of Godliness (Epiphany)—6, Work and Labour Contrasted (Septuagesima)—7, The Power of the Preaching of the Cross (Lent)—8, Walking through the Wilderness (Lent)—9, False Weights and False Measures (Lent)—10, Shrinking from the Call of Christ (Lent)—11, The Triumph of the Cross (Passion Sunday)—12, The Power of His Resurrection (Easter)—13, Self-consciousness (Easter)—14, The Years of the Right Hand of God—15, Idle Fears—16, The Burden of Life—17, Patience—18, The Wedding Garment—19, The Child of Promise—20, St. Paul—21, Life Saved, yet Lost—22, Life Lost, yet Saved—23, Lessons from the Desert Ways—24, Man not a Debtor to the Flesh—25, The Love of Christ—26, God's never-failing Providence—27, The Confession of St. Peter.

H. R. ALLENSON'S CATALOGUE 11

DOLE (CHARLES F.)—

THE COMING PEOPLE.
A Social and Religious Study of Life from the standpoint of the beatitude, "The meek shall inherit the earth." By CHARLES F. DOLE, Author of "The Theology of Civilisation." *Fcap. 8vo, 5s.*

Boston Herald.—"Is as sincere in logic as it is inspiring in cheer and hope."

The Spectator devoted its leading article to this book, and said:—"This is a **healthy and virile essay**, which the reader will be thankful to Mr. Dole for having given him. There are in the book the **outlines of ideas of which we shall probably hear a good deal in the future**, as the attempt to interpret the Christian world and the Christian spirit in terms of the modern doctrine of evolution becomes more developed."

Methodist Recorder.—"It is **distinctly refreshing** to read this book, written in a style quite admirable, and under the impulse of a generous and reverent spirit. This book ought to be widely read, and we are sure that he who begins the work will finish it. Mr. Dole has the insight that discerns principles, and a keen eye for facts."

The Inquirer.—"Dealing with great problems, it is manly, simple, and invigorating."

DOLE (CHARLES F.)—

THE THEOLOGY OF CIVILISATION.
By CHARLES F. DOLE, Author of "The Coming People," "The Religion of a Gentleman," etc. *Fcap. 8vo, 5s.*

Contents: Introduction—The Realm of Doubt—The Moral Structure of the Universe—The World of Opposites—Thorough-going Theism—The Good God—Great Questions—Rational Optimism—The Beginnings of Personality—What Personality is—The Cost of Personality—The Religion of the Man and the Religion of the Child—The Process of Civilisation.

The Methodist Times.—"Mr. Dole's book on 'The Coming People' was good, but this is *STILL BETTER*. It is an exceedingly inspiring and helpful book. It is valuable, not from a theological, but from a religious point of view. The theologian will often revolt from Mr. Dole's views, but the religious man will pass by such passages, and gain great stimulus as he reads."

The Expository Times.—"It is a new book, **full of new thoughts**. . . . It stirs new hopes within us."

The Literary World.—"We have found the volume a **thoughtful and stimulating** contribution to an important study of the true inward relation of the religious inquiries of our time with the fuller outlook of the modern as distinct from the mediæval outlook in the realm of life and thought. It involves an earnest treatment of many great questions and not a few real difficulties that harass some true thinkers and good men and women."

DOWEN (Dr. Z.)—

THE IDEAL CHURCH.
An Address by Dr. Z. DOWEN. *Crown 8vo, paper wrapper*, 6d.

H. R. ALLENSON'S CATALOGUE

EAMES (Rev. JOHN, B.A.)—

SERMONS TO BOYS AND GIRLS.

By JOHN EAMES, B.A. With complete index to subjects and illustrative anecdotes. *Crown 8vo, cloth*, **3s. 6d.**

Sunday School Chronicle.—"These addresses display considerably more culture than the majority of sermons to young people. They have attractive titles, and the style is simple. They would, we imagine, **be listened to with interest** by intelligent children."

Family Churchman.—"This collection of Sermons, all of them **brief, pithy, and practical**, appeals to many beside the young, though from their plainness and simplicity they are specially suited to those for whom they were intended."

Christian Commonwealth.—"Beautifully printed and bound. Subjects aptly chosen, interestingly handled, and the addresses **abound in happy illustration.**"

Freeman.—"'Sermonettes' well worthy of publication, simple, pointed, and full of apt illustration."

Christian World.—"Mr. Eames takes pains to be interesting, and **uses sensible illustrations**, keeping clear of questionable anecdotage."

Christian Age.—"Many a preacher to children might well take a leaf out of Mr. Eames' Book."

The Christian.—"Sermon literature for young people, whether to be read directly by them, or embodied in pulpit teaching for their benefit, is a useful and growing class. Many will welcome 'Sermons to Boys and Girls,' which contains **fifteen discourses, pointed and well constructed.**"

Methodist Times.—"**Examples of what children's** addresses ought to be—simple in language, but pointed in teaching."

EDWARDS (Rev. C.)—

A BOX OF NAILS FOR BUSY CHRISTIAN WORKERS.

Fresh Volume of Original Outlines and Bible Readings. By Rev. CHARLES EDWARDS, Chaplain to the Soldiers' Home, Winchester. With Introduction by SYDNEY WATSON. *Just ready. Third Edition, Ninth Thousand. Crown 8vo, cloth,* 160 *pages,* **1s. 6d.**

Contents: Assorted Nails for Busy Workers—Strong Nails for Building Purposes—Pointed Nails for General Use—Selected Nails in Monthly Packets—Bright Nails for Active Service—Special Nails for Fixing Pictures—Numbered Nails for Willing Workers.

Methodist Recorder.—"Will be time saving as **giving thought a definite direction.** We commend the book very heartily to **Local Preachers.**"

The Christian.—"Here are 'Nails of many sorts.' The pages abound in material for evangelists and other workers, **sound in substance and direct in aim.**"

The Sunday School Chronicle.—"A little volume which has struck us even more, so living and suggestive it is, is 'A Box of Nails.' There is an unfailing point, a keen edge about these outlines, as well as a genuine and earnest spirituality."

Expository Times.—"They are **good nails**, of sterling quality, and **well shaped.**"

EDWARDS (Rev. C.)—

New Book by the Author of "A Box of Nails."

TIN TACKS FOR TINY FOLKS,

and other Outline Addresses for Teachers, Preachers, and Christian Workers amongst the Young. By Rev. CHARLES EDWARDS. *Neat cloth, Crown 8vo,* 2s. 6d.

Methodist Times.—"We are thoroughly pleased with this book. It is **a mine of thought** and illustrations. He is seen to special advantage in his talks on birds."
Local Preachers' Magazine.—"We could wish this handbook were placed in the hands of every preacher. Even those who shape their own outlines will find abundant helpful ideas, and just the kind to kindle thought."
Sword and Trowel.—"It seems to us to be THE VERY THING."
Free Methodist.—"With such a book **no preacher need fear** the toil of adding to his sermon—a word to the children."
Sunday School Chronicle.—"These outline addresses, simple in their divisions, apt in illustration, and telling in application, will be found **full of suggestion and help** to teachers and superintendents."

ELLIS (J.)—

TOOLS FOR THE MASTER'S WORK.

Comprising 250 Sermon Outlines, Bible Studies, Children's Addresses, Sermonettes, Temperance Talks, etc., etc. Collected by J. ELLIS, Editor of "The Tool Basket," etc., etc. *Cloth bound, Gilt, Crown 8vo,* 160 *pages,* 1s. 6d.

A difficulty is often felt by those who have to prepare a sermon or lesson at a very short notice, as to the choice of a theme. These notes and outlines have been gathered from many sources, and grouped in a convenient form, with two indexes of subjects and texts, with the hope that they may prove to be of service to the great army of Ministers, Teachers, and Christian workers.

This is an **Entirely New Collection of Sermon Outlines**, largely contributed by bona-fide Preachers.

The Methodist Times.—"Our old friend, Mr. J. Ellis, has just issued **another valuable volume,** comprising over 250 Sermon Outlines, Bible Studies, Addresses and Sermonettes. Most of the Outlines are just the suggestions and hints we so often want, and leave abundant scope for the preacher's own work and thought."
The Outlook.—"'Tools for the Master's Work' should prove of great use."
The Scotsman.—"A useful little book for clergymen and missionaries."
The Local Preachers' Magazine.—"Mr. Ellis seems to have **excelled himself** in this volume. The best of these Outlines is that they are **not mere skeletons,** but suggestive thoughts, leaving plenty of room for the individuality of the speaker."
The Bookman.—"The work is carefully done and will certainly **prove a mine of wealth.**"
The Baptist.—"The author displays great ingenuity in analysis. The divisions are simple and make free use of catch words, which will be readily remembered."
The Perthshire Constitutional.—"This is a small volume containing between two and three hundred Sermon Outlines. They are from many different pens: sometimes the same text or subject is treated in two or three different ways, so that there is ample variety. One good point about the book is that it **does not say too much** at a time, room is left for the individual speaker so to use the Outline as to make it his own. Another good point is the fulness of its index; the reader can find subjects and texts at a glance."

ELLIS (J.)—

WALLET FOR PREACHERS, TEACHERS, AND CHRISTIAN WORKERS.

An entirely new series of Outlines of Addresses by J. ELLIS, compiler of The Tool Basket, etc., etc. *Fcap. 8vo*, **1s.**

ELLIS (J.)—

OUTLINES AND ILLUSTRATIONS.

For Teachers, Preachers, and Christian Workers. Comprising 600 Outlines of Addresses, Bible Readings, and Sunday School Talks, together with over 250 Illustrations and Incidents. Compiled by J. ELLIS. Being "Tool Basket," "Seed Basket," "Illustrations and Incidents" bound in one volume. *Handsome linen binding, Fcap. 8vo*, **2s. 6d.**

The Christian World.—"The volumes previously issued under the titles, 'Tool Basket,' 'Seed Basket,' and 'Illustrations and Incidents,' are here **conveniently bound together.**"

The Christian.—"Here is **the scaffolding** on which to build hundreds of addresses and talks, and we are convinced that many a puzzled labourer will arise and build after consulting these suggestive pages."

The Methodist Times.—"We have so frequently referred to these books in our columns that we need not do more now than wish the little volume the success it deserves. It is daintily bound, of a size convenient for the pocket, and comprises **Six Hundred Outlines and Addresses, Bible Readings and Sunday School Talks, together with Two Hundred and Fifty Illustrations and Incidents.**"

The Expository Times.—"Three little books—'Tool Basket,' 'Seed Basket,' and 'Illustrations and Incidents'—were lately published, and gladly welcomed. They were the **close-packed work of a genius** in this department. These three are now bound in one, and published attractively."

Local Preachers' Magazine.—"**A very treasury of helpful, well-arranged matter. Excellent in spirit and suggestiveness.**"

Wesleyan S. S. Record.—"We have commended the smaller volumes as they came out each at a shilling without reserve, and now the one volume is beautifully got up for 2s. 6d. It is full of wise suggestions, and dull must be the mind that is not sharpened by the facts, incidents, and outlines given in great profusion."

Out and Out.—"Hundreds of hints, outlines, and illustrations are here supplied in compact and attractive form. **A valuable storehouse of good things.**"

ELLIS (J.)—

ILLUSTRATIONS and INCIDENTS.

For Preachers, Teachers, and Christian Workers. Being a Collection of 250 Anecdotes and Facts, with Index of Subjects. *Fifteenth Thousand. Neat cloth, Fcap 8vo*, **1s.**

Methodist Recorder.—"A choice and well-arranged collection of anecdotes marked by much freshness, and **likely to be of service** to many busy workers in providing 'windows' for their lessons and discourses."

Sunday School Chronicle.—"Quite a number of the illustrations are new to us."

ELLIS (J.)—

SEED BASKET FOR MINISTERS,
SUNDAY SCHOOL TEACHERS, AND CHRISTIAN ENDEAVOURERS. Being a collection of Three Hundred Outlines, Seed Corn, Sunday School Addresses and Band of Hope Talks. By J. ELLIS, Editor of "The Tool Basket." *Twentieth Thousand. Neat cloth*, 1s.

Rev. F. B. Meyer.—"Deserves its name."
New Age.—"The work is well done."
Methodist Times.—"Will find this little book of great service."
Christian Commonwealth.—"A wealth of suggestion."
Primitive Methodist.—"Three hundred excellent outlines."
Free Methodist.—"A great deal pressed into little compass."
Methodist Times.—"The 'Seed Basket' is as good as the 'Tool Basket.'"
Baptist.—"Another admirable collection of helps."
Preachers' Magazine.—"Brief, bright, suggestive."
☞ **Expository Times.**—"Contains **at least a year's sermons** or addresses, easily made and sufficiently worth making your own."

ELLIS (J.)—

TOOL BASKET FOR PREACHERS.
300 Outline Addresses for Preachers, Sunday School Teachers and Open Air Workers. Being a Collection of Sermon Outlines, Pegs of Thought, Sunday School Addresses, Advice and Hints to Open-Air Workers and Temperance Advocates. Compiled by J. ELLIS. *Thirtieth Thousand. Strong limp cloth boards, Fcap.* 8vo, 1s.

Rev. Mark Guy Pearse says "Admirable: the sort of thing that is **invaluable** to busy workers."
Methodist Times.—"Clever, **suggestive**, valuable, and thoroughly practical."
Christian.—"Has achieved a well-merited success."
Literary World.—"Really useful."
Local Preachers' Magazine.—"This compact little book."
Church Sunday School Magazine.—"Simple and suggestive notes."
Family Churchman.—"Outlines clearly and intelligibly put."
Pray and Trust.—"Suggestive and pointed."
Young Man.—"A handy little volume."
Jamaica Churchman.—"A very attractive as well as useful basket."
Expository Times.—"**The quality is very good** and the number very great."
British Weekly.—"Nicely got up."

EVANS (A. JOHNSON, M.A.)—

A PRIMER OF FREE CHURCH
HISTORY. By A. JOHNSON EVANS, M.A. *Crown 8vo, cloth, clear type*, 2s. 6d.

A **Veteran Free-Churchman. Dr. John Clifford** says:—"Mr. Johnson Evans **has laid the Free Churches under a great obligation** for his true story of the origin and early developments of the Free Churches of England and the United States. He knows his facts, marshals them with skill and cogency, and in a spirit of justice and charity that will commend them. The great struggle for liberty of conscience is depicted with clearness and force. **The book should be read by our young Free Church people throughout the land.**"

A PRIMER OF FREE CHURCH HISTORY
(continued)—

A Teacher of Future Pastors. Rev. G. P. Gould, M.A., says:—"I hasten to say at once that **I welcome it cordially** as a very able and, within its limits, satisfactory piece of work. I am struck especially with the judicial tone preserved throughout, there is a most evident desire to be most scrupulously fair all round. I trust it will have a wide circulation."

A Pastor at Work. Rev. Charles Brown says:—"I have read with very great interest and pleasure the 'Primer of Free Church History' by Mr. Evans. It is very interesting and very fair, and eminently readable. **I am delighted with it**, and hope it will receive, as it certainly deserves, a very wide circulation."

Sword and Trowel.—"**An excellent handbook.** Our young men and women ought to be taught the history of their splendid heritage. **In this clear and cogent primer** they will learn how irreparable is the loss of those who forsake the spiritual for the merely fashionable and formal, who leave the Church for an establishment of the State."

Free Church Chronicle.—"Mr. Evans' aim is to interest 'the young people of all ages' in the Evangelical Free Churches, and **we think he has succeeded.** The book is a useful, interesting, and opportune compendium. **It can do nothing but good.**"

Expository Times.—"The only offence his book can give is by its brevity. We could take much more with profit and with pleasure. **It is welcome, and well done.**"

The Glasgow Herald.—"The book is in reality a very excellent short history of Nonconformity, from the great secession in the time of Henry VIII. to these latter days. The general trend of opinion throughout the world, as well as a large number of local circumstances, have contributed to give a temporary activity to the Free Church Movement in England and Scotland, and a **short and well-written volume like this** is distinctly useful, as setting forth historically the fundamental principles on which the movement is based. Some striking parallels are suggested between the Evangelistic and Catholic methods of controversy in these days and in the seventeenth century."

FAIRBAIRN (Rev. R. B., D.D.)—

OF THE DOCTRINE OF MORALITY IN RELATION TO THE GRACE OF REDEMPTION.
By Rev. R. B. FAIRBAIRN, D.D. *Crown 8vo,* 5s.

FAULKNER (R. E.)—

JOSEPH SIDNEY HILL (First Bishop
in Western Equatorial Africa). By R. E. FAULKNER. With an Introduction by the Right Rev. BISHOP STUART. *With Three Portraits. Second Edition. Large crown 8vo,* 3s. 6d.

C. M. Intelligencer.—"To a young man the story it tells should be an inspiration."

British Weekly.—"The strong, steadfast, kindly face that looks at you as you open this volume encourages to its perusal. And the promise of the frontispiece is amply fulfilled. **Whoever wishes to make the acquaintance of an admirable and loving man**, and to see what the Christian character in these latter days is, **should read this volume.**"

Literary World.—"This biography, well written and full of interest, is **calculated to stir very mingled feelings.** When Bishop Hill died at the early age of forty two, he had put into seventeen years of active ministerial life more zealous work than many a fellow-labourer has the opportunity or power, perhaps, to perform in a span far longer. Sprung from the people and apprenticed to a trade, it was a Southampton clergyman who recognised in the lad, John Hill, qualities that had promise. **Hill was of the stuff that gathers strength by difficulties.** The Church militant lost a son she could ill spare in John Sidney Hill."

H. R. ALLENSON'S CATALOGUE

JOSEPH SIDNEY HILL (continued)—

India's Women.—"Apart from its interest to all lovers of missionary work, the story of Bishop Hill is so **full of stirring scenes** and lively anecdotes as to compel the attention of the most casual reader."

Presbyterian.—"The perusal of it leaves the heart richer and better for having become acquainted with such a noble life."

Student Volunteer.—"We welcome this simple record of his Christ-like, unselfish and deeply sympathetic life."

Otago Workman.—"The simple story of an earnest life devoted to the noblest of callings and ending amid a halo of glory, reflecting a lustre on his whole previous career, and told in an unaffected manner by a discreet observer."

Forward.—"The chapters describing the Bishop's work amongst young men in New Zealand are specially interesting and instructive to young men."

Church Missionary Cleaner.—"We wish specially and earnestly to recommend the Memoirs of Bishop Hill. **It is just the book to give away**, particularly **to young men and boys.**"

Expository Times.—"Another missionary biography, and a good one."

Church Bells.—"The book should be read as an account of modern missions in some aspects, and also by any who are disposed to despair of humanity and to believe that the ages of heroism are passed away. This record will revive faith and restore hope in men and women, and is incidentally a strong piece of evidence in favour of the truth of the eternal gospel of the Son of God."

FORD (JOHN D., U.S.N.)—

AN AMERICAN CRUISER IN THE

EAST. By Chief Engineer JOHN D. FORD, U.S.N. (Fleet Engineer, Pacific Station), who was with Admiral Dewey at Manila. *Second Edition, including Battles of Cavite and Manila, with complete Index. One vol.*, 12mo, 536 *pages, cloth, fully illustrated*, 12s.

Describes in a simple and entertaining manner a cruiser's voyage to the Aleutian Islands, China, Korea, Japan, and the Philippines, with numerous photographic Illustrations and Maps, with accounts of life on an American warship, of the battles of the Yalu, of Cavite, and of Manila, and with map of the famous sea fight, drawn by a participant.

Army and Navy Journal.—"A straightforward and agreeable story, and a valuable as well as an entertaining book, and beautifully and abundantly illustrated."

The Outlook.—"A very entertaining volume: contains not only lively sketches of manners, places and institutions, but political and geographical information."

The Nation.—"An excellent book of travels. . . . There is a freshness in the relation and a cleverness of study and observation which make the narrative interesting and superior to the superficial tales of the ordinary globe-trotter."

FORSYTH (Rev. Dr. P. T., M.A.)—

THE HAPPY WARRIOR. By Rev.

Dr. FORSYTH, M.A. A Sermon preached as a Memorial Sermon upon the late Mr. W. E. Gladstone. *Crown 8vo*, 32 *pages*, **3d.**; *post free*, 3½d.

A fine inspiring address to young people.

British Weekly.—"The sermon is suggestive, bold, and warmly appreciative."

Methodist Times.—"A masterly memorial sermon."

FRUIT (JOHN PHELPS)—

THE MIND AND ART OF POE'S

POETRY. By JOHN PHELPS FRUIT, Professor of English Language and Literature. *Large crown 8vo, cloth*, **5s.**

B

GANT (F. T., F.R.C.S.)—
FROM OUR DEAD SELVES TO
HIGHER THINGS. By F. T. GANT, F.R.C.S. *Crown 8vo*, 2s. 6d.

A capital book for young men and women.
Literary World.—" The argument is illustrated by character sketches that are evidently portraits from life."
The Guardian.—" The author uses his technical knowledge and experience of human nature to a very good purpose. . . . In a series of very powerful descriptions no reader can fail to be impressed by a sense of the misery and bondage of sin, or fail to be helped by the hopeful possibilities of the soul's awakening."
Church Review.—" In the diagnosis of sin, this book has some value for the clergy; especially with regard to the sins of the flesh, of which the observant medical man may give a valuable diagnosis. This is especially true in the book before us. The terrible simultaneous degradation of body and soul is powerfully, but we fear accurately, described."
Christian.—" The works of the flesh and the lusts of sense are analysed with masterly skill, and the 'higher things' are described in a manner which rends the veil of Agnosticism in twain from the top to the bottom."

GIBBON (Rev. J. MORGAN)—
THE PULPIT. A Sermon and Address
to the Children. By Rev. J. M. GIBBON. Issued Monthly, 1d. *Post free*, 1½d.; or 12 months, 1s. 6d. Bound Volumes may be had as under:—

TWELVE SERMONS by Rev. J. M. GIBBON, selected from the monthly issues prior to 1899. *Fcap. 8vo, cloth*, 1s. 6d.; *post free*, 1s 9d.

VOLUMES FOR 1901, 1900, & 1899. Twelve different Sermons and Children's Addresses by Rev. J. M. GIBBON in each volume. *Fcap. 8vo, cloth*, 1s. 6d. *each*.

GIBBON (Rev. J. MORGAN)—
THE FOUR LAST THINGS. Four
Sermons on Death, Judgment, Hell, Heaven, by Rev. J. M. GIBBON. *Neat cloth*, 1s. *net; post free*, 1s. 2d.
Methodist Times.—" Lucid, fresh, and thoughtful sermons."
Christian.—" In 'Four Last Things' subjects of sublime and great import are discussed, not always in terms which we approve, nor to conclusions which we endorse, but uniformly, with reverence, and often helpfully."
Sunday School Chronicle.—" Worthy of careful reading."
Primitive Methodist.—" There is a vigour and freshness of thought that is captivating."

GRAY (Rev. Dr. GEO. Z.)—
THE SCRIPTURE DOCTRINE OF
RECOGNITION IN THE WORLD TO COME. By Rev. GEO. Z. GRAY, D.D. A book for the Bereaved. *Fifth Edition*. *Neat cloth*, 2s.

GREY (Rev. J. TEMPERLEY)—
A VILLAGE APOSTLE, AND
OTHER POEMS. By Rev. J. TEMPERLEY GREY. *Crown 8vo*, 2s. 6d.

H. R. ALLENSON'S CATALOGUE 19

GREER (Rev. DAVID H., D.D.)—
FROM THINGS TO GOD. Twenty-one Sermons by Rev. DAVID H. GREER, D.D., Rector of St. Bartholomew's Church, New York. *Crown 8vo, cloth*, 6s.

HABBERTON (JOHN)—
HELEN'S BABIES. By JOHN HABBERTON. 16*mo, cloth*, 1s.
A neat presentation of this healthy and humorous tale of child-life.

HALL (HARRIET M. M. [Mrs. Dr. NEWMAN HALL])—
VOICES, AND OTHER POEMS.
Square 16mo, artistic binding, bevelled boards, gilt edges, 2s. 6d. *net.*

HALLAM (Rev. FRANK)—
THE BREATH OF GOD. A Sketch Historical, Critical, and Logical of the Doctrine of Inspiration. *Crown 8vo, cloth*, 2s. 6d.
An able and well expressed summary of the results of the higher criticism on the Bible.

HALSEY (Rev. J.)—
THE SPIRIT OF TRUTH. Twenty-one Sermons by Rev. JOSEPH HALSEY. *Crown 8vo, neat cloth*, 5s.
The contents of this vigorous volume of sermons are as under :—
The Spirit of Truth—Ave Imperator !—The Ministry of the Cloud—The Foolishness of God—The Readiness of True Consecration—A Misinterpreted Verse and a Misapprehended God—A Cry from the Dust—Fishers of Men—The Fall of Jericho : Ancient and Modern—The Abundant Entrance—Divine Arrests in Service—The Reiterated Message and the Twofold Hearing—Social Contrasts — Jephthah ; or, Heredity's Victim and Time's Revenges — The Outcasts' Christ—Reticence not Indifference—Authority in Religion—The Comedy of the Calf—An Old Question with a New Answer—The Closed Book and the Rent Veil—The Many Voices and the One Message.

Christian World.—"Many readers of Mr. Halsey's ' Beauty of the Lord ' hoped to see more from his pen . . . Here is the second series as **filled with actuality and sanctified with common sense** as its predecessor."
New Age.—"It is a positive relief to come across something one can sturdily disagree with. Mr. Halsey is only wrong now and then, he is right in the main, and he puts his thoughts in a bright stimulating way, which gives to his book a great attractiveness."
Clergyman's Magazine.—"His style and mode of thinking are refreshing; buyers of sermons will spend their money wisely when they add this to their list."
South London Press.—"His views are expressed with remarkable lucidity, force, and courage."
Bradford Observer.—"**Original in the best sense**, they are the genuine utterances of a true man's mind and conscience, full of straight thinking and strong conviction, earnest and eloquent."
Clergyman's Magazine.—"A fresh and breezy book of sermons."
Liverpool Daily Post.—" Is fearlessly outspoken."

HANDLEY (Rev. S. B.)—
WHAT ENGLAND OWES TO THE PURITANS. By Rev. S. B. HANDLEY. *Crown 8vo, 36 pages*, 6d. *net; post free*, 7d.

Herts Congregational Magazine.—"Mr. Handley sums up his case, in the course of which he has marshalled an enormous number of facts in orderly, interesting, and compact array, by saying that now he trusts it is evident that England owes to the Puritans 'our ordered freedom and power of public opinion, our English Sabbath, and our English home.' We think he has abundantly proved his case, and to all who wish for an invigorating tonic in small compass for their Free Church faith we say, buy this well-informed little booklet."

Sword and Trowel. "We finished the perusal of these pages with the assurance of a lifetime confirmed, that 'our fathers were high-minded men.' The Protestants of to-day are in danger of forgetting their Puritan ancestry and the tremendous sacrifices which were made on behalf of civil and religious liberty, and the cause of God and truth. The Free Church Federation would do real service by scattering his little work broadcast over the land. The Nonconformist memory, like its conscience, needs stirring up; this little historical and descriptive work is admirably adapted for this purpose."

HARRIS (READER, K.C.)—
MEN'S SINS. An Address to Men only.
By READER HARRIS, K.C. *Second Edition. One Penny.*
Arranged to go into a court-shape envelope.

A trenchant, plain, and outspoken statement on social purity.

HERBERT (Rev. C.)—
WHEREFORE, O GOD? A Modern Esdras. By Rev. CHARLES HERBERT. *Ornamental wrapper, narrow 8vo*, 6d. *net; post free*, 7d.

Christian World.—"Man's labour, his sin and suffering, the mysteries of faith, of prayer, and of the Divine sacrifice come successively under review. The booklet is attractively written. Should be helpful to those on whom 'the riddle of the world' weighs heavily."

Coulson Kernahan.—"Very many thanks for so kindly sending me a copy. My opinion of the book itself you already know, and **I like it even better now that I have read it again in cold print.** I hope it will be a huge success. I must congratulate you on the get up. Mr. Allenson has produced it **admirably.** The cover design could hardly be improved upon."

Rev. F. A. Pring, Vicar of St. Luke's, Deptford, "begs for permission to serialise it in his local magazine, as it is so helpful for the needs of his district."

Prof. Whitehouse, Cheshunt College.—"The earlier chapters are very suggestive and show that you have been thinking ardently on the deepest themes."

Rev. J. H. Stanley, Great Baddow, Chelmsford.—"A valuable little book. The points raised are of the first importance, **the solutions offered are tersely and beautifully expressed.** I very earnestly commend the book, especially to young men."

Rev. H. H. Carlisle, M.A.—"Much pleased with it. Suggestive and timely, and likely to prove useful to thoughtful men. I shall put it into the hands of some I know to be perplexed about the mysteries."

Literary World.—"The author deals in a clever and very striking way with some **real religious difficulties.** There is much that is helpful and stimulating in these colloquies."

H. R. ALLENSON'S CATALOGUE 21

HERRON (Rev. G. D., D.D.)—

SOCIAL MEANINGS OF RE-
LIGIOUS EXPERIENCES. By Rev. Prof. G. D. HERRON,
D.D. *Crown 8vo, cloth,* 3s. 6d.

New Age (full page review).—"Dr. Herron is a fearless preacher of righteousness. The note struck is sufficiently evident from the title of the book."
Review of Reviews (full page review).—"Mazzini does not lack disciples, but Professor Herron, of Grinnell University, perhaps has grasped more thoroughly than any one else the inner meaning of his message. 'Social Meanings' is a book well worth reading."

HERRON (Rev. G. D., D.D.)—

BETWEEN CÆSAR AND JESUS.
Eight Lectures on the Relation of the Christian Conscience to the Existing Social System. By Rev. Prof. GEORGE D. HERRON, D.D. *Crown 8vo, cloth,* 3s. 6d.

Literary World.—"Dr. Herron is familiar to many thoughtful people in this country as a very earnest exponent and advocate of certain conceptions of the social and political claims of the Gospel of Christ. From first to last Dr. Herron writes with **intense resolution**, and with a **fine, pure passion** full of the enthusiasm of humanity, and with the adoration of Christ. The final chapter teems with noble and suggestive thoughts, which should be pondered earnestly by intelligent Christian men in England and America."

HERRON (Rev. G. D., D.D.)—

THE CHRISTIAN SOCIETY. By
Rev. Prof. G. D. HERRON, D.D. With Introduction by Dr. CHARLES A. BERRY (Chairman of the Congregational Union). *Crown 8vo, cloth,* 3s. 6d.

Christian World.—"Never in our day have we had the moral foundations and spiritual law of a Christian Society preached with such **prophetic fervour and power** as in this volume."

HERRON (Rev. G. D., D.D.)—

THE CHRISTIAN STATE. A Political Vision of Christ. By Rev. Prof. G. D. HERRON, D.D. *Crown 8vo, cloth,* 3s. 6d.

New York Critic.—"Dr. Herron is a man of power. He writes with immense enthusiasm and fine culture. Dr. Herron, like a prophet—a speaker of God, that he is—does not argue; **he appeals to one's moral nature**; he pleads, he commands."

HERRON (Rev. G. D., D.D.)—

THE NEW REDEMPTION. A Call
to the Church to reconstruct Society according to the Gospel of Christ. By Rev. Prof. G. D. HERRON, D.D. *Sixth Thousand. Crown 8vo, cloth,* 3s. 6d.

American Independent.—"A book to be read and pondered."

HOLDEN (CLARA M.)—
THE WARFARE OF GIRLHOOD.
A Series of Bright Papers for Girls. By Mrs. ROBERTSON LAWSON. *Handsomely bound, crown 8vo*, **1s. 6d.**

Christian World.—"The tone throughout is inspiring and practical."

HORNE (Rev. C. SILVESTER, M.A.)—
PRIMER OF CHURCH FELLOW-SHIP.
By Rev. C. SILVESTER HORNE, M.A. (*See* under Rev. William Pierce.)

HORNE (Rev. C. SILVESTER, M.A.)—
THE SPIRIT OF DIVES.
An Indictment of Indifference. A Sermon to Young Men and Women. By Rev. C. SILVESTER HORNE, M.A. 1d. ; *post free*, 1½d. (*Tracts for the Times*, No. 1.)

Literary World.—"An earnest sermon marked by frankness and wisdom."

HORNE (Rev. C. SILVESTER, M.A.)—
THE SOBRIETY OF HOPE.
In Praise of Optimism. A Sermon by Rev. C. SILVESTER HORNE, M.A. 1d.; *post free*, 1½d. (*Tracts for the Times*, No. 6.)

HORNE (Rev. C. SILVESTER, M.A.)—
THE LIFE THAT IS EASY.
A Course of Ten Sermons on the Christian Life to a Weeknight Congregation. By Rev. C. SILVESTER HORNE, M.A. *Crown 8vo, cloth*, **2s.**

This volume of sermons would make an acceptable gift to any one halting on the threshold of decision for Christ.

The Contents of this vigorous and freshly-written exposition of the Christian Life are as follows:—The Goal of Life—Fulness of Growth—The Mystery of Godliness—The Life that is Easy—Voices that Call to Life—The Master of Life—The Return to Self—Healing Health—The Power of Personality—Stability of Character—Means of Grace.

Presbyterian.—"The chapters are brief and very readable. Mr. Horne has given us a brilliant presentation of the Christian Life."
Christian Commonwealth.—"His style is remarkably like that of Dr. Culross, we could hardly pay him a higher compliment. Every page contains some original thought. The sentiment is purely evangelical."
Literary World.—"It is impossible to avoid the impression that this young preacher has **a message for the human conscience and Heart.** His manner of treatment is strenuous and intense. Is certain to be read and pondered by thoughtful young men and women."
Independent.—"It is a **vitalising, cheering, encouraging,** helpful volume."
Methodist Times.—"No one can read these pages without spiritual profit."
British Weekly.—"This suggestive volume of sermons."

H. R. ALLENSON'S CATALOGUE 23

HORWILL (Rev. H. W., M.A.)—
WANTED—AN ENGLISH BIBLE.
By Rev. H. W. HORWILL, M.A. 2d.; *post free*, 2½d. An Essay reprinted from *The Contemporary Review* by special permission of the Editor. (*Tracts for the Times*, No. 11.)

HORWILL (Rev. H. W., M.A.)—
FOUNDATIONS. A Sermon by Rev.
H. W. HORWILL, M.A. 1d.; *post free*, 1½d. (*Tracts for the Times*, No. 7.)
A fine and inspiring appeal to young people to build on Christ.

HORWILL (Rev. H. W., M.A.)—
LIGHT AND LEADING. Vols. I. and
II. (*See* under "Light and Leading.")

JAMES (Rev. G. HOWARD)—
TALKS TO YOUNG FOLK. Seven-
teen Addresses to Children. By Rev. G. HOWARD JAMES. With Index of Subjects and Anecdotes. *Crown 8vo, handsome cloth*, 2s. 6d.

Contents: "Greedy Dogs"—Truth Telling—How to Conquer Evil—Steadfastness—Good Words—Evil Words—A Lad who Helped Jesus—A Little Slave Girl—"For the Prize"—The Three "Phones"—Prayers that are not Heard—A Little Word of Great Meaning, "Amen"—What the Old Year says—The Snow: Its Wonders and its Service—The Snow: Its Might and its Parable—Jewels—A Child in the Pulpit.

Baptist Magazine.—"Mr. James has the happy knack of interesting."
The British Weekly.—"A volume of **simple sermons** for children."
Expository Times.—"Here are comradeship with the little ones, unabashed profusion of good story, **unforgetable lesson!**"
Christian Commonwealth.—"These talks are full of sound teaching, in simple homely language, enforced by **telling illustration.**"

JOHNSTON (WILLIAM A.)—
HISTORY UP-TO-DATE. A Concise
Account of the War of 1898 between the United States and Spain: Its Causes and the Treaty of Paris. By WILLIAM A. JOHNSTON. With Sixteen Photographic Illustrations and Portraits. *Crown 8vo, cloth*, 6s.

Daily Mail.—"A rather good account."
Manchester Guardian.—"Brevity, accuracy, and impartiality."

JONES (NEWTON)—

THE CAPTAIN ON THE BRIDGE.
And other Addresses to Children. By NEWTON JONES, Evangelist of the Sunday School Union. Illustrated with numerous Diagrams. *Small 4to, strong cloth*, 2s. 6d. *net ; post free*, 2s. 9d.

Rev. Thomas Spurgeon.—" A very helpful and suggestive book."

JOWETT (Rev. J. H., M.A.)—

THE DUTY OF BEING YOUNG.
An Address to Young People. By the Rev. J H. JOWETT, M.A. 1d.; *post free*, 1½d. (*Tracts for the Times*, No. 4.)

KEPHART (Rev. J. C., M.A.)—

CHART OF THE PUBLIC LIFE OF CHRIST.
Sixteen pages of Letterpress and Coloured Chart printed on strong bond paper, all neatly folded into a handy book for the pocket. Cloth limp, 2s. 6d.

Most valuable accompaniment to the Gospels. Shows at a glance the events of our Lord's Life by a coloured Diagram and a Harmony of the Four Gospels.

American Sunday School Times.—" There are evidences of great care. Mr. Kephart's book will be very useful."

KILBY (HENRY)—

TRIPS TO ALGERIA, HOLLAND, NORTH CAPE, HAMBURG AND LUBECK, THE HIGHLANDS, ITALY, THE NORTH SEA, POMPEII, THE UNITED STATES, AND CANADA.
By HENRY KILBY. *Illustrated.* 132 *pages, Demy 8vo, pictured boards*, 1s.

Chatty descriptions of visits to many interesting places.

LAWSON (Rev. W. ELSWORTH)—

HEROIC ENDEAVOUR.
A Word of Hope to Young Men. By Rev. W. ELSWORTH LAWSON. Two Addresses to Young Men, one a New Year's Address. *Neat enamel wrapper*, 6d.

Young Man.—" Of this book we may confidently say that it is one of great merit It is able, strong, and full of suggestion."
Christian World.—" An earnest sermon thoughtfully put together."

H. R. ALLENSON'S CATALOGUE 25

LEARMOUNT (Rev. JAMES)—
A New and Handsome Volume of Addresses to Children.

FIFTY-TWO ADDRESSES TO YOUNG FOLK.
By Rev. JAMES LEARMOUNT. *Neat cloth, crown 8vo*, 3s. 6d.

The great difference in the treatment of children to-day and of the earlier years of this century is continually being made evident by the forthcoming of various volumes that are especially interesting to the caretakers of the young. Mr. Learmount's volume is the latest to appear, and from its **abundance of happily chosen illustration and fund of anecdote** should prove of much use to the busy preacher or teacher in search of material to enlighten his own addresses. The volume, too, is **abundantly suited to** the actual **reading aloud** to small or greater gatherings of children, either **in the family circle** or class-room. A glance at the contents of the volume will readily show that Mr. Learmount has beaten a path for himself, and **as his subjects are fresh, so is his treatment of** them. A particularly strong feature of the **illustrations** is that very many of them are **drawn from the realm of science**, and in Mr. Learmount's hands, make a fascinating addition to the aids for speakers. The volume is further furnished with a comprehensive index. Many of these Addresses have already seen the light in the pages of *The Independent*, and it is largely on account of the many requests up and down the country from its readers, beside applications from those who have had the advantage of hearing them spoken, that this volume has been put forward with every confidence of being made heartily welcome.

The fifty-two subjects of Mr. Learmount's volume are:—1, Living Rainbows —2, Talking Sunbeams—3, The Cosmetic of Love—4, Castles in the Air—5, Pneumatic Lives—6, The Angel's Sin—7, An Immortal Heart —8, Glorified Dust—9, Carpe Diem—10, Human Lamps—11, A Human Menagerie—12, Bells on the Toes—13, Honour Bright—14, Nemesis 15, Real British Lions—16, Chameleon Lives—17, Clairvoyance - 18, Mesmerism—19, A Walk in Fairyland—20, Talking in Colours— 21, Sunny Lives—22, Little Parasites—23, Life's Chloroform—24, Fairies—25, Automatic Goodness—26, Growing Wings—27, Try, Try, Try Again—28, Children's Corners—29, Pace Makers—30, Armoured Cruisers—31, Uglification—32, Human Klondikes—33, Alive Inside— 34, Growing—35, The Third Finger—36. Moving Suns—37, Duty— 38, Cats—39, Dogs—40, Ladies and Gentlemen—41, Soldiers—42, An Iron Dress—43, Contentment—44, Sermons in Stones—45, Hobby-Horses—46, A Legend's Lesson—47, The Living Microphone—48, A Powerful Lever—49, Christmas Toys—50, Heaven's Christmas Lights —51, Robin Redbreast—52, Treasures of Memory—Index of Anecdotes and Illustrations.

The Examiner.—"The addresses are all rich in fresh and apt illustrations from science and legend, from literature and human life, and among all these there is not one "chestnut!" Ministers and others who have to speak to young folk should look into this volume."

The Pilot.—"Abundance of short and telling anecdotes, the value of which teachers will not be slow to recognise."

LEE (WM. E., M.R.C.S.E.)—

HUMAN BODY, THE, AND HOW
TO TAKE CARE OF IT. A Tract for the People. An Address delivered to the Fulham Y.M.C.A. By WM. E. LEE, M.R.C.S.E. *Crown 8vo, 22 pages*, 2d. ; *post free* 2½d.

Christian.—"An admirable tract."

LEWIS (Rev. F. WARBURTON, B.A.)—
THE UNSEEN LIFE. By Rev. F.
WARBURTON LEWIS, B.A. *Crown 8vo*, 2s. 6d.

New Age.—"Marked by thoughtfulness, spirituality, and that quality which our fathers called unction."

LIGHT AND LEADING. For Ministers,
Sunday School Superintendents and Teachers, Local Preachers and Bible Students. Vols. I. and II. edited by Rev. H. W. HORWILL, M.A. Vol. III. edited by Rev. G. CURRIE MARTIN, M.A., B.D., Reigate. *Small 4to size.* Vol. *I.*, 3s. 6d.; Vol. *II.*, 3s.; Vol. *III.*, 3s. 6d.

The object of "**Light and Leading**" is to bring, as far as possible, the **results of Modern Biblical Scholarship** and research within the reach of readers who do not know Greek or Hebrew, and to promote in general **the Reverent and Scientific Study** of the Scriptures, free from strained interpretation and theological bias. To supply practical hints respecting **Preaching** and **Public Speaking** for the help of beginners. To give **Self-taught Students**, especially in the department of sacred science, practical advice respecting the choice of books, methods of study, etc.

The Features include **Biblical Exposition;** Articles on **Methods of Teaching and Study;** Summaries of important Books, especially on Biblical and Educational Subjects; **Helps for Preachers** and Speakers, etc.

McKAY (Rev. G. P.)—
New Book on "The Last Things."
IMMORTALITY ON GOD'S
TERMS: Endless Life in Christ the Lord. By the Rev. GEORGE P. MCKAY. *Fcap. 8vo, cloth*, 1s.

Light and Leading.—"Fitted to provoke reflection and inquiry regarding a question of great importance. The writer entertains strong convictions, and offers excellent reasons for doing so. We can conceive of nothing in so small a compass, which could deal more incisively and comprehensively with the subject of 'Conditional Immortality' than this booklet does."

The Christian.—"Deeply solemn questions considered with befitting reverence."

Rev. J. Morgan Gibbon.—"A brave and timely utterance."

Rev. O. C. Whitehouse, M.A., Cheshunt College.—"An interesting and suggestive book. I agree in the main with its conclusions, which are those of Dale and Edward White."

Sir G. G. Stokes, Bart., LL.D., D.C.L., F.R.S.—"I quite agree with the author. For the last 30 years I have lived in the belief that this is the truth, and from time to time have been struck with the wonderful way in which the doctrine dove-tails into the whole system of the Christian Faith."

Rev. George Dana Boardman, D.D., New York.—"I like it for the truth of its doctrine, the fidelity of its exegesis, the clearness of its statements, and the homage it gives to the bestower of immortality."

MACKINNON (Colonel W. C.)—
SAADI SHIRAZI, A FEW FLOWERS
FROM THE GARDEN OF. Translations into English Verse of portions of THE BŪSTAN. By Col. W. C. Mackinnon. *Second and revised edition*, 3s. *net ; post free*, 3s. 3d.

H. R. ALLENSON'S CATALOGUE 27

MACLAREN (Rev. ALEXANDER, D.D.)—
SERMONS PREACHED IN MAN-
CHESTER. By Rev. ALEXANDER MACLAREN, D.D. *Second and Third Series, Fcap. 8vo,* 3s. 6d. *each.*

By arrangement with the publishers of these valuable books of the eminent Manchester preacher, Mr. Allenson has much pleasure in drawing attention to this important addition to his catalogue, and the very favourable reduction of 1s. on the published price of each of these books, which **long since earned a first place** among sermon literature, and even in comparison with the later work of Dr. Maclaren have never been excelled.

MANN (Rev. CAMERON)—
COMMENTS AT THE CROSS.
Six Lent Sermons. By the Rev. CAMERON MANN, Rector of Grace Church, Kansas City, U.S.A. *Crown 8vo, cloth,* 2s. 6d.

Contents: 1, The Comment of Indifference—2, of Hatred—3, of Despair—4, of Faith—5, of Superstition—6, of Thought—Appendix—The Comment of Love.

From the Preface.—"As far as I know, this is the first attempt to group together and treat as a whole the sayings of those who watched at the crucifixion."

MARRIAGE SERVICE ACCORD-
ING TO THE CHURCH OF ENGLAND. Printed in Red and Black, with presentation fly-leaf for name of the parties marrying. *In two styles, neat artistic cloth, gilt edges,* 6d. ; *paper, gilt edges,* 3d. *Postage,* ½d. *extra.*

MARTIN (Rev. G. CURRIE, M.A., B.D.)—
A CATECHISM ON THE TEACH-
ING OF JESUS. By Rev. G. CURRIE MARTIN, M.A., B.D. For use in Schools and Bible Classes. 16 *pages, stout wrapper, clear type,* 1d. ; *cloth,* 2d. *Post free,* 2½d.

About God—Himself—The Holy Spirit—Prayer and Worship—The Kingdom of God—Our Duty—Discipleship—Sin—His Own Death—His Resurrection and Second Coming—His Mission.

The answers are entirely in the words of Scripture (Revised Version).

Rev. Dr. Clifford says:—"This Catechism is one of the best I have seen. The questions are most skilfully arranged, and the answers are apt and effective. A **better catechetical guide** for the young in acquiring a knowledge of the teaching of Jesus **I cannot imagine.**"

Professor W. F. Adeney says:—" I hope indeed it may be of good service. **What a grand total of teaching.**"

Rev. Alfred Rowland says:—"**I like your Catechism**; I hope it may have a large circulation. The idea of stating essential Christian truths in the very words of the Founder of the Christian Religion is not only excellent in itself, but is well carried out."

MARTIN (Rev. G. CURRIE, M.A., B.D.)—
SERMONS TO CHILDREN ON
MOTTOES OF GREAT FAMILIES. *Crown 8vo, cloth,* 3s. 6d.

MARTIN (Rev. G. CURRIE, M.A., B.D.)—
LIGHT AND LEADING. Vol. 3.
See under "Light and Leading."

MEN, BOOKS FOR YOUNG. (*See*
under Phillips Brooks, Bryson, Davis, Faulkner, Gant, Lawson, Phillips.)

MERCER (Rev. HENRY F.)—
BREAD FOR THE BAIRNS. Outline
Addresses to Children. By the Rev. HENRY F. MERCER. *Royal* 16*mo, paper,* 1s. *net* ; *cloth,* 2s. *net. Interleaved for notes.*

Sunday School Chronicle.—" From the letters I receive there is an undoubted need for works of this sort, and I would counsel Christian workers to add this book to their stores. The addresses are brief outlines built up about a blackboard plan. The teaching is direct, strong, and true."

Scotsman.—" Simple and ingeniously devised religious lessons for children. It should prove helpful to ministers and Sunday School teachers."

MILLEDGE (Rev. SYDNEY)—
SNAP SHOTS FROM THE
STUDY. By the Rev. SYDNEY MILLEDGE. *Sq.* 16*mo, cloth, limp,* 1s. Twelve volumes of these simple Gospel messages to boys and girls are now ready. "Snap Shots from the Study" is published weekly, *price,* ½d. *Sent post free monthly, one copy for* 6 *months,* 1s. 9d. *Two copies,* 2s. 10d.

MILLS (B. FAY)—
GOD'S WORLD AND OTHER
SERMONS. Fifteen Representative Sermons. By B. FAY MILLS. *Crown* 8*vo, cloth,* 5s.

Literary World.—" Deserves attention as revealing something of the style and teaching of this very successful American evangelist. The appeals are driven home with many illustrations and incidents from Mr. Mills' own personal experience."

Expository Times.—" As inspiration, as electric spark, in short as sermons, they are everything."

Indian Church Quarterly.—" Brimful of telling anecdote and apt illustration. Most telling and pointed appeals."

MISSIONARY LIFE AND WORK
(*see* Bryson's "Roberts of Tientsin" (China) ; Davis's "Joseph Hardy Neesima" (Japan); Faulkner's "Joseph Sidney Hill" (New Zealand and W. E. Africa) ; Phillip's "Christian Chivalry" ; Pierce's "Dominion of Christ"; Brock's "Sidney Roberts Webb" (Congo).

Brighten the Children's Sunday.

MISSIONARY LOTTO. Consisting of Questions and Answers chiefly on the work of The London Missionary Society, arranged to instruct and entertain. It is an admirable means of communicating information, and provides something quite fresh which may be used on Sunday with the young people. *In box,* 1s. *net; post free,* 1s. 3d.

MONOD (WILFRID)—

HE SUFFERED; or Human Suffering Interpreted by Jesus Christ. Six Meditations for Holy Week. By WILFRID MONOD. *Royal 16mo,* 2s.

MORGAN (Rev. G. CAMPBELL)—

NEW COURT PULPIT. Issued Monthly. Contains Sermons and Notes by this popular preacher. 1d.; *post free,* 2d. *Twelve Sample Nos., post free,* 1s. 3d.

MORISON (JOHN, D.D.)—

COUNSELS TO A NEWLY-WEDDED PAIR. A Companion to the Honeymoon, and a Remembrancer for Life. By the late Dr. JOHN MORISON. *Handsomely bound in light ribbed cloth, neatly ornamented in gold, gilt edges,* 2s. 6d. *Thirty-second thousand.*
An old favourite as a wedding present.

NEEDHAM (E. S.)—

AN IMAGINARY SYMPOSIUM. Criticising Scepticism and Agnosticism. *Crown 8vo, cloth,* 2s. 6d.
Literary World.—" This is a very sprightly little book, not only entertaining but suggestive."

NEW ORTHODOXY, THE. Biblical, Theological, and Literary Articles aiding in the Reconstruction of the Christian Beliefs. *Vols. I. and II., 8vo,* 7s. 6d. *each.* Edited by Rev. ROBERT TUCK, B.A.

NEW TESTAMENT IN GREEK. A New and Revised Critical Edition based on the Texts of Tischendorf, Westcott and Hort, and Weiss, with Marginal References and Footnotes.
This is the Edition published by the Wurtemburg Bible Society.
Strongly bound in limp leather, tape sewn, gilt edges, round corners, 3s. 6d.
Strongly bound in semi-limp cloth boards, sprinkled edges, round corners, 2s. 6d.
This Greek Testament can also be had in ten parts, each bound strongly in limp cloth, suitable for the breast pocket, at 5d. *each, postage* 1d. *extra.*

NONCONFORMIST MINISTER'S
ORDINAL, THE. A fresh setting of the Preachers' Services for Baptismal, Marriage, and Funeral Services. **Large Type.** *Fcap. 8vo, neat cloth,* **1s.** *net; dark red cloth, gilt lettered,* **1s. 3d.** *net; black buckram, gilt lettered, very strong,* **1s. 6d.** *net; Turkey morocco, gilt edges and gilt lettered,* **3s. 9d.** *net; postage,* **2d.** *each extra.*
This book will go comfortably into a breast pocket.

Presbyterian.—"Judicious and devout."
Literary World.—"A work many Nonconformist ministers will be glad to know of and to possess. It is a handily and tastefully presented book; as convenient in size, type, and binding as could well be."
Evangelical Magazine.—"Will no doubt prove most valuable to the young minister, who on leaving college needs some such guide."
Primitive Methodist.—"When this ordinal is known we predict that it will be largely used."

NORTON (Rev. JOHN N., D.D.)—

OLD PATHS. Fifty-two Sermons. By
Rev. JOHN N. NORTON, D.D. A Course of Sermons for the Church's Year. Illustrated with numerous useful and telling anecdotes. *Large crown 8vo,* **6s.**

OUTLINE SERMONETTES ON
GOLDEN TEXTS. Forty-seven topics by—

Rev. Prof. W. F. Adeney, M.A.
Rev. W. J. Allan, M.A., B.D.
Rev. W. Armstrong.
Rev. W. W. D. Campbell, M.A.
Rev. John Eames, B.A.
Rev. Hugh Elder, M.A.

Rev. R. C. Ford, M.A.
Rev. A. R. Henderson, M.A.
Rev. G. Currie Martin, M.A., B.D.,
Rev. Sydney Milledge, M.A., and
Rev. E. Pearce Powell, M.A.

Reprinted from "Light and Leading," vol 3. Fcap. 8vo, cloth, **1s.**

PALMER (Rev. E. REEVES, M.A.)—
A Theology for the Twentieth Century.

CHRIST, THE SUBSTITUTE. A
Series of Studies in Christian Doctrine, based upon the Conception of God's Universal Fatherhood. By Rev. E. REEVES PALMER, M.A., Author of "The Development of Revelation." *Crown 8vo, cloth,* 418 *pages,* **7s. 6d.**

In this work the Author, from the starting point of the Universal Fatherhood, elaborates a system of Theology in which various doctrines—as Substitution, Forgiveness, Justification, Election, etc.—are presented in a manner hitherto unrecognised.
N.B.—The Author's former work, "The Development of Revelation,' was highly appreciated by the late Right Hon. W. E. Gladstone.

PALMER (JOSEPH)—
THE GOSPEL PROBLEMS AND THEIR SOLUTION. By JOSEPH PALMER. *Crown 8vo, cloth*, 400 *pages*, 6s.

Spectator.—"'The Gospel Problems and their Solution' proceeds on the theory that the Synoptic Gospels are the record of our Lord's utterances in Aramaic, while St. John gives those that were spoken in Greek. It is an elaborate piece of work, from which, whether he accepts its theory or no, **the student can scarcely fail to learn much.**"

Unitarian Bible Magazine.—" We have no hesitation in pronouncing this to be a most interesting volume. Not that we regard it as in any sense final. But it lays open before us in an honest and genuine manner, and very methodically too, the result of much thoughtful, laborious study made by one who has worked his way out of a narrow circle into a position of independent inquiry, and **shows a rare and valuable clearness** in the statement of every difficulty."

"The comparison of parallel passages in the Gospels our author makes is most suggestive. The use he makes of the hints supplied to students by the newly unburied papyrus fragments of Jesus' sayings; the careful collection of word differences that show the Greek complexion of John's Gospel; these, and many other points will make the book of some value to those who can catch an impulse to fresh enquiry, without being obliged blindly to adopt conclusions."

Glasgow Herald.—" Mr. Palmer, in a style which it is **a real pleasure to read**, and with learning which it is impossible not to respect, undertakes to prove that the narrative parts of the Gospels were written soon after, and for the most part immediately after, the events happened which they relate; and that the reports of Christ's longer addresses were taken down as they were spoken. Even the circumstances connected with the birth of Christ which no human being but Mary could know are not admitted to be exceptional. According to Mr. Palmer, they are admitted into the Gospel narratives only on the authority of written documents."

Guardian.—"A work of real value. We cannot, of course, endorse all the author's arguments or conclusions. But he has devoted many years to his task, and no one can deny that several of his points are new and important. **We are glad to call our readers' attention to his book as one that well deserves their study.**"

Baptist.—" Discussed with considerable ability, and the whole of the Gospels brought under a close critical review. There is much archæological information in the book concerning ancient writings, tablets, papyri, MSS., the use of shorthand in early times, etc., to illustrate and sustain various parts of Mr. Palmer's theory. He has certainly taken immense pains and spent much time in careful research, and the reader will find many lines of thought and study **worthy of the consideration of all Bible students.**"

Westminster Review.—"The chronological confusion in Luke is explained by the fact that in editing he got the slips mixed and the writer being no longer alive to assist him, he was not able to get them in their right order. It will be seen from this that **this is an original and entertaining work.**"

English Churchman.—" Indebtedness to other authorities for the strengthening of his view is admitted by Mr. Palmer, whose independent, devout and truth-seeking qualities go very far to secure our confidence and concurrence. **We cordially recommend his laborious endeavour,** and wish his book a wide circulation."

Family Churchman.—"This inquiry **will well repay careful reading,** and commend itself to many biblical students as the work of one of no little care, research, and ability, endued alike with a reverent mind and with a true love for God's holy and inspired Word."

Christian.—" A work which **will interest many Bible students.**"

PARKER (Rev. JOSEPH, D.D.)—
TO-DAY'S CHRIST. A Study in Reincarnation. By Rev. JOSEPH PARKER, D.D. A Companion to "To-Day's Bible." *Cloth*, 1s. 6d. *net; by post*, 1s. 9d.

PARKER (Rev. JOSEPH, D.D.)—

TYNE FOLK—MASKS, SHADOWS,
AND FACES. By Rev. JOSEPH PARKER, D.D. *Handsome cloth, crown 8vo*, 3s. 6d.

Methodist Times.—"We are glad to welcome his latest work. A charming series of Tyneside sketches. Readers cannot fail to be interested in the recollections so graphically set forth."
Literary World.—It is a collection of vigorous and simple stories, displaying intimate knowledge of the North Country folk and their ways."
Expository Times.—"Of all Dr. Parker's books, 'Tyne Folk' is the favourite. It is both himself and the folk, but chiefly himself of course. And he is himself the most interesting personality, both to himself and to us, that any of his books contain. The delight of it is that we have him when he does not know, and see him when he thinks we are looking at another."
From a chapter in "Studies in Texts" **Dr. Parker** says:—"Any one caring to know more about my early days, and the conditions in which I lived, should read 'Tyne Folk.' In this book I have given an almost literal account of the people who affected my earliest impressions and endeavours, and who thus created the atmosphere which surrounded my progress towards maturity. Oh, those old, old times, and old, old folks."

PARKER (Rev. JOSEPH, D.D.)—

JOB'S COMFORTERS, OR SCIEN-
TIFIC SYMPATHY. By Rev. JOSEPH PARKER, D.D. 6d. *net*; *post free*, 7d.

PARRY (Rev. JOHN, M.A.)—

THE PARISH DISTRICT VISITING
BOOK, AND SICK AND COMMUNICANTS' LIST. *Second Edition. Strongly bound in buckram cloth, round corners, for the pocket*, 2s. *net* ; *post free*, 2s. 3d.

PEARSON (Rev. SAMUEL, M.A.)—

AM I FIT TO TAKE THE LORD'S
SUPPER? By Rev. SAMUEL PEARSON, M.A. *Seventeenth Thousand.* 16 *pages, crown 8vo*, 1d.; *post free*, 1½d. 6s. *per* 100. (*Tracts for the Times*, No. 5.)

PERREN (Rev. C. H., D.D.)—
The Evangelist's Handbook.

REVIVAL SERMONS IN OUTLINE.
With Thoughts, Themes, and Plans, by eminent Pastors and Evangelists. Edited by Rev. C. H. PERREN, D.D. *Crown 8vo*, 344 *pages, cloth*, 3s. 6d.

Part I. 80 Pages on Methods.
SOME MODERN REVIVALS By Rev. JOHN R. DAVIES.
DIVINE AND HUMAN AGENCY IN REVIVALS. By Rev. JOHN GORDON, D.D.
THE PASTOR'S VALUE. By W. H. GEISTWEIT.
THE EVANGELIST IN REVIVALS. By Rev. E. A. WHITTIER.

H. R. ALLENSON'S CATALOGUE 33

REVIVAL SERMONS IN OUTLINE (continued)—
THE PEOPLE'S PART IN REVIVAL WORK.
HOW TO PROMOTE REVIVALS. By D. L. MOODY.
WORK PREPARATORY TO REVIVALS. By Rev. HERRICK JOHNSON, D.D.
REVIVALS—HOW TO PROMOTE THEM. From a Lecture by CHARLES G. FINNEY, D.D.
HOW TO SECURE A REVIVAL. By E. P. BROWN.
SOME HINTS ABOUT REVIVALS.
HOW TO AWAKEN FRESH INTEREST IN OUR CHURCHES. By D. L. MOODY.
HOW TO SAVE SOULS. By Rev. F. O. DICKEY.
PERSONAL WORK IN REVIVALS. By Rev. B. FAY MILLS.
EXPECTING CONVERSIONS. By IRA D. SANKEY.
DEFECTIVE REVIVAL WORK.
THE SUNDAY EVENING SERVICE. By Rev. ADDISON P. FOSTER, D.D.
THE INQUIRY MEETING. By D. L. MOODY. [SEEKERS.
HELPFUL PASSAGES FOR DIFFERENT CLASSES OF

Part II. 244 Pages of Outlines and Sketches of Revival Sermons. Forty-four Old Testament, seventy-one New Testament. In all one hundred and fifteen Outlines from approved Evangelists, such as J. W. CONLEY, R. A. TORREY, A. B. EARLE, J. L. CAMPBELL, JOHN McNEILL, J. WILBUR CHAPMAN, D. L. MOODY, E. W. BLISS, D. H. COOLEY, A. J. GORDON, J. H. ELLIOT, G. C. FINNEY, D. W. WHITTLE, A. F. BARFIELD, A. T. PIERSON, THE EDITOR, and others.

Sunday School Chronicle.—"A large number of Sermon Outlines adapted for Revival Services. Outlines gleaned from those whom God has used and owned in the blessed work."
Daily Chronicle.—"One great merit, they are brief."
Expository Times.—"Famous sermons all passed through a capable condenser."
Christian Age.—"Teems with excellent suggestions."
Methodist Times.—"To young men desirous of engaging in evangelistic work, we can highly recommend this volume."

PERREN (Rev. C. H., D.D.)—
SEED CORN FOR THE SOWER.

A Book of Thoughts, Themes, and Illustrations for the Pulpit and Platform. Original and Compiled by Rev. C. H. PERREN, D.D. With Complete Indices to Subjects, Texts, and Authors quoted. *Cloth boards*, 394 *pages*, 5s.
Is arranged in alphabetical order throughout, and is equipped with the following three good indices—Complete Index of Texts Illustrated—Complete Index of 250 Authors Quoted—Complete Index of Subjects Treated—thus making its contents easily available.

The Methodist Times.—"An admirable collection of thoughts and illustrations, compiled for the use of Christian workers. **One of the charms** of this book is **the absence of the stock illustrations**, common to works of this class. The value of the work is enhanced by the fact that the subjects are arranged in alphabetical order, and there are two exhaustive indices, one of authors and the other of texts. Rightly used, the book will be **a boon to preachers and teachers.**"

C

PHILLIPS (Rev. THOMAS, B.A.)—

CHRISTIAN CHIVALRY. A Missionary
Address to Young Men. By Rev. THOMAS PHILLIPS, B.A., Norwich. *An artistic Booklet. Enamel paper wrapper, narrow 8vo*, 6d.

Life of Faith.—"An address on Phil. iv. 13, specially addressed to young men. Workers among young men should bear this little work in mind."
Christian.—"Friends of missions might do well to distribute copies among young men."

PIERCE (Rev. WILLIAM), and HORNE (Rev. C. SILVESTER, M.A.)—

THE PRIMER OF CHURCH FELLOWSHIP.
By Rev. W. PIERCE and Rev. C. S. HORNE, M.A. *Fourth Edition.* For Use in the Independent Churches. *Cheap Edition*, 6d. ; *post free*, 7d. *Cloth*, 1s.

Rev. Principal Fairbairn, D.D., Oxford.—"Your little book is most timely. It is full of wisdom and of good feeling, and I know no book which speaks a more needed word. May it help our churches, and our young people in particular, to know what the Church really means and what their duties toward it."
Dr. R. W. Dale, of Birmingham.—"I have read with great interest the 'Primer' which you have just published. It is admirable from first to last. It is precisely the kind of book that Congregational ministers must desire to put into the hands of Church members, and of candidates for Church membership. It is a triumph of simplicity, clearness and earnestness."
Dr. R. F. Horton, M.A., Hampstead.—"I think the 'Primer' will be of the greatest use, not so much as a rigid text book for pastors and teachers to employ in classes, but as a model or pattern of the ground which has to be covered, and filled, according to the individual conviction, in instructing the young. For my own part, I mean to use it, just as it is ; but then, I am perhaps more in accord with you than many of our brethren would be ; they will be able to use it with equal profit, though in a different way. I hope the success of it will be very encouraging."
Rev. Alexander Maclaren, D.D., Manchester.—"I have read it with much interest, and think it extremely well adapted for the purpose intended. I shall recommend it in my own congregation and elsewhere as opportunity serves. I am sure that many pastors will join with me in thanking you for a very necessary and well-done piece of work."
Rev. Joseph Parker, D.D., London.—"This is an excellent idea. That Mr. Pierce and Mr. Horne have taken it up is to me a cheering sign of the times."
Word and Work.—"We gladly welcome the new and cheaper edition of 'The Primer of Church Fellowship,' by the Revs. William Pierce and C. Silvester Horne. Having already expressed our high opinion of it when published at one shilling, we rejoice to see this cheaper edition, and trust it will be scattered broadcast over the twofold section of Christendom, known as the Churches of the Congregational order. It is an admirable handbook to the privileges and duties of Church membership."

PIERCE (Rev. WILLIAM)—
Sermons on Missionary Work.

THE DOMINION OF CHRIST.
The Claims of Foreign Missions in the Light of Modern Religious Thought and a Century of Experience. By Rev. WILLIAM PIERCE. *Handsome cloth, large crown 8vo*, 3s. 6d. *Special edition, for distribution, stout paper*, 1s. *net*.

H. R. ALLENSON'S CATALOGUE 35

THE DOMINION OF CHRIST (continued)—

Contents: The Dominion of Christ — Patriotism and Missions — The Saviour of the World—The Vocation of the Missionary—Women as Missionaries—The Beckoning Vision—Place of Education as a Missionary Agency—Relation of the Churches to the Work of Foreign Missions — Foreign Missions and Christian Life and Thought — Physician and Evangelist—Forward—Complete Index.

Mr. Pierce's work would be found useful at any time, but should particularly be so now when the China mission field is in such a disturbed state. It would well form the basis of a short series of addresses for week-night services.

L.M.S. Chronicle (Rev. GEO. COUSINS).—"Earnest in spirit, enthusiastic and hopeful in tone, and thoroughly practical in aim. We heartily commend this book, and desire for it a large circulation."
Methodist Times.—"Clear, manly, and thoroughly Protestant."
Indian Christian Patriot.—"A really good book on Christian Missions."
British Weekly.—"Cannot fail to increase intelligent interest in the propagation of Christianity."
American Sunday School Times.—"A Pastor would find this book of great stimulative value."
Baptist.—"The position that the missionary is essentially an evangelist and not an educationalist is ably maintained. There is a vigorous plea for extended medical missions."
C. M. Intelligencer.—"A good and stimulating book."

PIERCE (Rev. WILLIAM)—

CHRISTIANITY AND ART. A Sermon by Rev. WILLIAM PIERCE. *Crown 8vo*, 16 *pages*, 1d. ; *post free*, 1½d. (*Tracts for the Times*, No. 2).

POTWIN (Prof. L. S.)—

HERE AND THERE IN THE GREEK NEW TESTAMENT. By Prof. L. S. POTWIN. *Large Crown 8vo*, 5s.

PRING (Rev. F. A.)—

THE MESSAGE OF THE INCARNATION TO THE NATION. Sermon by Rev. F. A. PRING, Vicar of St. Luke's, Deptford. *Crown 8vo*, 16 *pages*, 2d. ; *by post*, 2½d.

REICHEL (Rev. GEO. V., M.A.)—

WHAT SHALL I TELL THE CHILDREN? By the Rev. GEO. V. REICHEL, M.A. *Handsome cloth, crown 8vo*, 5s.

A new volume of Object Sermons and Themes, with many illustrative Anecdotes.

British Weekly.—"It is rather a nice book, and will be very useful to teachers and those who preach to children. The merit of the volume is that **it has freshness.**"

36   H. R. ALLENSON'S CATALOGUE

RIPON (Right Rev. Lord Bishop of [Dr. BOYD CARPENTER])—

THOUGHTS ON PRAYER. By
Right Rev. LORD BISHOP OF RIPON. *Fcap. 8vo, cloth,* 1s. 6d.

Contents: Necessity of Prayer—Times Adverse to Prayer—Heartwork in Prayer—Reality of Answers to Prayer—Efficacy of Prayer, etc.

Rock.— 'It deals with many important questions. Cannot but prove helpful to all who may bestow any attention upon them. We accord this volume a most hearty welcome."

RIPON (Right Rev. Lord Bishop of [Dr. BOYD CARPENTER])—

FOOTPRINTS OF THE SAVIOUR.
By Right Rev. LORD BISHOP OF RIPON. *Crown 8vo, cloth,* 2s. 6d. *New Edition, with Thirteen Illustrations printed separately on Art Studio paper. A very handsome gift book, and useful withal.*

Chapters on places visited by our Lord: Bethlehem—Cana—Sychar—Nazareth—Capernaum—Gennesaret—Decapolis—Bethany—Gethsemane—Calvary—Emmaus—Olivet.

ROTHERHAM (JOSEPH BRYANT)—
Valuable Aid to Bible Study.

THE EMPHASISED NEW TESTAMENT.
A New Translation designed to set forth the exact meaning, the proper terminology, and the graphic style of the sacred original; arranged to show at a glance **Narrative, Speech, Parallelism,** and **Logical Analysis;** and emphasised throughout after the Idioms of the Greek tongue, with select references and an appendix of notes. By J. B. ROTHERHAM. This version has been adjusted to the critical text ("formed exclusively on documentary evidence") of Drs. Westcott and Hort. *Third Edition. Crown 4to, double columns, 272 pages, cloth,* 10s. 6d.; *half roan,* 10s. *net; half morocco,* 12s. 6d. *net; whole limp morocco,* 16s. *net.*

The Christian Commonwealth.—We know of no translation which is of more service to ministers or to Bible students generally."

The British Weekly says:—"This is a painstaking work which deserves recognition. No page will be read without having a clearer light shed upon some passage or verse. . . . The book **is well worth study.**"

The Christian says:—"Many years ago Mr. Rotherham brought out a version of the New Testament critically emphasised, and some of us employed the book with interest and profit. The present work strikes us as following a better method than its predecessor. The title-page fairly describes the plan of the work. The typographical arrangement is very successful, emphasis being indicated by signs that are expressive without being cumbersom. "

The Christian, in a further review, says:—"It is a pleasure now to welcome the completed work, the third edition of a version which was first published twenty-five years ago. To many this version will be a great help, not only in study, but in devotional reading. Thoughtful Christian workers will appreciate the volume as a present."

ROYAL HELPS FOR LOYAL LIVING.
Daily Readings for a year. Scripture, Poetical, and Prose quotations from eminent writers of all time. 16*mo*, *cloth*, 3s. 6d.

SERMONS (*see* Banks, Battershall, Brooks,
Burrell, Carpenter (Boyd), Caws, Dawson, Dix, Eames, Gibbon, Halsey, Horne, James, Learmount, Lewis, Perren, Pierce, Pring, Reichel, Snell, Thew, Thomas (Evan), Thomas (H. Elwyn), Tipple, Tracts for the Times, Tyndall.

SERMON OR MANUSCRIPT
PAPER. THE PATERNOSTER SERIES.

The user of this paper enjoys the following special advantages: It is easily arranged by means of holes punched in the left hand margin, so allowing that a sheet of paper can be immediately inserted or abstracted at desire, and that without disturbance to any other sheet.

Small 4to Good Writing Paper, ruled faint lines and margin line, 1s. 6d. for 10 quires.

Octavo Good Writing Paper, ruled faint lines and margin line, 1s. for 10 quires.

Any special size and ruling made promptly to order.

SHELDON (Rev. CHARLES M.)—

IN HIS STEPS: What Would Jesus Do?
BY CHARLES M. SHELDON. With Preface by Rev. F. B. MEYER, B.A. *Handsome presentation edition, cloth gilt, bevelled boards,* 3s. 6d. *Cheaper editions,* 2s. 6d., 2s., 1s. 6d., 1s. *and* 6d.

Please ask for Mr. Meyer's Edition, which was the first to be on sale in England, and is the only authorised Edition in this country.

This remarkable social story, the thought of which is the application to all life of the test question, "What would Jesus do?" has had an extraordinary sale. In the guise of a dramatic story, the book makes a powerful appeal to the public conscience in the lines in which interest is now so deeply aroused—namely, the social conditions affecting the relations of employer and employee, rich and poor, the Christian and the world, the saloon and the voter, etc.

Dr. Clifford says:—"This is a living book. It has the fascination of a story, and the inspiration of a prophet's message. The thought of our time is just now crystallizing round the example of Jesus. No question is so urgent as 'What would Jesus do in my place and with my circumstances?' WE MUST ANSWER IT, and it is a real gain to see how others of our own day have answered it. The book will be of great service."

Extract from Mr. Meyer's Preface.—"The author's purpose is to draw attention to the ethical teachings of Jesus, and to enforce the necessity of compliance with them on the part of those who bear His Name. And who shall say that there is no need? 'In His Steps' will set its readers thinking, and lead to that self-questioning which is the first step towards life of the noblest quality. Because I enjoyed the book when I read it, and think it will lead many to reconsider and reconstruct their lives, I have pleasure in writing these prefatory commendations."

Sunday School Times.—"The reading of the book will search many a heart, and ought to lead to a simpler, holier, and more fully consecrated Christian life."

Christian Endeavour World.—"A fascinating tale, that draws and holds with straightforward winsomeness."

SHELDON (Rev. CHARLES M.)—

THE CRUCIFIXION OF PHILIP STRONG.

By CHARLES M. SHELDON. *Handsome presentation edition, cloth gilt, bevelled boards,* 3s. 6d. *Cheaper editions,* 2s. 6d., 2s., 1s. 6d., 1s. *and* 6d.

Chicago Herald.—"A fine piece of realistic writing."

Zion's Herald.—"The people wanted the Gospel, the old Gospel, without any reference to such things as the oppression of the poor, the rum traffic, gambling, industries, and the like. Philip's Gospel was too broad, too worldly, for his people, and they could not endure it. The story is wonderfully well told and has a double edge."

The Congregationalist.—"It is an argument, a plea, a panorama and a story all in one. The story is one of intense vigour and pathos. It will secure a very wide reading, and it should make a deep impression upon every reader and produce lasting fruit."

SHELDON (Rev. CHARLES M.)—

MALCOLM KIRK; or, Overcoming the World.

A Tale of Moral Heroism. By CHARLES M. SHELDON. *Handsome presentation edition, cloth gilt, bevelled boards,* 3s. 6d. *Cheaper editions,* 2s. 6d., 2s., 1s. 6d., 1s. *and* 6d.

This book tells the entrancing history of the regeneration of a lawless western town. The hero, Malcolm Kirk, embodies every element of courageous self-sacrifice. As one writer has said: "He glorifies and invites to one of the noblest types of heroism." The servant girl question is treated from a new standpoint in the character of Faith Kirk, and the liquor element receives some hard blows. Young people will read it over and over again with growing interest, and it should be in every Sunday School library.

SHELDON (Rev. CHARLES M.)—

THE TWENTIETH DOOR; or, Battling with Temptation.

By CHARLES M. SHELDON. *Handsome presentation edition, cloth gilt, bevelled boards,* 3s. 6d. *Cheaper editions,* 2s. 6d., 2s., 1s. 6d., 1s. *and* 6d.

Sunday School Journal.—"Its picture of youth struggling toward manhood in a hand-to-hand fight with robust temptations is of thrilling interest."

Golden Rule.—"No one can read it without feeling that few sermons would be more interesting or helpful than this story. I propose to read portions of this book referring to school life to my Sunday School class of boys at their next monthly meetings at my home. The author has a special gift in this way."

Religious Herald.—"The sturdy and conscientious manliness with which Paul decided all questions, his true and helpful friendship with his school and college room mate, together with the story of the home life of his mother, brother, and sister, make a story of great interest."

Congregationalist.—"It is a story of school and college life as well as of manly service and helpfulness in more than one sphere."

H. R. ALLENSON'S CATALOGUE 39

SHELDON (Rev. CHARLES M.)—

RICHARD BRUCE; or, The Life That
Now Is. By CHARLES M. SHELDON. *Handsome presentation edition, cloth gilt, bevelled boards*, 3s. 6d. *Cheaper editions*, 2s. 6d., 2s., 1s. 6d., 1s. *and* 6d.

This story of a young man's conflicts in his attempt to live up to a high ideal should interest all, particularly young men.

The Congregationalist.—"It is a truly powerful, practical, touching Christian narrative, creditable to the writer and engrossing to the reader. . . . He possesses real power as a delineator of character, skill in using incidents and wisdom in describing a natural, manly and inviting type of Christianity. Put the volume into your Sunday School library."

SHELDON (Rev. CHARLES M.)—

HIS BROTHER'S KEEPER; or, Christian Stewardship. By CHARLES M. SHELDON. *Handsome presentation edition, cloth gilt, bevelled boards*, 3s. 6d. *Cheaper editions*, 2s. 6d., 2s., 1s. 6d., 1s. *and* 6d.

The Religious Telescope.—"A striking book which relates how the perplexities of a great labour trouble led a rich young man to see that his money was not given him for his own individual pleasure and profit alone."

The Episcopal Recorder.—"The story is well-written, intensely interesting, and should incline the hearts of readers to take a wider view of this great problem."

SHELDON (Rev. CHARLES M.)—

ROBERT HARDY'S SEVEN DAYS;
or, A Dream and Its Consequences. By CHARLES M. SHELDON. *Handsome presentation edition, cloth gilt, bevelled boards*, 3s. 6d. *Cheaper editions*, 2s. 6d., 2s., 1s. 6d., 1s. *and* 6d.

Christian Work.—"The earnestness, the zeal, the solemnity, the kindliness, the Christianity, of that week's living are pictured with a skill and dramatic power that cannot fail to make readers feel as never before how solemn a thing it is to live."

The Congregationalist.—"It is a well conceived and powerfully written story, which should arouse lethargic Christians and do much to establish brotherliness and true views of this life and the next. Portions of the book are dramatic, and all of it is of great interest."

The Herald and Presbyter.—"The impossibility of making up in a week for the neglect of the opportunities of a lifetime is impressively shown."

SHELDON (HENRY C.)—

HISTORY OF THE CHRISTIAN CHURCH. By HENRY C. SHELDON, Professor in Boston University. 5 *vols., extra crown 8vo, cloth*, 42s.

    Vol. I.—The Early Church.
    Vol. II.—The Mediæval Church.
    Vols. III., IV., V.—The Modern Church.

Professor W. T. Davison, writing in **The Methodist Times.**—"The New Church History may be with confidence described as one of the clearest and most readable for the general reader anywhere obtainable, very useful to the elementary student as well as serviceable to more advanced students for its summaries, tables, and general surveys, while for a modern period it will be found interesting and valuable to all. We are sure that Methodist readers, at all events, will give Professor Sheldon's volumes the welcome on this side of the Atlantic which their brightness, force, comprehensiveness, and practical utility deserve."

SIME (Rev. A. H. MONCUR)—

WHAT THE CHURCH MIGHT BE.
A Sermon by Rev. A. H. MONCUR SIME. 16 *pages, crown 8vo*, 1d.; *post free*, 1½d. (*Tracts for the Times*, No. 13.)

SIN PUNISHED, BUT SINS FORGIVEN.
The simple way of Salvation of the first century, but now practically a New Theory of the Atonement. This sets forth from Scripture the two penalties for the infraction of God's laws—one *inevitable*, the other *conditional*. *Crown 8vo*, 1s.

SMITH (HANNAH WHITALL)—

THE OPEN SECRET; OR, THE BIBLE EXPLAINING ITSELF.
Nineteen Bible Readings. By Mrs. PEARSALL SMITH, Author of "The Christian's Secret of a Happy Life." A series of stimulating Bible studies. *Crown 8vo*, 326 *pages, sewed*, **2s. 6d.**
Contents: Our Saviour—God is Love—The Law and the Gospel—Assurance of Faith—Keeping Power of God—Rest of Souls—Consecration—God's Ownership—Fruit-Bearing—The Presence of God, etc.

SNELL (Rev. BERNARD J., M.A.)—

CITIZENSHIP AND ITS DUTIES.
A Sermon. By Rev. BERNARD J. SNELL, M.A., B.Sc. *Crown 8vo*, 16 *pages*, 1d.; *post free*, 1½d. (*Tracts for the Times*, No. 3.)

SNELL (Rev. BERNARD J., M.A.)—

WHY ARE WE INDEPENDENTS?
By Rev. BERNARD J. SNELL, M.A., B.Sc. Sermon preached on Free Church Sunday. *Crown 8vo*, 2d.; *post free*, 2½d. (*Tracts for the Times*, No. 8).

Western Daily Mercury.—"In these days of Anglo-Catholic reaction it is well to set forth the principles for which the Independents stand. The Rev. Bernard Snell has done this with effect in a powerful sermon in which he answers the question, 'Why are we Independents?'"

SNELL (Rev. BERNARD J., M.A.)—

THE WIDENING VISION. And other
Sermons. By the Rev. BERNARD J. SNELL, M.A., B.Sc. Including Thirteen Addresses to Children (Twenty-six Sermons in all). *Crown 8vo, neat cloth*, **3s. 6d.**

Manchester Guardian.—"It would be **difficult to find a better example** of the kind of preaching which finds favour at present as compared with that which was in vogue fifty years ago. There is no attempt at rhetoric, but serious, earnest thoughts on the real problems of life."

Independent.—"Evokes admiration for his manly downrightness and utter honesty. There is no special pleading. Free in style, fresh in illustration."

Christian World.—"The addresses to the children are very interesting and abound in good stories."

H. R. ALLENSON'S CATALOGUE 41

SNELL (Rev. BERNARD J., M.A.)—
THE ALL - ENFOLDING LOVE.
And other Sermons. By the Rev. BERNARD J. SNELL, M.A., B.Sc. Including Thirteen Addresses to Children (Twenty-six Sermons in all). In one vol. *Crown 8vo, neat cloth*, 3s. 6d.

Christian World.—"Mr. Snell here gives us thirteen of his **eminently vigorous sermons**, and a further instalment of the delightful words to children."
Sunday School Chronicle.—"Certain to find many readers by reason of the breadth of sympathy which characterizes it, the sane and practical gospel which it proclaims, and the simple directness of its style. The book is not only for the spiritual edification of Adult Christians, however. It contains thirteen sermons addressed directly to children, and if we have had favourable words to speak of the sermons to grown-up people, we have to say of these 'Words to Children' that they strike us as being **quite the best children's addresses we have read for many a day.**"

SNELL (Rev. BERNARD J., M.A.)—
THE GOOD GOD ("Le Bon Dieu").
Twenty-six Five-Minute Addresses to Children. By the Rev. BERNARD J. SNELL, M.A., B.Sc. (*Taken from the above two volumes.*) *Crown 8vo, neat cloth*, 2s.

Newcastle Daily Chronicle.—"Charming addresses to children, simple, homely, childlike instructions."
South London Press.—"Pervaded with warmth, kindliness, and sympathy."
Lloyd's News.—"Clearly and forcibly impresses his meaning on his little auditors."
Manchester Guardian.—"Bright and vigorous, full of stories drawn from a wide range, not seldom touched with humour."

SNELL (Rev. BERNARD J., M.A.)—
THE VIRTUE OF GLADNESS.
And other Sermons. By the Rev. BERNARD J. SNELL, M.A., B.Sc. Including Thirteen Addresses to Children (Twenty-six Sermons in all). In one vol. *Crown 8vo, neat cloth*, 3s. 6d.

Christian World.—"**Another welcome volume** from the courageous Brixton preacher."
Evangelical Magazine.—"Mr. Snell is one of the boldest, freshest, and most unconventional preachers in London, and it is evident from the healthy exposition of ethical and spiritual Christianity which we have in this volume where the secret of his popularity lies."
Manchester Guardian.—"There is much freshness of treatment in these discourses, which are mainly practical."
Christian Age.—"The Sermonettes to Children are charming productions; nothing could be better."

SNELL (Rev. BERNARD J., M.A.)—
THE FOUR LAST THINGS. By
the Rev. BERNARD J. SNELL, M.A., B.Sc. Four Sermons— 1, Death; 2, Judgment; 3, Heaven; 4, Hell. *Crown 8vo, neat cloth*, 1s.

STOWELL (Rev. J. HILTON, M.A.)—
WHAT IS A CONGREGATIONAL CHURCH?
A Sermon by Rev. J. HILTON STOWELL, M.A. 16 *pages, crown 8vo,* 1d. ; *post free,* 1½d. (*Tracts for the Times,* No. 12.)

STRONG (Rev. CHARLES H.)—
IN PARADISE; OR, THE STATE OF THE BLESSED DEPARTED.
By the Rev. CHARLES H. STRONG. *Crown 8vo, cloth,* 3s. 6d.

STRANGE ADVENTURE OF THE REV. WM. PANTON, PRIEST.
Crown 8vo, paper, sewed, 6d.

Methodist Times.—"Deeply interesting for a number of reasons. It is a polemic against Ritualism, powerful, yet filled with the tenderest spirit the reviewer has ever found in any controversial pamphlet. But it is also literature. The writer has also the gift of character drawing. It is a human document significant of much which cheers in these grey days."

THEW (Rev. JAMES)—
BROKEN IDEALS, AND OTHER SERMONS.
By Rev. JAMES THEW. *Crown 8vo, cloth,* 3s. 6d.

British Weekly.—"Mr. Thew's sermons are fresh and tender."

THOMAS (ALFRED)—
IN THE LAND OF THE HARP AND FEATHERS.
A Series of Welsh Village Idylls. By ALFRED THOMAS. *Handsome crown 8vo, art cloth, gilt top,* 6s. Uniform with "Bonnie Brier Bush" in style. *Cheaper edition, art linen boards,* 3s. 6d. ; *also in 4 parts,* 6d. *each, net ; postage* 1d. *extra.*

Daily Chronicle.—"Religion is the vital thing with these people, and one cannot read these papers without feeling something of the reality and beauty of it." "Full of sympathy." "Charming story." "Drawn by a loving hand."
Bradford Observer.—"Much simplicity and charm."
Baptist.—"Rustic homeliness, sincerity, generosity, and godliness of the people are seen in every chapter of the book."
New Age.—"Tells with charming simplicity and directness story after story of the village life of Wales."
Methodist Times.—"Marked by considerable power."
Westminster Review.—"Stories of the quaintest characteristics of the countryside, told with sympathetic appreciation, and not without a sense of humour."
Independent.—"As a modest and readable contribution to the study of Welsh life, this book is well worth a perusal."

THOMAS (Rev. EVAN)—
FOR LOVE'S SAKE.
By the Rev. EVAN THOMAS. *Crown 8vo, cloth,* 1s. 6d. *net ; post free,* 1s. 9d.

H. R. ALLENSON'S CATALOGUE 43

THOMAS (Rev. H. ELWYN)—

PULPIT TALKS TO YOUNG PEOPLE.
By the Rev. H. ELWYN THOMAS. *Crown 8vo, sewed*, 1s. 6d. *net.*

Glasgow Herald.—"The author is a Welshman, and his discourses combine in a very happy manner the fervid eloquence of the Welsh Pulpit with the breezy directness which is characteristic of some Congregational preachers. The subjects are such as young people like to hear discussed, and others such as they are the better for hearing about. . . . The book would be an excellent one to put in the hands of a young man, and may be recommended also to ministers as a specimen of the kind of preaching to which young people lend a ready ear."

Weekly Echo and Times.—"These addresses by a man of wide experience are just the thing either for young people themselves to read, or as food for reflection for those who have to teach the young."

Welsh Young Folk.—"The English language in all its beauty and simplicity is on these pages, and the preacher's utterances are exceptionally readable, racy, and humorous."

THOMAS (Rev. H. ELWYN)—

MARTYRS OF HELL'S HIGHWAY.
By Rev. H. ELWYN THOMAS. Introductory Preface and Appendix by Mrs. JOSEPHINE BUTLER. *Handsome cloth, crown 8vo*, 3s. 6d. *Second thousand, cheaper issue*, 2s. 6d.

The Star.—"Written with graphic and remorseless power, vigour of style, and thorough honesty of purpose."

Bradford Observer.—"All true reformers of every kind will wish it success."

Gentleman's Journal.—"The work is true, explicit, searching, and . . . earnest men will study it as a contribution towards the solution of an ever-engrossing problem. It ought to be extensively given to our Sunday Schools and public libraries."

Glasgow Herald.—"The contents are thoroughly in keeping with the title. . . . Written with quite a passionate earnestness."

Independent.—"A courageous book which will probably create great sensation."

The Christian.—"No one could read this unveiling of one of the blackest forms of calculating and fiendish iniquity without horror and indignation."

Christian World.—"Social reformers will find much help in its pages."

The Witness and the Day.—"It is **utterly impossible** to put it aside until it is finished. . . . Full of scorching sentences which burn their way into the reader's soul."

TIPPLE (Rev. S. A.)—

SUNDAY MORNINGS AT NORWOOD.
With additional Sermons and Prayers. By Rev. S. A. TIPPLE. *New edition, Crown 8vo*, 6s.

Congregational Magazine.—"The natural demand for discourses so wise in spirit and so excellent in form could not be satisfied by the issue of a single edition. The few added discourses of more recent date will increase the satisfaction of the old readers and of new."

British Weekly.—"There are more original ideas in Mr. Tipple's volume than in many which have rapidly run into nine or ten editions. Both the prayers and the sermons contained in it give evidence of a fresh, lucid, and forcible thinker. The sermons are short, very interesting, and always aim at impressing on the hearer one idea. **No connoisseur in sermons can fail to appreciate the fine quality of Mr. Tipple's Work.**"

Christian World.—"The first edition has long been out of print, and many will be glad to know that they can obtain these **rarely spiritual and suggestive** sermons. Two sermons are new, the one a reply to Tolstoi's literalism, the other on 'The Silence of Christ.'"

44   H. R. ALLENSON'S CATALOGUE

TRUMBULL (A. E.)—
MISTRESS CONTENT CRADDOCK. A Novel. By ANNIE ELIOT TRUMBULL. 305 *pages*, 12*mo*, *cloth*, 5s.

Manchester Guardian.—"A faithful picture of life in the early days of our colonies."
Spectator.—"A strong Puritan atmosphere."

TRUMBULL (A. E.)—
ROD'S SALVATION. By ANNIE ELIOT
TRUMBULL. Illustrated by CHARLES COPELAND. 12*mo*, *cloth*, 5s.

Springfield Republican.—"The volume entitled 'Rod's Salvation' contains four short stories, some of which are long enough to be fairly called novelets. . . . 'Rod's Salvation' is a good picture of longshore life, telling of the devotion of a sister to a scapegrace brother and well worthy a reading."
The Citizen.—"Miss Trumbull is blessed by a most delightful and unpretentious gift of story-telling. Her work suggests a twilight musician; she has a certain dainty humour in her touch."

TRUMBULL (A. E.)—
A CAPE COD WEEK. By ANNIE ELIOT
TRUMBULL. 12*mo*, *cloth*, 5s.

The keenness, quickness, and acuteness of the New England mind were, perhaps, never better illustrated than in her stories. Her conversations are at times almost supernaturally bright ; such talk as one hears from witty, brilliant, and cultivated American women—talk notable for insight, subtle discriminations, unexpected and surprised terms, and persuasive humour.
The Outlook.—"'A Cape Cod Week' contains an account of the adventures and achievements of three young women who sought the seclusion, silence, and scenery of Cape Cod, and who enlivened that remote and restful country by flashes of talk often brilliant, almost always entertaining. Miss Trumbull's work is delightful reading : the sameness of the commonplace and the obvious is so entirely absent from it."

TORREY (R. A.)—
GIST OF THE LESSONS, 1901.
A Concise Exposition of the International Sunday School Lessons for 1901. By R. A. TORREY, Superintendent of the Moody Bible Institute, Chicago. Author of "How to Bring Men to Christ," "How to Study the Bible," etc. *Size*, $5\frac{1}{2}$ by $2\frac{1}{2}$ *inches, most handy pocket companion. Strongly and serviceably bound*, 1s. *net*; *post free*, 1s. 2d.

This little book contains the **complete text** of each lesson with parts emphasised in heavier type, the **alterations of the Revised Version** also noted, and from $2\frac{1}{4}$ to $2\frac{3}{4}$ pages of **commentary and notes**, so that possessors of this book can, wherever they happen to be, use any passing minute in a study of next Sunday's lesson. Each study is accompanied by a pointed series of questions upon the lesson.
These studies are equally useful to speakers and others apart from the Sunday School connection, each study being a complete outline of a subject suitable for an address. Copies for 1900 can still be had.

TRACTS FOR THE TIMES.

Scottish Endeavour.—"Admirable for putting into the hands of thoughtful young people."

16 pages. Price 1d. *each ; post free,* 1½d.

1. **THE SPIRIT OF DIVES.** By REV. C. SILVESTER HORNE, M.A. An Indictment of Indifference.
2. **CHRISTIANITY AND ART.** By REV. W. PIERCE. A Repudiation of "Art for Art's Sake."
3. **CITIZENSHIP AND ITS DUTIES.** By REV. BERNARD J. SNELL, M.A. "Apathy is the Enemy."
4. **THE DUTY OF BEING YOUNG.** By REV. J. H. JOWETT, M.A., Carr's Lane, Birmingham.
5. **AM I FIT TO TAKE THE LORD'S SUPPER?** By REV. SAMUEL PEARSON, M.A. *Third Edition.* 17th Thousand.
6. **THE SOBRIETY OF HOPE.** By REV. C. SILVESTER HORNE, M.A.
7. **FOUNDATIONS.** By REV. H. W. HORWILL, M.A.
12. **WHAT IS A CONGREGATIONAL CHURCH?** By REV. J. H. STOWELL, M.A.
13. **WHAT THE CHURCH MIGHT BE.** By REV. A. H. MONCUR SIME.
14. **THE DEVIL IN KHAKI.** By REV. W. PEDR WILLIAMS.

Price 2d. *each ; post free,* 2½d.

8. **WHY ARE WE INDEPENDENTS?** By REV. BERNARD J. SNELL, M.A.
9. **THE HUMAN BODY, AND HOW TO TAKE CARE OF IT.** By W. E. LEE, M.R.C.S.E.
11. **WANTED—AN ENGLISH BIBLE.** By REV. H. W. HORWILL, M.A. Reprinted from *The Contemporary Review.*

32 pages. Price 3d. *; post free,* 3½d.

10. **THE HAPPY WARRIOR.** An Address to Young Men and Women, By REV. P. T. FORSYTH, M.A., D.D., Cambridge.

TUCK (MARY N.)—
WITH THE SOWERS IN AN EASTERN LAND. By Miss MARY N. TUCK, of the London Missionary Society, Berhampore, N. India. 24 *pages,* 3d. *net ; by post,* 3½d.

A most interesting and readable article of a personal visit to the native women of an Indian village. Suitable for reading at a Missionary Working Party.

TUCK (Rev. ROBERT, B.A.)—
(*See* under New Orthodoxy.)

TYNDALL (Rev. C. H., M.A., Ph.D.)—
The Eye as Well as the Ear.
OBJECT SERMONS IN OUTLINE.
Forty-five Topics for Children's Services and P.S.A's. By Rev. C. H. TYNDALL, M.A., Ph.D. With Introduction by the Rev. A. F. SCHAUFFLER, D.D. *Handsome crown 8vo*, 3s. 6d.

A new edition has been prepared to meet the demand for this particular book, which can claim to be the first of its kind in pointing to truth by means of the eye as well as the ear.

It is worth while to point out that if it is not possible or convenient to employ the object accompanying the text, these addresses and outlines of addresses of Dr. Tyndall's are so arranged that, by means of a slight description which is given in every case, the actual object can be dispensed with.

Independent.—"The lessons are well conceived and worked out with great ingenuity, and in good hands could not fail to be extremely effective. We advise pastors, Sunday School superintendents, and others who have young peoples' meetings in charge to examine this book."

American Congregationalist.—"Those pastors who are wrestling with the problem how to attract, interest, and influence young people may obtain valuable suggestions from this book."

Golden Rule.—"Everything is original and suggestive, no pains are spared in bringing together the things which can be made serviceable as symbols."

The Expository Times speaks of this as the "Great Kindergarten in the pulpit."

WEIDNER (Prof. R. F., M.A.)—
STUDIES IN THE BOOK. By Rev.
Prof. REVERE FRANKLIN WEIDNER, M.A. *12mo, cloth*, 2s. 6d. *each*.

NEW TESTAMENT. 3 Vols.
   Vol. I.—Historical Books. Seven General Epistles and Revelation.
   Vol. II.—1 and 2 Thessalonians, Galatians, 1 and 2 Corinthians, and Romans.
   Vol. III.—Colossians, Ephesians, Philemon, Philippians, Hebrews, 1 and 2 Timothy, and Titus.

OLD TESTAMENT.
   Vol. I.—Genesis.

WILLETT (H. L., Ph.D.)—
THE PROPHETS OF ISRAEL. By
Prof. HERBERT L. WILLETT, Ph.D., Instructor in Semitic Languages and Literature, and Dean of the Disciples' Divinity House in the University of Chicago. 156 *pages, cloth, fcap. 8vo*, 1s. 6d. *net ; post free*, 1s. 9d.

Each chapter of this admirable handbook is followed by a series of questions.

Christian Evangelist.—"We will venture the assertion that never before has so much information about the Hebrew prophets been condensed into one hundred and sixty pages."

H. R. ALLENSON'S CATALOGUE 47

WILLETT (H. L., Ph.D.)—

LIFE AND TEACHINGS OF JESUS.
By Prof. HERBERT L. WILLETT, Ph.D. 164 *pages, fcap. 8vo, cloth*, 1s. 6d. *net; post free*, 1s. 9d.

A good feature in this book is the series of questions appended at end of each chapter.

The Christian Evangelist.—"This book is the finest compendium of the facts in the life of Jesus, and the chief characteristics of His teaching, which we believe to be in print."

WILLETT (H. L.), and CAMPBELL (JAMES M.)—

THE TEACHING OF THE BOOKS;
OR, THE LITERARY STRUCTURE AND SPIRITUAL INTERPRETATION OF THE BOOKS OF THE NEW TESTAMENT.
By Prof. HERBERT L. WILLETT and Rev. JAMES M. CAMPBELL, D.D. 338 *pages, crown 8vo, cloth*, 6s.

This handbook has been prepared especially for advanced Bible Class work, but it is hoped that it may also be found useful to the pastor and general Bible student. The aim of the book is to get through the letter of Scripture to the spirit, through the shell to the kernel, through the bone to the marrow.

Bibliotheca Sacra.—"One of the most trustworthy and helpful books of introduction to the New Testament which has been published."
Christian Century.—"Its admirable combination of the critical and spiritual, expressed in clear and condensed literary style, makes it a valuable book."

WILLIAMS (Rev. W. PEDR)—

THE DEVIL IN KHAKI. A Sermon
by Rev. W. PEDR WILLIAMS. *Crown 8vo*, 1d. *; post free*, 1½d. (Tracts for the Times, No. 14.)

WOLFE (J. E.)—

GOLD FROM OPHIR. A New Series
of Bible Readings. Edited by J. E. WOLFE. With an Introduction by Dr. JAMES H. BROOKS. Contributed to by Dr. PENTECOST, Dr. A. J. GORDON, Prof. MOOREHEAD, Rev. F. B. MEYER, etc., *8vo, cloth boards*, 302 *pages*, 7s. 6d.

C. H. Spurgeon in **Sword and Trowel.**—"The owner of this fine vol. will have a warehouse of pulpit and platform furniture ready for use. Everything is condensed and analysed, so that there is not a line to spare. The doctrine is after our own heart, and the pervading spirit is one of downright earnestness."

INDEX OF AUTHORS' NAMES

	PAGE
BALLARD (Rev. Frank, M.A.)	3
BANKS (Rev. L. A., D.D.)	3
BATTERSHALL (Rev. W. W., D.D.)	5
BRIANT (W. B.)	5
BROCK (Rev. William)	5
BROOKS (Rt. Rev. Phillips, D.D.)	6
BROWN (Calvin S.)	7
BROWN (Rev. Charles)	7
BROWN (Ruth Mowry)	7
BRYSON (Mrs.)	7
BURRELL (Rev. D. J., D.D.)	8
CAMPBELL (Rev. J. M., D.D.)	8
CARPENTER (Rt. Rev. Boyd, D.D.)	8
CAWS (Rev. Luther W.)	9
CLARK (Rev. H. W.)	2
CLARK (Rev. R. W., D.D.)	9
COOK (Charles, F.R.G.S.)	9
COSTER (Rev. G. T.)	9
DAVIS (Rev. J. D., D.D.)	9
DAWSON (Rev. W.J., M.A.)	10
DE KAY (Charles)	10
DICKIE (Rev. John)	10
DIX (Rev. Morgan, D.D.)	10
DOLE (Rev. Charles F.)	11
DOWEN (Rev. Z., D.D.)	11
EAMES (Rev. John, B.A.)	12
EDWARDS (Rev. Charles)	2 and 12
ELLIS (John)	13
EVANS (A. Johnson, M.A.)	15
FAIRBAIRN (Rev. R. B., D.D.)	16
FAULKNER (R. E.)	16
FORD (John D.)	17
FORSYTH (Rev. P. T., M.A., D.D.)	17
FRUIT (John P.)	17
GANT (F.T., F.R.C.S.)	18
GIBBON (Rev. J. Morgan)	18
GRAY (Rev. Geo. Z., D.D.)	18
GREER (Rev. D.H., D.D.)	19
GREGORY (Miss)	2
GREY (Rev. J. Temperley)	18
HABBERTON (John)	19
HALL (Harriet M. M.)	19
HALLAM (Rev. Frank)	19
HALSEY (Rev. J.)	19
HANDLEY (Rev. S. B.)	20
HARRIS (Reader, K.C.)	20
HERBERT (Rev. Charles)	20
HERRON (Rev. Prof. G. D., D.D.)	21
HOLDEN (Clara M.)	22
HORNE (Rev. C. Silvester, M.A.)	22
HORWILL (Rev. H. W., M.A.)	23
JAMES (Rev. G. Howard)	23
JOHNSTON (W. A.)	23
JONES (Newton)	24
JOWETT (Rev. J. H., M.A.)	24

	PAGE
KEPHART (Rev. J. C., M.A.)	24
KILBY (Henry)	24
LAWSON (Rev. W. E.)	24
LEARMOUNT (Rev. James)	25
LEE (W. E., M.R.C.S.E.)	25
LEWIS (Rev. F. Warburton, B.A.)	26
MCKAY (Rev. G. P.)	26
MACKINNON (Col. W. C.)	26
MACLAREN (Rev. Alexander, D.D.)	27
MANN (Rev. Cameron)	27
MARTIN (Rev.G.Currie, M.A., B.D)	27
MERCER (Rev. Henry F.)	28
MILLEDGE (Rev. Sydney)	28
MILLS (B Fay)	28
MONOD (Wilfrid)	29
MORGAN (Rev. G. Campbell)	29
MORISON (Rev. John, D.D.)	29
NEEDHAM (E. S.)	29
NORTON (Rev. Jno. N., D.D.)	30
PALMER (Rev. E. Reeves, M.A.)	30
PALMER (Joseph)	31
PARKER (Rev. Joseph, D.D.)	32
PARRY (Rev. John, M.A.)	32
PEARSON (Rev. Samuel, M.A.)	32
PERREN (Rev. C. H., D.D.)	32
PHILLIPS (Rev. Thomas, B.A.)	34
PIERCE (Rev. Wm.)	34
POTWIN (Prof. L. S.)	35
PRING (Rev. F. A.)	35
REICHEL (Rev. George V., M.A.)	35
ROTHERHAM (J. B.)	1 and 36
SHELDON (Rev. Charles M.)	37
SHELDON (Prof. Henry C.)	39
SIME (Rev. A. H. Moncur)	40
SMITH (Mrs. Pearsall)	40
SNELL (Rev. Bernard J., M.A.,B.Sc.)	40
STOWELL (Rev. J. Hilton, M.A.)	42
STRONG (Rev. Chas. H.)	42
THEW (Rev. James)	42
THOMAS (Alfred)	42
THOMAS (Rev. Evan)	42
THOMAS (Rev. H. Elwyn)	43
TIPPLE (Rev. S. A.)	43
TORREY (Rev. R. A.)	44
TRUMBULL (A. E.)	44
TUCK (Mary N.)	45
TUCK (Rev. Robert)	46
TYNDALL (Rev. C. H., M.A., Ph.D.)	46
WEIDNER (Rev. Prof. R. F., M.A.)	46
WELSH (Rev. R. E.)	2
WILLETT (Rev. H. L., Ph.D.)	46
WILLIAMS (Rev. W. Pedr)	47
WOLFE (J. E.)	47

www.ingramcontent.com/pod-product-compliance
Lightning Source LLC
Chambersburg PA
CBHW022115300426
44117CB00007B/724